The Lost 116 Pages

The Lost 116 Pages

Reconstructing the
Book of Mormon's Missing Stories

Don Bradley

GREG KOFFORD BOOKS
SALT LAKE CITY, 2019

ISBN 978-1-58958-760-1 (paperback); 978-1-58958-040-4 (hardcover)
Also available in ebook.

Greg Kofford Books
P. O. Box 1362
Draper, UT 84020
www.gregkofford.com
facebook.com/gkbooks
twitter.com/gkbooks

Library of Congress Control Number available upon request.

Contents

In memory of those I have lost,
my little brother Charles
and my parents Edward and Patricia Bradley
&
for those I have found,
my sons Donnie and Nicholas.

INTRODUCTION

LOOKING FOR WHAT WAS LOST

In the early summer of 1828, the sole manuscript copy of centuries of Nephite history that Joseph Smith had translated from the golden plates and lent to his scribe Martin Harris disappeared from Martin's locked drawer and was never seen again. Joseph's response to the theft of this manuscript was pure anguish: "Oh, my God!" his mother recalled him exclaiming, "All is lost! all is lost!"[1]

The theft of this manuscript, comprising the first half of Mormon's abridged history of the ancient Nephites, raised fears that the thieves would attempt to use it to discredit any retranslation Joseph might do—fears confirmed by later revelation saying the conspirators had doctored the manuscript's words to create contradictions. Instead of retranslating Mormon's account from this manuscript, Joseph therefore *replaced* it with another, shorter account from Nephi. The resulting book, though still published under Mormon's name was now a hybrid. Mormon's original design for the book had been upended, and Joseph Smith's earliest words of written revelation were forever gone.

For Latter-day Saints ever since, the Book of Mormon's "lost 116 pages" have taken on a kind of mythical status, as if everybody knows part of the Book of Mormon is missing, but nobody knows what was in it. The surrounding mythos has spawned its own narrative of heroes and villains, with Martin Harris's wife Lucy being cast in the role of villain (or, for opponents of the faith, hero) for purportedly taking the manuscript and destroying it. The episode is often treated by former Mormons, and by irreverent observers like the creators of the "South Park" series, as if it is completely obvious that the skeptical ("smart, smart, smart") Lucy Harris burned the manuscript and that Joseph Smith's failure to reproduce the manuscript word for word displays a disingenuousness in his report of translating it. For Latter-day Saints, the manuscript loss and replacement take a very different meaning, displaying the hand of providence in Joseph Smith's life. The lost manuscript hovers spectrally at the edges of Latter-day Saint consciousness as an ever-present absence, and every once in a while rumors emerge that the hole has been filled by the lost pages being found.

---

1. Lavina Fielding Anderson, ed., *Lucy's Book : A Critical Edition of Lucy Mack Smith's Family Memoir*, 414–16.

The Story Behind This Book

As a child I remember learning in my Primary classes that Joseph Smith lost the first many pages of the Book of Mormon, and I recall asking, baffled, "What was in them?" That childhood curiosity later evolved into an effort to understand the part of the Book of Mormon we *do* have. What insight could I gain into the second half of Mormon's narrative by better understanding the first? How would this detail enhance my understanding of the small plates of Nephi account used to replace the first half of Mormon's account? Fifteen years ago I began hunting for work by other scholars on the subject and found mostly just a single brief book chapter devoted to the subject.[2]

Yet there *were* people who knew what was in the lost manuscript. Joseph Smith had translated it. Martin Harris and members of his family had read it. Had they shared with others any of the missing text's contents? Mormon had narrated the remainder of his account with occasional backward glances to his missing narrative, and the authors of what have become known as "the small plates of Nephi" that replaced this narrative had summarized it. What clues lay hidden in those accounts? If I gathered these clues like the pieces of a picture puzzle, what pictures of missing narrative would start to emerge? I assembled the known clues, dug for more, and analyzed what I'd found.

Methodology for Reconstructing the Missing Stories

The Book of Mormon's lost pages are not the first notable historical manuscript to go missing, and I am not the first scholar to attempt to reconstruct a missing text. The work of reconstructing lost texts has a long and venerable history. Scholars have many times attempted to map out missing portions of an ancient manuscript or extrapolate the overall plot of an ancient narrative from its surviving fragments or reflections in later texts. Such problems are confronted by scholars in a range of historical disciplines.

Biblical scholars seek to reconstruct the "J," "E," "P," and "D" strands of tradition behind the five books of Moses and the "Q" text, a common source that can be discerned behind the shared material in the Gospels of Matthew and Luke.[3] Classicists frequently work with fragmentary manuscripts that

---

2. While brief, this chapter was also extraordinarily useful, providing an initial starting point for my research. John A. Tvedtnes, *The Most Correct Book: Insights from a Book of Mormon Scholar*, 37–52.

3. For a description and examples of work on the textual strands within the Pentateuch, see Richard Elliott Friedman's *Who Wrote the Bible?* and *The Hidden Book in the Bible*. For work on "Q," see James M. Robinson, Paul Hoffmann, and John S. Kloppenborg, eds., *The Critical Edition of Q: Synopsis including the Gospels of Matthew and Luke, Mark and Thomas with English, German, and French Translations of Q and Thomas.*

require a *restitutio textus*.[4] Scholars of Chinese history and literature have engaged similar puzzles since at least 1772, when work began on the reconstruction of the great Yongle Encyclopedia.[5] Arabists and Islamicists attempt to reconstruct early Muslim sources and lost portions of medieval literary works.[6] Efforts to reconstruct the contents of missing texts have even been made in a Book of Mormon context, with BYU religion professor S. Kent Brown having attempted to reconstruct from the Book of Mormon's internal clues what was in Lehi's personal record spoken of by Nephi—a record that (as discussed in Chapter 6) overlaps the lost manuscript.[7]

Despite the frequency with which the problem of missing texts occurs for investigators of the past, a methodology for addressing the problem has yet to be systematically developed. As one practitioner has observed, efforts to "work out general principles of procedure" for textual reconstruction have achieved "only small results" so far, possibly because the methods vary widely depending on the text and because it is difficult to explain the methods used without demonstrating them in practice.[8]

Some of the methods used in this book, developed by the author, bear considerable similarity to those used in the reconstruction of classical Greek and Roman plays. A key method in both is to identify narrative patterns or structures in other texts by the same author (e.g., Mormon's available abridgment) or in works the author used as models (e.g., the biblical accounts of the Exodus drawn on by Mormon) and then situate the surviving fragments at the appropriate places in the structure. Thus, for example, Utah State University historian of ancient theater Mark L. Damen, extrapolates missing sequences of action from gaps in the plays of Menander based on how the playwright structures such sequences in his surviving plays and from the ways later playwrights modeled their own plays on Menander's.[9] Repeated structures in Mormon's

---

4. See, for example, the papers by Mark L. Damen discussed and cited below.

5. For details on this Herculean task and the emperor who decreed it, see Mark C. Elliott, *Emperor Qianlong: Son of Heaven, Man of the World*. Regarding similar efforts in the nineteenth century and today to reconstruct historic Chinese texts, see Edward L. Shaughnessy, *Rewriting Early Chinese Texts*, 195, 256; Robert F. Campany, *To Live as Long as Heaven and Earth: A Translation and Study of Ge Hong's Traditions of Divine Transcendents*; and T. H. Barrett, "On the Reconstruction of the *Shenxian zhuan*," 229–35.

6. Lawrence I. Conrad, "Recovering Lost Texts: Some Methodological Issues," 258–63; and Ella Landau-Tasseron, "On the Reconstruction of Lost Sources."

7. S. Kent Brown, "Lehi's Personal Record: Quest for a Missing Source," 19–42.

8. Campany, *To Live as Long as Heaven and Earth*, 127n29.

9. Mark L. Damen, "Translating Scenes: Plautus' Adaptation of Menander's Dis Exapaton," 205–31; and Mark L. Damen, "Reconstructing the Beginning of Menander's Adelphoi (B)," 67–84. Dr. Damen graciously corresponded with me about

abridgment of Nephite history and the Book of Mormon's repetition of the typological structures of the Bible make it possible to similarly extrapolate from the patterns of clues left for us within the published Book of Mormon text and combine these with external sources that provide fragments of the lost narrative.

Patterns in the available Book of Mormon narrative and in the way it appropriates biblical narrative provide templates for ordering the various narrative fragments into cohesive wholes. So, for instance, the presence of a Mosaic Exodus pattern in the available narrative of Lehi's journey makes this narrative a plausible context into which we can plug the report from someone who interviewed Joseph Smith Sr. of the building of a "tabernacle" in the wilderness early in lost narrative (see Chapter 8).

The presence in the current Book of Mormon of a brief small-plates replacement for the lost manuscript provides a narrative map on which many of the fragments of the lost manuscript's narrative can be pinned to provide a fuller picture of the early Nephite narrative. So, for instance, details from the extant text's narrative callbacks (such as the reference to Aminadi interpreting the writing on the wall of the temple in Alma 10:2) and from external sources (such as a statement by Martin Harris's brother about Muloch [see Chapter 14]), can be added at appropriate points to the small plates narrative.

The reasoning used in this process is known as inference to the best explanation.[10] Inference to the best explanation, frequently used in science and the staple of historical thinking, involves developing the simplest, most elegant and comprehensive model to explain the traces of the past left to us in historical sources.

While this book presents several new historical sources that are key to its reconstruction—sources I will begin introducing in Chapters 6 and 7—it also makes new use of older sources. Many of these are available in Dan Vogel's enormously useful *Early Mormon Documents* series. Still others appear in the Book of Mormon itself. Bringing new analytical questions to these old sources can enable them to speak afresh, disclosing previously unknown truths about the past, like an old acquaintance who has never related a certain story simply because we have never asked the right question. As philosopher of history Robin G. Collingwood explained, growth in our knowledge of the past does *not* come primarily through the finding of new documents; rather:

> The enlargement of historical knowledge comes about mainly through finding how to use as evidence this or that kind of perceived fact which historians have hitherto thought useless to them.[11]

---

the methods he employs in his work. Another analogous problem brought to my attention by classical historian Trevor Luke would be reconstructing lost portions of the ancient Greek "epic cycle."

10. Peter Lipton, *Inference to the Best Explanation*. It is also termed abductive reasoning.

11. Robin G. Collingwood, *The Idea of History*, 247.

Every study has its limitations. One limitation of this book is the necessary stylistic infelicity that the methodology of reconstruction requires that some evidence used in earlier reconstructions must be repeated again in later reconstructions where it is relevant. Another limitation is that the reasonable size of a single volume prevents me from laying out fully everything that can be gleaned about the Book of Mormon's lost text from the sources I have examined thus far.

The certainty of the conclusions that I can draw from those sources varies, with some—such as Ishmael's lineage from the tribe of Ephraim—approaching complete certainty, and others—such as the presence of the land of Sidom in the lost manuscript—being less certain. *All* historical reconstruction is probabilistic, and some facets of the past can be reconstructed with greater certainty than others. Because the models used in this book are probabilistic, they are capable of being improved indefinitely, and doubtless will be over time—including by some readers of this book.

Addressing Both Latter-day Saint
and Non-Latter-day Saint Audiences

Writing as a Latter-day Saint, expecting to be read to a good extent by other Latter-day Saints, and yet wanting this work to also be accessible to non-Latter-day Saints and contribute to wider scholarship involves decisions on how to balance various audiences and concerns. Given my own faith, and that this faith will be shared by many of my readers, I have elected to write about a work we mutually embrace as scripture in the language of faith. I speak of the golden plates as real physical objects, of Joseph Smith translating those plates, and of Mormon as a real voice speaking from the narrative in those plates. For non-Latter-day Saint readers, this particular language of faith may be a foreign tongue. Yet in other ways I have framed the work with these readers in mind.

As a scholar of religious studies and an historian of religion specializing in nineteenth-century America, rather than an archaeologist or historian of the ancient world, my methods are best suited to getting *at* the Book of Mormon text rather than to getting *behind* the text. Recognizing that my own expertise is focused in this way, and that a number of my readers will not be Latter-day Saints, I have made every effort to limit my work to reconstructing the Book of Mormon's lost contents using evidence compelling for both Latter-day Saints and non-Latter-day Saints.[12] This means omitting certain kinds of

---

12. Thus, for instance, when I include arguments in this book hinging on the Hebrew meaning of the name *Benjamin* in Chapter 15, I have first verified that this meaning, "son of the right hand," would have been available in biblical commentaries

potential evidence and focusing on other kinds. So, for instance, there may be Mesoamerican cultural practices that (given a Mesoamerican setting for the Book of Mormon) could illuminate the Book of Mormon's descriptions of the Nephite discovery of (the scrying instrument) the interpreters. Yet, since that Mesoamerican context is not one that all readers can agree is relevant, I have excluded such arguments. To present arguments that will work for readers across a range of worldviews, I have attempted to substantially limit, and where possible omit, from my arguments a presumed context of origin—something on which readers of various stripes will not agree. A seeming exception to this is that I frequently place the Book of Mormon in the world of the Bible. However, since it seems to me incontrovertible that the Book of Mormon both begins within the Bible and emerged in a world where the Bible was well known, this strikes me as both a well-grounded and a necessary context in which to examine it.

My methodology for reconstructing the Book of Mormon's lost text *does* assume that this text was consistent and coherent—an assumption that is both necessary[13] and warranted.[14] Yet, since that methodology only attempts to get *at* the text and not *behind* it, it does not require the reader to adopt a particular worldview as a precondition for understanding what was in the Book of Mormon's lost manuscript.

In this way, my approach in this volume is similar to that of textual critics of the Bible. A textual critic working on the Resurrection narrative at the end of the Gospel of Mark can take the reader *to* what the earliest text said, but cannot take the reader *beyond* what the earliest text said, to the actual Easter events behind it. I have endeavored to similarly take the reader *to* the account offered in the lost manuscript.[15]

---

of Joseph Smith's time in addition to being evident to speakers of biblical Hebrew. Similarly, arguments employed herein that depend on the details of the biblical world may be understood by non-Latter-day Saint readers as indicating that Joseph Smith was an unusually close reader of the Bible.

13. As Wolfgang Iser argued, the process of reading or interpreting a text assumes that the text has a fundamental coherence and seeks to find that coherence. Wolfgang Iser, *The Act of Reading: A Theory of Aesthetic Response*, 125.

14. Literary analyses of the Book of Mormon by Grant Hardy and John Christopher Thomas, among others, have demonstrated that the Book of Mormon can be profitably approached as a coherent narrative populated by self-consistent characters and narrated by personae who demonstrate distinctive motives and voices. Grant Hardy, *Understanding the Book of Mormon: A Reader's Guide*; John Christopher Thomas, *A Pentecostal Reads the Book of Mormon: A Literary and Theological Introduction*.

15. For further discussion of the methodological issues involved in doing history tied to religious claims, see the Introduction to Don Bradley, "American Proto-Zionism and the 'Book of Lehi': Recontextualizing the Rise of Mormonism."

The Structure of this Book

This book is divided into two parts. Part I, comprising Chapters 1-5, consists of a history *of* the lost pages. Chapters 1 and 2 narrate the coming forth of the Book of Mormon, telling the familiar story in an unfamiliar way in order to introduce background material needed to make sense of the lost manuscript's translation (Chapter 3) and theft (Chapter 4). Chapter 5 describes the physical manuscript itself, including an assessment of how much material it contained, arguing that this is more than has been assumed.

Part II, comprising chapters 6-15, consists of my reconstruction of the history *in* the lost pages—its missing stories. Chapter 6 describes the sources that have been identified as standing behind the lost manuscript and how this information can be used to help reconstruct some of the lost stories. This chapter also describes other sources used in the reconstruction, as well as more of the methodology of reconstruction, and introduces the meta-narrative of building a new, American Israel that runs across the succeeding five chapters. These chapters, 7-11, reconstruct the events in Lehi and Nephi's building of this new nation of Israel, including their exodus from Jerusalem at Passover, their construction of a new "tabernacle" in the wilderness, their division into a nation of seven tribes, their "conquest" of the new land, and their re-establishment of sacrificial worship in Nephi's temple. Chapters 12 and 13 make close use of the Book of Mormon's internal evidence to describe what can be known from the middle of the lost manuscript, including the narrative of the prophet Aminadi reading God's writing from the wall of the temple (Alma 10:2). The available evidence overwhelming focuses on the early part of the lost Book of Mormon text and the late part of the lost text. No identified nineteenth century source describes events from the *middle* of the lost manuscript, making this middle portion a much more obscure period in Nephite history.[16] Chapter 14 pieces together the lost manuscript's crescendo, the little known but vital story of Mosiah$_1$, leader of the Nephite exodus to Zarahemla and founder of the dynasty to which King Benjamin was heir. Chapter 15 fleshes out the early reign of Benjamin from the lost manuscript's final chapters and brings the narrative to the beginning of our available portion of Mormon's abridgment at Mosiah 1:1. A conclusion rounds out the book by distilling from the work of reconstruction new insights on the Book of Mormon and the Restoration.

---

16. The dearth of sources on the lost manuscript's middle contents is probably due to what are known as serial position effects in memory, including the primacy effect and the recency effect, by virtue of which people tend, respectively, to recall early or later items in a series or narrative better than middle items. My thanks to Nicholas Bradley for contributing to this insight.

Key Terms and Use of Scripture Citations

A number of key terms in this work merit clarification. The term "Original Manuscript" means the translation manuscript for the Book of Mormon produced by Joseph Smith's scribes at his dictation. Although the Book of Mormon's *lost* manuscript fits this definition, I generally reserve the term Original Manuscript for the *extant* portion of the translation manuscript. (The term "extant," often used in history and textual criticism, means "surviving" or "available." The extant portion of the Book of Mormon is the part available to us now, as distinguished from the lost manuscript.) The term "Printer's Manuscript" refers to a copy made from the Original Manuscript so the book could be typeset without once-again putting the manuscript in jeopardy of theft.

Although I generally use the term "lost manuscript" for the missing Book of Mormon text, the term has its disadvantages. It is awkward to speak of Joseph Smith translating "the lost manuscript," since the manuscript obviously wasn't lost while he was translating it. So when speaking of the manuscript *before* its loss I will generally refer to it as "the *initial* Book of Mormon" "manuscript," or "the initial manuscript." For the sake of smoothing out prose, I sometimes also refer to the lost manuscript as the "lost pages" as well.

"Book of Lehi" is another term used in this book, one that has sometimes been used a name for the entire lost manuscript. As used in this book the name "Book of Lehi" refers more specifically to the lost manuscript's opening portion, which (as discussed in Chapter 5) appears to have been titled "The Book of Lehi" and to have narrated the story of Lehi and perhaps also the subsequent story of his son Nephi.

Another set of unfamiliar names readers may encounter in these pages includes variant spellings for names from the Book of Mormon. As explained at appropriate points in the text, these variant spellings—particularly "Muloch" instead of "Mulek"—are the spellings given in the earliest manuscripts, as identified by Book of Mormon Critical Text director Royal Skousen.

Another usage of names that needs to be clarified is the use of first names for some figures involved in the coming forth of the Book of Mormon. After introducing the major players in the historical narrative surrounding the lost manuscript, I will generally use their first names. These historical figures are closely familiar to most of those who have read the Book of Mormon. The use of first names will also help to avoid confusion arising from the fact that people in the narrative often belong to the same family. Thus the name "Harris" could refer to Martin Harris or to his wife Lucy Harris.[17]

---

17. Note that Joseph Smith Sr. in my narrative will always be designated as such. Joseph Jr. will only be designated as such when necessary to distinguish him from Joseph Sr.

Scripture is cited frequently in this book, so it is necessary to spell out that all Bible quotations below are from the King James Version unless otherwise noted, and all italics in scriptural quotations are my own. Books of scripture cited parenthetically are abbreviated according to standard abbreviations used in the published standard works of the Church of Jesus Christ of Latter-day Saints.

For ease of distinction, this book follows standard conventions of capitalizing certain terms from the Bible, such as Exodus, Tabernacle, Promised Land, and Conquest. Using these conventions will help distinguish *Lehi's* exodus from the biblical Exodus, the Nephite promised land from the biblical Promised Land, and so forth.

The Purposes of this Book

As should be clear from everything said above, this book is a work of scholarship and not of inspiration. My conclusions, like all empirical conclusions, are subject to revision as the evidence grows. We will learn to make better use of the sources we have, including closer reading of our available Book of Mormon text. New sources will also be found that will require revision of existing interpretations—and also enable the confirmation and expansion of those interpretations. Already some of these working models for interpreting the evidence provide powerful explanatory tools in accounting for the data and integrating our understandings of the Book of Mormon.

My reconstructions of the lost manuscript are obviously not scripture, yet they may, and hopefully will, shed *light* on scripture. I personally believe that key pieces of the lost manuscript's content (most obviously those in the small plates but also those given in an interview by the Prophet's father, and others) were providentially preserved for that very purpose—so we could better understand the Book of Mormon text we have.

On one level, this is a book about the Book of Mormon's *lost* text, an attempt to satisfy some of my own thirst and that of others for knowledge about Joseph Smith's earliest recorded revealed text—the lost half of Mormon's abridgment. On another level this is a book about the Book of Mormon's *familiar* text, the canonized text that we as Latter-day Saints read, study, pray about, share with others, and seek to apply in our lives. The more we know about the missing first part of Mormon's book, the better we will grasp the portion we have. My greatest hope in presenting this book to the world is that better understanding the lost manuscript will enable us to better comprehend, appreciate, delve into, and live out this other testament of Jesus Christ, the Book of Mormon.

ACKNOWLEDGMENTS

No book is truly the product of only one person. With apologies to any whose contributions I may overlook, I offer gratitude to those who have helped me arrive here.

There are a handful of people without whom this book would not be in print. Case Lawrence—thank you for believing in me. Thank you so much as well to my sister Jen Bradley, to Jon La Lanne, to Mark Thomas, and to Nathan and Molly Hadfield. Nathan has contributed to this book in more ways than I can enumerate. He has been like Martin Harris, except in reverse—recovering my manuscript when I lost it.

This book benefited from two Hugh Nibley Fellowships from the Maxwell Institute for Religious Scholarship and additional grants from the Laura F. Willes Center for Book of Mormon Studies—for all of which I am so grateful.

Loyd Isao Ericson of Kofford Books has been a model editor. Thank you for understanding my vision for this book, my friend, and helping me make it real.

Michaelann Gardner was a crucial part of my life for much of the writing of this book. Others who were particular sources of support along the way are Karl Hale, Brian and Laura Hales, Brian Hauglid, Paul Hoskisson, Jerry Grover, Randy Paul, Dr. Stephen and Janae Thomas, Earl and Corrine Wunderli, Marcus and Annice North, and Steven and Judith Peterson.

My two greatest intellectual interlocutors over the years, who are also two of my very best friends, have influenced everything I do. This is for you, Trevor Luke and Maxine Hanks. I hope when you read this you see your fingerprints.

Many thanks to my graduate mentor and friend, Philip Barlow. Royal Skousen, Director of the Book of Mormon Critical Text Project, was a generous and unfailing source of knowledge, always answering my inquiries. My friend Mark Ashurst-McGee, of the Joseph Smith Papers Project, put me on to key evidence for the lost manuscript's contents—the Fayette Lapham interview of Joseph Smith Sr. Kirk Caudle assisted with the key insight behind the Passover context of Lehi's exodus. Thank you, Jody Livingston, for your brilliant illustrations and the ideas they sparked in me.

Allen Grover, Phil Brown, and Andrea Edwards—you helped me get started on the path that led here. Greg Kofford encouraged me to turn my research into a book. Among those who have been major sources of research and ideas and encouragement for this book are Clinton Bartholomew, Donnie Bradley, Drew Sorber, Alex Criddle, Lincoln Cannon, Anita Wells, Kim Berkey, Joe Spencer, Claire McMahan, Jeffrey Mahas, Neal Rappleye, and Colby Townsend. And thank you, thank you, thank you, Marie Thatcher for all your help in this. Hypatia was not a greater saint of scholarship than you.

Among the many others who have contributed in some way to my getting here, I gratefully acknowledge the late Jerry Ainsworth, Dr. Chris Bailey, Dr. Rob Beckstead, Kristen Beckstead, Dr. Kirt Beus, Chris Blythe, David Bokovoy, Book of Mormon Central, Joe Bowden, Matt Bowen, Matt Bradley, Sue Bradley, Dale Broadhurst, Debbie Brown, Dr. Jeff Brown, Richard Bushman, Dorothée Cannon, Stanford Carmack, James Carroll, Kevin Christensen, Hohn Cho, Roger L. Colton, Richley Crapo, Dr. Dan Daley, Mark Damen, Jeff Dunn, Steven Epperson, Corey L. Evans, the late Orceneth Fisher, Brant Gardner, Glenn Gardner, Michaelann Gardner, Nan Gardner, Gary Gillum, the late Clark Goble, Dave Golding, Ana Lisa Hale, Dallin Hales, Bill Hamblin, Allen Hansen, Grant Hardy, Heather Hardy, Dr. Scott Harris, Albert Hoffman, Jana Hoffman, Del Jay, Doreen Jay, Robin Jensen, Caleb Jones, Gracia Jones, Norm Jones, the Joseph Smith Papers Project, KC Kern, Rene Krywult, Alan Lafferty, Susan Lee (Aunt Susie), Bianca Lisonbee, Mike MacKay, Patrick McCleary, Justin Martinez, Russell Matero, Alan Miner, the Mormon Transhumanist Association, Jared Nelson, Lizza Nelson, Pedro Olavarria, Jacob Ostler, Jeremy Orbe-Smith, Dan Peterson, Jaxon Peterson , Kent Pickering, Adrienne Shaver, Geoff Slinker, Bryant Smith, Ben Spackman, Jonathan Stapley, Mike Standiford, Cathy Thomas, the late John Tvedtnes, Sid Unrau, Brian Whitney, Mark Wright, Allen Wyatt, and Carl Youngblood.

Thank you to my friends from the Camelot days of the Spencer scripture study, our little Zion—Joe and Karen Spencer, Michaelann Gardner, Donnie Bradley, James Egan, Diana Brown, Holly Huff, Christian Harrison, Edje Jeter, Sharon Harris—I miss you. Don Guam.

If as Joseph Smith once said, "Friendship is the grand fundamental principle of 'Mormonism,'" then I have been blessed with an ideally "Mormon" life. Friends who have helped me get me here just by being the open-hearted people they are Joe Spencer, James Egan, Trevor Luke, Bert Fuller, Logan Roane, Bryce Haymond, Kimberlee Galaxyy, Sarah Hilton, KJ Stone, Kirsten Williams, Jared Riddick, Karl Hale, and Lincoln Cannon.

Thank you to my parents, Don Brown and the late Patricia Thornhill Bradley and Ed Bradley. Because you made me who I am, everything I make is yours as well. Thank you, Dad (D.B.), for seeing the vision of what this was all about and cheering me on.

Donnie and Nicholas, thank you for letting me talk with you about all this, for giving me useful input, for the inspiration you've given your dad, and, when I needed it, the will to live. Everything I do is partly for you. And this is no exception.

Thank you, most of all, to the One who gave me the gifts to live, love, and discover.

Don Bradley

Part 1

The Lost Pages

CHAPTER 1

THE ARK OF THE NEW COVENANT

On the night of September 21–22, 1823, seventeen-year-old Joseph Smith experienced three visitations from an angel who told of a long-lost book of scripture written on golden plates and buried toward the top of a nearby hill. The book held the sacred history of ancient Israelites and others who had sailed to the New World centuries before Christ. This book, Joseph would learn by later revelation, was destined to "work a reformation" that would restore biblical faith as it had been "in the days of old."[1] The angel told him he would find the golden plates deposited with other sacred relics in a stone box that one early account called an "ark."[2]

Though the story may sound singular, and to some fantastical, it was nothing new under the biblical sun. Twenty-four and a half centuries before this angel sent Joseph Smith to the hill to recover the book of golden plates, the Israelite high priest Hilkiah discovered the Book of the Law or "book of the covenant" in the temple and sent it to King Josiah (2 Kgs. 22:8; 2 Chr. 34:14). This book was said to have been secreted by Moses some six centuries earlier "in the side of the Ark of the Covenant" with the stone tablets on which God had inscribed by his own finger the Ten Commandments, his covenant at Sinai (Deut. 31:25–26). When the young king learned the contents of the Book of the Law, he lamented that his people had "not hearkened

---

1. This text comes from the March 1829 revelation to Joseph Smith and Martin Harris now published in part as Doctrine and Covenants 5. The revelation was printed in full in the 1833 Book of Commandments and exists in a very early manuscript, dating to circa April 1829, just one month after the revelation was given. The revelation promised, "If the People of this Generation harden not their hearts I will work a *reformation* among them" (italics added). The earliest text, used here, is cited in H. Michael Marquardt, *The Joseph Smith Revelations: Text and Commentary*, 26–29.

2. John A. Clark, reporting on detailed 1828–29 narrations by Book of Mormon financier and scribe Martin Harris, wrote of Joseph Smith's discovery of the plates, "This book, which was contained in a chest, *or ark*, and which consisted of metallic plates covered with characters embossed in gold, he must not presume to look into, under three years." Clark, Letter to "Dear Brethren," August 24, 1840, in Vogel, *EMD*, 2:71; emphasis added. The primary definition given for "ark" in the 1828 Webster's dictionary was "a small close vessel, chest or coffer, such as that which was the repository of the tables of the covenant among the Jews" and another was "a depository." The stone vessel in which the plates had been deposited fits both. Noah Webster, *An American Dictionary of the English Language*, s.v. "ark."

unto the words of this book, to do according unto all that which is written concerning us" (2 Kgs. 22:13). Guided by the newfound "book of the covenant" (2 Kgs. 23:2) from out of the Ark of the Covenant, the king carried out the Josian Reform, a campaign to restore Israel's pure faith and renew its relationship with God. Josiah led his people in swearing an oath in the temple that they would "walk after the Lord, and keep his commandments . . . to perform the words of this covenant that were written in this book" (2 Kgs. 23:3). The book was intended to bring Israel into a "new covenant" written not on stone but on the heart.[3]

Like Josiah's mission to reform Israelite religion, which had been prophesied three centuries before his birth (1 Kgs. 13:2), Joseph Smith's role in working a reformation was anticipated centuries before by prophecies in the golden plates themselves and years before his birth by his paternal grandfather, Asael Smith, who had a premonition that one of his descendants would "promulgate a work to revolutionize the world of religious faith."[4] Joseph, like a new Josiah, would inaugurate his work of restoration and renewal with another newly-found book of scripture: "the new covenant, even the Book of Mormon" (D&C 84:57).

Sacred Things

Joseph found this new book of the covenant on the morning after the angel's appearance. Climbing the hill he would come to call Cumorah to the place the angel had indicated, Joseph pried up a large stone that proved to be the lid of the stone vault or "ark." Inside he found a collection of artifacts that the Book of Mormon calls "sacred things" (Alma 37:47), treasures similar in form and

---

3. For Josiah's reformation, see 2 Kings 22:8-20, 23:1-25, and 2 Chronicles 34:14-33, 35:1-19. For the new covenant written in the heart, see Jeremiah 31:31-34. Compare these with 2 Nephi 8:7, Mosiah 13:11, and Proverbs 3:3 and 7:3.

4. George Q. Cannon, *The Life of Joseph Smith the Prophet*, 32. Cannon identifies his source as a document written by "one who knew him [Asael Smith] and heard him speak," evidently referring to Asael's grandson George A. Smith. Although this document has not been identified, George A. Smith left other, similar accounts. See George Albert Smith, "Sketch of the Autobiography of George Albert Smith," 101; George A. Smith, August 2, 1857, *Journal of Discourses*, 5:102. Asael's son John recorded a similar recollection in about 1839. John Smith, Journal, in Vogel, *EMD*, 1:562. And Joseph Smith reported in his history, "My grandfather, Asael Smith, long ago predicted that there would be a prophet raised up in his family, and my grandmother was fully satisfied that it was fulfilled in me. My grandfather Asael died in East Stockholm, St. Lawrence county, New York, after having received the Book of Mormon, and read it nearly through; and he declared that I was the very Prophet that he had long known would come in his family." Joseph Smit et al., *History of the Church of Jesus Christ of Latter-day Saints*, 2:443.

historical function to the regalia of a political dynasty and the relics of a temple priesthood, such as the "holy things" of the biblical tabernacle and temple.

Most prominent among the artifacts in the stone box were the plates, which appeared to be made of gold, reversing the composition of the biblical sacred book and its box. Mount Sinai's tablets were of stone and laid in an ark of gold; the hill Cumorah's were of gold and laid in an ark of stone. The plates, witnesses reported, were partly sealed shut and were engraved with hieroglyphics, in the grooves of which was a "black, hard stain" that contrasted the characters against the golden page.[5] According to one of these witnesses, the prophet's father, Joseph Smith Sr., the volume's back plate detailed an alphabet of its characters.[6] Charles Anthon, who was shown a facsimile of this back plate, recognized in it characters like those of multiple alphabets and described it as decorated with "various delineations of sun, moon, stars, &c."[7]

The golden book's title page or front cover displayed symbols in which the prophet's father tantalizingly perceived "the masonic implements," referring, at minimum, to two symbols that are indispensable to Masonry and have an ancient provenance before it—the compass and the square.[8]

Resting on top of this symbolically inscribed plate were what Joseph would learn from the Book of Mormon to call "the interpreters" (Ether 4:5, Mosiah 28:20).[9] Through these he would later translate, or "interpret," the book from

---

5. Orson Pratt, January 2, 1859, *Journal of Discourses*, 7:30–31. A similar description was given by Francis Gladden Bishop: "The characters are rubbed over with a black substance so as to fill them up, in order that the dazzling of the gold between the characters would not prevent their being readily seen." Francis Gladden Bishop, *An Address to the Sons and Daughters of Zion, Scattered Abroad, Through All the Earth*, 48. While Bishop claimed to base his description on a vision of the plates, his understanding of the plates' appearance was undoubtedly informed by his close association with Martin Harris.

6. Fayette Lapham, "Interview with the Father of Joseph Smith, the Mormon Prophet, Forty Years Ago. His Account of the Finding of the Sacred Plates," 305–9, in Vogel, *EMD*, 1:462.

7. Charles Anthon to William E. Vibbert, August 12, 1844.

8. Notably, some scholars argue that Joseph Smith Sr., who related this description of the Masonic implements on the golden plates, was himself a Freemason. See Cheryl L. Bruno and Joe Steve Swick III, *Method Infinite: Freemasonry and the Mormon Restoration*. For the ancient provenance of the compass and square as symbols and architectural tools, see Hugh W. Nibley, *Temple and Cosmos*, 167–304.

9. Lapham, "Interview," in Vogel, *EMD*, 1:462. Joseph Smith Sr. reportedly described the interpreters resting on top of the plate inscribed with the compass and square and under a "lid." His interviewer, Fayette Lapham, understood this "lid" to be a lid or cover on the book of plates, a protective and apparently blank top plate. Lapham reports that both the back plate and the second plate on which the interpreters sat were engraved,

the plates. The interpreters were a pair of crystalline lenses with an associated breastplate. After Joseph first brought the interpreters home, he held the object out to his mother. Lucy "took the article in my hands" and "examined" it, testifying later, "I have seen and felt also the Urim and Thummim." In her history Lucy also related that her son "handed me the breastplate wrapped in a thin muslin handkerchief," through which she could "see the glistening metal" and "feel its proportions." She would therefore testify to a Nauvoo visitor, "I have likewise carried in my hands the sacred breastplate."[10]

It is likely that Joseph's father, Joseph Sr., enjoyed a similar privilege of examining these Nephite relics, making Lucy's descriptions of the relics, and likely those of Joseph Sr. as well, the most accurate in the historical record. Joseph Sr. reportedly described the lenses of the interpreters as "diamonds," which likely refers to crystals having a diamond-like appearance.[11] Supporting this understanding Lucy similarly characterized them to a Nauvoo visitor by noting that "[t]hey *resemble* two large bright diamonds."[12] In her history she described them more fully in her history as "two three cornered diamonds" that were framed in silver and "connected with each other in much the same way, as old-fashioned spectacles."[13] They could be

---

but he says nothing about engravings or other details on the lid plate, other than that the interpreters lay under it. Other accounts of the plates say nothing of a blank top plate or a protective lid over the plates other than the lid of the stone *box* in which they were found. It is most likely this top stone of the box, rather than to a protective top plate of the book, that Joseph Smith Sr.'s description referred. On this, most probable, understanding, the plate inscribed with compass and square was the top plate of the set, and the interpreters sat on top of this plate, immediately under the lid of the box.

10. Henry Caswall, *The City of the Mormons; or, Three Days at Nauvoo, in 1842*, 26. Lavina Fielding Anderson, ed., *Lucy's Book: A Critical Edition of Lucy Mack Smith's Family Memoir*, 389–90.

11. Lapham, "Interview," in Vogel, *EMD*, 1:462.

12. Caswall, *City of the Mormons; or, Three Days at Nauvoo, in 1842*, 26; emphasis added.

13. Anderson, *Lucy's Book*, 379. See also Mosiah 28:13; Joseph Smith—History 1:35. In an interview fifteen years after Lucy's account, Martin Harris reportedly described the interpreters as "round." Yet this same interview has Harris also describe them as "white, like polished marble, with a few grey streaks" and "not so thick at the edges" and says he "never dared look into them by placing them in the hat," details suggesting that either Martin conflated the Nephite interpreters with Joseph Smith's other seer stones or the interviewer conflated them and combined Martin's descriptions of separate seeing instruments into a single, garbled hybrid. One of these stones was egg-shaped; the other was white, flecked with other colors, matching the description *of the interpreters* given by Harris. Both seer stones were often placed in Joseph's hat to exclude external light. The interpreters, as described in Chapter 3, were used differently. A final, and I believe decisive, indication that the 1859 interview text describing the stones of "the

attached to a breastplate, also contained in the box, by a rod which held them in front of the user's eyes.[14]

The interpreters closely paralleled two of ancient Israel's temple artifacts: the stone tablets of the Ten Commandments and the biblical Urim and Thummim. As the Book of Mormon would unfold the story of the interpreters to Joseph Smith when he translated it, they were given to the brother of Jared, a founder of the Jaredites, whose exodus from the tower of Babel in about 2000 BC led them to their promised land in the New World. Like the inscribed stone tablets in the Ark of the Covenant, the Jaredite interpreters had been given by the hand of God on a mountaintop and hallowed by the touch of His finger. The interpreters also were equivalent in structure and function to the biblical Urim and Thummim, which similarly consisted of a pair of stones attached to a breastplate worn in the temple by the high priest, who consulted it to learn God's will.[15]

Each lens of the spectacles Joseph Smith found with the plates was an interpreter or seer stone that amplified the abilities he had as a seer. Joseph had previously obtained two other seer stones of lesser splendor and scope but identical function—a white stone, from near the shore of Lake Erie, to which he had been led by vision, and a brown stone, which he recovered while digging a well for his Manchester neighbor Mason Chase.[16] (To distinguish these latter two stones from the two he found in the stone box, we will hereafter

---

interpreters" was actually based on Joseph's *seer stones*, is that Martin here speaks of the stones in question as stones to which he had access—stones he *could* place "in the hat" if he "dared." While this accurately describes both of Joseph's seer stones, which Martin saw on a routine basis and sometimes handled, it does not accurately characterize the interpreters, which—like the biblical temple relics—were considered too sacred for Joseph to be shown to or used by unauthorized persons. As reported in the Book of Mormon itself, "the things are called interpreters, and no man can look in them except he be commanded, lest he should look for that he ought not and he should perish" (Mosiah 8:13). For a description of Joseph Smith's use of his seer stones, see Chapter 3. For the Harris interview, see "Mormonism---No. II," 163–70.

14. Anderson, *Lucy's Book*, 379. See also William Smith, interview with J. W. Peterson and W. S. Pender, 1921.

15. For the function of the biblical Urim and Thummim, see Cornelis Van Dam, *The Urim and Thummim: A Means of Revelation in Ancient Israel*.

16. For the significance of Joseph Smith's white seer stone, see Don Bradley, "Joseph Smith's First Vision as Endowment and Epitome of the Gospel of Jesus Christ (or Why I Came Back to the Church)." The identity of Joseph's white stone as the one recovered by Lake Erie and the significance of this stone will be further discussed in the author's work-in-progress provisionally titled "Acquiring an All-Seeing Eye: Joseph Smith's First Vision as Seer Initiation and Ritual Apotheosis."

refer to the stones from the box as "interpreters" and apply the term "seer stones" only to the stones he found at Lake Erie and in the Chase well.)

An equally curious instrument Joseph found in the stone vault was a brass ball with two spindles, an instrument the Book of Mormon would call the "Liahona" and describe as functioning like a compass (1 Ne. 16:10, 2 Ne. 5:12, Mosiah 1:16, Alma 37:38). Finally, also within the stone box was a sword, which the book would designate "the sword of Laban" (Mosiah 1:16) in ironic homage to the previous owner whose head it had removed.

When Joseph eagerly attempted to remove these relics, he was repulsed by an unseen force and told by the reappearing angel that he could not yet obtain them but must come back one year later. Like the biblical high priest who accessed the Ark of the Covenant behind the veil of the Holy of Holies once each fall on the Day of Atonement, Joseph was to visit the sacred depository in the Hill Cumorah on the same day every year, the autumnal equinox.[17]

Purification

Joseph visited the sacred repository at the opening of each autumn in 1824, 1825, and 1826, each time a year older and wiser but still forbidden to take the plates into his custody.

Why the delay? On Joseph's first visit to the hill, the divine messenger told him that he was not yet sufficiently purged of worldly motives, such as the desire for material benefit. A large quantity of gold within reach would seem like a dream come true for a boy from an indigent farm family. Despite his family's hard work, farm life was inherently insecure—as the young Joseph knew too well. Within his own memory the world had seen the year-long volcanic "winter" of 1816 ("the Year without a Summer") and the consequent crop failure that caused what has been called the "last great subsistence crisis in the western world."[18] This famine threatened mass starvation in the northeastern United States and forced the Smith family's exodus from New England to western New York. The material woes Joseph experienced were compounded by the nation's first serious financial panic, or depression, during which the teenager would have seen the pages of Palmyra's newspaper fill with notices

---

17. For the high priest visiting the Ark annually on the Day of Atonement, see Leviticus 16 (especially verses 12–13, 29–34).

18. John D. Post, *The Last Great Subsistence Crisis in the Western World.* The 1816 climate change and famine are believed to have been caused principally by the colossal eruption of Mount Tambora. Clive Oppenheimer, "Climatic, environmental and human consequences of the largest known historic eruption: Tambora volcano (Indonesia) 1815," 230–59.

of foreclosure against farm families like his.[19] The desire to escape the poverty and backbreaking labor of the farm motivated some to supplement their daily farm labor with nighttime quests for buried treasure, a venture for which they reaped only a harvest of irony: more backbreaking labor. These dreams of buried treasure offer a window into the quiet desperation of people like the Smiths, who tried to extract a stable living from ground cursed with instability.

By 1825, as Joseph Smith was just entering manhood, he became involved with a band of such "money diggers," who embraced him in the hope that his reported special gifts would prove useful to their quest.[20] In fall 1825, he was hired to go to Harmony, Pennsylvania, on the New York-Pennsylvania state line, to help well-to-do farmer Josiah Stowell search for a reputed lost Spanish silver mine. When later asked about his treasure searching, Joseph, writing as editor of the *Elders' Journal*, did not deny it; rather, in response to the frequently asked question, "Was not Jo Smith a money digger[?]" he answered, probably thinking of his employment with Stowell, "Yes, but it was never a very profitable job to him, as he only got fourteen dollars a month for it."[21]

Being in the frequent company of money diggers would do little to heighten a poor adolescent's focus on the spiritual wealth within a book of golden plates, but Joseph's visions had attested that the plates, and his gift, had much more than a mundane value. By the winter of 1826, he was reportedly "mortified" that his divine gift should have been put to such banal and superficial use.[22] He soon left Stowell's employment to follow in the steps of another Josiah. Though he retained for a time his associations with those who continued to dig, Joseph, now twenty, abandoned quests for material treasure and fully prepared himself to acquire the sacred book of plates.

During or after his fourth visit to the hill, on September 22, 1826, the angel directed Joseph to a companion better suited to a future prophet: Emma

---

19. The Smiths would lose their farm to foreclosure soon after Joseph's third visit to the hill in 1825. For a classic study of the depression of the late 1810s and early 1820s, see Murray N. Rothbard, *The Panic of 1819: Reactions and Policies*.

20. Joseph Smith's involvement in treasure searching is well documented. See, for example, Richard L. Anderson, "The Mature Joseph Smith and Treasure Searching," 489–560; Ronald W. Walker, "Joseph Smith: The Palmyra Seer," 461–72; Ronald W. Walker, "The Persisting Idea of American Treasure Hunting," 427–59; and Richard Lyman Bushman, *Joseph Smith: Rough Stone Rolling*, 48–52.

21. This question and its answer were published by Joseph Smith as editor of the *Elders' Journal*. See Joseph Smith, "Elders Journal: Joseph Smith Jr. Editor," 42–44.

22. Joseph Smith Sr. is reported to have said that he and his son Joseph Jr. were "mortified that this wonderful power which God had so miraculously given him" had been hired out for pecuniary use. W. D. Purple, "Joseph Smith, the Originator of Mormonism. Historical Reminiscences of the Town of Afton," in Vogel, *EMD*, 4:135.

Hale. Joseph had met Emma in Pennsylvania in 1825 when boarding with her family while he was employed by Josiah Stowell. The angel told Joseph that in order to obtain the plates on his final visit to the hill he must bring Emma with him—as his wife.[23]

Recovering a Lost Book

A year later, Joseph, married and matured beyond questing for treasure, approached his final visit to the hill with every expectation of success. At long last he received the plates and sacred relics from the ark that had borne them safely through fourteen centuries. While Emma waited nearby, the angel gave Joseph a strict charge to keep the plates out of profane hands or sight.[24] As reported by Joseph's mother, the messenger warned that Joseph must "be watchful and faithful" because "wicked men" would "lay every plan and scheme that is possible" to take the plates from him.[25] Joseph's scribe, Martin Harris, added that the angel particularly warned Joseph regarding "wicked men" with whom he had previously associated, and against whom he must now guard: "[H]e must quit the company of the money-diggers. . . . [T]here were wicked men among them. He must have no more to do with them."[26]

Subsequent events would prove the money diggers, especially the Smiths' neighbor Samuel T. Lawrence, to be among those whom the angel had warned about. The diggers' efforts began even before Joseph removed the plates from the hill. Brigham Young recounted conversations with a money digger, likely Luman Walter, who searched for the plates on the hill in the days just before Joseph recovered them.[27] And Joseph Knight Sr., the friend and benefactor whose wagon Joseph drove to the hill to retrieve the plates, reported that Samuel Lawrence had previously "[b]in to the hill and knew about the things in the hill and he was trying to obtain them." Knight also

---

23. Henry Harris, "Statement," 252; Lapham, "Interview," in Vogel, *EMD*, 1:462; Kyle R. Walker, "Katharine Smith Salisbury's Recollections of Joseph's Meetings with Moroni," 14–15.

24. Anderson, *Lucy's Book*, 376–77. Joseph Lewis and Hiel Lewis, "Mormon History. A New Chapter, About to Be Published," 1.

25. The quote is from Lucy Mack Smith. Anderson, *Lucy's Book*, 376–77, 388.

26. "Mormonism---No. II," 168.

27. Brigham Young reported that an associate of the Palmyra treasure diggers from another town, probably referring to Luman Walter of Pultneyville and later Sodus, New York, also went to the hill in the days before September 22, 1827, in a vain effort to acquire the plates for himself. Brigham Young, February 18, 1855, *Journal of Discourses*, 2:180; Brigham Young, July 19, 1857, *Journal of Discourses*, 5:55. For the "conjuror's" probable identity as Luman Walter, see Vogel's introduction and annotation to these accounts in Dan Vogel, ed., *Early Mormon Documents*, 3:335–38.

recalled that before Joseph retrieved the relics, Joseph was "some afraid of him [Lawrence] that he mite be a trouble to him" and "therefore sint his father up to Sams as he Called him near night to see if there was any signs of his going away that night."[28] Neither Samuel Lawrence nor any of the other would-be robbers caused trouble that night, but in the weeks ahead Lawrence would take a leading part in their efforts to get the plates away from Joseph, whom they believed had stolen the plates from *them*.

Honor among money diggers, it seems, dictated that anything drawn from the ground by one member of a digging group belonged to all. Regarding the diggers' sense of ownership over the plates, Martin later told an interviewer:

> The money-diggers claimed that they had as much right to the plates as Joseph had, as they were in company together. They claimed that Joseph had been traitor, and had appropriated to himself that which belonged to them. For this reason Joseph was afraid of them.[29]

Joseph had suspected even before he received the angel's charge on September 22, 1827, that his erstwhile friends would attempt to take the plates, and he feared being waylaid en route by former digging associates and losing the plates just as he received them. Even with the assurance from his father that Lawrence was settled in for the night, Joseph thought it best to hide the plates in a hollowed-out tree rather than take them home. He would bring the interpreters home that same day but chose to wait several days to return and retrieve the plates.[30] When he did go to retrieve them, he wrapped them in his frock and set out for home. On the way he was attacked, but he managed to fend off the attackers and escape with just a dislocated thumb and the sacred trust still in his hands.[31] Thus failed the first of many attempts to steal the plates.

When he successfully got the precious plates home, Joseph kept them literally under wraps. Surprised, his father asked, "What, Joseph, can we not see them?" But Joseph demurred, vowing to be faithful to the angel's instructions and show the plates only as commanded, though he allowed his family to heft and feel the plates through the frock or after they were transferred into a pillowcase.[32] Not until years later would anyone else see the plates fully, and even then only select witnesses.

---

28. Joseph Knight Sr., "Manuscript of the History of Joseph Smith," in Vogel, *EMD*, 4:14–15.

29. "Mormonism---No. II," 166.

30. Lucy Mack Smith describes Joseph showing her the interpreters the next morning, indicating that he brought those home directly from the hill. Anderson, *Lucy's Book*, 378–79.

31. Anderson, 385–86.

32. C. E. Butterworth, "The Old Soldier's Testimony. Sermon preached by Bro. William B. Smith, in the Saints' Chapel, Detroit, Iowa, June 8th, 1884," in Vogel,

Ancient Israel's Ark of the Covenant and associated holy things were draped with a veil or wrapped when removed from the temple sanctuary, especially when the Tabernacle (the temple's portable counterpart) was moved from place to place (Num. 4:4–20). Similarly, the sacred things Joseph retrieved from the stone ark were to be kept covered in public. Both the Old World and the New World relics as a rule were to be seen and touched only by those appointed. For the relics of Sinai's ark this meant primarily the high priest, who accessed the biblical Ark during the most sacred feast, the Day of Atonement, while for the relics of Cumorah's ark, it meant Joseph.[33]

The Golden Plates and Jewish Festivals

Joseph's fulfillment of a role like that of the biblical high priest comes into sharper focus when we consider *when* he completed his acquisition of the plates: September 22, 1827. This date corresponded to "the first day of the seventh month" in the Jewish calendar and is also the date of the Jewish Feast of Trumpets, which inaugurated the fall Jewish festival season and prepared for the Day of Atonement. Joseph therefore retrieved the plates from their ark the day Jews celebrated God inscribing the Law on stone tablets with His finger on Mt. Sinai, a fitting occasion for God to begin bringing forth a lost book inscribed on golden tablets by way of stones He had touched with His finger on Mt. Shelem (Ether 3).[34]

After retrieving the plates from their ark, Joseph secreted them in the hollowed out tree for "about ten days."[35] The timing once again evinces a larger design. The days from the Feast of Trumpets to the Day of Atonement, known as "the Days of Awe" or "Days of Repentance," are a period of reconciliation and preparation for the Day of Atonement—a preparation period of *ten days*.[36] At the end of this period, on the Day of Atonement, the biblical high priest clad himself in white linen and the breastplate and Urim and Thummim, donned a crown with an engraved gold plate to "bear the iniquity of the holy things" (Ex. 28:36–37), and performed the symbolic sacrifices of

---

EMD, 1:505. Joseph Smith's sister Katharine similarly recalled that he had been "forbidden" to show the plates. Katharine Smith Salisbury, Letter to "Dear Sisters," in Vogel, *EMD*, 1:569; Herbert S. Salisbury, "Things the Prophet's Sister Told Me," in Vogel, *EMD*, 1:569.

33. On penalty of death, only the priests were to see the "holy things" before they were covered (Num. 4:4–20).

34. Lenet Hadley Read, "Joseph Smith's Receipt of the Plates and the Israelite Feast of Trumpets," 110–20.

35. Willard Chase, "Willard Chase Statement, Circa 11 December 1833," 246.

36. Reuven Hammer, *Entering the High Holy Days: A Complete Guide to the History, Prayers, and Themes*, 1–11, 22. See also Leviticus 23:23–38.

atonement. He then entered the Holy of Holies, sprinkling the atoning sacrificial blood on the Ark of the Covenant, propitiating God for the remission of Israel's sins (Lev. 16; Num. 29:7–11).[37]

At this same festival season in 1827, four millennia after its institution by Moses, Joseph Smith took home the golden plates, reuniting them with the Nephite "Urim and Thummim" to translate a book that would "talk of Christ," "rejoice in Christ," "preach of Christ," "prophesy of Christ," and show the remnant of Israel "to what source they may look for a remission of their sins" (2 Ne. 25:26).

37. The various connections between the coming forth of the Book of Mormon and Jewish worship in the Hebrew Bible may help to account for a focus among Latter-day Saints of this period on the work of gathering the Jews to an American New Jerusalem, as documented in Don Bradley, "American Proto-Zionism and the 'Book of Lehi': Recontextualizing the Rise of Mormonism."

CHAPTER 2

THE SEALED BOOK

At home Joseph secured the plates in a small chest, which he then concealed. To keep a closer watch over the plates, he began working in the fields with his father instead of hiring out as a laborer. He was devoted to protecting the plates, and his family was as zealous as he.[1]

Yet the Smiths held the golden plates precariously, a fact of which no one was more keenly aware than they. Much of the time the golden record was stored in a wooden chest hastily hidden on the Smith property. The Smiths did their best, moving the plates from hiding place to hiding place and even setting up decoys to distract the raiders who descended on their house and farm. But their human inadequacy to safeguard a divine record from dozens of determined foes was transparent.

As the record came from the angel's hands into their hands, its security dropped dramatically. When Moroni, the record's last author, hid it in the hill centuries before, he did not leave it unprotected. Rather, in some of his final words on the plates he declared that he would soon "seal up" the record (Moro. 10:2). According to Noah Webster's 1828 dictionary, to "seal up" the book means simply "to inclose; to hide; to conceal" or "to keep secret."[2] As a scriptural example of the latter sense, Webster points to the divine instructions given to Daniel concerning his all-encompassing vision: "Shut up the words, and seal the book even to the time of the end" (Dan. 12:4). Webster could as well have cited the heavenly voice to John the Revelator, also the recipient of a universal vision: "Seal up those things which the seven thunders uttered, and write them not" (Rev.10:44). In this sense, the Book of Mormon had been "sealed up" and "kept back because of the wickedness of the people . . . hidden because of iniquity" (D&C 6:26–27), and a portion of it was to remain so even after Joseph completed his work of translation (2 Ne. 27:7; Ether 3:25).

There is, however, a stronger sense in which the plates had been sealed up by Moroni, and it is one more immediately relevant to the Smiths' predicament. "Sealing up" in the Book of Mormon often refers to a prophet consecrating sacred texts and objects into divine care to protect them against discovery, recovery, and tampering (1 Ne. 14:26; 2 Ne. 26:17, 27:22, 30:3; Ether 3:28, 4:5, 5:1; Moro. 10:2). Webster captured part of this meaning: "To mark as

---

1. Lavina Fielding Anderson, ed., *Lucy's Book: A Critical Edition of Lucy Mack Smith's Family Memoir*, 387–89.
2. Noah Webster, *An American Dictionary of the English Language*, s.v. "seal."

one's property, and secure from danger."[3] The Book of Mormon describes both God and the devil sealing *people* in this sense, with its prophets warning their audiences that either Christ or the devil will "seal you his" (Mosiah 5:15; Alma 34:35). Additionally, Book of Mormon prophets themselves could seal on God's behalf and mark something as divine property. In this sense, the book of scripture prophesied that Joseph Smith would "seal up" the plates "*unto the Lord*" after completing his translation from them (2 Ne. 27:22; 30:3).[4]

This notion of sealing up a sacred record to God has parallels in the biblical text. In the Bible, a document that was sealed (usually in wax, with the sender's stamp or seal pressed into it) could legally be opened only by the intended recipient.[5] Thus the sealed book in the Book of Revelation could not be opened by John, nor by anyone else except the Lamb of God (Rev. 5:1–7; 6:1). Similarly, the golden plates, being "sealed up unto the Lord" and thus authoritatively marked as his, were removed from human keeping and became a divine *possession*. They could be unsealed and returned to human possession only by God, or as Joseph Smith's experience indicates, by God's angelic agent.

When giving the plates over to Joseph, the angel explained the great drop in the plates' security that came with this action, and exhorted Joseph to almost superhuman effort to keep them safe:

> Now you have got the Record into your own hands, and you are but a man, therefore you will have to be watchful and faithful to your trust, or you will be overpowered by wicked men, for they will lay every plan and scheme that is possible to get it away from you, and if you do not take heed continually, they will succeed. While it was in my hands, I could keep it, and no man had power to take it away; but now I give it up to you. Beware, and look well to your ways, and you shall have power to retain it, until the time for it to be translated.[6]

The responsibility thus placed on Joseph and his family was extreme. The plates had come from angelic care and would return to angelic care when they left the possession of the Smiths. But for now *they* were to be the guardian angels of the gap, keeping the book as safe in their hands as it had been in heavenly hands.

---

3. Webster, s.v. "seal."

4. Nephi prophesies that after Joseph Smith has "sealed up unto the Lord" this record he will also "hide up unto the Lord" the record (2 Ne. 30:3). This sequence of "sealing up" a record and then "hiding up" likely means that after the record has been spiritually consecrated to God's keeping, it is then *physically* put out of the prophet's possession, and thereby into God's possession in being buried in the depths of the earth. In other places the Book of Mormon uses the phrase "hide up unto the Lord," without additional talk of "sealing up," to refer to this same process of consecrating objects into God's care.

5. John W. Welch, "Doubled, Sealed, Witnessed Documents: From the Ancient World to the Book of Mormon," 391–444.

6. Anderson, *Lucy's Book*, 376–77, 388.

"Wicked Men"

Soon after Joseph's recovery of the relics, his father learned that the local money diggers were meeting with a "conjuror" from another town to aid their scheming after the plates. Joseph Smith Sr. located the gathered men nearby at Samuel Lawrence's house and listened as they devised "plans to find 'Joe Smith's goldbible [sic].'" Defying the eavesdropper, the visiting conjuror, probably Luman Walter, of Pultneyville, "bawled out at the top of his voice, 'I am not afraid of any body—we will have them plates in spite of Joe Smith, or all the devils in hell.'"[7]

These raiders, described by Lucy Mack Smith as "a large company of men well armed," descended on the Smith property several times.[8] The Smiths took pains to hide the plates from them, concealing the golden book in the cooper's shed, under the floor of the house, or beneath the hearth, as Joseph was prompted through divine guidance. Martin Harris related one such instance:

> After they had been concealed under the floor of the cooper's shop for a short time, Joseph was warned to remove them. He said he was warned by an angel. He took them out and hid them up in the chamber of the cooper's shop among the flags. That night some one came, took up the floor, and dug up the earth, and would have found the plates had they not been removed.[9]

By such means Joseph successfully kept the plates in his possession. The Palmyra money diggers, and also the Pultneyville conjuror who had sworn to get the plates despite "all the devils in hell," were outwitted by an angel.

To lose the plates to the money diggers even temporarily would have disastrously negated the purpose of its centuries-long sealing protection. In the biblical narratives, the purpose of sealing a document was to ensure its purity. The document's unbroken seal attested that it had not been opened or tampered with by any unauthorized persons.[10] The sealing up of records by Book of Mormon prophets achieved the same effect. By making God the record's lawful possessor and placing it in his care, the process of sealing up preserved it from corruption at the hands of those who "seek to destroy the things of God" (2 Ne. 26:17). Nephi, on viewing the same panoramic vision

---

7. Anderson, 381–82. Brigham Young also described efforts by this "conjuror" to obtain the plates. Brigham Young, February 18, 1855, *Journal of Discourses*, 2:180; Brigham Young, July 19, 1857, *Journal of Discourses*, 5:55. The "conjuror" is also mentioned in connection with attempts to steal the plates in a reminiscence by Joseph's sister Katharine. Kyle Walker, "Katharine Smith Salisbury's Recollections of Joseph's Meetings with Moroni," 15–16.

8. Anderson, *Lucy's Book*, 391–92.

9. "Mormonism---No. II," in Vogel, *EMD*, 2:307.

10. Welch, "Doubled, Sealed, Witnessed Documents," 391–444.

of human history as John the Revelator, learned from an angel that others too had been "shown all things" and the records of their visions had been "sealed up *to come forth in their purity*" (1 Ne. 14:26).

In this way the records on the golden plates contrast sharply with the Bible. Across the millennia the biblical writings were transmitted by human beings—some good, some bad, all fallible—and thus subject to corruption. In the process, Nephi reported seeing in vision, these writings had "many covenants of the Lord . . . taken away" by a "great and abominable church" (1 Ne. 13:26). Yet over these same millennia, the writings on the plates were in divine keeping. The Book of Mormon could thus come forth from the plates in divinely guaranteed purity through Joseph Smith to *restore* the covenants lost from the Bible. It could, that is, unless the plates fell into the hands of those, like the money diggers, who might mar them. Even if the plates were not harmed or altered, they would no longer have an unbroken provenance of trustworthy safekeeping: their purity would be suspect. Until the plates were returned to angelic care, no small weight rested on the Smiths. Fortunately, they did not have to bear it alone.

When Joseph obtained the plates the angel not only warned of enemies but also promised friends that would assist him in both keeping the plates from harm and later publishing the writings they contained. According to Martin Harris, the angel told Joseph "to go and look in the spectacles, and he would show him the man that would assist him," and when he did so, "he saw myself, Martin Harris, standing before him."[11] Lucy Mack Smith related how Martin first became directly involved with the project. On October 6, 1827, two eventful weeks after Joseph recovered the plates, Joseph looked into the interpreters, saw Martin through them, and requested his mother to carry an urgent message to Martin about the plates.[12] Lucy's identification of the timing of this event is significant. Given that Joseph retrieved the plates from their protective ark on the Feast of Trumpets, the first day of the seventh month in the Jewish calendar, fourteen days from that retrieval was the *fifteenth* day of the seventh month, evoking God's commandment to Moses to hold a new feast at this time after the Feast of Tabernacles and the Day of Atonement. The new festival was the Feast of Tabernacles:

---

11. "Mormonism---No. II," in Vogel, *EMD*, 2:307.

12. At a conference of the Church on Wednesday, October 8, 1845, Lucy described this event as occurring "eighteen years ago last monday." This detail places it on it October 6, 1827, exactly two weeks to the day from Joseph's final visit to the hill. Norton Jacob, Journal, October 8, 1845, in Vogel, *EMD*, 1:225. For Lucy's written account of this incident, see Anderson, *Lucy's Book*, 395–402. For Martin's, see "Mormonism---No. II," in Vogel, *EMD*, 2:308–9.

[I]n the fifteenth day of the seventh month, when ye have gathered in the fruit of the land, ye shall keep a feast unto the Lord seven days. . . . Ye shall dwell in booths seven days; all that are Israelites born shall dwell in booths: That your generations may know that I made the children of Israel to dwell in booths, when I brought them out of the land of Egypt: I am the Lord your God. (Lev. 23:39–43)

This feast commemorated the Israelites' forty years of wandering and trial during the Exodus. While the temple in Jerusalem stood, all Jews were required to make pilgrimage there for the feast.

The themes of trial and journey commemorated in this feast on October 6, 1827, intertwined with what was then occurring in the lives of those working to bring forth the book of plates. During the period after Joseph had gotten the plates but before he had brought them home to safety, the Smiths endured a period of trial that rose to the level of high drama as they fended off literal raids of their home by robbers. And the message Joseph sent to Martin that first day of the Feast of Tabernacles was that Martin was to undertake his own storied sacred journey: Joseph "had got the Plates & he wanted him to take an alphabet of the characters & carry them to the learned men to decipher."[13]

Joseph was poorly positioned to do any work of his own with those characters while the plates were in constant jeopardy. It was fortuitous, or providential, that his father-in-law Isaac Hale had cooled his anger over Joseph eloping with Emma and offered the couple a house to live in and land to farm on his property in Harmony, Pennsylvania. In late October, Emma's brother Alva Hale arrived with his wagon to help the couple move. They made plans to leave for Harmony on Monday, November 3, apparently spreading this as their expected departure date to decoy the robbers. Instead, according to Martin, they left on Saturday, "the first of November," also the date of a traditional Christian feast known as All Saints Day.[14] Joseph and Emma's period of trial and affliction in protecting the plates—from when they lifted the plates from their hilltop ark to when they got them safely away from their adversaries—was thus an even forty days. Like each of the previous dates on which they took a new step in the process of bringing forth the golden plates, this timing had biblical significance. Moses endured forty days of fasting on the sacred mountaintop to acquire the sacred tablets he would place *in* the Ark (Ex. 34:28; Deut. 9:9, 11, 18, 25; 10:10), paralleling the larger forty *years* of Israel's affliction in the wilderness. Elijah fasted forty days on "Horeb, the mount of God" before encountering Him in the "still, small voice" (1 Kgs.

13. Norton Jacob, Journal, October 8, 1845, in Vogel, *EMD*, 1:225.

14. Anderson, *Lucy's Book*, 348; "Mormonism---No. II," in Vogel, *EMD*, 2:310.

19:8–12). And Jesus endured forty days of fasting and temptation in the wilderness to commune with God (Matt. 4:2; Mark 1:13; Luke 4:2).

Before the couple's departure, a supportive Martin assisted them in paying off their debts and gave them fifty dollars for their journey and "to do the Lord's work."[15] The initial period of constant vigilance for the safety of the plates having been successfully navigated, Joseph, Emma, and the plates now passed out of the money diggers' reach and into the protection of family and friends.

"Sealed by the Hand of Moroni"

For Joseph Smith, Harmony was aptly named. Here there would be no more former money-digging colleagues laying claim to the golden plates. No longer needing to hide the sacred treasure from thieves who break in and steal, he could begin work on translating it. Between his November 1827 arrival in Harmony and a visit from Martin Harris in February 1828, Joseph transcribed characters from the plates, reportedly doing so behind a curtain so he could unwrap the plates while still keeping them veiled from public view.[16] In this way he prepared a facsimile of the characters for Martin to take to educated men in the larger cities to the east.

It may be that Joseph had some hope that the learned men would succeed in translating the plates' alphabet and provide him with a key to decipher the book.[17] However, as we will see, a good deal of evidence indicates he knew they would fail but understood that their failure was necessary to fulfill prophecy and allow his own translation work to move forward.

Martin took the facsimile of the final, sealed plate first to politician, scholar, and world traveler Luther Bradish in Albany and then to the distinguished scholars Samuel Mitchill and Charles Anthon in New York City.[18]

---

15. Anderson, *Lucy's Book*, 400–401; "Mormonism---No. II," in Vogel, *EMD*, 2:310.

16. Early accounts by both John A. Clark and Charles Anthon indicate that Joseph made the character transcriptions from behind a curtain. John A. Clark to "Dear Brethren," August 24, 1840, in Vogel, *EMD*, 2:264; Charles Anthon to E. D. Howe, February 17, 1834, 270–72; Charles Anthon to Thomas Winthrop Coit, April 3, 1841, in Vogel, *EMD*, 4:384.

17. Joseph's father reportedly told Fayette Lapham that an alphabet of the characters was contained on the last leaf of the book of plates and that this was sent to the learned. And Joseph's mother described him wanting the plates' "Egyptian alphabet" translated. Fayette Lapham, "Interview with the Father of Joseph Smith, the Mormon Prophet, Forty Years Ago. His Account of the Finding of the Sacred Plates," in Vogel, *EMD*, 1:463; Anderson, *Lucy's Book*, 393, 402.

18. For a detailed examination of Martin Harris's journeys with the character transcript, see Richard E. Bennett, "'Read This I Pray Thee': Martin Harris and the Three Wise Men of the East," 178–216.

According to Anthon, the document carried by Martin Harris was a "transcript of a page of the Golden Bible"—i.e., a facsimile of a single plate from the set Joseph had recovered.[19] But which plate? Joseph's mother recalled him wanting to send an "alphabet" from the plates,[20] and Joseph's father recounted that such an alphabet was contained on the last plate of the book of plates.[21] Fitting together the various puzzle pieces provided by Anthon, Joseph Sr., and Lucy Mack Smith, it appears that what Joseph sent to the scholars was a transcript or facsimile of the concluding plate.[22]

This facsimile, which appears to have been lost early in Joseph Smith's prophetic career, should not be confused with the still-extant and widely circulated "Caractors" document—a small scrap of paper on which are written seven horizontal rows of Book of Mormon characters.[23] Though commonly (mis)identified as the Anthon transcript, the "Caractors" document does not fit any of the descriptions provided by Anthon, nor the similar description provided by an anonymous 1850s informant who reported also seeing it.[24] Instead, the plate facsimile shown to Anthon—which had characters displayed "in one or two parallel columns," was adorned with depictions of the "sun, moon, and stars"—was a different document.[25] Six years after examining the facsimile Anthon described it as consisting of "all kinds of crooked characters disposed in columns." It included "crosses and flourishes" and characters from "various alphabets." In Anthon's later account he described characters from Hebrew and Greek. On Martin's report Anthon had said "they were Egyptian, Chaldaic, Assyriac, and Arabic" (JS—H 1:64).[26] The characters were "arranged in perpendicular columns, and the whole ended in a rude delineation of a circle divided into various compartments, decked with various strange marks." Anthon saw in this circular design an echo of

---

19. Charles Anthon to William E. Vibbert, August 12, 1844.

20. Anderson, *Lucy's Book*, 393, 402.

21. Lapham, "Interview," in Vogel, *EMD*, 1:463.

22. It is also possible that Joseph Smith's transcription provided facsimiles of *multiple* plates, including the bottom plate of the sealed portion of the stack and an additional plate or plate from the top of the stack.

23. See Chapter 4 for further discussion of the fate of the character transcript taken by Martin Harris to Charles Anthon.

24. An informant told Orsamus Turner that Martin Harris had shown him "the manuscript title page" [i.e., the transcription of a plate]. On it were drawn, rudely and bunglingly, concentric circles, between above and below which were characters, with little resemblance to letters." Orsamus Turner, *History of the Pioneer Settlement of Phelps and Gorham's Purchase*, in Vogel, *EMD*, 3:52.

25. Anthon to Vibbert, August 12, 1844.

26. Anthon to Howe, February 17, 1834.

Aztec calendar from Alexander von Humboldt, *Researches Concerning the Institutions & Monuments of the Ancient Inhabitants of America*, 1814, plate XXIII.

"the Mexican Calender given by Humboldt," meaning the Aztec calendar published by Alexander Von Humboldt in 1814.[27]

In 1841 Anthon would again describe the paper Harris presented him:

> The characters were arranged in columns, like the [C]hinese mode of writing, and presented the most singular medley that I had ever beheld. Greek, Hebrew, and all sorts of letters . . . were intermingled with sundry delineations of half moons, stars, and other natural objects, and the whole ended in a rude representation of the Mexican zodiac.[28]

"An informant," possibly Charles W. Brown, reported to Orsamus Turner that Martin had shown him the facsimile Joseph had drawn, which the informant understood to transcribe the plates' "title page." He described it as containing "concentric circles, between, above, and below which were characters, with little resemblance to letters."[29] This account of a circular symbol on the plates facsimile resembles Anthon's description of a symbol resembling the Aztec calendar, which consisted of a sun symbol surrounded by concentric circles and divided into symbol-laden compartments by the sun's rays.

27. Anthon to Howe, February 17, 1834; Alexander [von] Humboldt, *Researches Concerning the Institutions & Monuments of the Ancient Inhabitants of America, with Descriptions & Views of Some the Most Striking Scenes in the Cordilleras!*, plate XXIII.

28. Anthon to Coit, April 3, 1841.

29. Turner, *History of the Pioneer Settlement*, in Vogel, *EMD*, 3:52.

Martin's Kirtland, Ohio, neighbor and confidant Francis Gladden Bishop, who acquired considerable information from Martin, gave this description in 1850:

> On the last plate . . . is a circle with rays proceeding from it resembling the sun, as commonly sketched, and around this circle are twenty-four circles more, but of a different character from the first, as each of these circles is composed of figures resembling stars, and half-moons—as, a star, then a half-moon, and so continued until the twenty-four circles are complete.[30]

Bishop, whose close relationship with Martin Harris will be explored in Chapter 5, would have known something of the final plate's design from Martin's descriptions of its facsimile. His report disagrees with Anthon's in placing the circular symbol at the center of the plate, rather than the end, but it agrees that this symbol was present and consisted in part of concentric circles.

These various descriptions of the plates facsimile are confirmed by a description offered by Fayette Lapham, based on his 1830 interview with Joseph Smith Sr. He said that the facsimile the Prophet took from the golden plates reportedly reminded one observer of an Ottoman Turkish travel certificate:

> The remaining pages were closely written over in characters of some unknown tongue, the last containing the alphabet of this unknown language. Joseph, not being able to read the characters, made a copy of some of them, which he showed to some of the most learned men of the vicinity. All the clue he could obtain was from George Crane [Palmyra resident and near neighbor to Charles Bradish, brother of Luther Bradish], who said he had seen a Pass that had been given to Luther Bradish, when traveling through the Turkish dominions; and he

---

30. Bishop's mention of twenty-four circles on the seal of the plates parallels the "four and twenty elders" of John the Revelator's vision (Rev. 4:4; 19:4) and the twenty-four Jaredite plates found in the Book of Mormon by Limhi's people and abridged by Moroni as "The Book of Ether" (Mosiah 8:9; Alma 37:21; Ether 1:2). Francis Gladden Bishop, *An Address to the Sons and Daughters of Zion, Scattered Abroad, Through All the Earth*, 48. Bishop offers a description of the entire set of golden plates. Both Anthon and Turner's informant agree with Bishop's account in describing a circular design, including concentric circles and the sun, moon, and stars. Bishop's description also agrees with Joseph Smith Sr.'s in placing an "alphabet" on the plates, and again with Anthon in having the characters arranged in columns "from the top downwards," rather than in rows running from left to right or right to left. Bishop's description, however, differs from that of Joseph Sr. in placing the plates' alphabet on the front plate or title page, rather than on the final plate with the circular figure. And unlike Anthon, who consistently recalled the facsimile ending with the circular figure, Bishop places it in the center of the final plate. Bishop understood the final section of the plates to be part of the "sealed portion" discussed later in this chapter. Thus, in his understanding, the final plate of the set, the one containing the circular design, was also the last plate of the sealed portion.

thought the characters resembled those of that Pass. Accordingly, Joseph went to Franklin-county, and saw Mr. Bradish, who could not read the strange characters, but advised him to return home and go into other business.[31]

Scholar Michael MacKay has identified a letter from Luther Bradish indicating that "his passport-like certificate from the Ottoman Empire was written in Turkish and included a Turkish seal."[32] Following up on George Crane's comparison of the plates facsimile with this certificate, Martin would later take that facsimile to Bradish in Albany. Bradish doubtless compared the facsimile to his travel certificate, and there is no account of him indicating a close match between the two documents, but there is reason to believe there were in fact similarities that had led to the document being taken to Bradish in the first place. As noted by Erin Jennings, who has located two Ottoman Turkish travel certificates of unknown date, "Turkish passes did somewhat resemble Anthon's description of the characters document" in having circular symbols (seals) and representations of moons and stars.[33]

My own search for Ottoman Turkish travel certificates from near the time of this event has identified such a certificate from 1844 with striking similarities to the descriptions of the plates facsimile. This passport contains two large representations of the crescent moon and star that were symbols of that empire, three circular-seal stamps, a large central circular or oval symbol composed of twenty-four smaller circles, each containing a seven-pointed star and calligraphic Ottoman Turkish script, a form of Perso-Arabic.[34] No wonder George Crane saw similarities between the plates facsimile and a "Turkish pass"! While Joseph Smith almost certainly would never have seen an Ottoman Turkish travel certificate prior to transcribing the characters and symbols from the plates, it appears that such certificates coincidentally shared with that facsimile several similar Arabic-like characters, representations of the sun and the moon, and circular designs including one with twenty-four circles.

Based on the plates facsimile's reported similarity to a Turkish travel certificate and agreeing descriptions of the facsimile by Orsamus Turner's informant, Gladden Bishop, and Charles Anthon, the final plate in Cumorah's book almost certainly contained a complex circular design including concentric circles and astronomical representations. Anthon attempted to explain

---

31. Lapham, "Interview," in Vogel, *EMD*, 1:463.

32. Michael Hubbard MacKay, "'Git Them Translated': Translating the Characters on the Gold Plates," 83–116.

33. Erin B. Jennings, "Charles Anthon—The Man Behind the Letters," 171–72.

34. Photograph of 1844 Ottoman passport in author's possession. This document was auctioned as a collector's item via eBay. Image recovered from Google image cache December 29, 2016. Notably, Arabic was one of the languages Anthon reportedly identified on the plates facsimile (JS–H 1:64).

this design as a variant on the Aztec calendar, but the Book of Mormon suggests another possibility. Moroni, the concluding author, finishes the book by saying he is about to "seal up these records" (Moro. 10:2). On the book's title page, which Moroni had written previously, he says the book was primarily "written by the hand of Mormon" but would ultimately be "sealed by the hand of Moroni." As discussed at the beginning of this chapter, sealing a text included being certified authentic and pure and kept in the safe possession. This involved the use of a distinctive symbol, such as one engraved on a signet ring that could be pressed into wax. Because of this timeworn practice of impressing a distinctive symbol onto a document, the word "seal" has come to refer not only to the physical impression or stamp made on a document but also to the symbolic design of the impression itself. Thus, for example, the Great Seal of the United States on the back of a dollar bill includes the familiar symbol of a circle enclosing a pyramid and all-seeing eye. From biblical times down to the present, such symbolic seals have often taken circular form.

The complex circular symbol on the golden plates was said by Bishop to have been affixed specifically to the back of the brother of Jared's "sealed record."[35] This is consistent with Joseph Smith's description of the position of the Book of Mormon title page within the plates stack, which identifies the title page as appearing at the "end" of the Nephite record but identifies this as being found at the *top* of the plates.[36] It is also consistent with David Whitmer's detailed description that the front section of the book of plates was the Nephite Book of Mormon, while the back section was the brother of Jared's sealed book.[37] The various descriptions of a circular seal on the bottom plate would thus dovetail beautifully with the Lord's instructions to the brother of Jared to "write things and *seal* them up" (Ether 3:37).

Moroni similarly reported that the final thing he would do with his own Nephite record was to "seal [it] up" (Moro. 10:2). Moroni's seal on the plates is possibly reflected in the descriptions of the plates, just as the brother of Jared's apparently is. Joseph Sr. described symbols occurring on the *front* plate, which we have argued minimally included compass and square. And granting the descriptions by Joseph Smith, David Whitmer, and others that the bottom of the plates stack was the Jaredite sealed record and the top of the

---

35. Bishop, *An Address*, 48.

36. Joseph Smith wrote in the draft *History of the Church*, "I wish also to mention here, that the Title Page of the Book of Mormon is a literal translation, taken from the very last leaf, on the left hand side of the collection or book of plates, which contained the record which has been translated; the language of the whole running same as all Hebrew writing in general." "Joseph Smith, History, 1838–1856, Volume A-1 [23 December 1805–30 August 1834]."

37. Abner Cole, "Gold Bible, No. 6," 127.

stack was the Nephite record, this is precisely where we would expect to find a seal affixed to the plates by Moroni.

These sealings of various portions of the book of plates apparently involved a physical action as real as the engraving of words on the plates. Just as the Book of Mormon's text was primarily "written by the hand of Mormon," so it would be "sealed by the hand of Moroni" (Title Page) in part by engraving a sacred symbolic seal on the top plate, just as the brother of Jared, apparently, engraved a seal on the bottom plate. These physical actions of affixing sacred seals to the plates symbolically represented or enacted the prophets' delivery of their plates into divine care.

"Read this, I Pray Thee"

On his return from taking the plates facsimile to Luther Bradish, Samuel Mitchill, and Charles Anthon, Martin Harris claimed that Anthon certified in writing that the facsimile contained genuine ancient characters from a blend of Old World scripts, something Anthon would later, and dubiously, deny.[38] In an 1834 letter to E. D. Howe, Anthon said of Harris, "He requested an opinion from me in writing, which of course I declined giving."[39] But Anthon seriously undercut the credibility of this denial when he wrote seven years later that when Harris asked for an opinion in writing, "I did so without any hesitation," asserting now that the opinion he gave was that the document was a hoax.[40] While Anthon consistently tried to distance himself from the plates transcript that has become connected with his name, his *strategies* for creating that distance varied between denying that he providing a certificate of authenticity and affirming that provided a certificate of *in*authenticity.

On one account from Joseph, Anthon not only certified the authenticity of the characters themselves but also the correctness of a translation Joseph had made of some of those characters. Writing in 1839, Joseph recounted Martin saying upon his return from New York City that he had shown Anthon the characters and their translation.[41] In contrast to this reminiscence, Joseph's 1832 recollection omits the translation and appears to imply that he did not begin translating until after Martin returned from his trip:

---

38. Anthon to Howe, February 17, 1834; Anthon to Coit, April 3, 1841.

39. Anthon to Howe, February 17, 1834.

40. Anthon to Coit, April 3, 1841.

41. Joseph Smith et al., *History of the Church of Jesus Christ of Latter-day Saints*, 1:20. It should be noted that Martin Harris's "own account" of the character transcript episode that Joseph quotes in his history was not a written account, but represented the oral account Martin gave on his return, as Joseph remembered it. This is indicated by Joseph's his wording: "I refer to his own account of the circumstances *as he related them to me after his return* which was as follows."

[H]e returned to me and gave them to me to translate and I said I cannot for I am not learned but the Lord had prepared spectacles for to read the Book[;] therefore I commenced translating the characters.[42]

Concurring with Joseph's early memory, a later letter by Martin suggests that he *initially* brought Anthon just the character transcription.[43] Likewise, six years after the event Anthon also claimed that Harris presented him not with a translation but with just a transcription, and that "no translation had been furnished at the time by the young man with the spectacles."[44]

This apparent contradiction yields two plausible solutions: First, it is possible that Joseph did preliminary translation work during his early examination of the alphabet on the final plate, deciphering individual characters with the aim of creating a dictionary or key to the language on the plates.[45] Consistent with this, Anthon at one point recalled hearing that Joseph had done some translating but says that none accompanied Martin's facsimile. This statement by Anthon, in tandem with Martin's later failure to report taking a translation to Anthon on his first visit, suggests the possibility that Joseph may have been more accurate in remembering he had *made* some preliminary translation of characters than in recalling that he had *sent* this translation with Martin.

---

42. Joseph Smith, "History, circa Summer 1832."

43. The one first-person account by Martin Harris that mentions him taking a "translation" to Anthon confuses the word "translation" with the word "transcription." Having been asked about taking the "translation" to Anthon, Martin wrote in response that "the translation that I carried to Prof. Anthon *was copied from these same plates,*" indicating that he is referring to a transcription (copying) of the characters rather than a translation (interpretation of their meaning). Martin's assumption that the word "translation" here actually referred to the *transcription* of the characters would have been natural if, in fact, a transcription was all he took to Anthon on this occasion. Martin Harris to H. B. Emerson, November 23, 1870; emphasis added.

44. Anthon to Howe, February 17, 1834.

45. Joseph's encounter with an "alphabet" on the golden plates is echoed in his later work with Egyptian papyri. Joseph's journal for October 1, 1835 indicates that he and his scribes Oliver Cowdery and W. W. Phelps attempted to compile an "Egyptian alphabet" in connection with his translation of the Book of Abraham. Dean C. Jessee, Mark Ashurst-McGee, and Richard L. Jensen, eds., *The Joseph Smith Papers, Journals, Volume 1: 1832–1839,* 67. These labors resulted in the production of three largely identical manuscripts, each individually titled "Egyptian Alphabet" and written in the hands of these three men respectively. These documents are located in the Joseph Smith Papers, Church of Jesus Christ of Latter-day Saints Archives, Salt Lake City, Utah. For a discussion of these and related documents, see Brian M. Hauglid, *A Textual History of the Book of Abraham: Manuscripts and Editions.*

Second, we can also reconcile the various accounts by positing that Joseph's later memory collapsed two distinct events into one. Martin, according to Anthon, visited him *twice*, first to bring the untranslated characters, and again to bring the completed translation—the published Book of Mormon.[46] Martin thus *did* take to Anthon both a transcription of the characters and their translation—just not at the same time. Perhaps Joseph, recalling that Anthon had seen both a transcription and a translation, mistakenly conflated these separate incidents into a single incident.

Regardless of whether Anthon saw a translation in early 1828 (rather than just in 1830), and regardless of whether Joseph had yet begun to make one by this point, Anthon did see, and was baffled by, the characters. His curiosity piqued, the professor inquired further about the finding of the record on which the singular characters were written. When Martin told him that it was a sacred record, to which the finder had been led by an angel, Anthon tore up the certificate he had written. Now skeptical of the record's existence and unable to translate from the facsimile in any case, Anthon requested that the record itself be brought to him for a proper examination. Martin, according to Joseph, "informed him that part of the plates were sealed, and that I was forbidden to bring them," upon which Anthon replied, "I cannot read a sealed book" (JS–H 1:65).

Anthon's bafflement at the characters of this sealed book is understandable. In addition to the plates being sealed up in the sense of being withheld or belonging in divine care, they were also sealed up by being written in a language no living person knows: "[Y]e shall write them and shall seal them up, that no one can interpret them; for ye shall write them in a language that they cannot be read" (Ether 3:22–24). The Book of Mormon was recorded in what was called "reformed Egyptian," in which characters derived from Egyptian were used to record Hebrew words. Mirroring this untranslatable language in which the Book of Mormon was recorded on the golden plates, the Book of Mormon includes within itself an account of another set of plates—this time containing a vision of humanity's complete past and future given to the brother of Jared— that had been written in an unknown Jaredite language that required divine translation. Both these books, written as they were in unknown languages, were held under an informational lock, which could be opened only by the proper key—not a scholarly attempt at translating their alphabets, but a divine "interpreter" or set of "interpreters" like those provided with the plates. Fittingly, Joseph described this object found with the plates to his mother as "the key."[47]

---

46. Anthon to Howe, February 17, 1834; Anthon to Coit, April 3, 1841.
47. Anderson, *Lucy's Book*, 378–79, 389.

That revelatory key, or set of keys, was not immediately put to use in translating the plates. Rather, Martin first took a facsimile of the last plate, including the alphabet, to see if learned men could translate it, and thus provide a different kind of key by which to translate—a linguistic key. Joseph initially attempted a similar approach in his 1835 work with the Egyptian papyri connected with the Book of Abraham, and used the key provided by that effort in later efforts at non-revelatory, linguistic translation.[48]

Martin's travels with this facsimile and particularly his exchange with Anthon had a striking correlation to Isaiah's words about a sealed book:

> [T]he vision of all is become unto you as the words of a book that is sealed, which men deliver to one that is learned, saying, Read this, I pray thee: and he saith, I cannot; for it is sealed: And the book is delivered to him that is not learned, saying, Read this, I pray thee: and he saith, I am not learned. (Isa. 29:11–12)[49]

Joseph's later accounts show that he recognized after the fact how delivering the Book of Mormon characters to learned men connected with Isaiah's prophecy. But could he have also recognized it before the fact?

Joseph may have stumbled blindly into prophecy; or, as one prophet fulfilling the words of another, he may have walked into it deliberately, with prophetically open eyes. Connecting the sealed book in his possession to the sealed book of Isaiah's prophecy would have been simple. And Joseph would have readily, and painfully, recognized himself in "him that is not learned." At this point in his life, according to Emma, Joseph struggled at reading unfamiliar names and "could neither write nor dictate a coherent, well-worded letter."[50] Since the prophecy's "unlearned" man was to be tasked with reading the book only after the "learned" declared himself unable, the unlearned Joseph may have understood that only after allowing learned men to try translating would he be given full permission and power to translate.

Significant evidence supports this interpretation. First, in Oliver Cowdery's 1835 version of Joseph's history in *The Messenger and Advocate*, he reported

---

48. Having derived "Egyptian Alphabet" documents from his Book of Abraham translation effort, Joseph Smith later used a variant version of the "Egyptian Alphabet" to attempt a linguistic translation of the "Kinderhook plates," possibly suggesting how he may have envisioned using the alphabet from the plates to translate the Book of Mormon in 1828. Don Bradley and Mark Ashurst-McGee, "Joseph Smith and the Kinderhook Plates," 93–115; and Don Bradley and Mark Ashurst-McGee, "'President Joseph Has Translated a Portion:' Joseph Smith and the Mistranslation of the Kinderhook Plates," 452–523.

49. In the Book of Mormon version of this prophecy, the "vision of all" is described as a complete revelation of all of sacred history and the future: "a revelation from God, from the beginning of the world to the ending thereof" (2 Ne. 27:7–8).

50. Joseph Smith III, "Last Testimony of Sister Emma," 290.

that Joseph knew early on that Isaiah 29 would have to be fulfilled before he could translate. According to Oliver, the angel had told Joseph in 1823:

> [I]t was . . . [his] privilege, if obedient to the commandments of the Lord, to obtain, and translate the same by the means of the Urim and Thummim, which were deposited for that purpose with the record. "Yet," said he, "the scripture must be fulfilled before it is translated, which says that the words of a book, which were sealed, were presented to the learned; for thus has God determined to leave men without excuse, and show to the meek that his arm is not shortened that it cannot save."[51]

Consistent with this, Emily Colburn Austin, an early Saint and an in-law to Joseph Knight (who also assisted with the translation), later recalled that even before Joseph obtained the plates,

> He declared an angel had appeared to him and told him of golden plates, which were hidden up to come forth on a certain day; and . . . it was that which Isaiah the prophet had spoken of; a vision which should become as the words of a book that is sealed; which was delivered to one that was learned, saying: "Read this, I pray thee."[52]

Given Austin's reminiscence, and particularly Oliver Cowdery's early history, it appears that Joseph anticipated "the learned" would be helpless to make sense of the characters, and that he sent the characters, not to have them translated, but to fulfill the words of Isaiah and thus, stepping into this prophecy as its unlearned man, acquire power to translate them himself.

This conscious attempt to fulfill scripture had precedent *in* scripture. The New Testament Gospels offer several examples of purposeful fulfillment of prophecy. For example, in the Gospel of Luke Jesus commands his disciples to carry swords to fulfill a prophecy that the messiah would be reckoned a transgressor and renegade (cf. Isa. 53:12). When two of the disciples take up swords, Jesus declares this enough to fulfill the prophecy (Luke 22:36–38). In another, the Gospel of John narrates that Jesus spoke some of his last words on the cross ("I thirst") in order "that the scripture might be fulfilled" (John 19:28)—meaning Psalms 69:21: "They gave me also gall for my meat; and in my thirst they gave me vinegar to drink."[53]

Latter-day Saints would later follow such scriptural precedents, aiming to fulfill scriptural prophecies of building the New Jerusalem, making the desert

---

51. Oliver Cowdery, "Letter IV," 80.

52. Emily M. Austin, *Mormonism; or, Life Among the Mormons*, 34.

53. The Gospels also report other instances of Jesus intentionally fulfilling prophecy. In Matthew 26:52–56 Jesus tells Peter he will allow himself to be arrested in order to fulfill prophecy, and in Matthew 21:1–9 Jesus rides into Jerusalem on a donkey and a colt to fulfill a prophecy of Zechariah (Zech. 9:9).

blossom as the rose, and taking the Gospel to every nation. Near the close of his prophetic career, Joseph would declare his intention to fulfill a prophecy of Daniel: "I calculate to be one of the Instruments of setting up the Kingdom of Daniel, by the word of the Lord, and I intend to lay a foundation that will revolutionize the whole world."[54] In this same way, near the beginning of his mission the young prophet Joseph took Isaiah's prophecy as *a plan of action*.

Martin also entered prophecy, but perhaps less knowingly. An 1829 news article by the Rochester printers with whom Martin had recently discussed publishing the Book of Mormon said Martin had gone "in search of some one to interpret the hieroglyphics, but found that no one was intended to perform that all important task but Smith himself."[55] Martin, on this early account, originally expected that scholars would translate the characters and only realized after their failure that Joseph was to do the translation. Several years after this account, Palmyra minister John A. Clark similarly recalled that Martin realized on returning from New York City that Joseph, not the learned, would translate the plates. Clark also claimed that Martin viewed this as the fulfillment of scripture. Yet the scripture Martin then had in mind, and which he quoted to Clark, was not Isaiah 29, but 1 Corinthians 1:27–29:

> God hath chosen the foolish things of the world to confound the wise; and God hath chosen the weak things of the world to confound the things which are mighty; And base things of the world, and things which are despised, hath God chosen, yea, and things which are not, to bring to nought things that are: That no flesh should glory in his presence.[56]

When asked years later by an interviewer if he had seen the Isaiah 29 connection at the time of his first visit to Anthon, Martin reportedly responded that he had not "but that Joseph Smith had shown that chapter to him *after his return*."[57]

Although Martin did not join Joseph in seeing the Isaiah connection as events transpired, it appears that Charles Anthon did. A man well-versed in the foundations of Western culture, Anthon lived in a Bible-saturated age and

---

54. Joseph Smith, May 12, 1844, in Andrew F. Ehat and Lyndon W. Cook, *Words of Joseph Smith: The Contemporary Accounts of the Nauvoo Discourses of the Prophet Joseph*, 367.

55. "Golden Bible," 70–71.

56. John A. Clark, Letter to "Dear Brethren," August 24, 1840, in Vogel, *EMD*, 2:267. Confirming that Martin Harris used 1 Corinthians 1:27–29 to validate the uneducated Joseph Smith's calling to translate the Book of Mormon, Martin cited this same passage to Anthony Metcalf for the same purpose some four and a half decades later, in an 1873–74 interview. Anthony Metcalf, *Ten Years Before the Mast. Shipwrecks and Adventures at Sea! Religious Customs of the People of India and Burmah's Empire. How I Became a Mormon and Why I Became an Infidel!*, in Vogel, *EMD*, 2:348.

57. Metcalf, *Ten Years*, in Vogel, *EMD*, 2:347; emphasis added.

showed a studied knowledge of biblical texts in his writing.[58] Anthon's biblical literacy and personal devotion are evident from his work on *A Classical Dictionary* by John Lemprière, which under Anthon's new editorship greatly multiplied in biblical substance and increased in devotional style.[59] The man was clearly scripturally savvy enough to connect Harris's talk of a "sealed book" with Isaiah's prophecy of "the book that is sealed" (Isa. 29:11).

Anthon's accounts of Martin's visit are written with disdain—and wit. Alluding to Joseph working with the plates while veiled by a curtain, Anthon lampooned him by playing on a common idiom describing one who uses secrecy to deceive, calling him "the individual 'behind the curtain.'"[60] Given the satirical spirit and verbal wit of Anthon's accounts, his reported retort to Martin about the sealed book rings true—if one imagines it delivered in a tone of scoffing irony.

The words of the "learned" in Isaiah's prophecy found an echo in Anthon's retort precisely *because* Anthon was sufficiently learned to know them, and intellectually disdainful enough of Joseph's prophetic claims to mock them. Anthon's jest was thus a learned one, but not a wise one. Having played out the textual script for Isaiah's "one that is learned," Professor Anthon stepped, or stumbled, into prophecy in a way that would make him the primary ex-

---

58. See, for instance, Charles Anthon, *A System of Ancient and Medieval Geography for the Use of Schools and Colleges*, 43–44, 665–88.

59. In roughly eight hundred pages, Lemprière's 1822 edition of *A Classical Dictionary* mentions Israel twice, Jeremiah and Isaiah collectively three times, "our saviour" four times, and "scripture" ten times. Anthon's 1825 edition, without adding to the length, mentions Israel four times, Jeremiah and Isaiah collectively three times, "our saviour" twelve times, and "scripture" twenty-three times. Anthon's 1842 edition, while adding three-quarters to length of those earlier editions, adds new religious content proportionally much more, now mentioning Israel ten times, Isaiah and Jeremiah collectively sixteen times, "our saviour" thirty times, and "scripture" forty-three times. (This may be contrasted with the insignificant change in religious content between Lemprière's own successive editions, as when the 1822 edition added one new mention of scripture and one of Isaiah over the previous edition.) Anthon's work shows him to have had knowledge of and devotion to the Bible. J. Lemprière, *A Classical Dictionary; Containing a Copious Account of all the Proper Names Mentioned in Ancient Authors* (1820, 1822, 1825); Charles Anthon, *A Classical Dictionary; Containing a Copious Account of all the Proper Names Mentioned in Ancient Authors* (1842).

60. Anthon to Coit, April 3, 1841. The idiom of secret and presumably deceptive action being performed "behind the curtain" was in use since at least the early eighteenth century, when it appeared multiple times in the works of Jonathan Swift. And a search in Google Books shows it abundantly in use by the time of Anthon's 1841 letter. That Anthon purposely played on this idiom in the letter is evident from his use of quotation marks around the phrase "behind the curtain."

ample of the learned fool in the Book of Mormon's more extensive version of the Isaiah text.[61]

Anthon was a devout Christian, a teacher, and a leading contributor to his field of knowledge. For what, then, does the Book of Mormon condemn him? Certainly not for his learning. The Book of Mormon affirms the value of being learned in its very first verse, where the prophet Nephi declares that he is able to create his sacred record precisely because he had been "taught somewhat in all the learning of my father" (1 Ne. 1:1). And the book's primary author, Mormon, declares that his childhood diligence at becoming learned was part of the reason he was chosen to keep his people's records—and hence to write the Book of Mormon (Morm. 1:2). Nor is Anthon condemned for being an intellectual—one immersed in the life of the mind. Book of Mormon prophets exhort their audiences to greater openness and intellectual engagement with such [exhortations] as "open . . . your minds" (Mosiah 2:9) and "awake and arouse your faculties, even to an experiment" (Alma 32:27).

What Anthon is condemned for in the Book of Mormon is pride and over-concern for his personal advancement and reputation. Anthon, according to the Book of Mormon variation, will not let Martin take the certificate with him but instead insists on seeing the plates for himself "because of the glory of the world and to get gain" (2 Ne. 27:16). If Martin could truly bring him an ancient record, Anthon would get credit for identifying the find's value. But if Martin could not, then Anthon had nothing to gain and much to lose in his professional life by letting Martin take the certificate. Had his certificate circulated with the Book of Mormon, this would have harmed Anthon's reputation in the academic circles of his day, which, like Anthon himself, rejected modern prophetic claims and visits of angels. Yet by taking the certificate back and destroying it Anthon ensured that his most enduring reputation—among the millions of Latter-day Saints for whom his name is a household word—would be as the man who certified the Book of Mormon characters and then reversed himself out of concern for his reputation.

Though an upstanding and productive man, Anthon became the stand in the Book of Mormon's example of pride and self-seeking that can afflict those of great education and intellectual achievement.[62] Anthon, and the elites whose weaknesses he is used to represent, would thus not have the plates. Rather, the Lord would bring them forth through "him that is not learned."

---

61. The Book of Mormon offers a much more detailed version of this prophecy, with more obvious parallels to Martin Harris's visit to Charles Anthon and the translation of the Book of Mormon (2 Ne. 27:6–26; cf. 2 Ne. 9:28; 28:15.)

62. The Book of Mormon also condemns social stratification based on wealth and "chances for learning" (3 Ne. 6:12).

And then, the prophecy proclaims, "the wisdom of their wise and learned," like Anthon, "shall perish" (2 Ne. 27:16, 26).

In addition to explaining Anthon's error, the Book of Mormon variation of Isaiah's prophecy also explains why the plates themselves could not just be turned over to Joseph Smith's and Charles Anthon's generation. It was held back "because of the things which are sealed up, the things which are sealed shall not be delivered in the day of the wickedness and abominations of the people. Wherefore the book shall be kept from them" (2 Ne. 27:8). The seemingly redundant statement that the "things which are sealed" will not be delivered "because of the things which are sealed up" actually distinguishes "sealing" and "sealing up" as two distinct actions. While the plates were sealed up, in the senses of being held back in divine care and written in unreadable script, they were also sealed in two additional ways. We have already seen that the brother of Jared sealed his record (included by Moroni with the larger set of golden plates, likely with the circular seal on the back or bottom plate), and Moroni sealed the Nephite plates by hand as well, perhaps with his own symbolic seal on the top plate. But a subset of the plates had previously been sealed in the sense of being put under physical binding or lock. Both Joseph and his mother describe a portion of the plates being bound shut.[63] And Book of Mormon witness David Whitmer gave the most precise description of this sealing. Less than two years after seeing the plates, Whitmer described them to a Palmyra newspaper editor as

> divided equi-distant, between the back & edge, by cutting the plates in two parts, and united again with *solder*, so that the front might be opened, as it were by a hinge, while the back part remained stationary and immoveable, and in this manner remained to him and the other witnesses a *sealed book*, which would not be revealed for ages to come, and that even the prophet himself was not as yet permitted to understand.[64]

This physical seal or lock on the section of plates containing the higher, still hidden, or sealed up revelation prevented it from being viewed or tampered with, certifying the purity of its contents for the day when it would at last come forth.

The prophecy also indicates three more times that the book would be held back from full and permanent possession by Joseph's generation because of the sealed content held in reserve for future generations:

> [T]he book shall be kept from them . . . .neither shall he deliver the book. *For* the book shall be sealed by the power of God, and the revelation which was sealed

---

63. Joseph Smith, "Church History," 706–8, 710; Henry Caswall, *The City of the Mormons; or Three Days at Nauvoo in 1842*, 26–27.

64. Cole, "Gold Bible, No. 6," 126.

shall be kept in the book until the own due time of the Lord . . . . And the man shall say: I cannot bring the book, *for* it is sealed. . . . *Touch not the things* which are sealed, for I will bring them forth in mine own due time; for I will show unto the children of men that I am able to do mine own work. *Wherefore*, when thou hast read the words which I have commanded thee . . . then shalt thou seal up the book again, and hide it up unto me, *that* I may preserve the words which thou hast not read, until I shall see fit in mine own wisdom to reveal all things unto the children of men. (2 Ne. 27:8, 10, 17, 21–22)

Bearing a message for which no one was yet fully prepared, the plates would not be given to Joseph's generation; rather, as a March 1829 revelation proclaimed, they would be "reserved . . . for a wise purpose in me, and it shall be made known unto future generations; but this generation shall have my word" (D&C 5:9–10). The plates could not be taken to Charles Anthon for examination, put in a museum, nor even yet be kept in a temple. Joseph's generation was to have only the sacred *word* from the plates, or a portion of it, to prove their faith and readiness for the complete book of plates (2 Ne. 27:8; Ether 4:6, 13–16; cf. 3 Ne. 26:9–10).

Once the sealed portion was translated, the golden plates' full spiritual freight would be delivered. There would then be no future purposes or generations for which to hold them in divine and angelic reserve and out of human hands. No longer would the book need to be kept from them; it could be delivered into lasting human care, perhaps housed like the biblical stone tablets in a temple. But Joseph and his generation were to have them only on loan, and to read only the portion of Nephite history he was called to translate. Joseph, like Anthon, had stepped into prophecy. To Joseph, Book of Mormon's Isaiah prophesied, the Lord would say, "The learned shall not read them, for they have rejected them, and I am able to do mine own work; wherefore thou shalt read the words which I shall give unto thee" (2 Ne. 27:20).

CHAPTER 3

TRANSLATING THE NEPHITE RECORD

After showing the character facsimile to Anthon and other scholars, Martin Harris returned home to Palmyra in February or March 1828. He then, in company with his wife Lucy Harris, journeyed to Harmony, Pennsylvania, to return the character transcript to Joseph Smith and report on what the scholars had been able—and unable—to tell him. With "the learned" having failed to read the characters, the task of translation fell to Joseph alone, and Martin effectively implored Joseph, as he had the linguistic scholars, "Read this, I pray thee." It may be at this time (as Joseph's 1832 history and the Book of Mormon's extensive text of Isaiah 29 imply) that Joseph discovered he could interpret the characters himself by scrutinizing them through the spectacles (or "interpreters") he had found with the plates.

In Harmony, Lucy reportedly made herself a nuisance by insisting that she must see the plates and eventually "ransacking every nook and corner about the house—chests, trunks, cupboards, &c." and searching the nearby woods in order to get a glimpse of the plates.[1] After two weeks, Martin took Lucy home for a much deserved rest. There, he planned another trip to Harmony—this time alone. Though he had recently traveled to Harmony, Philadelphia, and New York City, then back to Palmyra, back to Harmony, and back yet again to Palmyra, Martin now arranged his affairs so that he could return to make a more extended stay in Harmony and serve as Joseph's scribe for the translation effort.[2]

While Martin arranged things at home in March and into mid-April 1828, Joseph was not idle. Whatever preliminary study of the characters he may have made in earlier months, he now translated in earnest, dictating the first stories of the Book of Lehi, not to the imminently expected Martin, but to the immediately present Emma. Her identity as the scribe for the first portion of the book is indicated by her recollections of the translation:

> When my husband was translating the Book of Mormon, I wrote a part of it, as he dictated each sentence, word for word, and when he came to proper names he could not pronounce, or long words, he spelled them out. . . . Even the word Sar[i]ah he could not pronounce at first, but had to spell it, and I would pronounce it for him.

---

1. Lavina Fielding Anderson, ed., *Lucy's Book: A Critical Edition of Lucy Mack Smith's Family Memoir*, 405.
2. Anderson, 404–7.

When he stopped for any purpose at any time he would, when he commenced again, begin where he left off without any hesitation, and one time while he was translating he stopped suddenly, pale as a sheet, and said, "Emma, did Jerusalem have walls around it?" When I answered, "Yes," he replied "Oh! I was afraid I had been deceived." He had such a limited knowledge of history at that time that he did not even know that Jerusalem was surrounded by walls.[3]

These incidents underscored for the educated Emma how unlearned she believed her husband to be and thus how divinely aided he must have been in dictating the complex Book of Mormon text. Her account also points to the content then under translation. Joseph would have first encountered, and struggled to pronounce, the name of Lehi's wife, Sariah, not in 1 Nephi, but at the opening of the lost pages. (In any case, the handwriting in the Original Manuscript when Sariah's name is first used in 1 Nephi is not Emma's but Oliver Cowdery's.) Similarly, the walls of Jerusalem would not have first been mentioned 1 Nephi but again early in the lost pages. (The handwriting when Jerusalem's walls are first mentioned in 1 Nephi is also not Emma's and is likely that of one of the Whitmer brothers.[4]) Furthermore, 1 Nephi was translated in June 1829, after Joseph moved from Harmony, Pennsylvania, to Fayette, New York. Emma did not immediately accompany him in this move, but joined him later, making it impossible for her to have been the scribe for early 1 Nephi.[5] Emma was thus the scribe for the very opening narratives of the lost pages, where Lehi's family, including Sariah, were first introduced, and where the narrative of Nephi slipping in through the walls of Jerusalem to get the brass plates would first have been told. This made her the first scribe for the translation of the Book of Mormon as a whole.

Emma's accounts also tell us where they did this work together: in their marital home, most likely in the house's low-ceilinged "chamber," or "upper room," sometimes preparing the room by hanging veils marking off sacred space.[6] For the biblically minded Joseph, doing such sacred work in the

---

3. Emma Smith Bidamon, interviewed by Edmund C. Briggs, in Edmund C. Briggs, "A Visit to Nauvoo in 1856," 454.

4. Royal Skousen, *The Original Manuscript of the Book of Mormon: Typographical Facsimile of the Extant Text*, 14.

5. Of Joseph and Oliver Cowdery's late-May 1829 move to Fayette, New York, Lucy Mack Smith wrote, "Joseph and Oliver set out without delay; leaving Emma to take charge of affairs during her husband's absence." Anderson, *Lucy's Book*, 449–50.

6. Anthon's 1834 and 1841 accounts both have Martin Harris telling him that Joseph transcribed the characters "in the garret of a farm-house," behind a curtain or veil. Charles Anthon to E. D. Howe, February 17, 1834, in Vogel, *EMD*, 4:378–79; Charles Anthon to Thomas Winthrop Coit, April 3, 1841, in Vogel, *EMD*, 4:384. Harmony-area locals reported to Frederick Mather that Joseph also dictated the translation to

chamber of the house would almost surely have evoked Jesus's "upper room" celebration of the Feast of Unleavened Bread that inaugurated both Passover and the institution of the sacrament of the Lord's Supper. And it foreshadowed Joseph's own later institution of the endowment in the "upper room" of his Nauvoo red brick store (Mark 14:12–25; Luke 22:7–23).

The accounts are less specific on *when* Joseph and Emma's work shifted focus from the transcribing and examining the plates' alphabet to full-blown translation of the opening narratives of the Nephite record. Joseph placed the start of his subsequent translation work with Martin Harris in "about" mid-April, but (as detailed below and in Chapter 5) by this point Joseph had been working for a number of days in dictating to Emma and his other early scribes.[7]

While no source identifies the date when Joseph and Emma began translating the account of Lehi's exodus, the dates that *can* be identified earlier in their bringing forth of the Book of Mormon evince a clear pattern that enables us to conjecture intelligently when they began translating. On the timetable presented from the historical sources in Chapters 1 and 2, *each step in Joseph and Emma's early work of bringing for the Book of Mormon was keyed to dates significant in the Hebrew Bible*, particularly dates significant in the Jewish festival calendar. At the Feast of Trumpets, they retrieved the plates from their stone ark; on the Day of Atonement, Joseph brought the plates home; at the Feast of Tabernacles, Joseph looked into the priestly "interpreters" and sent for Martin to request he take characters from the plates to the learned; and forty days after recovering the plates on Trumpets, Joseph and Emma removed the plates from the Manchester environs in which they had lain for 1500 years and took them to Harmony.

Given that the first three events in the coming forth of the Book of Mormon were keyed to the exact dates of Jewish festivals, and the fourth event was keyed to one of those festivals at the biblically significant interval of forty days, we might reasonably anticipate that further events in the Book of Mormon's coming forth would be similarly keyed to such festival occasions. Joseph and Emma's initial translation work a few weeks before mid-April suggests such a sacred occasion in the Jewish calendar that would fit the pattern of their earlier work and befit a work written "to the convincing of Jew and Gentile that Jesus is the Christ," the Messiah. On March 29, Passover began with the time for the slaying of the Paschal lamb.

Reuben Hale, Martin Harris, and others in "the little low chamber" of his house. Frederick G. Mather, "The Early Mormons. Joe Smith Operates at Susquehanna."

7. A more precise timeline for the translation work on the initial manuscript will be explored in Chapter 5.

"I Will Prepare unto My Servant a Stone"

Although Joseph had shielded himself and the plates from view while transcribing their characters, Emma makes no mention of a curtain as Joseph dictated the translation to her. Instead it is evident from her accounts that during this time he principally used his brown seer stone, which, unlike the interpreters, he was not obliged to keep hidden from the view of others.[8]

Unlike Joseph's earlier efforts at copying an alphabet of the reformed Egyptian symbols, translating from the plates by way of this seer stone did not require him to work directly with the plates. Instead he received a visual or conceptual *revelation* of the book's contents. Thus the scene in the translation room, as Emma described it to her son Joseph III, was as follows:

> In writing for your father I frequently wrote day after day, often sitting at the table close by him, he sitting with his face buried in his hat, with the stone in it, and dictating hour after hour with nothing between us. . . . The plates often lay on the table without any attempt at concealment, wrapped in a small linen table cloth, which I had given him to fold them in.[9]

While an observer unacquainted with Joseph's translation process may think he seemed more interested in what was at the bottom of his hat than what was on the plates, a glimpse into the world of "seeing" provides context to his actions. We can better understand the *outside*, observable translation process (peering into seer stones in a hat) by considering the *inside*, unobservable process (its phenomenological and symbolic dimensions—i.e., what he experienced and how that experience was supposed to affect him).

"Sight to Translate"

The process of translation and also that of receiving "thus saith the Lord" revelation through the seer stone involved, as the term "*seer* stone" suggests, a visual experience of some kind for the person using it. Various reports from people who were positioned to hear Joseph's account of the experience indicate that as he looked at the seer stone he *saw* the words of translation.

Like his use of the seer stone, this idea that Joseph spiritually saw the translation has sometimes been a matter of controversy. Joseph's visionary seeing of the translation is believed by some to exclude him from having any role in formulating the language of the translation, such as the selection of words. This exclusion of a role for Joseph Smith in the process is viewed as problematic for three reasons: First, such a process would not make Joseph Smith a *translator* at all, but merely a *reader* of the Book of Mormon. Second,

---

8. Joseph Smith III, "Last Testimony of Sister Emma," 289–90.
9. Smith, 289–90.

portions of the translated Book of Mormon text are written in Joseph Smith's rural, upstate-New York idiom, including grammatical errors common to that idiom.[10] Third, such a process would contradict Joseph's "thus saith the Lord" revelations that describe the processes of revelation and translation as allowing and requiring the prophet's mind to be active in these processes.[11]

We will see that there is ample evidence that Joseph Smith's translation process did involve a visionary component, but first we should distinguish the *fact* of Joseph Smith seeing from *interpretations* of how that experience is produced. Research in visual perception indicates that the *experience* of sight does not occur in the eyes, but, like the experience of seeing something in memory, in the mind. This research also demonstrates that the experience of sight involves the mind's active *construction* of images, rather than merely their passive *reception*.[12]

The common understanding of visual perception would allow Joseph to see something on the seer stone only if the stone emitted photons that struck his retina. But in reality his seeing these words written in the ink of "spiritual light"[13] requires no such thing. We do not know the underlying process by which these images were produced, nor the extent to which Joseph Smith's own cognitive and spiritual faculties were used in generating them.

The question of *whether* Joseph Smith saw symbolic images of the translated words is entirely distinct from *how* those images were produced. Were Joseph's cognitive processes involved in selecting or crafting what he saw? That Joseph Smith could have worked out, or "studied out" (D&C 9:8), the words of translation then seen them reflected back to him through the interpreters (and presumably also the seer stone) was suggested by Elder B. H. Roberts in the beginning of the twentieth century:

---

10. See Royal Skousen, "The Original Language of the Book of Mormon: Upstate New York Dialect, King James English, or Hebrew?" 28–38.

11. A revelation through Joseph Smith to Oliver Cowdery during the translation of the Book of Mormon instructs Cowdery on how to translate, stating that as part of the process of arriving at the translation text, "you must study it out in your mind" (D&C 9:6–9). And a November 1831 revelation through Joseph refers to his revelations as being in "his language," which because of its "imperfections" other church members wished to improve upon or "express beyond" (D&C 67:5). Each of these revelations characterizes the process of divine manifestation as one in which the revelator's mind is active in clothing that manifestation in words.

12. For a fuller discussion of these issues as they relate to the translation of the Book of Mormon, see Brant Gardner, *The Gift and Power: Translating the Book of Mormon*, 259–78.

13. David Whitmer, *An Address to All Believers in Christ*, 11.

The translation thought out in the seer's mind may also have been reflected in the interpreters and held there until recorded by the amanuensis, all of which would be incalculably helpful. But since the translation is thought out in the mind of the seer, it must be thought out in such thought-signs as are at his command, expressed in such speech-forms as he is the master of.[14]

Whatever the deeper information processes underlying the translation, the evidence is overwhelming that Joseph Smith experienced and reported to others a visual or visionary aspect to his translation process. Joseph left no written firsthand details of his translation process but referred to it in distinctively visual terms, describing himself as reading the plates through spectacles and a seer stone and by virtue of his gift as a *seer*—a word whose very construction denotes one who sees (Mosiah 8:16–17). One of his revelations even described him having "power and *sight* to translate" (D&C 3:12).[15]

In addition to *implying* that he saw something while translating, Joseph almost surely *told* those around him during the translation something about his process and experience. It is difficult to imagine Joseph doing something as odd and counterintuitive as looking into his hat day after day while translating without offering any rationale for this practice to his wife or other scribes and companions who assisted him. A number of those who assisted with or witnessed the translation, and others who spoke with Joseph about it, left accounts detailing the process, likely as it had been described to them by Joseph. Three of those who spoke with Joseph Smith about the process—David Whitmer, Ezra Booth, and Truman Coe—reported explicitly that he told them he *saw* the words.[16]

In addition to these secondhand reports are twenty-two other accounts, given by eight different persons, which say Joseph saw the translation without explicitly identifying him as their source. Joseph is, however, the im-

---

14. B.H. Roberts, *Defense of the Faith and the Saints*, 1:281.

15. In its earliest known versions, this revelation (originally given circa July 1828) says Joseph Smith had been given "*right* and power to translate" the Book of Mormon. This was intentionally changed to "sight and power," but it is unclear whether this was an evolution of the text or the restoration of a lost original reading.

16. Ezra Booth, an alienated Mormon writing in 1831, reported Joseph's claim that "in translating . . . [t]he subject stands before his eyes in print." Ezra Booth, "Mormonism—No. III." Kirtland minister Truman Coe, whose account of visual translation via the interpreters will be given in full below, concludes the account with, "This is the relation as given by Smith." Truman Coe, "Mormonism," 2. David Whitmer reported in that "*Joseph said*" that in the darkness of his hat "a spiritual light would shine forth" from the seer stone and something like a parchment "would appear before Joseph, upon which was a line of characters from the plates, and under it, the translation in English." J. L. Traughber Jr., "Testimony of David Whitmer," 341.

plied source of all such accounts, since those making the accounts either got their information from Joseph or from others they believed got information from him. Since Joseph alone had the experience of translation, only information believed to trace to him could have been considered reliable. These witnesses include three of Joseph's translation scribes (Martin Harris, Oliver Cowdery, and John Whitmer), his brother William, translation witnesses David Whitmer and Elizabeth Whitmer Cowdery, and a benefactor of the translation effort, Joseph Knight Sr.[17]

"The Light which Shineth in Darkness"

What did Joseph see? Joseph reportedly saw the English translation for each reformed Egyptian character from the plates written on the surface of his seer stone, not in ink, but in letters of "spiritual light."[18] Joseph's seer stone was like that of the prophesied Gazelem, which was to "shine forth in darkness unto light" (Alma 37:23). The accounts and Joseph's translation practices suggest that he could perceive and focus on the spiritual light more easily in the absence of *distracting physical light*.[19] A dark room would have thus been an optimal place for his work as a translator, but such conditions would have hindered the scribe's work. Joseph adopted a compromise measure, working in a well-lit room so his scribe could see the page while using a hat to shield his seer stone from light. To do this, he placed the stone in the bottom of his stovepipe hat and rested his face over the brim, enabling him to look at the stone in the dark.

The effect reportedly wrought by the spiritual light within the darkness was transformative. The Book of Mormon hieroglyphs, as Joseph and other witnesses described them appearing on the plates, were set out in *black* against a

17. These accounts may be found in John W. Welch, *Opening the Heavens: Accounts of Divine Manifestations, 1820–1844*, Documents #23, 45, 55, 56, 76, 81, 83, 84, 85, 86, 88, 89, 90, 93, 94, 95, 96, 97, 98, 101, 108, 112, 116, and 176.

18. David Whitmer reported, "Joseph Smith would put the seer stone into a hat, and put his face in the hat, drawing it closely around his face to exclude the light; and in the darkness the spiritual light would shine." Whitmer, *An Address*, 11. Another account by Whitmer speaks of the translation appearing in "bright luminous letters." James H. Hart, Letter to the Editor, in Vogel, *EMD*, 5:108. In one of the earliest detailed accounts of how Joseph Smith translated, Joseph Knight, Sr., who helped support the Smith family financially during the translation, wrote, "Now the way he translated was he put the urim and thummim into his hat and Darkned his Eyes then he would take a sentence and it would apper in Brite Roman Letters then he would tell the writer and he would write it." Joseph Knight Sr., "Manuscript of the History of Joseph Smith," in Vogel, *EMD* 4:17–18.

19. Accounts of the light shining in the darkness are given in the previous note. A number of other accounts also mention Joseph using his hat to "exclude the light." See, for example, William Smith, *William Smith on Mormonism*, 10.

bright background of *gold*.[20] Conversely, the translated images or words that appeared as Joseph looked at the seer stone occluded in his hat were light against darkness. Thus through the stone, the record's original, untranslated state was inverted: its meaning, previously hidden in characters literally and figuratively "as dark as Egypt"[21] now stood written in strokes of light, words ablaze against a black page of ambient darkness.[22] Like the development of a negative into a photograph, transposing dark with bright, Joseph Smith's process of translation rendered, in place of the opaque hieroglyphs that had baffled the learned professors, lucid English words intelligible to the unlearned prophet.

This illumination of the visual faculties by which Joseph perceived the spiritual light both represented and brought about the illumination of his understanding. In both vision and knowledge Joseph went from uncomprehending darkness into light. It is perhaps this unity of the symbol with the process being experienced and symbolized that is most striking about Joseph Smith's reported experience as translator.

Several of Joseph Smith's early revelations, which were also given through the spiritual light shining in darkness from the seer stone, evoke and develop this symbolism inherent in their mode of delivery. One such revelation through Joseph in 1829 for his brother Hyrum instructed Hyrum to believe "in the power of Jesus Christ, or in my power which speaketh unto thee: for behold it is I that speaketh: behold I am the light which shineth in darkness, and by my power I give these words unto thee" (D&C 11:10–11).

Thus the medium through which this revelation was received—words of light appearing on the stone amid darkness—is invoked in the revelation itself to authenticate the revelation's message and identify its divine author. The luminous words seen by Joseph in the seer stone were given by the power of him who *is* "the light which shineth in darkness," "the power of Jesus Christ."

---

20. Orson Pratt reported that the Eight Witnesses of the Book of Mormon, who attested to handling the golden plates, "describe these plates as being about the thickness of common tin, about eight inches in length, and from six to seven in breadth" and having "[u]pon each side of the leaves of these plates . . . fine engravings, which were stained with a black, hard stain, so as to make the letters more legible and easier to be read." Orson Pratt, January 2, 1859, *Journal of Discourses*, 7:31.

21. The phrase "dark as Egypt," a nineteenth-century idiom, was used by Joseph Smith to describe the total darkness he experienced on looking into the hat after Martin Harris surreptitiously swapped out the seer stone for another, similar-appearing rock. See Edward Stevenson's account of his 1870 interview with Martin Harris in Edward Stevenson, "One of the Three Witnesses," 4.

22. Compare this to Alma 37:23—"I will prepare unto my servant Gazelem, a stone, which shall shine forth in darkness unto light, that I may discover unto my people who serve me, that I may discover unto them the works of their brethren."

Written by the Finger of God

A revelation to Joseph Smith five years after he obtained the golden plates similarly underscores the divinity of both the Book of Mormon and his early first-person divine revelations by invoking their mode of delivery. The Lord, in this revelation, refers to "the Book of Mormon and the former commandments which I have given" as "*that which I have written*" (D&C 84:57), affirming these texts' *authority* by identifying himself as their *author*, he having spiritually written them as they appeared on the seer stone.[23]

The symbolic value of spiritual writing appearing on the stone exceeds merely identifying the divine source of the Book of Mormon and the revelations. The writing of God's words on stone also evokes one of the foundational stories of biblical religion—the writing of the Ten Commandments "by the finger of God" on the stone tablets at Sinai.[24] It is no wonder then that Joseph Smith's revelations through the seer stone were known to the earliest Latter-day Saints as "commandments" (and hence their first compilation as "The Book of Commandments"). The biblical parallel was not lost on the early Saints, nor was its implication—that the spiritual communications that appeared on Joseph's seer stone were no less authoritative and divine than those written by God's finger on Moses's stone tablets.

Piercing the Veil: A Glimpse of Translation by the Interpreters

Emma appears to have been one of four relatives (by blood or by law) who wrote for Joseph during the translation. After her initial scribal work, two of her brothers also assisted, with the scribes perhaps rotating irregularly across translation sessions. Emma's older brother, Alva Hale, evidently took

---

23. God is similarly quoted in the Bible, using the phrase "which I have written" with reference to law he wrote for Moses on the tablets at Sinai (Ex. 24:12; cf. Hosea 8:12). The Book of Mormon version of Isaiah uses similar phrasing, varying from the King James Version's reference to the righteous as "the people in whose heart is my law" with the reading "the people in whose heart I have written my law" (Isa. 51:7; 2 Ne. 8:7).

24. The phenomenon of something shining after coming in contact with the divine presence is another parallel between Joseph Smith's translation phenomenology and the story of God writing on his finger on the stone tablets at Mount Sinai. As described in the Book of Exodus, after Moses' exposure to the presence of God as God touched the stone tablets, his face shined (Ex. 34:29–30). The grooves of the stone tablets, where God had written, were subject to the same literally illuminating divine influence, but the narrative does not report that these also shined, but this is precisely the effect of His touch in the parallel incident of the Lord touching the stones brought to him by the brother of Jared on another mountaintop (Ether 3).

up the pen to assist, though very briefly,[25] and her youngest brother, Reuben Hale, did a fair amount of work as scribe, reportedly taking dictation for Joseph on a number of occasions.[26] Joseph also credited his younger brother Samuel Smith with providing some (probably brief) service as a scribe.[27]

On "about" April 12, 1828, according to Joseph's recollection, Martin Harris returned and began work as the principal scribe for the translation, continuing to write for Joseph until about June 14, 1828.[28] In translating with Martin's help, Joseph used the interpreters, which apparently required a more elaborate physical setup.[29] While translating through the seer stone allowed Joseph to leave the plates wrapped up or in a distant hiding place, translating through the interpreters required the plates to be physically pres-

---

25. Three evidences support Alva Hale's scribal service to Joseph Smith being brief. First, very few sources report that Alva served as a translation scribe. Second, David Whitmer, one of the only sources attributing a scribal role to Alva, says his service was brief. "Revelation Revisers," 7. Third, although Emma's son Joseph Smith III appears to have heard that this uncle had been one of the scribes and she acknowledged that Alva "may have written some," she did not then recall him serving as a scribe. Emma Hale Smith Bidamon, in Smith, "Last Testimony," 289–90.

26. "Joe Smith would write the translation from his plates upon a slate, or dictate what to write, and others would copy upon paper. His assistants were witness Martin Harris and brother-in-law Reuben Hale. The translating and writing were done in the little low chamber of Joe Smith's house." Frederick G. Mather, "The Early Mormons. Joe Smith Operates at Susquehanna," in Vogel, *EMD*, 4:355 (compare similar Mather quote in Vogel, *EMD*, 4:364). Also, Smith, "Last Testimony," 289–90, and Knight, "Manuscript of the History," in Vogel, *EMD*, 4:18.

27. In his earliest recorded history Joseph reported this of the translation work before Martin Harris's scribal tenure: "[N]ow my wife had writen [sic] some for me to translate and also my Brother Samuel H Smith." Joseph Smith, "History, circa Summer 1832."

28. "History, 1838–1856, volume A-1 [23 December 1805–30 August 1834]." These dates are almost certainly not exact, and it is unclear how Joseph recalled or arrived at the specific dates of April 12 and June 14. Likely he arrived at these dates by anchoring the beginning and ending of Martin's scribal tenure to other events, for which he had recorded or well-remembered dates. As discussed further below, June 15, 1828, was the birth (and death) date for Joseph and Emma's oldest child. If he recalled that Martin left shortly before the child's birth, Joseph would have arrived at June 14 as the outside date on which Martin could have gone. Another family event, the April 9 death of Emma's uncle Reuben Hale in North Franklin, New York, about 75 miles from Harmony, could have similarly anchored the inauguration of Martin's scribal work. Joseph may have keyed his memory of Martin's first scribal work to Hale's death or funeral.

29. Simplifying Joseph's shifts from the seer stone to the interpreters and then eventually back to the seer stone, Emma described him to one inquirer as having used the interpreters for "the part that Martin Harris lost." Emma Smith Bidamon to Emma Pilgrim, March 27, 1870, in Vogel, *EMD*, 1:532.

ent and uncovered. To prevent anyone from seeing the open plates, a veil was placed between Joseph and the scribe so that these sacred things, like the holy things of the biblical temple, could be shielded from common gaze.[30]

Fortunately, several people heard detailed descriptions of these objects from Joseph Smith, and a few reportedly also felt or saw some of the items for themselves. Joseph Smith's parents fit both categories. Joseph's mother and father saw the interpreters and the book of plates, respectively, and also heard him describe these objects immediately after he first saw them.[31] The interpreters, as described by Lucy Mack Smith in earlier chapters, were translation "keys" of triangular shape—"three cornered diamonds." And we have learned from Joseph's father that these interpreters lay on the top plates of the book, which was engraved with symbols, minimally including compass and square.[32]

Over this plate with the compass and square symbols were laid the two transparent triangles described by Joseph's mother—the interpreters. The placement of the triangular interpreters over the depictions of compass and square is fitting—perhaps literally—and suggests another layer to the compass

---

30. The law given in the Hebrew Bible specifies that the Ark of the Covenant and other "holy things" were to be veiled when carried from place to place, and that, on penalty of death, only the priests were to see them before they were covered (Num. 4:4–20).

31. The entire Smith family handled the plates wrapped in a cloth when Joseph brought them back from the hill. Joseph Smith Sr., along with two of his other sons, testified to having seen and handled them, turned the leaves of the plates, and seen the engravings on them. And, as quoted in the text below, Lucy Mack Smith reported seeing and handling the interpreters through a thin muslin handkerchief.

32. Fayette Lapham reported learning the following about the plate the interpreters rested on: "On the next page were representations of all the masonic implements, as used by masons at the present day." Fayette Lapham, "Interview with the Father of Joseph Smith, the Mormon Prophet, Forty Years Ago. His Account of the Finding of the Sacred Plates," in Vogel, EMD, 1:462. As discussed in greater detail in Chapter 1, any set of "the masonic implements" would minimally contain the two essential implements of compass and square, without which a lodge could not be opened. As further discussed in that note, a representation of "the masonic implements, as used by masons" of that day would likely also include a book with compass and square placed on it; the pillars of Solomon's temple; an apron; the name of God; the sun, moon, and stars; and might include the beehive, the Star of David, and the Ark of the Covenant. The association of these symbols with Freemasonry would not puzzle most Latter-day Saints of the present, since these symbols are familiar from scripture. Indeed, most of these "Masonic" symbols were drawn by Freemasons from the Bible. Symbols that in the 1820s evoked Freemasonry for Joseph Smith Sr. have different meanings to later Saints. To Latter-day Saints since 1832, for instance, sun, moon, and stars are not associated with Freemasonry, nor even only with the many biblical passages that mention them, but with the celestial, terrestrial, and telestial kingdoms (D&C 76).

and square symbolism of the relics. Triangular interpreters could potentially be placed over the compass and square engravings so as to align perfectly with them, one interpreter aligned with the compass, the other with the square.[33]

The interpreters and the engravings would have aligned, not by coincidence, but by design. The plates were made to go with the interpreters and to be translated with them (Ether 3:23–24). Compass and square symbols on the plates would have represented and provided a place for the interpreters, which would fit them as a key fits a lock.

Adding yet another layer to the compass and square symbolism of the interpreters is the structure of the larger device that contained them. According to Lucy Mack Smith, the triangles or "three-cornered diamonds" were set in curved frames "which were connected with each other in much the same way, as old-fashioned spectacles."[34] By Joseph Smith's day, spectacles that sat on the bridge of the nose and looped over the ears, like our familiar modern eye-glasses, were common. What Joseph's mother meant by "old fashioned" has two likely candidates: the first are rivet or scissor spectacles that folded on a simple rivet and were still in use at the time, though were becoming increasingly rare; the second was the lorgnette, a type of spectacles held to the eyes by a handle that were still commonly used. Because the interpreters were said to be connected to a rod—which could conceivably be used as a handle—a comparison to the lorgnette may seem apt; however, it was likely to the folding spectacles, rather than the lorgnette, that Lucy was comparing the interpreters. While "old-fashioned" to us, the lorgnette continued very much in vogue through the nineteenth century, and what Lucy had remarked as being old-fashioned about the interpreters was not that they could be attached to a handle but how their two lens frames attached to *each other*: the frames of the interpreters were "*connected* . . . in much the same way as old-fashioned spectacles"; this suggests that the spectacles lacked the solid bridge over the nose common to later spectacles and instead folded over a hinge. It was these folding spectacles that were older in style, rarer in use, and readily identifiable as "old-fashioned" at the time Lucy used this term. If the interpreters were like rivet spectacles, they would have had a hinge that, like a compass, allowed their lenses to fold in and over one another, or to fold out, allowing them to be opened to a right angle, or, in builder's terms, to the square.

An obvious challenge to this description of a hinged device is that gravity would tend to pull the lenses down under the hinge, where they would hang use-

---

33. A fit between the inscribed compass and square symbols and the interpreters would not require that the symbols and the interpreters be the same size. An interpreter could be overlaid onto the corresponding symbol, at least in part, if the interpreter and symbol had the same angle.

34. Anderson, *Lucy's Book*, 379.

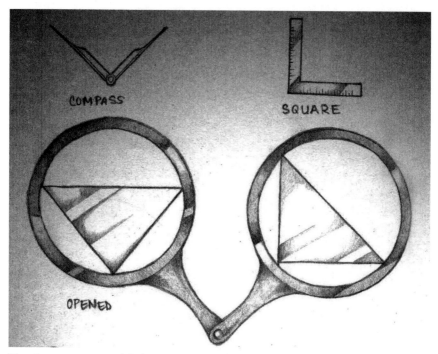

The interpreters, modeled on Lucy Mack Smith's description resembling "old-fashioned spectacles," in unfolded position. Artist's rendition courtesy of Jody Livingston, Peculiar People Illustrations.

lessly. When attached to the rod, the device would have required a catch to hold the lenses in position in front of the eyes. In holding the lenses in place, a catch would have also given them a default position and distance from one another. The default width to which it would open would depend on how close to the eyes it was intended to be used and how wide-set the user's eyes were expected to be.

Some nineteenth-century reports say that the lenses of the interpreters were set too wide for Joseph's eyes, making it uncomfortable for him to use them simultaneously while they rested on the rod. Joseph's father, a wearer of spectacles himself, reportedly said the interpreters were set one and a half inches wider than the lenses of ordinary spectacles, indicating either that Joseph was not using it in the way intended by its inventor or that the device holding the interpreters was designed for a person of extraordinary size.[35] Perhaps the most obvious default position for the device would be for the lenses to fall open to a right angle (90 degrees), by opening 45 degrees to each side. This position would also have familiar symbolic value, making the device a compass opened to the position of the square.

---

35. Lapham, "Interview," in Vogel, *EMD*, 1:462.

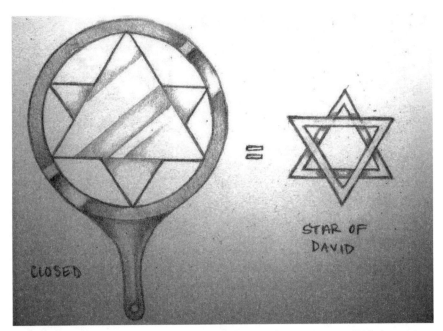

The interpreters, modeled on Lucy Mack Smith's description, in folded position. Artist's rendition courtesy of Jody Livingston, Peculiar People Illustrations

The evidence provided by the prophet's parents thus suggests the interpreters embodied the compass and the square on three levels: (1) the engravings on the plate upon which the interpreters rested, (2) the shapes of their lenses, and (3) the adjustability of their frame to form angles corresponding to both compass and square.

In addition to compass and square, the interpreters could be evoked or embody other symbols. A hinged device with triangles that fold over one another could be used to form the symbol of a star. So, for example, two equilateral triangle lenses folded diametrically opposite to one another would create the Star of David.

Depending on the orientation of the lenses, the use of the interpreters could also evoke the symbol of the all-seeing eye. With an equilateral-triangle lens oriented with its base at the bottom during the interpreters' use, the user's eye would be framed in a triangle in precisely the way the symbol of the all-seeing eye is most often depicted.[36]

Considering the shape and engineering of the interpreters can also extend our understanding of the "sealing up" of the plates, and of the interpreters

---

36. Notably, Joseph Smith referred to his white seer stone as "an All-Seeing Eye." W. D. Purple, "Joseph Smith, the Originator of Mormonism," 3, in Vogel, *EMD*, 4:133–34.

"with" the plates, as commanded by the Lord of the brother of Jared: "[T]hese two stones will I give unto thee, and ye shall seal them up also with the things which ye shall write" (Ether 3:23). We have seen that one way the book of plates was sealed up was by its final author affixing a sacred symbol to it—a seal. While the plates required the *adding* of such a seal, the interpreters could acquire such a seal by being *folded into* it, as how superimposing two triangles can create a star like the Star of David. The Star of David, which appeared occasionally in Jewish contexts as early as the seventh century BC, often encompassed within a circle, was traditionally identified as a "seal."[37] A strikingly similar image would emerge if two triangles were folded over one another in the manner of "old-fashioned spectacles," rendering a star within the circle of the interpreters' rims. The interpreters' apparent capacity to be folded up *into* a seal seems one likely way they could be sealed up.

If the interpreters were sealed up in this sense, what did it mean for them to be sealed up *with* the plates? If compass and square engravings on the top plate constituted a seal on the plates, and the interpreters, folded together, constituted a seal in themselves, then the two seals could be aligned as corresponding seals and thus sealed up together. Such an alignment and sealing up of the interpreters with the plates would have fittingly implied that they were the necessary "key," to use Joseph's term, by which the plates could be sealed or unsealed, their contents revealed or hidden with God.

Such a *sealing* of the plates using sacred Nephite temple relics that Joseph described to his mother as a "key" prefigures concepts of sealing, by sacred keys, in a temple context, that Joseph would not begin to introduce formally for a decade and a half after his recovery of the plates. Yet such concepts and language were present in fundamental ways from the time Joseph visited Cumorah to remove these sacred relics from the Nephite ark and begin to reveal their contents to the world.

The Breastplate and Its Symbolism

The connection of the interpreters, and their compass and square symbolism, to the breastplate also bears some exploration. Found with the interpreters in Cumorah's stone ark and designed to hold them, this breastplate clearly bore the same relationship to interpreters as the biblical high priest's breastplate did to the Urim and Thummim. The high priest's breastplate was part of a larger set of holy garments God commanded Moses to make:

---

37. Joseph Gutmann, *The Jewish Sanctuary*, 21–22. This study is Section XXIII: Judaism, of the Iconography of Religions, produced by the Institute of Religious Iconography of the State University Gronigen, Netherlands. See also Herbert M. Adler, "The Jews in Southern Italy," 111–15. Gershom Scholem, *Kabbalah*, 362–68.

And thou shalt make holy garments for Aaron thy brother. . . . And these are the garments which they shall make; a breastplate, and an ephod, and a robe, and a broidered coat, a mitre, and a girdle . . . that he may minister unto me in the priest's office. (Ex. 28:2, 4)

The ephod was the garment to which the breastplate attached. The mitre (a priestly headdress or cap, also called "the crown") has its own parallel to the priestly treasures of Cumorah's ark. On the mitre's front, resting over the forehead, was an engraved gold plate with the words "Holiness to the LORD" (Ex. 28:36–37; 39:30).

The accompanying breastplate was to be made of "fine twined linen," with various colors (Ex. 28:15). In it were set stones on which were engraved the names of the tribes of Israel, so the high priest could "bear the names of the children of Israel in the breastplate of judgment upon his heart" (vv. 17, 21, 29). Also attaching to the breastplate were the two stones named the Urim and Thummim (Lev. 8:8).

Paralleling this biblical holy garment to which the Urim and Thummim attached was the breastplate to which the Book of Mormon interpreters attached. According to Lucy Mack Smith, it "extended from the neck downwards, as far as the centre of the stomach."[38] William Smith, who heard about the interpreters and breastplate from both his mother Lucy and his brother Joseph, reportedly told John W. Peterson that the interpreters connected to the breastplate via a rod attaching to the shoulder and that the interpreters could be carried in "a pocket . . . prepared in the breast-plate on the left side immediately over the heart."[39] Thus, when not in use, the interpreters would sit on the left side of the chest. When connected to the rod, they would unfold a few inches apart above and in front of the breastplate, likely with a "compass"-formed triangle lens opening to one side and a "square"-formed triangle lens to the other.

In using the breastplate and interpreters, Joseph was, in effect, putting on the high priestly garments and acting in the place of the biblical high priest. The physical setup required for him to use these in the translation was somewhat elaborate. Joseph prepared the room for the work of translation via the interpreters by hanging a curtain or veil across the upper room of his home, to

---

38. In her memoir Lucy wrote of the breastplate, "It was concave on one side, and convex on the other, and extended from the neck downwards, as far as the centre of the stomach of a man of extraordinary size. It had four straps of the same material, for the purpose of fastening it to the breast, two of which ran back to go over the shoulders, and the other two were designed to fasten to the hips. They were just the width of two of my fingers, (for I measured them,) and they had holes in the end of them, to be convenient in fastening." Anderson, *Lucy's Book*, 389–90.

39. "Statement of J. W. Peterson Concerning William Smith," May 1, 1921, in Vogel, *EMD* 1:508–9.

veil himself and the plates from the scribe, as he would later hang a veil in his red brick store to prepare the room for endowment ceremonies.[40] Within this veiled translation space, as within the Tabernacle and Solomon's Temple, the sacred artifacts could be bared and used. Behind the veil, Joseph donned the breastplate and attached to it the interpreters, or, as he later called them, the Urim and Thummim.[41] Because translator and scribe were at differing levels of readiness for the divine presence, they had to interact through the veil with Joseph dictating the revealed words to Martin, and Martin recording them and repeating them to Joseph for him to confirm that they were correct.[42]

---

40. The use of a curtain to veil the spectacles and plates while these were in use is reported in 1834 and 1841 by Charles Anthon and in 1840 by John A. Clark, who describes it as a "thick" curtain. Anthon to Howe, February 17, 1834, in Vogel, *EMD*, 4:378–79; Anthon to Coit, April 3, 1841, in Vogel, *EMD*, 4:384. John A. Clark, Letter to "Dear Brethren," August 24, 1840, in Vogel, *EMD*, 2:268.

41. In his 1839 history, Joseph Smith describes the interpreters, calling them "the Urim and Thummim" and indicating that they attached to the breastplate: "[T]here were two stones in silver bows—and these stones, fastened to a breastplate, constituted what is called the Urim and Thummim" (JS–H 1:35). For the term "Urim and Thummim" applied to the interpreters in Joseph Smith's revelations, see D&C 17:1. Early manuscripts of this revelation probably used the term "interpreters," but the earliest extant version, from the 1835 Doctrine and Covenants, used "Urim and Thummim." Richard S. Van Wagoner and Steven C. Walker argue: "The Nephite interpreters were not referred to as Urim and Thummim until 1833, when W. W. Phelps first equated the two in the first edition of the *Evening and Morning Star*." Richard S. Van Wagoner and Steven C. Walker, "Joseph Smith: 'The Gift of Seeing,'" 53. However, Brant Gardner sensibly cautions that the Phelps piece likely demonstrates only "the first time the association appeared in print," noting "that the term was very likely current earlier among the community" and that "Phelps may have merely repeated what had become an oral convention among the Mormons." Gardner, *The Gift and Power*, 128n27. There are few explicit mentions of Joseph Smith wearing the breastplate while using the interpreters. See William Smith interview with J. W. Peterson and W. S. Pender in "Statement of J. W. Peterson Concerning William Smith," in Vogel, *EMD*, 1:508–9.

42. Clark, Letter to "Dear Brethren," in Vogel, *EMD*, 2:268. Truman Coe, reciting Martin Harris's early account of translation by the interpreters, stated that during this process "a thick curtain or blanket was suspended" between them. Joseph would "look through his spectacles, or transparent stones, and would then . . . repeat what he saw, which, when repeated aloud, was written down by Harris, who sat on the other side of the suspended blanket." Although Coe's repeated use of "repeat" is confusing, he appears to say that Joseph would dictate the words of translation he saw, upon which Martin would repeat them back to Joseph before recording them. That Joseph had his scribes verify the text with him by repeating it back is also verified by accounts from translation witness David Whitmer and by manuscript evidence

The only detailed description of the process of translation by the formidable interpreters comes from an 1836 letter of Kirtland, Ohio, minister Truman Coe shortly after Coe had interviewed Joseph Smith:

> The manner of translation was as wonderful as the discovery. By putting his finger on one of the characters and imploring divine aid, then looking through the Urim and Thummim, he would see the import written in plain English on a screen placed before him. After delivering this to his emanuensi, he would again proceed in the same manner and obtain the meaning of the next character.[43]

This account does not identify the hand that literally or figuratively wrote the words of translation on "the screen placed before him." However, this identification was made elsewhere when the Book of Mormon was described by revelation to Joseph Smith as "that which *I* have written"—referring to God as the writer (D&C 84:57). Fittingly, then, Joseph's own action in this divine writing process parallels that of the Lord: as Joseph touches a character on the gold plates with his finger, the Lord writes its interpretation upon the veil with *His* finger.

Coe's recital of the Prophet's translation account is also significant in its mechanical details about the functioning of the interpreters, which, as reported, produced a visual effect similar to that of a slide projector or a nineteenth-century slide lantern: a small image that "would appear on the lenses"[44] was projected in much larger form onto the screen or veil in front of him. This fulfilled quite literally the Lord's prophecy to the brother of Jared about the interpreters: "I will cause in my own due time that these stones shall *magnify* to the eyes of men these things which ye shall write" (Ether 3:24).[45]

---

from the surviving portions of the original manuscript of the Book of Mormon, by Royal Skousen. Whitmer, *An Address*, 12; "Mormonism. Authentic Account of the Origin of The Sect from One of the Patriarchs," 1; Royal Skousen, "Translating the Book of Mormon: Evidence from the Original Manuscript," 61–93.

43. Coe, "Mormonism,"1.

44. An obituary for David Whitmer reported that when "Smith would put on the spectacles . . . a few words of the text of the Book of Mormon would appear on the lenses." Combining the details provided by Whitmer and Coe, we arrive at images being projected via the lenses onto the veil. "The Last Witness Dead!" 3.

45. The slide lantern, or "magic lantern," was an early type of image projector, invented in the mid-seventeenth century. Significantly, the lenses of the interpreters may have been convex on both sides, like those of a magnifying glass. In 1850, Francis Gladden Bishop, who then had Martin Harris as a follower, had described the interpreters as "convex on either side." In 1859, Martin Harris reportedly described them as thicker in the center but "not so thick at the edges." Francis Gladden Bishop, *An Address to the Sons and Daughters of Zion, Scattered Abroad, Through All the Earth*, 48. "Mormonism---No. II," 165–66.

The interpreters would have projected images onto the screen most visibly when outside light was excluded. Indeed, the defining function of a screen in Joseph's day was not to provide a surface for the projection of images but to *screen out* external light. A screen, as defined in the Noah Webster's 1828 Dictionary, was "any thing that separates or cuts off inconvenience, injury or danger; and hence, that which shelters or protects from danger, or prevents inconvenience. Thus a screen is used to intercept the sight, to intercept the heat of fire or the light of a candle." In this it was equivalent to a veil, whose function was also to separate: "A cover; a curtain; something to intercept the view and hide an object." Both could be employed to "intercept the sight" or "view."[46]

The "screen placed before him" during the process of translation by the interpreters was thus not just an internal movie screen in Joseph's mind; it was a physical obstruction—the veil or blanket that needed to be hung in front of him to screen out interfering light.[47] Joseph translated, on the reports conveyed by Pomeroy Tucker, "behind a blanket-screen drawn across a *dark corner* of a room" to screen out physical light.[48] The blanket or veil in front of Smith thus functioned both like the doors of a darkened movie theater, blocking out distracting and interfering light, *and* as the movie screen onto which the images were projected. The full visual and emotional effect of this process, if imagined, is striking. Equilateral-triangle and right-triangle lenses project their light onto the veil. And incandescent letters appear one by one against the blackness as if written by an unseen hand—another manifestation of "the light which shineth in darkness."[49]

The curtains or veils behind which Joseph translated via the interpreters thus appear to have had several functions: shielding the sacred objects from outside gaze, facilitating Joseph's perception of the subtle spiritual light by reducing natural light, providing a screen or canvas onto which the words written in this light could be projected and magnified, and marking off sacred space in which Joseph could use the breastplate and interpreters.

Yet, in marking a boundary between sacred space and ordinary space, the veil did more than separate. A boundary is not only a marker of separation, but also a point of contact. The veil between sacred and profane, higher and lower, provided the point of contact between Martin and Joseph, and between Joseph and the Lord. Through the veil, the spiritual veil symbolized

---

46. Noah Webster, *American Dictionary of the English Language*, s.v. "screen" and "veil."

47. Coe's reference to a "screen placed before" Joseph is comparable to Anthon's "curtain before him."

48. Pomeroy Tucker, *Origin, Rise, and Progress of Mormonism*, 36; emphasis added.

49. The writing by God's finger on this veil might fruitfully be compared to the writing on the wall of the temple "by the finger of God" in the Nephite story of Aminadi (Alma 10:2). See Chapter 13.

by the physical curtain, Joseph communicated with the Lord. Wearing the breastplate and consulting the interpreters, Joseph would touch with his finger each of the engravings—the mysterious alphabetic characters, the "crosses and flourishes," the esoteric "implements." And the Lord wrote by his own hand each symbol onto the veil. The Lord then unfolded the symbol's meaning, "writing" it also on the veil.

The very veil that divided higher and lower also provided a place for conveying knowledge from higher to lower. Boundaries of sacred space had been similarly marked off with cloth in the ancient biblical Tabernacle and Solomon's temple, where a veil was hung before the Holy of Holies, in which the high priest, wearing the breastplate and Urim and Thummim, approached the Ark of the Covenant on the Day of Atonement to perform his most sacred responsibilities.

As a translator, Joseph Smith—secluded behind a veil like that concealing the Ark, wearing a breastplate like that of the Jewish high priest, and consulting two stones that paralleled the stones of the biblical Urim and Thummim—took on the high priest's mediatory role as revelator, consulting God on behalf of others through instruments and sacred space consecrated to that purpose. In this way, the translation space acted as a makeshift tabernacle.

Joseph would again construct such sacred space in the 1830s by building an actual temple in Kirtland, Ohio, where he would introduce ordinances of washing and anointing and where, behind a drawn veil, he and Oliver Cowdery would enter the Lord's presence. He would construct another sacred edifice in the 1840s when he built the Nauvoo Temple, with its still more profound and sweeping sacred rituals. But the first temple space Joseph Smith constructed was where he translated the lost book in the upper room of his house, the space demarcated by a hanging veil and hallowed by God's presence manifest in His hand reaching out to write on the veil.

CHAPTER 4

THE MANUSCRIPT THEFT

Despite having been missing for nearly two centuries, investigations into the disappearance of the Book of Mormon's lost manuscript have scarcely been done at all. Instead, Martin Harris's antagonistic wife Lucy Harris has been generally assumed to be the only suspect worth considering, and the case was closed before it was ever opened. This chapter will open the case of the Book of Mormon manuscript theft, exploring in detail how the manuscript came to be stolen and examining the evidence for the identity of the thieves.

The story of the manuscript's loss begins where we left off in the story of its translation. Joseph Smith and Martin Harris carried out their respective roles in the translation process for several weeks, but practical considerations entailed that sooner or later they must pause. Emma was about to deliver the couple's first child, and Martin was feeling pressure to return home after having parted with his children and wife and forsaken his farm for most of the spring. It also appears that Joseph and Martin were running out of paper.[1]

In anticipation of a break in the work, Martin requested that he be permitted to take the translation manuscript home with him to show others.[2] He likely also requested to again take the plate facsimile that he had shown to Anthon. Such permission would enable him to display both the characters, which "the learned" could not read, and the translation, which Joseph *had* read from the plates.[3] That Martin took the Anthon transcript and lost it with the translation manuscript is suggested by two considerations: no one describes seeing that transcript after 1828, and none of the still-existing transcripts match the one described by Anthon.[4]

In response to Martin's request to take the documents, Joseph petitioned God for permission but was denied through the interpreters. At Martin's urging, Joseph asked again, resulting again with the same answer. After further

---

1. Joseph Knight Sr., "Manuscript of the History of Joseph Smith," in Vogel, *EMD*, 4:19. Joseph Knight recalled giving Joseph "a little money to Buoy paper" in January 1829. Since, as discussed below, little if any translation work was done during the remainder of 1828 after the manuscript loss, this suggests that Joseph was already low on paper for translation when the work halted in June 1828. The paper used for the translation is further discussed in the following chapter.

2. Joseph Smith, "History, circa Summer 1832."

3. John A. Clark, *Gleanings by the Way*, 222–28.

4. Charles Anthon to E. D. Howe, February 17, 1834, in Vogel, *EMD*, 4:377–81. Charles Anthon to Thomas Winthrop Coit, April 3, 1841, in Vogel, *EMD*, 4:382–86.

teasing from Martin, and as the translation neared a pause, Joseph agreed to make a third inquiry, upon which permission was finally granted for Martin to show others the manuscript, along with a commandment that it be limited to only five designated family members: "his brother Preserved Harris, his own wife, his father, and his also mother, and a Mrs Cobb a sister to his wife."[5] Before taking the manuscript, Martin had to covenant to obey "the word of the Lord" that restricted the manuscript's audience to those five.[6]

Martin's repeated requests were, in part, responsible for the manuscript loss. Had he settled for the first or second answer, the curious reader would not be holding the present book in his or her hands but would instead be reading a version of the Book of Mormon that contains many of the missing stories this volume intends to reconstruct. Given the risks and severity of the consequences of Martin's actions, a question crucial to understanding the loss of that book is: Why was Martin Harris so insistent on taking the manuscript home with him after already having been told no by God twice?

Trouble in the Harris Home

An obvious reason for Martin Harris to take the manuscript back with him was to satisfy skepticism at home. Martin's wife had been doubtful of, and even antagonistic toward, Joseph Smith's claims. Additionally, Martin's time away from his home and farm raised skepticism about *him*. From the family's perspective, Martin Harris was a man gone mad.[7] Martin's various travels in the winter of 1828 to authenticate the character transcript (between Palmyra, Harmony, Albany, Philadelphia, and New York City) and his subsequent journeys that spring to act as Joseph's scribe would likely have taken about eight weeks in just travel time alone.[8] On top of these, Martin spent some eight weeks of the spring actually scribing for Joseph.[9] Martin thus sacrificed much of his winter and nearly his entire spring to assist with the translation, and the particular time period Martin chose to leave the farm to serve as a translation scribe was startling. The winter of 1827–28, which has been called "a season

---

5. Joseph Smith et al., *History of the Church of Jesus Christ of Latterday Saints*, 1:21.

6. Smith, "History, circa Summer 1832."

7. Pomeroy Tucker, *Origin, Rise, and Progress of Mormonism*, 54.

8. Elden Watson estimates that Martin spent forty days traveling with the character transcript. This was followed by a journey to and from Harmony with his wife Lucy, which was then followed with his trip to begin scribing for Joseph and his return trip after scribing, each of these two round trips adding about eight days, bringing the estimated total to fifty-six days—eight weeks. Elden Watson, "Approximate Book of Mormon Translation Timeline."

9. Stanley Kimball, "The Anthon Transcript: People, Primary Sources, and Problems," 327.

of extraordinary climatic anomalies," was so unseasonably warm as to bring an early planting season in the eastern United States, moving planting in upstate New York forward to mid-April. The time that Martin was assisting Joseph would have rivaled harvest as the busiest time of the year for a farmer in that region.[10] During the time of his absence from the farm Martin, who had a reputation as an expert farmer, should have been carrying out or at least overseeing the work of harrowing, plowing, planting, and otherwise preparing his ground to ensure the fall yield of the flax, beans, pumpkins, corn, and other grains on which his livelihood depended.[11] Instead, Martin spent that exact period—from about April 12 through June 14—scribing the translation.

Planting season, however, was not all Martin missed at home. While in Harmony with Joseph, Martin was absent from something even more momentous: the May 8 wedding of his daughter Lucy Jr. to Flanders Dyke in Palmyra.[12]

Evidence that Martin's absence from these family events was causing trouble at home is visible in what Martin's wife was doing in his absence. On May 13, five days after Martin failed to show up to give his daughter's hand to Flanders Dyke, a deed *from* Martin for eighty acres of his land appears in the Palmyra land records. The deed is made out to Martin's cousin and brother-in-law, Peter Harris (Lucy's brother; Martin and Lucy were biological first cousins). With this deed appears another, from Peter Harris to *Lucy* for the same eighty acres of what had been Martin's land. This succession of deeds from Martin to Peter then from Peter to Lucy provided an indirect way for Martin to convey her dowry land to Lucy, circumventing laws about joint marital property. But how could Martin deed his land, even indirectly, to Lucy in his absence? The deeds in question were originally executed on November 29, *1825*.[13] After their original signing, Lucy held onto these deeds for nearly three years before she felt the need to record them. Her

---

10. Cary J. Mock et al, "The Winter of 1827–1828 over Eastern North America: A Season of Extraordinary Climatic Anomalies, Societal Impacts, and False Spring," 87–115. My thanks to Geoff Slinker for bringing this paper to my attention.

11. The month of May, which Martin Harris spent entirely at scribing for Joseph, was not only a crucial time for planting but also an optimal time for haying. Information about farming in Palmyra area was provided by Donald Enders and Emily Utt, both of the LDS Historic Sites Division. Personal communication from Emily Utt, July 20, 2011.

12. Their marriage was announced in the May 9, 1828, *Wayne Sentinel.*

13. Indenture, Martin Harris to Peter Harris, Wayne County, New York, November 29, 1825; and Indenture, Peter Harris to Lucy Harris, Wayne County, New York, November 29, 1825. New York Land Records, Wayne County, Deeds 1827–1828, Vol. 5, Family History Library, Salt Lake City, Utah. I am grateful to Michael H. MacKay for first putting me on to this source, and to Marie Thatcher for tracking it down.

sudden recording of these deeds to give them full legal efficacy immediately after Martin missed their daughter's wedding communicates her intentions as clearly as any words could have. Upon her husband's failure to show up for the wedding, Lucy acted to give herself financial independence from Martin. She was taking an initial step toward separation.

When Martin *did* return home a full month after his wife took this step, he was walking into a firestorm—and he knew it. In view of his absence from both his agricultural seed and his generational seed, and the consequent estrangement between him and his wife, Martin's insistence to Joseph that he *had* to take the manuscript home becomes understandable. Martin told his son from his second marriage, Martin Jr., "many times" that "he obtained the manuscript to show to his wife in order to convince her of the truth of the B[ook] of M[ormon], as she was very bitter against the work."[14] When we realize the magnitude of Martin's absences from the family, the reason for his wife's bitterness becomes clear.

After making such tremendous sacrifices at his family's expense, Martin needed some way of demonstrating to the family that he had not lost his mind but had stayed away from farm and family, and even his daughter's wedding, for a good cause—for a book that would do good in the world and would sell sufficiently for the family to recoup their growing investment in it. To have any hope of reconciliation with his wife, he needed something to show for his absence.

The Crime

Likely using Martin or Joseph as a source, Lucy Mack Smith provides us with some details of what transpired when Martin went home with the manuscript. On his arrival in Palmyra, Martin "was not slow" in acting on his hard-won permission to show the manuscript to the five designated family members.[15] But because the purpose of bringing the document home was to palliate his family by showing them the impressive contents of the book, he more than likely stretched the permission to include other family members aside from the five, including the daughter and new son-in-law whose nuptials he had missed for the book's sake.

Lucy Harris was apparently pleased with what she saw and heard of the manuscript, and she gave him permission to lock it in her bureau, which was

14. Reported in William Wallace White, Journal, May 15, 1904. My thanks to Nathan Hadfield for making me aware of this source, and to Corey L. Evans for sharing it with me.

15. Lavina Fielding Anderson, ed., *Lucy's Book: A Critical Edition of Lucy Mack Smith's Family Memoir*, 420.

presumably the most secure location in their house. However, shortly after Martin arrived back in Palmyra with the manuscript, "a very particular friend" called on him while Lucy was out, and Martin did not know where the bureau key was. The friend's curiosity "was much excited" and he "earnestly desired to see" the manuscript. Martin, for his part, was eager to please the friend by displaying the fruit of his scribal labors. Not wanting to wait for Lucy to return, Martin broke into his wife's bureau by picking the lock, and in the process he both "injured his lady's beaureau [sic] considerably" and violated the covenant he had made with God. On his wife's return and discovery of the damage to her bureau, "an intolerable storm ensued." Martin took possession of the manuscript again, storing it in "his own set of drawers where he had it at his command" and showing it to "any good friend who happened [to] call on him."[16] According to Martin's later recitation about the manuscript pages, during this time "he read them in the evenings to his family and some friends," afterward always being sure "put them in his bureau in the parlor, locking both bureau and parlor, [and] putting the keys of each in his pocket."[17]

After following this routine one night and then leaving for a few days' trip, Martin never saw the manuscript again. When he went to retrieve the manuscript upon his return, it was gone. He cross-examined his wife and frantically tore open beds and pillows, but all to no avail. If Lucy Harris knew anything, she would not admit to it even under duress.[18]

Before this loss, another, of a much more personal nature, occurred for Joseph and Emma in Harmony. Shortly after Martin's departure, their first child was born—and died. Joseph nursed his weak and grief-stricken wife through the weeks that followed, but as time wore on without word from Martin, another burden weighed on Joseph's mind. Emma, knowing her husband's worry over the book, urged him to leave her in her mother's care and go to Palmyra to learn what detained Martin.[19]

Joseph's 1839 history implies that he had good reason to worry at this time that letting Martin take the manuscript had led to disaster. Joseph recounted that after Martin left with the manuscript the angel came and rebuked Joseph for asking permission again to let Martin take the manuscript after being twice refused. In consequence of this impertinence, Moroni took from him the sacred relics and suspended his gift of seeing.[20]

---

16. Anderson, 421.

17. William W. Blair, footnote comment in Lucy [Mack] Smith, *Biographical Sketches of Joseph Smith the Prophet, and His Progenitors for Many Generations*, 131.

18. Anderson, *Lucy's Book*, 418, 422.

19. Anderson, 412.

20. Smith, *History of the Church*, 1:21–22.

During Joseph's journey of a few days by stagecoach from Pennsylvania to the Palmyra-Manchester area he was so distressed over the loss of his child, his wife's poor health, and the feared loss of the manuscript that he scarcely slept. When he neared Manchester, a kindly fellow passenger who feared Joseph would fall asleep in the forest along the way and come to disaster insisted on helping him home. Over the final miles, the stranger led him by the arm, since Joseph "would fall asleep as he was walking along, every few minutes," according to his mother's account.[21]

Shortly after daybreak when Joseph had rested a bit, he sent for Martin Harris. The Smiths expected Martin to join them at eight o'clock for breakfast. He arrived four and a half hours later, "his hat drawn over his eyes." Lucy Mack Smith's dramatic account of what occurred during his visit cannot be improved on:

> At length he entered the house. Soon after which we sat down to the table, Mr. Harris with the rest. He took up his knife and fork as if he were going to use them, but immediately dropped them. Hyrum, observing this, said "Martin, why do you not eat; are you sick?["] Upon which, Mr. Harris pressed his hands upon his temples, and cried out, in a tone of deep anguish, "Oh, I have lost my soul! I have lost my soul!"
>
> Joseph, who had not expressed his fears till now, sprang from the table, exclaiming, "Martin, have you lost that manuscript? have you broken your oath, and brought down condemnation upon my head, as well as your own?"
>
> "Yes, it is gone," replied Martin, "and I know not where."
>
> "Oh, my God!" said Joseph, clinching his hands. "All is lost! all is lost! What shall I do? I have sinned--it is I who tempted the wrath of God. I should have been satisfied with the first answer which I received from the Lord; for he told me that it was not safe to let the writing go out of my possession." He wept and groaned, and walked the floor continually.
>
> At length he told Martin to go back and search again.
>
> "No," said Martin, "it is all in vain; for I have ripped open beds and pillows; and I know it is not there."
>
> "Then must I," said Joseph, "return to my wife with such a tale as this? I dare not do it, lest I should kill her at once. And how shall I appear before the Lord? Of what rebuke am I not worthy from the angel of the Most High?"[22]

Joseph did have to return to his wife with report of the manuscript's disappearance, but he was unable to tell her who had taken it. Any evidence of who the thief or thieves might be was lacking, and while Martin suspected his wife, Lucy Harris denied participating in or knowing anything about the theft.[23]

---

21. Anderson, *Lucy's Book*, 414–16.
22. Anderson, 418–19.
23. Anderson, 422.

Joseph's initial revelation responding to the manuscript's disappearance (D&C 3) given in the weeks following said nothing of the thieves. However, a later revelation (D&C 10:1–37) recorded in May 1829 identified the theft as the work of a conspiracy of "wicked men" who had altered the words Joseph translated.[24] Readers of the revelation appear to have typically imagined the conspirators physically doctoring the original manuscript, taking up lying pens to add invasive text beside or over top of that recorded by Joseph's scribe. On this reading, the revelation describes a rather clumsy effort to discredit the Book of Mormon: the conspirators would try to palm off as the unmodified translation manuscript a document on which obvious interpolations had been made, with counterfeit words written over and crammed into the narrow spaces between the authentic words.

But Joseph's revelation does not describe the conspirators against the Book of Mormon making these sorts of interpolations on the manuscript they had taken. Rather, it says they had altered the manuscript's "words." The *words* of the translation could be altered in two ways, either by tampering with the original pages or by copying some of them onto fresh pages, imitating the scribe's handwriting but introducing variant wording into the new copy. Whatever the challenges of convincingly mimicking the handwriting of Martin Harris or other scribes, it would have been less daunting than trying to pass off insertions and overwriting as the original text on the translation manuscript. The more intelligible strategy of (mis)copying the manuscript is a better candidate for what the revelation calls the conspirators' "cunning plan" (v. 23).

The revelation attributes to those who conspired to steal the manuscript several ignoble motives: They had acted in "anger" (v. 24) "to destroy" Joseph (v. 6), to get "the glory of the world" (v. 19), and to avoid "shame" they feared the book's publication would cause them (v. 19). These men, the revelation said, had been misled by Satan, who whispered to them the accusation against Joseph—"[H]e hath deceived you" (v. 29). So they set a trap for Joseph: when he retranslated and published the Book of Mormon they would identify and publish discrepancies between it and their altered text to show that he had "contradicted" himself in his two pretended translations (v. 31). In this way, Satan would "stir up" (v. 32) people to anger against Joseph so they would not believe God's words, and "thus Satan thinketh to overpower your [Joseph's] testimony in this generation, that the work might not come forth in this generation" (v. 33). This revelation about the stolen manuscript was published in part in the Preface to the 1830 Book of Mormon to explain to readers why

---

24. My analysis of the timing of Doctrine and Covenants 10 has been assisted by a 2011 internship with the Joseph Smith Papers Project, where discussions with Michael MacKay and Robin Jensen helped clarify my thoughts.

Nephi's "small plates" had been substituted for the missing first portion of Mormon's abridgment.[25]

The Suspects

Lucy Harris has long been the chief, if not the *only*, identified suspect in the theft of the initial Book of Mormon manuscript. Her role in the theft, however, has been assumed more than argued and has been favored to the exclusion of other possibilities. While Lucy may or may not have been involved with the theft, she is just one of multiple potential suspects who also had access to Martin and motives to abscond with the manuscript.

Lucy Harris

Lucy Harris was a strong-willed woman that Lucy Mack Smith described as having an "irrascible temper."[26] Lorenzo Saunders, who claimed to know Lucy Harris but did not seem to share Lucy Smith's dislike of her, similarly described her as "pretty high on combativeness."[27] This temper and combativeness of Lucy Harris is known to have taken other dramatic measures to separate her husband from the Book of Mormon project. About three months before the June 1828 manuscript theft, she reportedly colluded with an accomplice to discredit the Book of Mormon by stealing the Anthon

---

25. In addition to replacing the lost manuscript with another text, Joseph took another step that appears to have been aimed at foiling the conspirators described in Doctrine and Covenants 10. Early in June 1829, when Joseph had finished translating Mormon's abridgment, he dispatched one of those assisting him to go to Utica to secure a copyright for the book. There are four oddities in how this was done. First, acquiring a copyright for a book was not usually considered necessary at the time and not usually done. Second, the book was not yet complete. Third, Joseph's assistant, presumably at his behest, insisted that not just the book's title as required by law, but its entire title page, be transcribed into the copyright application. Fourth, the copyright, thus acquired, technically did not cover Nephi's small plates! The title page transcribed into the copyright record explicitly identified Mormon's record as the work to be copyrighted—making no mention of Nephi's text—and the small plates text mostly had not been translated. What the copyright specifically protected was the translation of Mormon's abridgment. Since the lost manuscript was, Joseph tells us, part of Mormon's abridgment, the lost manuscript would have been protected by the copyright Joseph obtained. It thus appears that Joseph's decision to pursue a copyright for the Book of Mormon text was aimed at stopping the conspirators from publishing the stolen manuscript. For copyright law at the time see Nathaniel Hinckley Wadsworth, "Copyright Laws and the 1830 Book of Mormon," 77–96.

26. Anderson, *Lucy's Book*, 421.

27. Lorenzo Saunders, interviewed by E. L. Kelley, in Vogel, *EMD*, 2:149.

transcript, which the manuscript thief or thieves probably stole again.[28] And several months after the manuscript theft, around early spring 1829, she attempted to stop Joseph Smith from resuming the translation by suing him for defrauding Martin of his money with spurious claims to possess and translate ancient gold plates.[29] Given these actions, it is reasonable to think she may have taken similarly dramatic action to stop the book's translation while the manuscript was stored in her home and plausibly within her reach.[30]

The claim that Lucy had stolen the manuscript appeared in print within three years of the theft.[31] Early Palmyra rumor said Martin had interrogated his wife about the manuscript and vented his anger at her over its disappearance, resulting in the couple's separation and enduring bitterness toward one another.[32] Martin reportedly shared his early belief that his wife had taken the manuscript and given it to others with Palmyra Episcopal minister John A. Clark,[33] and, according to one statement, Martin came to believe late in life that Lucy had taken the manuscript and burned it.[34] This is backed up by Lorenzo Saunders, who claimed to have heard her actually confess to doing so.[35] Harris family tradition similarly describes her taking the manuscript and burning it.[36]

Lucy's access to the manuscript, motivation, alienation from Martin, early suspicion, reported confession, and family tradition make a strong case of her

---

28. Anderson, *Lucy's Book*, 404.

29. Anderson, 440–45.

30. Lucy Harris's early distaste for the book that absorbed her husband's time and resources only grew with time. Five years later, after she and Martin had separated and he had gone on a mission to proselytize people to the Book of Mormon, she wrote, "The man has now become rather an object of pity; he has spent most of his property, and lost the confidence of his former friends. If he had labored as hard on his farm as he has to make Mormons, he might now be one of the wealthiest farmers in the country. He now spends his time in travelling through the country spreading the delusion of Mormonism, and has no regard whatever for his family." Lucy Harris, "Statement," 256.

31. "The Progress of Mormonism," 173. Of forty-four known nineteenth-century sources regarding the stolen manuscript, over one-third (fifteen of them) identify Lucy Harris as the thief.

32. John A. Clark to Dear Brethren, August 31, 1840, in Vogel, *EMD*, 2:269–70. Jesse Townsend to Phineas Stiles, December 24, 1833, in Pomeroy Tucker, *Origin, Rise, and Progress of Mormonism*, 288–91; "Old Newspapers--No. 24," in Vogel, *EMD*, 2:342; "Old Newspapers--No. 25," in Vogel, *EMD*, 2:343.

33. John A. Clark, Letter to "Dear Brethren," August 31, 1840, in Vogel, *EMD*, 2:269.

34. William Pilkington, "A Dying Testimony Given by Martin Harris."

35. Lorenzo Saunders, interviewed by E. L. Kelley, November 12, 1884, in Vogel, *EMD*, 149.

36. Frances Magee, Oral History, interviewed by Mike George, n.d., in Linda Sillitoe and Allen D. Roberts, *Salamander: The Story of the Mormon Forgery Murders*, 154.

being the manuscript thief. However, there are reasons to be suspicious of the allegations. First, her motive to steal the manuscript, and particularly to steal and then destroy it, is not unequivocal. Before the manuscript disappeared, Lucy's opposition to the Book of Mormon was inconsistent, becoming permanently entrenched only after Martin blamed its disappearance on her. When Joseph first recovered the plates, Lucy Harris reportedly volunteered money to the Smiths to help with the book.[37] She was also apparently "pleased" with its contents when she was finally able to view the manuscript, and this report is consistent with the circumstances.[38] Martin Harris evidently perceived such a positive shift in his wife's attitude when he entrusted the manuscript to her care, even to the point of allowing her exclusive control over its access, since she, not he, initially held the key. And, notably, *the manuscript did not disappear while in Lucy Harris's care.* It was not until after Martin took the manuscript back into his own care, securing it in his own bureau, that it disappeared. And even when Martin blamed her for the manuscript's later disappearance, he did not believe his wife's attitude toward it to be such that she would destroy it; he instead believed she had given it to others.[39]

Later in life, according to one source, Martin did come to believe his wife had both taken the manuscript and burned it.[40] However, there are reasons to be skeptical of this 1934 affidavit by William Pilkington reporting on an 1874 or 1875 interview with Harris. Written over a century after the original events, and even some six decades after the conversation it reports, Pilkington's recollection seems to rely heavily on Joseph Smith's published history of the manuscript loss rather than Martin,[41] pointing to the likeli-

---

37. Anderson, *Lucy's Book*, 395.

38. Anderson, 420.

39. Clark, Letter to "Dear Brethren," August 31, 1840, in Vogel, *EMD*, 2:269. It may be posited that Martin's view that the stolen manuscript was not destroyed but given to others grows out of Joseph Smith's May 1829 revelation indicating that the manuscript was still in existence (D&C 10). But John A. Clark is reporting on conversation he had with Martin Harris in *1828*, and thus prior to this revelation. And, as shown later in the chapter, Martin Harris actually rejected Doctrine and Covenants 10, apparently because it called him "a wicked man." It would thus not have been the source of Martin's interpretation of the manuscript loss.

40. Pilkington, "Dying Testimony of Martin Harris."

41. Pilkington almost certainly would not have recalled precisely the names of those to whom Martin was to show the manuscript without consulting Joseph Smith's published history. And the range of translation dates he attributed to Martin's narrative reflect the approximate dates estimated by Joseph in his history. Pilkington also follows closely Joseph Smith's version of the Anthon incident from his 1839 history, which, as shown above in Chapter 2, varies from Martin's known recitations of the event. See Joseph Smith, et al., *History of the Church of Jesus Christ of Latter-day Saints*, 1:20–1.

hood that it was also influenced by the common rumor of Lucy Harris burning the manuscript—a rumor that became only more prevalent during the twentieth century. Complicating the affidavit even further, just four years later Pilkington recounted in his 1938 autobiography that Martin thought the manuscript to have been stolen *from* his wife and taken into unknown hands.[42] It is unclear whether Martin told either story.[43]

Moreover, only one of the available sources claims an admission from Lucy herself. In this 1884 account, Palmyra resident Lorenzo Saunders was quite emphatic about hearing Lucy confess to stealing and burning the manuscript:

> I was as well acquainted with Martin Harris's wife, as well as I was with my own wife. & know what course she took, & when she burned up those papers. I heard her say she burned the papers. she was pretty high on combativeness. . . . she says she burned them up. And there was no mistake, but she did. They never was found; never came to light. I lived till I was 43 years old right there; & she never denied of burning the papers. He brought them home to proselyte her & she burned them.[44]

Unfortunately, Saunders's report of having acquired his information directly from Lucy is also problematic. Despite Saunders's claimed closeness to Lucy, the life circumstances of Saunders and Lucy do not make it obvious that they should have known one another. Lucy lived on the opposite side of Palmyra from Saunders and was fifteen years his senior, the two being at the time of the theft respectively thirty-two and seventeen. In addition, Saunders claim that Lucy never denied burning the papers the entire time he lived in Palmyra (until he was 43—i.e., 1854) loses steam against the facts of Lucy's having denied and of her death nearly two decades earlier in 1836.

Further, contrary to Saunders's assertion that Lucy "never denied" taking the manuscript, she reportedly denied any complicity in the theft on multiple occasions around the time of its occurrence, was still denying it several years later (within a few years of her death), and even denied it to fellow opponents of the Book of Mormon. Lucy Mack Smith, undoubtedly basing her account

---

42. William Pilkington, Autobiography, 1934–1939.

43. It is similarly difficult to establish the reliability of the supposed Harris family tradition of Lucy stealing and burning the manuscript. This tradition was reported in the 1987 book *Salamander*, a semi-novelized account of the Mark Hofmann forgery investigation. The authors of *Salamander* cite Frances Magee, a widow of a Martin and Lucy Harris descendant, telling an investigator in the mid–1980s that Lucy had stolen and burned the Book of Mormon's lost pages. With nearly a century and a half separating the manuscript theft and Magee relating her understanding of the Harris family tradition, the lack of additional evidence corroborating the tradition's provenance and the possibility of it being influenced by outside sources makes Magee's account too unreliable. Frances Magee, Oral History, 154.

44. Saunders, interview by Kelley, November 12, 1884, in Vogel, *EMD*, 2:149.

on Martin's July 1828 confession to the Smiths about losing the manuscript, said that even under Martin's stringent questioning about the theft, his wife had "solemnly averred that she did not know anything about it whatever."[45] In 1833, Lucy Harris was approached by D. P. Hurlbut for information that would undermine the faith Martin now advocated. Given the widespread rumors that she had taken it, it seems implausible that Hurlbut failed to ask about it. The only indication of what she told him on the question appears in the book begun by Hurlbut and completed in 1834 by E. D. Howe, *Mormonism Unvailed*: "The fact respecting the lost manuscript, we have not been able to ascertain. They sometimes charged the wife of Harris with having burnt it; but this is denied by her."[46] Although Howe does not directly address the claim that Lucy had burned the manuscript, his admission that the manuscript's fate was yet unknown to him indicates that Lucy had denied to Hurlbut either stealing or destroying it.

If not from Lucy Harris, where did the rumor that she had stolen and burned the manuscript originate? The first known source attributing the manuscript theft to Lucy Harris is a May 1831 article in the *Geauga Gazette*, a newspaper printed near the early Mormon gathering place of Kirtland, Ohio. The *Gazette* article, as reprinted in the *Philadelphia Album*, reported:

> We are told that the wife of the prophet Harris, refused to be a Mormonite, and he has left her among 'the Gentiles.' She it was who purloined several pages of the first revelation, and which, by the direction of the angel, have never been supplied.[47]

The fact that this report was published near Kirtland rather than in New York points to the gathering saints—not the Palmyra rumor mill—as its source. There, the saints had a ready source of information and opinion on the subject: Martin Harris. The *Gazette* article in which Martin and Lucy Harris were mentioned was about the incoming Mormons, many of whom would have had access to Martin's views on the disappearance of the manuscript. But the *Gazette*'s likeliest source was Martin himself, who had come to Kirtland from Palmyra in March 1831, briefly traveled back to Palmyra, and then returned to Kirtland around the time of *Gazette* article. If Martin had spoken to the *Gazette*, it would not have been the only newspaper he had spoken to, as other sources show Martin to have had dealings with the area's

45. Lucy Smith, "Preliminary Manuscript," in Anderson, *Lucy's Book*, 422.

46. Eber D. Howe, *Mormonism Unvailed*, 22.

47. "The Progress of Mormonism," 173. This account states that it was a reprint of an article in the "Tuesday" issue of the *Painesville Gazette* (i.e., the *Geauga Gazette*). The original article likely appeared in the Tuesday, May 24, 1831, issue of the *Geauga Gazette*. (No extant copy of this issue of the *Gazette* is known to the author.)

newspapermen during his early days in Kirtland.[48] While Martin had begun blaming his wife shortly after the manuscript disappeared in 1828, this belief appears to have been more of a suspicion on his part than something he could warrant from direct evidence. If Martin had good evidence pinning the deed on his wife, he presumably would not have blamed the less likely suspect that he focused his suspicions on during his later years: an angel.[49]

Given the tense marital circumstances that led to Martin bringing the manuscript home, it is understandable that he would have suspected his wife of the theft. Adding to this, Martin would have been *motivated* to believe she was the thief in order to deflect blame from himself. Joseph Smith believed that the theft was a direct result of Martin breaking his covenant with God by showing the manuscript to persons other than those he was permitted to.[50] In addition, the revelation that blamed the manuscript's disappearance on "wicked men" had also called Martin himself "a wicked man," making him loath to accept the revelation and shoulder some degree of responsibility for the loss of a book of scripture. If Martin could pass the blame to someone who he had been authorized to show the manuscript, then he could possibly claim that he was not to blame. Given Lucy's easy access to the manuscript, she was not just a *plausible* suspect but a *perfect* scapegoat for Martin to absolve himself with. While Martin was undoubtedly giving his real opinion in suspecting his wife of the theft, his interpretation of the events was most certainly influenced by both their marital problems and the very human tendency to deflect blame.

Although those writing about the manuscript theft have largely followed Martin Harris's initial identification of Lucy Harris as the thief, it appears that Martin himself may have abandoned this theory quite early. While Martin was making this accusation as early as 1828 and up until 1831, after that time no report exists of Martin making this claim outside William Pilkington's contradictory secondhand accounts a century later. Martin did speak of the theft in various later interviews, but in those he offered no opinion on the identity of the thief.

In the end, what most persuaded Martin of Lucy's innocence was her continued denial until the moment of her death. Speaking to a congregation in

---

48. During a visit to Kirtland earlier in 1831, Martin Harris presented to Eber Howe's *Painesville Telegraph* office a copy of the Articles and Covenants of the Church for publication. Howe complied with Martin's request, publishing the Articles and Covenants in the April 19, 1831, issue of the *Painesville Telegraph*, but added a critical introduction. "The Mormon Creed," in Larry E. Morris, comp., *Documentary History of the Book of Mormon*, 37–40.

49. See the discussion of the Martis Harris Jr. account below.

50. Smith et al., *History of the Church*, 1:21.

Rexburg, Idaho, twenty-nine years after his father's death, Martin Harris Jr.—the elder Martin's from a later marriage—said of his parents and the lost manuscript:

> [A]fter he had read it [the manuscript] to her [his wife] he locked it up in a drawer & put the key on a chain which he carried around his neck. He then had occasion to go away on business for a few days & when he came back he went to get it & it was gone, he at once accused his wife of having taken it but she declared positively that she had not touched it & knew nothing about it & on her death bed she still declared that she had never seen them & knew nothing about them & she called God to witness the truth of her statement. He said as far as he could see, the lock had not been tampered with.[51]

As a devout Quaker whose every word was supposed to be spoken as if under oath, Lucy Harris seems unlikely to have gone to her grave repeating lies. Or at any rate, Martin Harris, despite knowing well the difficult aspects of his estranged wife's temperament, was unable to believe she would blatantly lie on her deathbed. As a result, Martin—the first person to postulate that Lucy had taken the manuscript—came to reject this explanation.

Unable to believe either that Lucy had lied about the theft or that his own breaking of his covenant had jeopardized the manuscript's safety, Martin developed a highly idiosyncratic theory of the manuscript's fate. He came to hold that the initial contents of the Book of Mormon disappeared the same way they had originally appeared. As reported by Martin Jr.: "[I]t was always a mistery [*sic*] to him what became of them but his theory was that an angel came & took them."[52] Clarifying this unusual understanding, and demonstrating Francis Gladden Bishop's tendency to echo back to Martin the very things Martin had told Bishop, the latter claimed in 1851 to know by revelation who had taken the manuscript from Martin Harris: an angel, "whose name was Nephi, who was the same Holy Angel who first appeared to Joseph" had taken "the manuscript of the 116 pages, which was translated by Joseph." Bishop thus confirmed to Martin what Martin already believed[53]

Although Martin abandoned his earlier belief that Lucy had stolen the manuscript, the seeds of her suspicion that he sowed began to take root. In 1851, the same year Bishop mirrored Martin's claim about an angel taking the manuscript, Orsamus Turner built on Martin's earlier explanation of who

---

51. William Wallace White, Journal, May 15, 1904. While it might be argued that Martin Harris told this story to his children to avoid implicating their mother in the theft, it should be noted that Lucy Harris was not the mother of the informant here. Martin Harris Jr. was the son of Martin Harris and Caroline Young Harris, sister of Brigham Young.

52. William Wallace White, Journal, May 15, 1904.

53. Francis Gladden Bishop, *An Address to the Sons and Daughters of God Scattered Abroad, Through All the Earth*, 27–28.

took it and added further speculations: "With sacriligious [*sic*] hands, she [Lucy Harris] seized over an hundred of the manuscript pages of the new revelation, and burned or secreted them."[54] Turner's tentative, qualified conjecture, nearly a quarter century after the manuscript theft, is *the first time anyone had suggested in print that the manuscript may have been destroyed.* Five years later a Manchester local who had read Turner echoed his words, but added a preference for one of Turner's two speculations on the manuscript's fate: "[H]is wife, who was an unbeliever, seized them, and either burned or secreted them—it was supposed the former."[55] Eleven years later, Pomeroy Tucker improved still further on the certainty of Turner's burning speculation by eliminating the other possibility: "Thus exercised, she contrived, in her husband's sleep, to steal from him the particular source of her disturbance, and burned the manuscript to ashes."[56] This would be repeated until there was no question in anyone's mind. Lining up the sources chronologically, we observe a trend: *the further we get from the actual theft, the more certain the rumors become of Lucy Harris taking the manuscript and burning it.*

Since Lucy Harris's possible role in the theft is unclear, the long tradition of her certain guilt is unwarranted. None of the accounts of her having stolen it can be reliably traced to a confession from her. To the contrary, given her antagonism toward Joseph Smith and the Restoration, Lucy *had motive to claim credit for the manuscript theft even if she did not do it.* A confession from Lucy to having stolen and destroyed the manuscript would have dealt a serious blow to the credibility of Joseph Smith's revelations—which pinned the deed on "wicked men" who had *not* destroyed the revelation but "altered" it. Such a confession would have also vindicated Mrs. Harris by demonstrating that the religion her estranged husband had used their family fortunes to build up was based on delusion. In place of such confession, Lucy Harris's continued denial of having committed the theft ultimately convinced the one person who had the greatest reason to blame her for the crime, and who had started the rumors of her guilt in the first place—her estranged husband Martin.[57] While her continued denial and lack of corroborating evidence is not proof of her innocence, those should give us reason to be open to other suspects.

---

54. Orasmus Turner, *History of the Pioneer Settlement of Phelps and Gorham's Purchase*, in Vogel, *Early Mormon Documents*, 3:52.

55. "Mormonism in Its Infancy," ca. Aug. 1856, in Vogel, *EMD*, 3:61.

56. Tucker, *Origin, Rise, and Progress of Mormonism.*

57. Pomeroy Tucker acknowledged that Lucy Harris refused to acknowledge the theft at first, writing years later, in 1867, "For years she kept this incendiarism a profound secret to herself, even until after the book was published." But Tucker never discloses to whom and when, if ever, Lucy Harris ultimately confessed her reputed role in the theft. Tucker, *Origin, Rise, and Progress of Mormonism.*

Flanders Dyke

Another potential suspect of the manuscript theft is Lucy and Martin Harris's son-in-law Flanders Dyke, whose missed wedding to Martin's daughter was a factor in Martin wanting so desperately to take the translation manuscript home. The romance of Flanders Dyke and Lucy Harris Jr., however, has another close connection to the manuscript loss that has not yet been discussed: it prompted the theft of one of the documents involved in the translation of the Book of Mormon. Lucy Mack Smith recounts:

> A young man by the name of Dikes, had been paying some attention to Miss Lucy, Martin Harris's oldest daughter. To this young man Mr. Harris was quite attached, and his daughter Lucy was by no means opposed to him; but Mrs. Harris, of course, was decidedly upon the negative. However, just at this crisis, a scheme entered her brain which materially changed her deportment to Mr. Dikes. She told him, if he would manage to get the Egyptian characters [the character transcript taken to Charles Anthon] from Mr. Harris's possession, and procure a room in Palmyra for the purpose of transcribing them, and then bring her the transcript, that she would consent to his marriage with her daughter Lucy.
>
> To this, Mr. Dikes cheerfully consented, and suffice it to say, he succeeded to her satisfaction, and thus received the promised reward.
>
> When Mr. Harris began to make preparations to start for Pennsylvania the second time, with the view of writing for Joseph, his wife told him that she had fully decreed in her heart to accompany him. Mr. Harris, having no particular objections, informed her that she might do so; that she might go and stay one or two weeks, and then he would bring her home again, after which he would return, and resume his writing for Joseph. To this she cheerfully agreed.
>
> But Mr. Harris little suspected what he had to encounter by this move. The first time he exhibited the characters before named, she took out of her pocket an exact copy of the same; and told those present, that "Joe Smith" was not the only one who was in possession of this great curiosity, that she had the same characters, and, they were quite as genuine as those shown by Mr. Harris. This course she continued to pursue, until they arrived at Joseph's.[58]

Lucy Mack Smith likely heard of these events from both her son Joseph and Martin, but the narration she gives also bears her stamp. Fiercely loyal to her prophet-son, Lucy Smith painted those who opposed him in the darkest of colors. Nowhere is this truer than in her descriptions of Martin's wife. Lucy Smith's telling of events makes Lucy Harris the epicenter of the resistance Joseph experienced while attempting to bring forth the Book of Mormon, including an 1829 Palmyra effort to discredit his claim to have the plates.[59] Describing the origin of this opposition, Lucy Smith writes of Lucy Harris:

58. Anderson, *Lucy's Book*, 404–5.
59. Anderson, 440–41.

[S]he mounted her horse, flew from house to house through the neighbourhood, like a dark spirit, making diligent inquiry wherever she had the least hopes of gleaning anything, and stirring up every malicious feeling which would tend to subserve her wicked purpose. Having ascertained the number and strength of her adherents, she entered a complaint against Joseph, before a certain magistrate of Lyons.[60]

Yet while Lucy Smith confidently identified Lucy Harris as the source of this organized opposition, Martin characterized it more generally:

[I]n March [1829] the People Rose up & united against the Work[,] gathering testimoney against the Plates & Said they had testimony Enough & if I did not Put Joseph in Jail <&his father> for Deseption[,] they Would me[.][61]

Martin did not identify a single instigator for this opposition but attributed it to a broad group. Given Lucy Mack Smith's tendency to turn the merely paranoid Lucy Harris almost into someone truly malicious, "like a dark spirit," her jarring report that Mrs. Harris swapped a copy of the Anthon transcript for her daughter's hand in marriage should be viewed with suspicion.

Yet the narratives in Lucy Mack Smith's history are not manufactured out of whole cloth; they represent actual, if occasionally distorted, events. Stripping Lucy Smith's narrative of her rather extreme view of Lucy Harris we find the probable core event: in early spring 1828, Flanders Dyke, whether on his own initiative or Lucy Harris's, curried favor with his potential mother-in-law by purloining and duplicating the character transcript for her.[62]

Lucy Smith's account, while somewhat fuzzy on what Lucy Harris hoped to accomplish with the duplicate character transcript, implies that the latter claimed to have gotten the characters from a modern source—probably hoping to convince others that Joseph also obtained the characters from such a source, rather than from ancient gold plates.[63] Within four months after Flanders Dyke reportedly stole and copied the character transcript in order to discredit Joseph Smith and the Book of Mormon, an unidentified person is said to have done the same thing with the translation manuscript for the same purpose. The thief or thieves who took the translation manuscript probably also stole the same document Dyke had, taking the transcript along with the translation, since, as noted earlier, that transcript appears to have not been seen by anyone after 1828. While the identity of this thief is unknown, such theft, copying, and attempted discrediting of Book of Mormon documents, including the character transcript, would not have been a new misdeed for

60. Smith, *Biographical Sketches*, 131.
61. "Testimony of Martin Harris, 1870."
62. Anderson, *Lucy's Book*, 404.
63. Smith, *Biographical Sketches*, 122.

Flanders Dyke, who not only had a personal history of such behavior, but also opportunity, motive, and a *later* pattern of property theft.

Martin, who reportedly showed the manuscript to any friend who asked, is almost sure to have shown the translation manuscript to his new son-in-law who was living in a house on Martin's property at the time.[64] Although Martin reportedly felt "quite attached" to Flanders,[65] the latter had cause to feel slighted by his father-in-law, on behalf of himself and his new bride, and, like Lucy Sr., had a rationale for feeling threatened by Martin's involvement with the Book of Mormon. Flanders, whose earlier cooperation with his mother-in-law points to him to sharing her skepticism about the book, would have also been concerned with the Harris family's financial fortunes. Now positioned to inherit from Martin's estate through Lucy Jr., he had particular reason to guard that estate against large investments from which he was not confident of a return.

Beyond the ability and motivation to steal the manuscript, Flanders also soon earned a reputation for theft. In August 1830, seven months after E. B. Grandin printed the Book of Mormon, the same press printed an article for the *Wayne Sentinel* warning readers to "Look Out for a Swindler":

> Flanders Dyke absconded from Palmyra, Wayne county, N.Y. on Saturday night the 7th inst. after having virtually swindled divers persons to the amount of about *one thousand dollars.* Dyke had resided in this town for about five or six years, and had managed to marry the daughter of a wealthy and respectable farmer. He soon afterwards obtained a lease of his father-in-law's farm, for a term of years (not yet expired,) on very favorable terms, and appeared to be in the full tide of prosperity. By the aid of the credit which these circumstances acquired for him, he bought such property of his neighbors, and goods from the stores, as he could get trusted for, promising generally the avails of a crop of wheat which he had on the ground. He harvested his wheat—carried a quantity to market, for which he received the cash—obtained advances in money and goods on account of the remainder—and on the night above stated, having accumulated in cash and property about $1000, started, in company with a young man of the name of *Asa Hill,* for Michigan. They were pursued the next day, and on the Monday morning following, most of the property, in the charge of Hill, was overtaken and secured a few miles west of Batavia. Dyke, anticipating the pursuit, had a few hours previously taken another route, and thereby escaped with most of the money. ...
>
> This is the *fifth* similar trick that has been played off upon people in this vicinity within a few years, *by persons belonging to the same family!* Their names should be recorded for the benefit and security of the public:-- *Samuel Dyke,* senior, once a saddler and trunk maker by trade, now a man of no steady employment. *Samuel Dyke,* jr. saddler, stage-driver, &c.—last heard from in Canada.

---

64. For more about Flanders and Lucy Dyke's house on Martin Harris's property, see the discussion below of the June 30, 1828, deed to Flanders Dyke.

65. Anderson, *Lucy's Book,* 404.

James Dyke, a *rat* saddler, runner for canal boats, &c. *John Biggs*, son-in-law to Samuel Dyke senior, baker, went to Buffalo—known in Canandaigua. And last, though not least in knavery, *Flanders Dyke*, the chief subject of this notice.
Palmyra, N. Y. Aug. 16, 1830.

*Printers throughout the United States and in Michigan and Canada, are requested to insert or notice the above.[66]

Dyke later went back to Palmyra, perhaps returning more of the unjustly taken money and goods, but his return and any restitution he may have made did not end his days of scheming after property. A decade after this incident, Dyke again appeared in the newspaper, this time with a reward offered for his capture after his escape from the Palmyra jail where he had been held for "obtaining property on false pretences [*sic*]."[67]

A possible indication that Martin had his own suspicions of Dykes's role in the manuscript theft appears in the historical record near, and likely immediately after, the theft. On June 30, 1828, perhaps two weeks after Martin returned home with the manuscript in hand, Martin and Lucy Harris executed a deed to Dyke for the house and land on which he was living. The timing of this conveyance suggests a settling up of accounts during a parting of the ways. Lucy had secured her own separate maintenance from Martin in May, recording his earlier deed to her. When their alienation was completed with the manuscript loss, and Martin's suspicions focused on her, no further steps were necessary for Lucy to live separately from Martin. But if Dyke had also fallen under Martin's suspicions in the wake of the manuscript's disappearance, a settlement between the two men would have been needed. The house and land on which Dyke and Lucy Harris, Jr. lived belonged to Martin, and up to this point Dyke had apparently lived on this property by Martin's good graces. But good graces, it appears, were no longer sufficient. Now it would require $200.[68]

Thus, a few lines of evidence suggest that Dyke took part in the manuscript theft. Dyke apparently fell under Martin's own suspicions, had unusually close access to the stolen documents, multiple motives for stealing them, a personal résumé that included stealing and copying one of these documents in order to discredit it, and a subsequent record of entrepreneurial activities that placed his hands in other people's pockets.

---

66. "Look Out for a Swindler," 3.

67. "$25 Reward," 4.

68. Indenture, Martin Harris and Lucy Harris to Flanders Dyke, Wayne County, New York, June 30, 1828. I am grateful to the intrepid Marie Thatcher for finding this source for me.

"A Very Particular Friend"

Another person whose possible role in the theft should be considered is Martin Harris's "very particular friend," mentioned but not named by Lucy Mack Smith. In her account, this friend displayed an especially keen interest in the book, calling on Martin "shortly after he got there" with the manuscript, "much excited" and "earnestly" desiring to see it. Martin, for his part, was recklessly eager to share the manuscript with this friend, and at the friend's urging compromised the manuscript's safety by damaging its secure compartment and established a precedent for sharing the manuscript with persons outside of the family.[69]

Joseph Smith, sharing either knowledge or surmise, later attributed the theft to persons to whom Martin had shown the manuscript pages beyond the permitted five: "[H]e did shew them to others and by stratagem *they* got them away from him."[70] Joseph's ascription of the theft to "stratagem" is telling, and hints at what he understood to have occurred. "Stratagem," as defined in the Webster's dictionary of the time, referred to "an artifice . . . ; a plan or scheme for deceiving an enemy" or "a trick by which some advantage is intended to be obtained."[71] Simple theft—someone sneaking in and taking the manuscript while Martin was away—would not seem to qualify. What stratagem, then, did Joseph Smith think had been used to part Martin from the manuscript? Joseph, in company with his mother, had heard Martin's July 1828 confession of mishandling the manuscript and therefore knew that the urging of a "very particular friend" had led him to compromise the manuscript's security. It is likely in this incident that Joseph detected a trick.[72]

Although Lucy does not provide the identity of Martin's mischief-making friend, there is at least one likely candidate among Martin's known associates—someone from the very group of money diggers who had previously attempted to steal the golden plates.

The Money Diggers

The money diggers, as we saw in the previous chapter, had particular reason to take interest in the book translated from the plates and to undermine its success. Their sense of entitlement to the plates made the book derived from it a natural object of their curiosity, and in some cases their ire.[73] At

---

69. Anderson, *Lucy's Book*, 421.

70. Smith et al., *History of the Church*, 1:21.

71. Noah Webster, *Noah Webster's First Edition of an American Dictionary of the English Language*, s.v. "stratagem."

72. Anderson, *Lucy's Book*, 418–21.

73. "Mormonism---No. II," in Vogel, *EMD*, 2:307.

least one of the diggers is known to have opposed the book quite actively the following year, and to have still taken action against it as late as 1833.

Early in 1829, several months after the manuscript disappeared, Joseph's former fellow treasure seeker Peter Ingersoll was willing to perjure himself in order to stop the translation and publication of the Book of Mormon and get Joseph jailed.[74] The occasion for Ingersoll's perjury was a lawsuit against the Prophet. Though Martin refused to join in on the suit against Joseph, his wife Lucy was, not surprisingly, quite willing. In her memoir, Lucy Mack Smith recounted some of the court proceedings, as rehearsed to her:

> The witnesses, being duly sworn, the first arose and testified, that Joseph Smith told him that the box which he had, contained nothing but sand; and he, Joseph Smith, said it was gold, to deceive the people.
>
> Second witness swore, that Joseph Smith had told him that it was nothing but a box of lead, and he was determined to use it as he saw fit.
>
> Third witness declared, that he once inquired of Joseph Smith what he had in that box, and Joseph Smith told him that there was nothing at all in the box, saying, that he had made fools of the whole of them, and all he wanted was, to get Martin Harris's money away from him, and that he (witness) was knowing to the fact that Joseph Smith had, by his persuasion, already got two or three hundred dollars.[75]

This testimony, particularly that of the first witness, should be compared to the 1833 affidavit sworn by Peter Ingersoll regarding Joseph Smith:

> [H]e made me his confident [sic]. . . . One day he came, and greeted me with a joyful countenance—Upon asking the cause of his unusual happiness, he replied in the following language: "As I was passing, yesterday, across the woods, after a heavy shower of rain, I found, in a hollow, some beautiful white sand, that had been washed up by the water. I took off my frock, and tied up several quarts of it, and then went home. On my entering the house, I found the family at the table eating dinner. They were all anxious to know the contents of my frock. At that moment, I happened to think of what I had heard about a history found in Canada, called the golden Bible; so I very gravely told them it was the golden Bible. To my surprise, they were credulous enough to believe what I said. Accordingly I told them that I had received a commandment to let no one see it, for, says I, no man can see it with the naked eye and live. However, I offered to take out the book and show it to them, but they refuse[d] to see it, and left the room." Now, said Jo, "I have got the damned fools fixed, and will carry out the fun." Notwithstanding, he told me he had no such book, and believed there never was any such book, yet, he told me that he actually went to Willard Chase, to get him to make a chest, in which he might deposit his golden Bible. But, as

---

74. Anderson, *Lucy's Book*, 443–44.
75. Anderson, 444.

Chase would not do it, he made a box himself, of clap-boards, and put it into a pillow case, and allowed people only to lift it, and feel of it through the case.[76]

Ingersoll's distinctive claim that Joseph Smith deceived others by palming off a box of sand as a box containing the golden plates seems to identify him with the witness making a similar claim at the 1829 trial. However, while Ingersoll alleged that Joseph had spontaneously concocted the golden plates story to fool his family about what was in the bag of white sand, testimony from the Smiths and others shows that Joseph described his quest for the plates over a period of four years before he ever claimed to take possession of them. This leaves Ingersoll's affidavit either at minimum a gross misremembering of what Joseph allegedly told him or a deliberate act of perjury.

Though the identities of Ingersoll's fellow witnesses is not yet clear, they were likely fellow money diggers who would have shared his enmity toward Joseph and been able to plausibly claim he had confided with them about the treasure he claimed to have found. Having worked together in searching treasure in the dark of night and later conspired with one another to steal the plates, Ingersoll and his collaborators could have easily put together a small conspiracy to put Joseph in jail and thus get the revenge they sought.

By deceiving others in order to discredit and avenge themselves on a presumed deceiver, Ingersoll and his companions fell under the condemnation pronounced by Joseph's revelation on the manuscript thieves: "Verily, verily, I say unto you, wo be unto him that lieth to deceive because he supposeth that another lieth to deceive, for such are not exempt from the justice of God" (D&C 10:28). Furthermore, the revelation's "wicked men" who stole the manuscript in "anger" and conspired to destroy his work evoked the angel's warnings about "wicked men" among the money diggers who would try to steal the plates. It also paralleled the money diggers in their secretiveness, describing them as men who "love[d] darkness rather than light" because darkness cloaked their evildoing (D&C 10:21).[77] Similarly, money diggers usually hid their digging activities under cover of night to keep the location of their treasure secret. For the "wicked men" of the angel's warning to become also the "wicked men" of the revelation would require only that they expand their conspiracy of theft against the book of plates to include the book taken *from* the plates.[78]

---

76. Peter Ingersoll statement, 1833, in Eber D. Howe, *Mormonism Unvailed*, 236.

77. Joseph Smith added this description of the conspirators in a revelatory expansion to the revelation in the 1835 Doctrine and Covenants.

78. Doctrine and Covenants 10 further links the conspirators to the money diggers when it implicitly groups Martin with the conspiring wicked men by calling him "a wicked man," because "he has sought to take away the things wherewith you have been entrusted; and he has also sought to destroy your gift" (vv. 6–7). However, given Martin's continued support of Joseph and selection to be one of the witnesses of the golden plates,

Adding to the suspicion of the money diggers being connected to the manuscript theft, Martin himself had personal connections with these men. In his 1859 interview with Joel Tiffany, Martin related various stories he had heard from "these money-diggers" that suggest a close association with several of these men: "These things . . . were told to me in confidence, and told by different ones, and their stories agreed."[79] Judging from his further comments, the money digger to whom Martin was closest was Samuel Lawrence, to whom Martin attributed stories about the diggers' remarkable experiences.[80]

Martin's involvement with the money diggers in general, and Lawrence in particular, may have even passed beyond mere conversation about treasure quests and into actual spadework. Ole Jensen, who knew Martin during his later years in Utah, recalled his account of a dig in the Hill Cumorah in the weeks after Joseph obtained the plates:

> I will tell you th a wonderful thing that happened after Joseph had found the plates: three of us took a notion to take some of tools and go to the hill and hunt for some more boxes or gold or something, and Indeed we found a stone box; we got quiet [*sic*] excited [p. 4] about it; and dug quiet [*sic*] carefully around it; we were ready to take it up: but behold <<by>> some unseen power it slipped and back into the hill;[81] we stood there and looked at it; One of us took a crowbar and tried to hold <<drive>> it through the lid to hold it; but it glanced and only broke one corner off of the box.
>
> Some time that box will be found and you will see the corner broken off; then you will know I have told you the truth.[82]

While Jensen could have conflated a dig that Martin had merely heard about with one he had participated in, Martin was positioned to finance such a dig and was well acquainted with several of Palmyra area's active money diggers, particularly Samuel Lawrence, making his involvement entirely plausible. And

---

it seems unlikely that the revelation was intended to cast Martin as a co-conspirator of the theft. Rather, Martin seems to be classed with the wicked men who attempted to dispossess Joseph of the plates and other sacred things because his misdeeds facilitated theirs. Regardless of whether he intended to help the conspirators, he did.

79. "Mormonism---No. II," in Vogel, *EMD*, 2:307.

80. "Mormonism---No. II," in Vogel, *EMD*, 2:307.

81. In his 1859 interview with Joel Tiffany, Martin Harris did not acknowledge having encountered such a "slippery treasure" while digging himself but recounted hearing about them from the money diggers: "It was reported by these money-diggers, that they had found boxes, but before they could secure them, they would sink into the earth." "Mormonism---No. II," in Vogel, *EMD*, 2:304.

82. Ole A. Jensen, "Testimony of Martin Harris (One of the Witnesses of the Book of Mormon)," in Vogel, *EMD*, 2:376. Brigham Young described this or a very similar dig, as it had been recounted to him by Porter Rockwell, the son of Manchester money digger Orin Rockwell. Brigham Young, June 17, 1877, *Journal of Discourses*, 19:37.

just as Martin was well positioned to finance a dig, Lawrence, who was reputed to be a seer in his own right and to whom Joseph had reportedly shown the site on the hill where he had found the stone box, was well positioned to lead one.[83] By keeping such company, and not breaking off these connections after the angel warned of conniving persons among them, Martin risked letting would-be thieves with a vendetta against Joseph into his confidence—and home.

Samuel Lawrence

It is quite likely among the money diggers, and particularly in the person of Samuel Lawrence, that we will find Martin's "very particular friend," who arrived at his door soon after he returned home with the manuscript and for whom he eagerly wrested the manuscript from its bonds of lock and key and of covenant obligation.

Beyond his helping lead the efforts to steal the gold plates from Joseph, Lawrence proved willing to avenge himself for real or imagined injury by taking another person's property. On April 17, 1833, three years after the publication of the Book of Mormon, Lawrence was indicted for "fraudulently secreting property."[84] The events behind the fragmentary court record of the indictment, as reconstructed by the late Rich Troll, are as follows: Samuel Lawrence, an agent for his brother-in-law Abner Cole's Rochester newspaper *The Liberal Advocate* (formerly the Palmyra *Reflector*) refused to deliver copies of the newspaper to a subscriber against whom he apparently had a vendetta, perhaps even pocketing the subscription money.[85] Around this time, Lawrence's employment with *The Liberal Advocate* was terminated, and a few months later he was indicted on the subscriber's charge of theft.[86] This incident—combined with Lawrence's belief that Joseph had wronged him in withholding his rightful share of Cumorah's treasure and that he was justified in trying to steal the plates—adds plausibility to Lawrence feeling similarly justified in secreting the manuscript.

Samuel Lawrence had clear motive, a direct connection with both Martin Harris and the book of plates, and a known instance in the few years following the manuscript theft of taking or withholding property illegally in order to get what he believed was due to him—or to exact revenge when he did not. He fits the profile of the thieves sketched in the near-contemporaneous revelation, almost certainly belongs in a set of persons whom the victim, Joseph Smith, believed had taken the manuscript (the unauthorized viewers), and makes an identifiable

---

83. Knight, "Manuscript of the History of Joseph Smith," in Vogel, *EMD*, 4:14–6.

84. Oyer and Terminer Minutes, 1824–1845, 92, in Vogel, *EMD*, 3:186.

85. Rich Troll, "Samuel Tyler Lawrence: A Significant Figure in Joseph Smith's Palmyra Past," 73–74, 85–86.

86. Wayne County, New York court record, April 17, 1833.

candidate for Martin's "very particular friend," who, whether by accident or by stratagem, compromised the manuscript's security and likely facilitated its theft.

The Revelatory Explanation for the Manuscript Loss

Joseph Smith's revelation on the stolen manuscript, published as Doctrine and Covenants 10, explains its theft on both historical and theological levels: Satan inspired wicked men to take the Book of Mormon manuscript and alter its text to produce contradictions that would impugn Joseph Smith's abilities as a translator; and God allowed this theft but had foreseen it and used it providentially, holding in reserve a back-up record that would more than fill the gap left by the corrupted text. This explanation, held by believers in the Book of Mormon consistently since the revelation was given, has often been an object of criticism by nonbelievers who see it as a transparent dodge to avoid having to reproduce the lost pages.

Support for the revelation's explanation will almost certainly continue to be a matter of faith and not of historical analysis. The tools of history are ill-suited to answering questions like "Were those who stole the Book of Mormon manuscript inspired by Satan to discredit the book?" or "Was the theft foreseen by God and factored into His plan for the book?" It is beyond the realm of historical scholarship to prove or disprove the explanation given by the revelation for the manuscript loss. However, it *is* within the scope of scholarship to assess why those involved in the emergence of the Book of Mormon found this explanation quite believable.

The revelatory explanation of the manuscript loss was believable to its earliest audience—those assisting Joseph Smith in bringing forth the Book of Mormon—because this explanation fit comfortably within the context of surrounding events. The revelation states that the translation manuscript had been taken by a group of "wicked men" acting in conspiratorial secrecy (D&C 10:8); that these individuals were motivated to prevent the publication of the Book of Mormon and harm and discredit its translator (v. 19); and that they would do so by doctoring the translated text, likely by introducing variations while copying it so the two versions would contradict (vv. 10–18).

Those supporting Joseph Smith in protecting, translating, and publishing the Book of Mormon would have also been unsurprised by the idea of conspirators taking the translation manuscript in order to introduce contradictions and thereby discredit it. Lucy Harris and Flanders Dyke had conspired to steal the character transcript, copy it, and use the copy to discredit Joseph's claims. Furthermore, those who pressed Martin to sue Joseph in March 1829 portrayed Joseph as self-contradictory and aimed to reveal his deception in claiming to possess the plates and being able to translate them.[87]

---

87. "Testimony of Martin Harris, 1870."

Altogether, the revelation said nothing that would have seemed unusual or surprising. The one novel explanation in the revelation is that of the conspirators hoping to discredit Joseph by producing a *variant* copy that would make it appear that Joseph was unable to reproduce the same translation. However, even this does not greatly diverge from the earlier conspiracy of discrediting the Book of Mormon by copying the character transcript. This new element in the revelation would have made particular sense to the early believers in light of the Book of Mormon theology of sealing up sacred records.

As explained in Chapter 2, a sacred text that had been sealed up was in the care of God and angels and was thus incorruptible so long as the seal remained in force. But a sacred text that passed through impure hands was tainted, thereafter falling under the suspicion that it had been corrupted. Nephi's panoramic vision of human history showed him that some records were "sealed up, to come forth in their purity," but the Bible, in passing through the hands of "the great and abominable church" built by the devil, was altered and many "plain and precious things" taken from it (1 Ne. 13:26–28; 14:23–26). Therefore, what had happened to the initial Book of Mormon manuscript was the opposite of sealing up. Rather than sealing up the translated pages unto the care of God, who would protect them and keep them pure, Joseph had unwittingly "delivered them up, yea, that which was sacred, unto wickedness," into the hands of wicked men who were inspired by Satan to *corrupt* the scriptural text.

The *suspicion* that the sacred text could have been corrupted by passing through the hands of the wicked would have arisen naturally from the theology and practice of sealing scriptural records described in the Book of Mormon. What the revelation did was to confirm this suspicion and instruct that, because of the modification of the sacred text, Joseph should not retranslate the stolen pages.

Narrowing the Mystery

Although the mystery of the missing Book of Mormon manuscript cannot at this time be definitively solved, those who actively opposed the Book of Mormon at the time of the theft and had plausible means to carry it out can be identified. Outside the improbable event that the manuscript was stolen by enemies to the Book of Mormon who are largely invisible in the historical record, those complicit in the manuscript theft likely include one or more of the persons discussed above. If we cannot yet identify the thief or thieves, we can at least narrow the probable suspects to two relatively small groups: Harris family insiders and Palmyra-area money diggers.

CHAPTER 5

THE LONG BLUE LOST MANUSCRIPT

The lost manuscript, it turns out, had both an unexpectedly striking appearance and a surprising length. Existing evidence allows us to piece together details about this lost object, including its length and both the size and color of the paper that it was written on. While thought by many to be just a brief record of Lehi's ministry, the lost manuscript was the first *half* of Mormon's abridgement and probably significantly longer than its traditional description as "116 pages."

The Blue Foolscap Manuscript

Joseph Smith and Martin Harris both reported that the lost manuscript was recorded on foolscap, writing paper cut to about 13x17 inches and named for its traditional "fool's cap" watermark.

> Mr Harris having returned from this tour he left me and went home to Palmyra, arranged his affairs, and returned again to my house about the twelfth of April, Eighteen hundred and twenty eight, and commenced writing for me while I translated from the plates, which we continued untill the fourteenth of June following, by which time he had written one hundred and sixteen <pages> of manuscript on foolscap paper.[1]

> By means of the urim and thummim "a pair of large spectacles," as Mr. Harris termed them, the translation was made, and Mr. Harris claims to have written, of the translations as they were given by Smith, "116 solid pages of cap [foolscap]." The remainder was written by others.[2]

Additional details from Martin on the physical appearance of the lost manuscript come to us by way of his longtime associate Francis Gladden Bishop, who published extensive descriptions of Book of Mormon artifacts, drawing much of his information from Martin.[3] Martin, in turn, supported Bishop's writings through the early 1850s, even serving as a "witness" to the accuracy of Bishop's reports.[4] When Bishop published a description of the

---

1. History of Joseph Smith (Mulholland draft).
2. Martin Harris interview in "A Witness to the Book of Mormon," August 28, 1870, in Vogel, *EMD*, 330.
3. Bishop's use of Martin Harris as a source is documented at length in Chapter 7.
4. For Martin Harris as "witness" to Bishop's writings, see Francis Gladden Bishop, *A Proclamation from the Lord to His People Scattered throughout all the Earth*, 1–2. For Martin's support of Bishop, see the description by Brigham Young, an uncle to Martin Harris through Martin's second marriage (to Young's niece Caroline), in

lost manuscript in 1851, it included a statement from Martin pronouncing the description "correct in every particular." [5] And what was the description that Martin endorsed? That the "manuscript was on ruled paper of a blueish [*sic*] cast and foolscap size, the writing course [*sic*] and heavy."[6]

The accuracy of this description is evidenced by Martin's continued support of Bishop after it was published under Martin's imprimatur.[7] If Bishop's published description of blue, lined paper was false, no one would have known this better than Martin, who had been principal scribe on the manuscript for nearly two months, had borrowed it to show to others, and had read it aloud to family and friends in the evenings.[8] Bishop's description of the manuscript pages is inherently plausible, with blue foolscap paper being common in the day. Palmyra-area historical expert Don Enders responded to Bishop's description with the observation that "lined paper with a blue tint would be a typical practical sort of paper available in the average bookseller stores in that area."[9] Lined paper with a blue tint was a typical writing paper available from John H. Gilbert and Pomeroy Tucker, who operated a bookstore in Palmyra in 1828, and from James Bemis in Canandaigua, a central distributor for paper products in the area. Martin could have purchased such writing paper from these and other merchants.[10] Blue paper existed in both low-medium and fine grades of paper quality depending on the dye used. Since the paper was reportedly lined and intended to be used for the recording of a sacred text, it seems likely that Martin as financier would have purchased the higher-quality paper for this important undertaking.[11]

The Manuscript Length

The Book of Mormon's lost manuscript is popularly thought to solely be an extended account of Lehi's life written on a manuscript of 116 pages. However, this description of its contents is incorrect, and the description of its page length

---

Brigham Young, April 17, 1853, *Journal of Discourses*, 2:127. See also H. Michael Marquardt, "Martin Harris: The Kirtland Years, 1831–1870," 29–30.

5. Francis Gladden Bishop, *An Address to the Sons and Daughters of Zion*, 28.

6. Bishop, *An Address*, 28.

7. Bishop, *A Proclamation from the Lord*, 1–2.

8. Blair, footnote comment in Lucy [Mack] Smith, *Biographical Sketches of Joseph Smith*, in Vogel, *EMD*, 1:367–68.

9. Emily Utt to Don Bradley, July 20, 2011, relaying information from Don Enders.

10. Utt to Bradley, July 20, 2011.

11. This method of "blueing paper" is said to have originated in Holland and was widely practiced in the eighteenth and nineteenth centuries. Irene Brückle, "Historical Manufacture and Use of Blue Paper"; Roy Perkinson, "Summary of the History of Blue Paper"; Charles Thomas Davis, *The Manufacture of Paper: being a Description of the Various Processes for the Fabrication, Coloring, and Finishing of Every Kind of Paper*, 473–76.

is likely incorrect as well. The Book of Mormon's internal evidence shows that the lost manuscript *began* with Lehi, and then covered the ensuing *four and a half centuries*, into the reign of King Benjamin—the same time period covered by the small plates account that replaces it. (See Chapter 6.) Accordingly, a revelation instructing Joseph Smith on how to replace the stolen manuscript commands him to "translate the engravings which are on the plates of Nephi, down even till you come to the reign of king Benjamin, or until you come to that which you have translated, which you have retained" (D&C 10:41).

The Book of Lehi?

In the summer of 1829, as the Book of Mormon headed to the press, Joseph Smith encountered an urgent problem for which he drafted a temporary fix that has proven to be remarkably permanent. Joseph's dilemma was this: Mormon's original, intended structure for his book was broken. With 450–460 years of Mormon's total abridgement of 920 years having been stolen, *half* of Mormon's narration was gone.[12] And while a substitution was made for the missing narrative, it was not replaced with a full account or with Mormon's own words. Readers thus needed to be oriented to the difference in authorship and narrative styles between Nephi's first-person small plates account and Mormon's third-person abridgement. In Mormon's original, *intended* structure, the book was straightforwardly what its name said—the Book of *Mormon*—that is, an account by Mormon. With Nephi's small plates replacing the first part of Mormon's abridgement, the resulting work, while still published under the name "The Book of Mormon," was now a *hybrid* written partly by Mormon and partly by Nephi and the small plates scribes. Without an explanatory preface, readers would go directly from learning on the title page that the book was an abridgement by Mormon—"The Book of Mormon, Written by the Hand of Mormon"—to finding on the next page the first-person narration of an entirely different author—a story beginning, "I, Nephi".

Joseph's task was to step into the gap between Mormon and Nephi and construct a provisional bridge between the two. Joseph did this in the form of a preface that was included in the first edition of the Book of Mormon and then discarded from future editions. This task, however, was trickier than it would appear. What had made it possible to replace Mormon's lost account, which had been abridged from a larger record called "the plates of Nephi," was a complex system of records that included another, shorter record, also called "the plates of Nephi." In a revelation Joseph received around this time on how to deal with the manuscript loss, the Lord told him to "translate

---

12. The precise time period covered by the lost manuscript is further discussed in Chapters 6 and 15.

the engravings which are from the *plates of Nephi*" (D&C 10:41), which the revelation distinguishes from the lost "abridgment from the *account of Nephi*" (v. 44) taken from what the Book of Mormon also calls "the plates of Nephi" (1 Ne. 9:2; W of M 1:3; Mosiah 1:6). While we have a modern convention of distinguishing "the large plates of Nephi" from "the small plates of Nephi" to help make sense of this, imagine how confusing it would have been to readers encountering the book for the very first time and confronting the two records *called by exactly the same name.* If in the preface Joseph had chosen to use the identical names for these records used in the Book of Mormon itself, he would have explained to the reader that the lost manuscript was taken from "the plates of Nephi" and replaced by "the plates of Nephi," making it appear to readers that the lost manuscript was replaced with itself.

Contrast the confusion of introducing two identically named "plates of Nephi" with Joseph's explanation in the preface to the first edition of the Book of Mormon:

> I translated, by the gift and power of God, and caused to be written, one hundred and sixteen pages, the which I took from the Book of Lehi, which was an account abridged from the plates of Lehi, by the hand of Mormon; which said account, some person or persons have stolen and kept from me, notwithstanding my utmost exertions to recover it again—and being commanded of the Lord that I should not translate the same over again . . . but behold, the Lord said unto me, . . . thou shalt translate from the plates of Nephi, until ye come to that which ye have translated, which ye have retained; and behold ye shall publish it as the record of Nephi.[13]

Instead of confusing the reader with two "plates of Nephi," Joseph distinguishes the source behind the lost manuscript as "the plates of *Lehi*" and reserves the name "plates of Nephi" only for the small plates that replaced it. With this substitution, readers would now realize that the lost manuscript was taken from one source and replaced using another.

How complete was this explanation? The discontinued use of both the preface in subsequent editions of the Book of Mormon and Joseph's own discontinued use of the terms "Book of Lehi" and "plates of Lehi" suggest that he was not satisfied with the solution. While these terms provided a *serviceable* description for quickly explaining what had occurred, they were ultimately replaced with the more precise distinction of the "large plates" and the "small plates" of Nephi.

Why then did Joseph refer to the plates of Lehi and Book of Lehi? Immediately there seems to be two problems with these designations. First, outside the first-edition preface, the source behind Mormon's abridgement is indicated to be the (large) "plates of Nephi" (e.g., Mosiah 1:6; 3 Ne. 5:10;

---

13. *The Book of Mormon: An Account Written by the Hand of Mormon, Upon Plates Taken from the Plates of Nephi* (1830), iii–iv.

D&C 10:39). Second, calling the whole lost manuscript "the Book of Lehi" implies that the four and a half centuries it covered were contained in a single intra-Book of Mormon book comparable to the First Book of Nephi or the Book of Alma. This would drastically differ from Mormon's remaining abridgment that divides material into much smaller units in the form of multiple individual books named for the principal record keeper of each given period. While he sometimes has two generations of record keepers in a single book, only when giving the extremely summary 4 Nephi does he abridge more than two generations of record keeping in one book. Given that the *same* narrator abridged both the Book of Mormon's lost text and its published text, we have reason to expect that the same pattern of division into smaller units would have been followed throughout. In the lost manuscript Mormon should thus present us not only with a "Book of Lehi," but also with the books of many other record keepers across the dozen generations it covered. Joseph's use of the term appears to err on the side of simplifying for readers the complexity of the book they were about to encounter.

Analysis of the available manuscripts of the Book of Mormon shows the original first two chapters of the Book of Mosiah to be lost. Our current Mosiah 1 was originally identified as "Chapter III," and Chapters I and II cannot be located. As discussed at length in Chapter 15, these original first two chapters of Mosiah appear to have been part of the lost manuscript.[14] Thus, while the

---

14. On an alternate reading, the missing first two chapters of the Book of Mosiah could also be understood, in light of Doctrine and Covenants 10:41, as material Joseph translated before lending Martin the manuscript but which Joseph "retained." The verse instructs Joseph to replace the lost manuscript by translating "the engravings which are on the plates of Nephi, down even till you come to the reign of king Benjamin, or until you come to that which you have translated, which you have retained." Could Mosiah, Chapters I and II be the "retained" portions? Neither Joseph nor Martin mention Joseph withholding part of the translation manuscript from Martin. And no retained manuscript has been identified. But a larger difficulty with this reading emerges when we place Section 10 in its chronological context. The idea that verse 41 refers to a portion Joseph withheld from Martin emerged when it was believed that the revelation had been given in summer 1828 shortly after the manuscript loss. In that context, reference to a retained portion of the manuscript would indeed mean there was a part of the 1828 translation work that Joseph held back from Martin. But recent scholarly work on Section 10 identifies it as a revelation received in late April-early May *1829*, when the Joseph had done copious additional translation work after the manuscript loss. In that context, the obvious referent for "that which you have translated which you have retained" is not a hypothetical portion of the lost manuscript that Joseph didn't lend to Martin, but, rather, the *post-*1828 translation manuscript that Joseph retained because it was received *after* the manuscript loss. When Section 10 is read in context, there is no evidence for Joseph

lost manuscript evidently *included* a Book of Lehi, the entire manuscript cannot accurately be *equated* with that book. Instead of providing an entire description of what was lost, Joseph appears to have simplified for readers the complexities surrounding the Book of Lehi. The Book of Lehi would have been the *first* book contained in the lost manuscript rather than the *only* book contained in it.

Similarly, Joseph Smith's use of the term "plates of Lehi" was perfect for distinguishing the lost manuscript from its replacement, but inadequate as a full description of the lost manuscript's source. That manuscript's "Book of Lehi" would, indeed, have drawn on "the plates of Lehi," just as Joseph said. The portion of Nephi's large plates that abridged Lehi's record could accurately be called "the plates of Lehi" on the same logic by which Jacob describes "the Book of Jacob" as written on as "the plates of Jacob," even though the larger record in which they were found was the (small) "plates of Nephi" (Jacob 3:14). As David Sloan explained:

> If the large plates of Nephi began with Lehi's record, this portion of the large plates could accurately be called the plates of Lehi. . . . [A]lthough Nephi made the large plates of Nephi and wrote on them, the portion of the large plates upon which he copied the record of Lehi was referred to as the "plates of Lehi." Therefore, Mormon's abridgment of Lehi's record found on the large plates could accurately be described as "an account abridged from the plates of Lehi, by the hand of Mormon."[15]

Joseph's identification of the lost manuscript with "the Book of Lehi," taken from "the plates of Lehi," presented the reader with real data, but simplified this data to the point that readers came away from it with a mistaken sense of clarity. The contents of the lost manuscript and their source-record had each been given a name that effectively distinguished them from their "plates of Nephi" replacement. But the names used were stand-ins for a much more complex set of books and records that Joseph could not so readily explain. It is perhaps for this reason that Joseph left the preface behind with the Book of Mormon's first edition. But, for better and for worse, the preface's terminology has endured, suggesting that the Book of Mormon's lost manuscript was far narrower than its actual scope as the first half of Mormon's abridgement.

Why 116 Pages?

The preface Joseph added to the Printer's Manuscript was also where he introduced the description of the lost manuscript as 116 pages. Viewing that figure in context of the preface, and of the Printer's Manuscript more broadly, raises questions about this figure's adequacy.

Smith withholding part of the 1828 translation manuscript—it was all borrowed, and all lost. For the dating of Section 10, see "Revelation, Spring 1829 [D&C 10]."

15. David E. Sloan, "The Book of Lehi and the. Plates of Lehi," 269–72.

The preface's purpose of bridging the gap between Mormon and Nephi did not require an accurate page count. Even the most approximate description of the lost manuscript would have served the intended purpose. Given the preface's hurried production and use of simplified stand-in information for the Book of Mormon's actual complexity, it would not be surprising if the preface's page tally served simply as a placeholder for the lost manuscript's actual, and likely unknown, page count.

Examining the preface in context suggests that the 116 figure was, in fact, such a placeholder. When this figure is put in the larger context of the manuscript in which it was introduced, a striking, almost certainly non-random coincidence emerges. The length Joseph gives for the lost manuscript happens to be the exact length of the manuscript that *replaced* it. When the Book of Mormon Printer's Manuscript was prepared for publication, the length of the small plates text (1 Nephi through Words of Mormon) that substituted for the lost text came out to a full 116 pages, spilling over just two and a half lines onto page 117.[16] This precise match between the replacement manuscript's known page count and the lost manuscript's *reported* page count pages raises the question of just where Joseph acquired the 116-page figure. Given that the Book of Mormon describes the small plates narrative as a "small account" (W of M 1:3), it is improbable that both the initial manuscript and its abbreviated replacement would be the same length.

By the time Joseph wrote the preface, the manuscript had been missing for a year; without the lost manuscript to consult, he would likely have been unsure how long it had even been. Furthermore, the pages of the lost manuscript may not have been numbered,[17] and even if they were it is not clear that Joseph would have noted this number and recalled it a year later. Instead, a page count that Joseph *could* readily access while writing a preface for the Printer's Manuscript is that for the small plates in the Printer's Manuscript.

---

16. "Printer's Manuscript of the Book of Mormon, circa August 1829–circa January 1830."

17. Stanford Carmack, who works closely with Royal Skousen, helpfully wrote to the author offering reasons to believe the lost manuscript was paginated. Carmack notes that (1) the later, 1829 Original and Printer's manuscripts paginated; (2) Martin Harris may have added some of the page numbers to the Printer's Manuscript; and (3) pagination would have made sense in order to keep so many pages in order. I am skeptical that the 1829 scribal practices, led by the more literarily savvy Oliver Cowdery, indicate what Martin did as scribe in 1828. And if Martin Harris had paginated the lost manuscript, and remembered that it was 116 pages long, it seems unlikely that his brother would have believed that Martin had scribed for "near 200" pages of that manuscript, as discussed later in this chapter. Personal communication from Stanford Carmack, email, June 27, 2019.

Checking the length of the lost manuscript's replacement was one way to attempt a rough estimate of the lost manuscript's length.[18]

---

18. The Book of Mormon's Printer's Manuscript (P) was copied from the translation manuscript, its Original Manuscript (O), so that the type for the first-edition Book of Mormon could be set from P. The idea that Joseph Smith may have derived the 116 page count from the P version of the small plates was first suggested by Brent Lee Metcalfe. This argument was later critiqued by Royal Skousen. Skousen argued that Joseph Smith *could not* have gotten the page count of 116 for the small plates from P because when the preface was written, Oliver Cowdery would have only copied the pages needed to typeset the first signature of the printed book. Skousen extrapolated from later data points in Oliver's production of P that he produced P only as needed for the typesetting of the Book of Mormon. Skousen's most significant data point for concluding that Oliver produced P only as needed is that from Helaman 13:17 through the end of Mormon, O was used for this purpose in place of P, suggesting that Oliver may have fallen behind in his copying of P. Skousen has recently rejected that earlier interpretation, presenting in its place the brilliant hypothesis that P was temporarily unavailable to the typesetter because it was taken to Canada to secure a Canadian copyright for the Book of Mormon. This new data suggests to me the need to rethink whether Joseph could have derived the 116 figure from P. It was formerly posited that Oliver produced P only as needed, and was therefore unable to have P ready in time for the typesetting of Helaman 13:17f. On Skousen's new timeline, he estimates that the typesetter would have reached Mosiah 26:28 (page 160 of P) at the same time Cowdery and his assistant copyists produced P for Alma 36 (page 261), placing the copyists a hundred pages ahead of the typesetter. Skousen's finding of a probable connection between the typesetter's use of O and the Canadian copyright trip similarly indicates that the copying of P was completed well *ahead* of the typesetting—i.e., that P was produced all the way through the end of the book (page 464 of P) by the time the typesetter had reached Helaman 13:17 (page 356). It is thus clear that Oliver Cowdery did *not* wait to produce P just as it was needed for the typesetting, opening the prospect that Oliver could have gotten a considerable head start in the copying process between the end of the translation in late June and the beginning of typesetting around late August. Given Oliver's potential to begin producing P two months ahead of the typesetting and that Oliver finished copying P *at least* 108 pages ahead of the typesetting, it is now perfectly reasonable to think that Oliver had reached *page* 116 in the copying process (the end of the small plates) before Joseph would have written the *number* 116 in his preface to P. Seen in this light, there is no anomalous coincidence in the lost manuscript and the small plates both being described as 116 pages. The relationship is not coincidental but causal—Joseph likely derived the 116 figure for the lost manuscript from the length of its replacement. See Royal Skousen's review of Metcalfe, "Critical Methodology and the Text of the Book of Mormon," 121–44; and Royal Skousen, "Why was one sixth of the 1830 Book of Mormon set from the original manuscript?" 93–103. (Note that the ideas here of what Royal Skousen's newest findings mean for the figure 116 are solely the interpretation of the present author, and not findings presented by Skousen.)

Although Joseph appears not to have continued to use the terms "Book of Lehi" and "plates of Lehi" to refer to the lost manuscript, he did continue to use "116 pages" to describe the replaced section.[19] For example, in his 1832 history Joseph writes of Martin: "[I]t came to pass that after we had translated 116 pages that he desired to carry them to read to his friends."[20] Similarly, in his official history (written 1838–39), Joseph says that Martin had been his scribe until "he had written one hundred and sixteen <pages> of manuscript on foolscap paper."[21] Of note here is that Joseph writes in this history as if Martin had served as the manuscript's sole scribe when his wife Emma and others had also acted as scribes during this period—including Emma's brothers, Alva Hale and Reuben Hale, and Joseph's brother, Samuel Smith. As in the preface, in his histories Joseph aims for *simplicity* rather than *precision*. We see this concern again when Joseph was invited by his brother Hyrum to tell about coming forth of the Book of Mormon in an October 1831 conference of the Church. There, Joseph reportedly "said that it was not intended to tell the world all the particulars of the coming forth of the book of Mormon, & also said that it was not expedient for him to relate these things &c."[22]

Altogether, the likelihood that Joseph did not even know the length of the lost manuscript, the shared total page count of the Printers Manuscript, time constraints in the writing of the preface, and Joseph's preference for functional simplicity over precision points to the 116-page figure being a quick estimate rather than an accurate description.

Given the cultural ubiquity of the term "lost 116 pages," it's worth asking why Joseph may have used this figure if the actual page count were unknown. Indeed, why cite a page count at all? Joseph did not write the preface for historians but for new readers of the Book of Mormon, and his purpose in

---

19. Martin Harris also sometimes used the term "116 pages" to refer to the lost manuscript. Given Martin's practice of following Joseph's language usage, this appears to be Martin using "lost 116 pages" as a *name* used for the lost manuscript, following Joseph's usage, rather than Martin making the assertion that this was the manuscript's precise page count. (Use of "lost 116 pages" as a *name* for the lost manuscript is ubiquitous, as in the title of the present book and in the scribal insertion in the minutes of Emer Harris's sermon, discussed later in this chapter, where the scribe uses "116 pages" as the name for a manuscript that Emer Harris had said contained "near 200 pages.") For a similar example of Martin following the lead of Joseph's terminology, see the Martin Harris letter to H. B. Emerson where he uses Joseph's 1838-1839 History term "translation" to refer to the *transcription* of the characters taken from the plates. Martin Harris to H. B. Emerson, November 23, 1870, in Vogel, *EMD*, 2:336.

20. Joseph Smith, "History, circa Summer 1832."

21. "History, 1838–1856, volume A-1 [23 December 1805–30 August 1834]."

22. "Minutes, 25–26 October 1831."

writing was not to act as the most thorough historical source, but to assure readers that the sacred book they held in their hands was adequate to the purposes it was divinely sent forth to achieve. In this context, citing the length of the small plates as a stand-in for the length of the lost manuscript evokes an equivalence between the two: they were comparable. Whatever its limitations as a historical source, the preface succeeded in addressing immediate confusion and questions that may have arisen from the theft and its remedy.

The Lost 200 Pages?

All Book of Mormon manuscripts—the lost manuscript, the fragments of Original (replacement) Manuscript, and the complete Printer's Manuscript copy of the original—were written on foolscap paper of 15–17 inches by 12–13.5 inches. In our extant Original and Printer's Manuscripts, the sheets vary slightly around a median size of approximately 16 inches by 13 inches. These were folded so that one sheet constituted two pages. We can thus estimate how much text would have fit into a given number of pages in the lost manuscript using the complete Printer's Manuscript.

A single page from the Printer's Manuscript compared to the printed page in a modern Latter-day Saint edition generally produces between 1 and 1.25 typeset pages, averaging about 1.15 printed pages per manuscript page. Using this ratio, 116 pages of manuscript would correspond to something around 133 printed pages, whereas 200 pages of manuscript would correspond to about 230 printed pages, and so on.

That the lost manuscript exceeded the traditional count was affirmed by Martin Harris's brother Emer Harris. On April 6, 1856, Emer, an early Utah pioneer, spoke at a Utah Stake conference in Provo on the rise of the Church and coming forth of the Book of Mormon. There, Emer told his audience that his brother had scribed for "near 200 pages" of the initial Book of Mormon manuscript before it was lost. By this time, the 116-page number was already quite well established in the Latter-day Saint mind, having appeared in both the preface of each of the initial five thousand copies of the Book of Mormon and in the serialized History of the Church in the *Times and Seasons*.[23] As an 1830 convert and early 1830s missionary (serving with his brother Martin), Emer had possessed his own copy of that first edition and distributed many others. In fact, by 1856 the term "116 pages" had been so entrenched that the clerk taking minutes of Emer's address subsequently inserted the subject header "116 P" at the top of the page, even though Emer had contradicted that number in his actual sermon.[24] Emer's variance from this number would

---

23. "History of the Church," 785.
24. General Minutes, April 6, 1856, Provo Utah Central Stake.

thus be knowing and deliberate, a variance indicating that he believed he had more accurate information on the lost manuscript's length than that reported in the first-edition preface. And Emer had privileged access to information through his brother who intimately knew the physical details of the lost manuscript—and knew them even better than Joseph Smith.

While it was Joseph who dictated the translation of the golden plates by looking at his translation instrument, it was Martin who handled the manuscript pages, transcribing the translation onto them over a period of some two months. Following this work, Martin borrowed the manuscript, which he, unlike Joseph, was able to read at his leisure and share with family and friends.[25] As financier of the translation project, the prosperous Harris probably also purchased the necessary writing supplies—including the foolscap paper—when journeying from Palmyra to Harmony in April 1828 to serve as Joseph's scribe.[26]

---

25. Joseph Smith undoubtedly received financial support from Martin for his family's immediate needs while Martin boarded with the Smiths during his scribal tenure in April–June 1828. But taking time away from planting in the spring meant that Joseph would have lower yields at harvest time. He would therefore have needed to rely on continuing assistance during and after the following fall. But when the manuscript loss brought the work to a halt, Martin no longer had incentive to contribute to a project that appeared to have fizzled out. That Joseph took considerable time away from his farming in the spring of 1828 is suggested both by his progress on the translation during that time and by his destitution after the following harvest season. Joseph's material needs in early 1829 were such that around "the first of the winter 1828" he and Emma journeyed to see Joseph Knight for assistance, in February his father and his brother Samuel made about an eight-day round-trip journey through the New York winter to bring him provisions, in late March 1829 Knight gave him money for provisions and writing paper, in early April Oliver Cowdery brought down funds from his school-teaching job to help Joseph avoid eviction, and in late April 1829 Joseph and Oliver sought further provisions from Knight. An unusually urgent need for money and food might also explain why Joseph slaughtered farm animals for meat in September while his neighbors waited till November. And Joseph later recalled that he and Emma had become "reduced in property" prior to Cowdery's arrival. If Joseph's lack of provisions in the winter is indicative of the time he had invested in farming the previous planting season, he had spent that season largely engaged in pursuits he placed as even higher priorities, chief among which was surely the translation. For Joseph and Emma's poverty following his extended translation work with Martin Harris, see Mark Lyman Staker and Robin Scott Jensen, "David Hale's Store Ledger: New Details about Joseph and Emma Smith, the Hale Family, and the Book of Mormon," 102–4.

26. That Harris purchased paper for the early translation effort is also suggested by the description, given by Martin Harris associate Gladden Bishop and supported by Harris, of the initial manuscript as written on lined paper "of a blueish cast," which suggests the paper was fancy and expensive rather than typical. The purchase of expensive writing paper by Harris is far more likely than its purchase by Smith.

Emer's account of Martin scribing for nearly two hundred pages would align with the quantities in which paper was sold at the time. While paper was sold in variously sized units, the quantity of paper purchased for the translation was likely in "quires," which both the Webster's dictionary of that year and typesetter John H. Gilbert indicate to have been units of twenty-four sheets.[27] These sheets were folded to produce two pages per sheet, making one quire equal to forty-eight pages.[28] Emer's report that Martin recorded "near two hundred pages" indicates four quires, 192 pages.

Emer's account also aligns with what can be inferred about the proportion of paper used up in the translation effort of the lost manuscript. When Joseph resumed the translation, he promptly needed more paper—indicating that Joseph and Martin had essentially used up the paper already purchased for the project.[29] Combined with Emer's report, it seems likely that Martin had purchased four quires and that Joseph and Martin consequently paused their work when the resulting 192 pages were substantially or completely used up. This would account for why Joseph needed more paper when he resumed the translation, explain how Emer could know that Martin had scribed for almost two hundred pages, and help account for why Joseph and Martin paused the translation work when they did.

Emer's account further aligns with what an interviewer recalled Martin reporting. Five years after interviewing Martin in 1875, Simon Smith wrote the Prophet's son Joseph III, telling him that Martin "said also that he had acted as scribe for your father when he was translating from the plates by the Urim and Thummim nearly one third of what is published."[30] While Simon Smith misremembered *which* text Martin produced, implying it was the published text rather than the lost text, his memory dovetails precisely with *how much* text Emer credited his brother with scribing. The total manuscript length of the published Book of Mormon is a little over 460 pages. Coupled with Emer's

---

27. The sale of paper by the quire is reflected in a conversational vignette recorded in a period newspaper: "Mister, what is the price of paper here?" "Twenty five cents a quire." "How many sheets is there in a quire?" "Twenty-four." *The Livingston Journal* (Oct. 1, 1834): 4; Noah Webster, *American Dictionary of the English Language*, s.v. "quire." John H. Gilbert identifies 48 pages of the Book of Mormon manuscript (i.e., 24 folded sheets) with "one quire." John H. Gilbert, "Joe Smith. Something About the Early Life of the Mormon Prophet. Story of the Mormon Bible From the Man Who First Printed It. The Men Who Figured in Its Production and Publication," in Vogel, *EMD*, 2:519.

28. Gilbert, "Joe Smith," in Vogel, *EMD*, 2:519.

29. Joseph Knight recalled that in January 1829 he "gave . . . Joseph a little money to Buoy paper to translate." Joseph Knight, Sr., "Manuscript of the History of Joseph Smith," 4:19.

30. Simon Smith, "Martin Harris' Testimony," 43.

estimate, the total manuscript length including the lost portion would have come to nearly 660 pages, making Martin's scribal efforts nearly one-third of the full manuscript length, just as Simon Smith recalled Martin reporting.

Notably, this nearly two hundred pages of lined foolscap paper scribed by Martin would account for only a portion of the entire lost manuscript, pushing its total length well beyond that figure. While Emer says that his brother had scribed for almost two hundred pages, Martin was only the last in a line of lost-manuscript scribes who contributed to the manuscript's total length.

Time Covered by the Lost Manuscript

Another vital clue to the lost manuscript's length is the period of Nephite history that it covered. The small plates account, which fills the gap left by the lost manuscript, begins with Lehi's calling (around 600 BC) and ends during the reign of King Benjamin (around 124 BC). The chronology of Benjamin's reign is a vital clue to how much time the lost manuscript covered. Benjamin's son, Mosiah$_2$, began his reign around 124 BC and held it for nearly thirty-three years.[31] If we assume that Benjamin reigned for a similar period of time, he would have taken the place of his father, Mosiah$_1$, around 157 BC.

The lost manuscript ended somewhere in the middle of Benjamin's reign, with the original first two chapters of the Book of Mosiah. When Joseph resumed his translation, he continued where he left off, picking up at the start of what was then numbered Book of Mosiah, "Chapter III." This chapter begins, "And now there was no more contention in all the land of Zarahemla, among all the people who belonged to king Benjamin, so that king Benjamin *had continual peace all the remainder of his days*" (Mosiah 1:1), and this implies that the lost initial two chapters of this book narrated the contentions during Benjamin's reign and that some additional time of peace had passed before the narrative resumes. Given an inferred coronation date for Benjamin of around 157 BC, the lost manuscript's narrative about him likely reached somewhere into the range of 150–140 BC, placing the lost manuscript's chronological endpoint in this range. (For more on the missing period of Benjamin's reign, see Chapter 15.)

Beginning about 600 BC and ending sometime around 150–140 BC, these 450–460 years of lost narrative comprised almost exactly half of the 921 years narrated by Mormon as an abridgment from the large plates. With the

---

31. Mosiah$_2$'s reign of 33 years is given in Mosiah 29:46. Chronology for King Benjamin can be estimated from the Book of Mormon's published text. My estimate of 124 BC follows the estimates by *The Encyclopedia of Mormonism* and the Scripture Committee of the Church of Jesus Christ of Latter-day Saints. John P. Pratt, "Book of Mormon Chronology," 169–71. *The Book of Mormon: Another Testament of Jesus Christ* (1981), 164.

published portion of Mormon's abridgement from the large plates (Mosiah–4 Nephi) comprising just under 300 manuscript pages, if we assume a comparable level of detail, the abridgment's lost first half would also have been similar in length—not 116 pages, but rather nearly 300.[32]

The Lost 300 Pages?

This estimate of 300 pages is complicated by both the prophet Mormon's focus on the coming of Christ to the Nephites, devoting scores of pages to the events of a single week, and his including only a few pages about the utopian, uneventful three centuries that follow. We can thus probably better estimate the average number of pages Mormon wrote per decade in the lost manuscript by basing our estimate on Mormon's earlier abridgement before the coming of Christ. For example, when Mormon continued his narration of the Book of Mosiah after the lost manuscript, he covered about thirty-three years in twenty-eight manuscript pages, for an average of about 8.5 pages per decade.[33] If Mormon gave the same degree of detail before the point where the lost manuscript ended that he did immediately after it ended, his writing about the previous four and a half centuries in the lost manuscript would have comprised about 382 pages.

If, on the other hand, the lost manuscript was only 116 pages, then Mormon would have written an average of only 2.6 pages per decade over the first four and half centuries of Nephite history. For this to be the case, Mormon would have needed to more than triple the amount of space he was giving per decade between the lost manuscript and the subsequent part of the Book of Mosiah. Given no obvious reason for Mormon to drastically change the degree of coverage he gave to events as he moved from the middle of Benjamin's reign to the later part of Benjamin's reign and the reign of Mosiah$_2$, it is reasonable to assume a fair level of consistency between how much he wrote in the lost manuscript and how much he wrote in the available portion of the Book of Mosiah

---

32. Mormon's abridgment covers pages 117 through 413 in the only complete version of the Book of Mormon manuscript, the Printer's Manuscript.

33. This count includes only the main, abridged text covering from 124 BC to 91 BC. I have omitted "the Record of Zeniff" and "the account of Alma" and his people in the wilderness since these cover a wider time period, do not represent abridgment from the large plates, and include additional narrators besides Mormon. The chapters included are Mosiah 1–9 and 25–29. These cover roughly pages 117–131 and 157–169 of the Book of Mormon Printer's Manuscript.

The Manuscript's Length via the Time Spent Translating It

Another reason to believe that the lost manuscript was considerably longer than 116 pages is the time required to produce the manuscript. Various accounts have been given of the production time and the work done by Joseph Smith's scribes, including dates given by Joseph for Martin's scribal work.

Martin Harris's Scribal Tenure

A decade after translating the Book of Mormon, Joseph reported in his history that Martin returned to serve as scribe "on about the twelfth of April, Eighteen hundred and twenty eighth and commenced writing for me while I translated from the plates, which we continued untill [*sic*] the fourteenth of June following."[34] This would have provided a sixty-four day window for their work together (allowing for both working and resting days).[35]

Joseph indicates with his "about" phrasing that the opening date of April 12 date was an approximation. If Martin set out for Harmony in early or mid-April, he may have intended to do scribing for Joseph and still return in time for his daughter's upcoming wedding on May 8—but then failed to return as he got caught up in the translation work or waited for Joseph to change his mind on letting Martin take the manuscript. Leaving Palmyra after mid-April would not have allowed him to stay in Harmony and assist in scribing, and it would have instead required him to return for the wedding as soon as he arrived. A mid-April timing for Martin's journey to Harmony is further supported by the fact that Martin was leaving his farm in Palmyra early in the planting season, when his time would have been at a premium. Even with travel by stagecoach, the quickest mode of transportation and the most likely one for a wealthy man, the journey was four days each way. The eight-day round trip was costly to his work, so his time investment likely would have necessitated him doing substantive scribing in order to make the journey worthwhile. Thus, if he anticipated at least eight days of translation work—in return for his eight-day investment of travel—before returning in time for the wedding,

---

34. Joseph Smith, History Draft, 1839, in Vogel, *EMD*, 1:71.

35. Joseph Smith does not appear to have had an earlier written record of those translation dates to draw upon in writing this account in his History. Yet a significant event might have offered a benchmark for memory: the death of Emma's uncle Reuben Hale in North Franklin, New York (about 60 miles from Harmony), occurred on April 9. Joseph's scribes during this period had primarily been members of the Hale family, so this event could have paused the translation work if Emma, Alva, Reuben (the deceased's namesake and perhaps Smith's main scribe at the time), and Joseph himself traveled to attend the funeral. If Martin Harris arrived shortly after the translation break caused by the uncle's funeral, Joseph could have remembered that as a beginning date for his translation work with Harris.

Martin would have needed to leave Palmyra no later than April 18, placing him in Harmony around April 22, ten days after the date recalled by Joseph Smith. It seems unlikely that the pragmatic Martin would have left Palmyra after this date, and far more likely that he would have left still earlier, as soon as he could arrange his affairs in Palmyra. He likely left Palmyra in time to be there in mid-April to allow as much time as possible to work with Joseph.

Joseph was less tentative about when his work with Martin ended and specifically cited June 14. His precision here is likely due to the birth and death of Joseph and Emma's son Alvin on the next day.[36] As Emma's labor and delivery loomed, a pause in the work was inevitable; and if Joseph and Martin were about out of paper then the pause in their work was timely.[37] Therefore, Joseph placing the end of their collaboration on the day before the June 15 birth of his son makes sense.

If Martin left Palmyra on April 12 and began his trip home on June 14, then the *maximum* length of Joseph and Martin's translation period could have been no more than sixty days. On the other end, we can also estimate the *minimum* amount of time Martin would have been in Harmony as a scribe. Assuming he planned to have at least as many translation days in Harmony as travel days (while still returning home for his daughter's May 8 wedding), then April 22 would have been the latest he would have arrived in Harmony. With Joseph benchmarking the conclusion of the lost manuscript's translation the day before his son's birth, it seems reasonably certain that their work together lasted to at least within a *week* before the birth, placing Martin's departure no later than June 8. These limiters would give Joseph and Martin a minimum window of forty-seven days together. To account for any overlooked factors, we could even adjust that down to an even six weeks, or forty-two days—a full one-third shorter than the time range reported by Joseph himself.

Joseph Smith's Translation Rate

We can estimate what Joseph's translation rate over those forty-two to sixty translation days would have been using two later periods of translation work as our guide: (1) Joseph's June 1829 work to produce the manuscript of the small plates consisting of some 116 pages; and (2) his April–May 1829 work with Oliver Cowdery on Mormon's abridgement.

A full year after Martin ceased scribing on the lost manuscript, in June 1829, Joseph finally translated the small plates account that would replace

---

36. Alvin Smith Gravestone, June 15, 828.

37. Additional paper would not have been difficult to obtain from local merchants, but high-quality paper might have been, and the need to acquire more paper would have provided a natural pausing point for the work.

it.[38] During that month, Joseph was also occupied with many other endeavors, including moving from Harmony, Pennsylvania, to Fayette, New York (a journey by wagon of four or more days), dictating five revelations to his scribes (D&C 14–18), a day of traveling to Palmyra followed by at least one day of negotiation with printers, another day of traveling to Rochester followed by at least one day of negotiating with printers, a day of traveling back to Palmyra to make an agreement for the printing with E. B. Grandin, and then a day's trip returning to Fayette. In addition to all of this, he had a title page printed and filed with the copyright office, shared the Book of Mormon message with others, and made multiple trips to Seneca Lake (nine miles roundtrip) to baptize new converts.[39]

Not surprisingly, Joseph later noted that his translation efforts during this period were intermittent:

> Mean time we continued to translate, at intervals, when not necessitated to attend to the numerous enquirers, that now began to visit us; some for the sake of finding the truth, others for the purpose of putting hard questions, and trying to confound us, among the latter class were several learned Priests <who> generally came for the purpose of disputation.[40]

Making allowance for travel and printing preparations and other distractions—considerations Joseph did not have to deal with while producing the lost manuscript—the number of days available to him for translation work would have been reduced by at least a dozen, leaving no more than eighteen days on which Smith could have translated. In that time, or less, he was able to produce the 116 pages of the small plates translation at a rate of about 6.5 pages per day.[41]

---

38. Joseph appears to have concluded his translation of the end of the Book of Moroni, at the end of the Book of Mormon, in late May 1829 and begun his translation of the small plates in early June, after relocating to Fayette, New York. John W. Welch, "The Miraculous Timing of the Translation of the Book of Mormon," 79–125; Elden Watson, "Approximate Book of Mormon Translation Timeline."

39. A stagecoach, for which the horses were exchanged for fresh horses every ten to twelve miles, could make the journey between Palmyra-Manchester and Harmony in four days. A wagon for which the beasts of burden were not exchanged would necessarily take significantly longer. A journey by stage between Harmony and Fayette should have taken three days, so I am estimating at least a four-day journey by regular wagon. Staker and Jensen, "David Hale's Store Ledger," 89.

40. Joseph Smith, History, 1838–1856, A-1:25.

41. While a complete page count for the Original Manuscript cannot be made due to water damage, a visible page number on the extant fragmentary pages of that manuscript shows that the small plates account in the Original Manuscript was three or four pages longer than that in the Printer's Manuscript. Brent Metcalfe, "The Priority of Mosiah," 395n1.

If we use a comparable rate of translation for both the replacement pages and the lost pages, then Joseph Smith's work with Martin Harris during a minimum six weeks of work would have produced a manuscript of about 270 pages. And this figure omits all pages Smith had already translated with the assistance of his four previous scribes, again suggesting a total manuscript size of around 300 pages or more.

An even better estimate of Joseph's translation rate can be made from his efforts in April to May of 1829—following his return to translating after a nine-month hiatus following the loss of the earlier manuscript. During this time there were fewer interruptions than he would have had in June, making this our best indicator of Joseph Smith's translation pace. The translation appears to have resumed in March 1829 with Martin Harris serving as scribe for what is now the first chapter of the published Book of Mosiah. However, our best timeline for measuring the translation begins in early April when Oliver Cowdery became Joseph's primary scribe, likely beginning at Mosiah 7, just after King Benjamin's sermon.[42] For this period we have two clear dates and matching texts to calculate a translation rate. According to Joseph, he and Oliver began translation work together on April 7. In addition, Oliver provides a concluding benchmark, noting that by May 15 they had translated "the Savior's ministry to the Nephites," which ends at 3 Nephi 29.[43] Thus, over a thirty-nine day period between April 7 and May 15, Joseph and Oliver translated from about Mosiah 7 through about 3 Nephi 29, just over 282 manuscript pages at a rate of about 7.23 pages per day. If Joseph and Martin worked at a rate comparable on the lost manuscript to that of Joseph and Oliver, then in 42 days they could have produced about 303 manuscript pages. This, of course, would have been on top of whatever Joseph had produced with his previous scribes—again suggesting that the lost manuscript was over 300 pages.

Of course, it could be that Joseph's early translation rate was lower than his later translation rate. As the Prophet gained experience translating and his scribes gained experience with taking dictation, they probably became more efficient in their respective tasks. However, by the time Martin had become a scribe, Joseph had already garnered translation experience with four others. Furthermore, the halt in the translation work after the manuscript loss would have offered Joseph hardly any additional translation experience between

---

42. Using John W. Welch's estimate that Joseph and Oliver started their April 7 translation work at Mosiah Chapter 1, they would have covered Mosiah 1 through 3 Nephi 29 between April 7 and May 15. In my analysis I am using a slightly more conservative translation-rate estimate based on Dan Vogel's argument that Joseph and Oliver began at Mosiah Chapter 7. Welch, "The Miraculous Timing," 79–125; Dan Vogel, *Joseph Smith: The Making of a Prophet*, 167.

43. Oliver Cowdery, "Left Kirtland on the 16th," 3–6.

Martin and Oliver, making a substantial increase in translation pace between Martin and Oliver unlikely.[44]

Positing that Joseph and Martin produced just 116 pages during their six-week scribal tenure on the initial manuscript would also require positing that Joseph promptly and inexplicably tripled or even quadrupled his translation rate when resumed the translation.[45] And this actually *understates* the acceleration required of Smith by the 116-page-manuscript hypothesis, for two reasons: first, the assumption of a six-week scribal tenure for Martin Harris is almost certainly too brief; and second, the calculated tripling or quadrupling of the rate assumes, wrongly, that Martin produced *all* 116 pages, rather than being the manuscript's fifth scribe.

Earlier Scribes of the Lost Manuscript

Nineteenth-century sources identify Alva Hale, Samuel H. Smith, Emma Hale Smith, and Reuben Hale as early scribes who worked on the lost manuscript. Alva Hale's scribal work on the lost manuscript was recalled by both David Whitmer and Emma. The latter, however, was less certain, saying that Alva "may have written some"—indicating he may have scribed for Joseph for as little as a single sitting and likely not for more than a handful of occasions.[46] Samuel H. Smith's scribal tenure was mentioned by Joseph just four years after the fact in his 1832 history. When Joseph reported that his wife Emma "had written some for me to translate," he added "and also my brother Samuel H. Smith."[47] Emma Smith's scribal service garnered significant mention from her husband and from Lucy Mack Smith, Joseph Knight, and David Whitmer.

---

44. The only translation work between June 1828 and April 1829 attested to in contemporaneous sources is the "few pages" Smith was to translate in March 1829 before stopping for a season (D&C 5:30).

45. Personal communication from Dan Vogel, January 8, 2015.

46. Joseph Smith's son, Joseph III, had evidently heard report of Alva Hale's early scribal work. When, in an 1879 interview with Joseph III shortly before her death, Emma Smith omitted Alva's name from a list of Book of Mormon scribes, her son prompted her with a follow-up question, "Was Alva Hale one?" Mrs. Smith indicated in response that she did not recall his scribal work though he "may have written some." Joseph III's question suggests he had previously heard (perhaps from his mother) that Alva Hale had served as a scribe and was following up on that recollection. David Whitmer, who was not present during the translation of the lost manuscript, had heard word that Alva Hale served as scribe but opined that Hale must have written only "a small portion." Joseph Smith III, "Last Testimony of Sister Emma," 289–90, in Vogel, *EMD*, 1:541. David Whitmer, "Revelation Revisers," *St. Louis Republican* 77 (16 July 1884): 7, in Vogel, *EMD*, 5:129–30.

47. Joseph Smith acknowledges the scribal service on the lost manuscript only of those who continued as believers in its divinity. He mentions Emma and Samuel

Emma reported taking dictation for her husband on the lost manuscript over a number of occasions: "I frequently wrote day after day," she reported, implying that she had transcribed her husband's dictation over multiple periods of consecutive days. Reuben Hale's work as scribe was more remembered in local memory than Emma's (whose efforts appear to have been unknown outside their immediate family and friends). His scribal service is described by Harmony residents Joseph F. McKune and Samuel Brush, in addition to garnering mention from Emma and from Joseph Knight. Brush recalled having found Reuben "often" engaged in scribal work on the translation when he called to see him. Reuben's scribal work, like Emma's, appears to have been frequent. Given the sources that indicate Emma Hale Smith and Reuben Hale scribed frequently for Joseph over a period of weeks, their scribal output theoretically could have rivaled Harris's output over his more than six weeks of work.

The various lines of evidence we have explored have all produced similar outcomes. When we consider the amount of time *covered* by the lost manuscript, we find that Mormon's abridgement for that period should have totaled 282 to 390 pages. When we consider the time *spent* translating the lost manuscript, we find that Joseph's translation output should have totaled well over 300 pages. When we consider insider reports, which have Martin alone scribing for "near 200 pages," after four other scribes had done their part, we again arrive at a manuscript that could readily total over 300 pages. None of our lines of evidence point to a manuscript of only 116 pages; instead, they all point to something well beyond that figure.

The historical record offers plenty of uncertainties, and we encounter one here. We do not know the length of the lost Book of Mormon manuscript and are thus left to infer it. Rather than engage the admittedly messy process of drawing inferences from the surviving traces of the past, some may prefer the certainty of relying on a stated figure, even if that figure is problematic. Doing so will not make the questions on this issue disappear. If we accept the traditional page count for the lost manuscript of 116, then we need to account for why, right at the break between the Book of Mormon's lost text and its available text, Mormon suddenly multiplies the degree of detail he gives in his narration and Joseph Smith suddenly triples his translation speed, and we need to account for why Martin's brother, despite knowing the traditional count of 116, goes with another number instead.

Smith, who were steadfast believers, but omits Alva and Reuben Hale, who believed at first but did not ultimately become followers of the new scripture.

Far More than 116 Pages

Emer Harris's report that his brother scribed for "near 200 pages" makes perfect sense in relation to all the evidence cited above. In addition, the pages recorded by four scribes previous to Martin could conceivably have rivaled Martin's output of nearly 200 pages, which means that Joseph's total lost translation could have pushed 400 pages—three and half times the traditional 116-page enumeration! This is not to say that the lost manuscript *was* 400 pages long, but to say that it plausibly *could have been*. However, if we assume that the work of Emma and the other earlier scribes lasted nearly half as long as Martin's and thus reasonably producing about half as much text (or something approaching 100 pages), the initial manuscript would have still totaled a little under 300 manuscript pages. This would equate to nearly 345 printed pages in our present Book of Mormon text and would mean that the lost part of the Book of Mormon was about two-thirds the length of the text we now have. For a comparison, if you imagine that we had lost everything from 1 Nephi through nearly the end of the Book of Alma, then you will have a pretty good idea of how much text we would then be missing.

The original first half of the Book of Mormon was almost certainly, far, far more than 116 pages. It contained a richness of narratives, themes, and details about journeys, struggles, revelations, lineages, priesthoods, kings, and queens that can illuminate the Book of Mormon text we have, but that would remain unknown until we could begin to assemble the various historical puzzle pieces providentially left to us.

That is, until now.

Part 2

The Missing Stories

CHAPTER 6

RECONSTRUCTING THE LOST MANUSCRIPT

The structure for the Book of Mormon anticipated by Joseph Smith and his scribes changed as the book's text unfolded across the translation process. What likely began with a simple third-person narrative found early in the translation became increasingly complex as it began to include various narrative forms. This change in style is perhaps best exemplified by the third-person narration of the lost manuscript being replaced with the first-person accounts by Nephi, Jacob, and Jacob's descendants—a style similar to the writings of the Book of Mormon's final two authors, Mormon and Moroni. This radical and fundamental change to the book's initial structure caused by the insertion of the manuscript's small-plates replacement was necessitated by the manuscript theft. By better understanding this change, we can also have a better understanding of what it was changing from.

The Small Plates as the Replacement Solution

Joseph Smith's short-term response to the manuscript's theft was to continue dictating the Book of Mormon narrative where he had left off in the early part of the Book of Mosiah. Several weeks into this work, Joseph received a revelation that sidestepped possible snares awaiting him from the thieves and solved both the problems that would arise from reproducing the stolen manuscript and those that would arise from *not* reproducing it.

Addressing Joseph, the revelation commanded him to "not translate again those words which have gone forth out of your hands" (D&C 10:30). The rationale for this forbearance was that Joseph's enemies were not only intending to use the stolen manuscript to test his abilities as a translator, they were also intending to rig the supposed test against him by altering the manuscript. Rather than a test, this was a trap. If Joseph was unable to exactly reproduce the translation (a feat that would be difficult if, as suggested by D&C 9:8–9, Joseph had to "study out" the exact wording of the text), then they could have used the stolen manuscript to point this out against him. If Joseph was able to reproduce the translation exactly, then by altering the text they could claim that he was unable to do so.

The revelation handily solved this problem of not *reproducing* the stolen text by instructing Joseph to *replace* it with another account covering the same time period. This replacement text would be the accounts in "the plates of Nephi" (D&C 10:38–45). While Joseph had previously encountered the term "plates of Nephi" during the translation process, it had there referred to the source behind the lost manuscript and the rest of Mormon's abridgment (Mosiah 1:6; Alma 37:2, 44:24; Morm. 1:4). It was not until Joseph began dictating the lost manuscript's "plates of Nephi" that it became clear that *these* "plates of Nephi" were not the ones mentioned in the earlier manuscript. The replacement text identifies itself as a record engraved on "plates of Nephi" (1 Ne. 9:2) but distinguishes these from the "other" plates of Nephi—those that served as the source of Mormon's abridgment (Morm. 1:4).

The "plates of Nephi" or "record of the people of Nephi" from which the title page indicates Mormon abridged his book, including the lost manuscript, are described as a vast, near-comprehensive record of Nephite history. The *other* "plates of Nephi"—those that *replace* the lost manuscript—are described by Mormon as a "small account of the prophets, from Jacob down to the reign of this king Benjamin, and also many of the word of Nephi" (W of M 1:3) and designated as "small plates" by Jacob, the second author to write on them (Jacob 1:1–2).[1] Within its text the small plates record's existence is represented as a divine providence, with Nephi averring that "the Lord hath commanded me to make these plates for a wise purpose in him, which purpose I know not" (1 Ne. 9:5). The account's purpose, while unknown to its narrators, is evident to historically informed readers: it was to fill the gap left by the lost manuscript.

With the revelation saying the lost text was abridged from the large plates of Nephi, it expressly commanded Joseph to not "translate again those words which have gone forth from your hands" in order to not "bring forth the same words" again (D&C 10:17, 30). Thus, Joseph's ability to instead translate the small plates account enabled him to fill the gap left by the lost manuscript without violating the revelation's injunction.

Mormon's Segue

The loss of the initial manuscript and consequent substitution of the small plates changed and complicated the Book of Mormon's structure. Though the book's title page pronounces it "The Book of Mormon, written by the hand of Mormon," the content that immediately follows the title page, "The [First] Book of Nephi," is introduced with the explanation, "I Nephi wrote this record." This switch between narrators necessitated Joseph adding a preface to the initial publication to preempt any confusion this discrepancy might bring to readers. (See Chapter 5.)

---

1. The use of the "large plates" and "small plates" terminology evolved out of Jacob's references to the "plates of Nephi" translated as 1 Nephi through the Words of Mormon as "the small plates upon which these things are engraven" and to the "plates of Nephi," containing the more detailed, non-extant account, as "the larger plates" (Jacob 1:1; 3:13).

In addition to the change of narrators between the title page and Nephi's introduction in his opening book, another explanation or bridge was required between the first-person accounts in the Book of Omni and the resumption of Mormon's third-person abridgement in the Book of Mosiah. It is between those two books that Mormon, mentioned on the title page, finally makes his appearance in the text. In The Words of Mormon, he explains why he spliced the intrusive small plates into his record. Though he had already presented a (now lost) narrative of the same period covered by the small plates in his abridgment, Mormon found the small plates "pleasing" because they included detailed prophecies of Christ, suggesting that such prophecies had been subtler or less evident in the earlier lost manuscript narrative (W of M 1:4).

Mormon's explanation of why he included the small plates with his record also hints at the kind of providence that had led Nephi to create the small plates in the first place:

> I do this for a wise purpose; for thus it whispereth me, according to the workings of the Spirit of the Lord which is in me. And now, I do not know all things; but the Lord knoweth all things which are to come; wherefore, he worketh in me to do according to his will. (W of M 1:6)

He then concludes his Words with a recap of the narrative about King Benjamin that he had provided in the original (now lost) Chapters I and II of the Book of Mosiah:

> And now I, Mormon, proceed to finish out my record, which I take from the plates of Nephi; and I make it according to the knowledge and the understanding which God has given me. (v. 9)

In doing so, Mormon bridges from the very brief small-plates synopses of Mosiah₁'s reign and Benjamin's early reign to our Mosiah 1:1.[2]

Mormon's Source for His Abridgement

The revelation instructing Joseph Smith on how to proceed with the translation informs us that the lost narrative was taken from a detailed Nephite record inaugurated by Nephi himself. It reminds its early audience members who were familiar with the lost manuscript's content that the manuscript mentioned this more detailed source:

---

2. This bridging function is also filled, less overtly, by Amaleki's conclusion to the Book of Omni, which immediately precedes Mormon's Words. Amaleki covers Benjamin's early reign, summarizing the same incidents of military and spiritual conflict that Mormon covers after him (Omni 1:23–25). Mormon thus oddly duplicates Omni's narrative bridge to Mosiah. While somewhat redundant, the duplication creates for the reader a more immediate narrative continuity between the small plates and Mormon's abridgment.

And now, verily I say unto you, that an account of those things that you have written, which have gone out of your hands, is engraven upon the plates of Nephi; yea, and you remember it was said in those writings that a more particular account was given of these things upon the plates of Nephi. (D&C 10:38–39)

The manuscript thieves, the revelation adds, "have only got a part, or an abridgment of the account of Nephi" (v. 44).

As discussed earlier, attempting to map all references to the "plates of Nephi" in this revelation onto "the plates of Nephi" discussed in the Book of Mormon can produce confusion. Read in light of the subsequently dictated Book of Mormon texts, the revelation seems ambiguous regarding which "plates of Nephi" it was instructing Joseph to translate in order to fill the gap created by the manuscript theft. Despite the ambiguity, it clearly identified which account the lost narrative was based on by reminding its original audience that the lost text identified its source as the "more particular account" (i.e., the fuller, more detailed account) of Nephite history—that is, Nephi's large plates.

Characteristics of the Large Plates Account

Doctrine and Covenants 10 describes the narrative in the lost manuscript as an abridgment of the large plates of Nephi. According to Noah Webster's contemporaneous *American Dictionary of the English Language* published in 1828—the same year Joseph Smith dictated and lost the initial Book of Mormon manuscript—to "abridge" was "to make shorter; to epitomize; to contract by using fewer words, yet retaining the sense in substance."[3] Thus, according to the revelation, the lost narrative that Joseph translated from the golden plates was a condensed version of the narrative contained in Nephi's large plates, offering fewer words and minutiae but with the same essential narrative substance.

In short, the large plates were not the golden plates that Joseph translated—they were the source of Mormon's abridgment that he engraved onto the plates in Joseph's possession. As the source for the abridgment, the characteristics ascribed to the large plates should similarly describe the lost narrative, including the perspective and concerns "of the kings, or those which they caused to be written" (Jarom 1:14) filtered through the prophetic perspective of the editor-narrator Mormon.[4] Representing an abridged record of Nephi's dynasty, the lost narrative would adopt that dynasty's point of view.

---

3. Noah Webster, *American Dictionary of the English Language*, s.v. "abridge."

4. The phrase "which they caused to be written" suggests that the kings sometimes dictated what was to be written onto the large plates. Similar phrasing is used to describe Joseph Smith's process of dictating the Book of Mormon translation to scribes (D&C 10:11), King Benjamin dictating his sermon to scribes who then spread the written text to others (Mosiah 2:9), and Nephi having his brother Jacob's sermon recorded (2 Ne. 11:1).

The "small plates of Nephi" account that Joseph Smith translated to fill the lost-manuscript gap describes the large plates mostly in contrast to the small plates themselves. While Nephi does not distinguish the two sets of plates by name, calling both simply "the plates of Nephi," he does distinguish them by purpose. Nephi says that the small plates "are not the plates upon which I make a full account of the history of my people" (1 Ne. 9:2). Thus, although he titles his first small plates account "The [First] Book of Nephi: His Reign and Ministry," he soon makes clear that the record is to focus more on "the ministry and the prophecies" (v. 3).[5] Accordingly, he offers very little about his reign. It is Nephi's "other plates," he explains, that were to convey more of his own reign and the subsequent "reign of the kings" and "the wars and contentions of my people" (vv. 2–4). Nephi distinguished his small plates ministerial record from his comprehensive large plates record in how he described the small plates, what he recorded on the small plates, and what he commanded his brother Jacob to record on the small plates. The small plates were to skimp on history, that is, on narrative, and incorporate primarily preaching and prophecy:

> Nephi gave me, Jacob, a commandment concerning the small plates . . . ; that I should not touch, save it were lightly, concerning the history of this people. . . . For he said that the history of his people should be engraven upon his other plates, and . . . if there were preaching which was sacred, or revelation which was great, or prophesying, that I should engraven the heads of them upon these plates, and touch upon them as much as it were possible. (Jacob 1:2–4)

Continuing to draw contrasts, Nephi distinguishes the record of his ministerial highlights in the small plates from the detailed record of his life and his nation in the large plates. He thus writes in his small account that he had written "a more history part" on his other plates, so that if readers "desire to know the more particular part of the history of my people they must search mine other [large] plates" (2 Ne. 4:14; 5:33). It was on those, Nephi says, that he engraved many of his and his father's teachings (4:14) and also "the record of my father, and also our journeyings in the wilderness, and the prophecies of my father; and also many of mine own prophecies" (1 Ne. 19:1). They also contain "the genealogy of [Lehi's] fathers, and the more part of all our proceedings in the wilderness" (v. 2). So, "the things which transpired before" Nephi made the small plates and began building a ship—in other words, most of Lehi's narrative and all of his wilderness exodus—"are, of a truth, more particularly made mention upon the first [large] plates" (v. 2).

---

5. Nephi's statement that the small plates' ministerial purpose was revealed to him only "after" he had made them may be intended to explain why he gave his record the somewhat misleading title "The Book of Nephi, His *Reign* and Ministry."

Nephi, however, is careful not to distinguish these records too sharply, lest the reader conclude that the subject matter of the small plates is sacred while that of the large plates is secular. He clarifies: "I do not write *anything* upon plates save it be that I think it be sacred" (1 Ne. 19:6). The small plates skimp on narrative, conveying primarily prophecy, doctrinal exposition, and biblical quotations. The large plates, like the narrative books of the Hebrew Bible, provide primarily *sacred history*. In short, rather than the distinction between the small plates and the large plates being one of a spiritual account and the other of a secular account, the two were more akin to the distinct genres of scripture in the Hebrew Bible. The large plates share a similarity to the historical books (such as Kings and Chronicles), whereas the small plates "which contained this small account of the prophets" (W of M 1:3) share a similarity to those histories' contemporaneous prophetic books (such as Isaiah and Jeremiah).

Mormon's abridgement in the lost manuscript did not so much zero in on highlights as try to tell a complete story of Lehi and the early Nephites and God's dealings with them. Less detailed than the large plates account it undertakes to abridge, and not as focused on discourse and prophecy as the small plates, the lost manuscript offered a more holistic account of Nephite history, filling its pages with the Nephites' encounters with God, with the Lamanites, and with one another.

Implications from Joseph Smith's Preface

As discussed in Chapter 5, in order to avoid confusing the reader, Joseph Smith oversimplified his description of the lost pages in his preface to the first printing of the Book of Mormon. Though imprecise, his writing that they consisted of "one hundred and sixteen pages, the which I took from the Book of Lehi, which was an account abridged from the plates of Lehi, by the hand of Mormon" nevertheless sheds light on some of the lost narrative's content.

Joseph writes in his preface that the lost narrative was, like most of the extant text that followed, an abridgment "by the hand of Mormon." These continuities in narrator identity and presentation (i.e., as an abridgment of larger records) suggest that the lost narrative was stylistically similar to Mormon's continued abridgement found in Mosiah through 4 Nephi. Like the latter, the lost manuscript would have been narrated in the third-person—one that was presumably anonymous, with Mormon seeming to wait to introduce himself until his work of abridgment is nearing completion by telling readers, "Behold, I am called Mormon" (3 Ne. 5:12).[6]

---

6. As discussed above, the large plates (and thus Mormon's abridgement) may have been modeled on that of the historical books of the Bible (e.g., Exodus, 1 and 2 Samuel, 1 and 2 Chronicles), which are anonymously narrated. If so, the original intent was likely

In this the lost manuscript contrasts with the first-person narration in the small plates accounts, beginning in the voice of Nephi, whose account is told from the perspective of the second generation of Lehi's family and centers its attention there. Thus, Nephi tells in detail how *he* received for himself a version of God's covenant with his father Lehi (1 Ne. 2:16–24) but never provides the narrative of how *Lehi* had received the covenant in the first place. To the extent that Lehi's story is told in this account, it is first filtered through Nephi's perspective. Mormon's narration at the beginning of the lost manuscript almost certainly gave greater attention to Lehi's experiences than Nephi does in his small plates account and provided a narration that made use of both of their perspectives.

Joseph's use of the terms "Book of Lehi" and "plates of Lehi" in his preface, though inadequate in characterizing the lost manuscript as a whole, tells us something about how the narration therein *opened*. While Joseph stretched this term by using it as a label for the entire lost manuscript, he almost certainly did not simply create the name for the preface. The lost manuscript evidently began with "the Book of Lehi," suggesting that it centralized Lehi more than Nephi. This "Book of Lehi," in turn, represented material abridged from Nephi's detailed large plates account that may have included Lehi's personal record.[7] Thus the kind of detail regarding Lehi that Nephi says he is *not* including from his father's record—his earliest dreams and visions (1 Ne. 1:16), his genealogy (6:1), the details of his exodus (v. 3)—very likely *were* included in the lost manuscript (19:2).

The Hebraic Lost Manuscript

One indication of what was in the lost Book of Mormon manuscript is the impact that the manuscript had on the earliest Latter-day Saints who interacted with it. When those involved in the translation of this manuscript made statements about the lost pages before the rest of the Book of Mormon was translated, those statements should reflect the lost content. Significantly, at the time Joseph Smith and Martin Harris worked on the translation, persons in conversation with them at the time recount hearing them characterize the book and its purpose in surprisingly *Hebraic* terms.

The first of these accounts, one of the earliest affidavits commenting on Joseph Smith and the Restoration, reports Joseph's own characterization of his prophetic mission during this time. According to this account, Joseph

---

to have the book be anonymously narrated until the reader reaches the narrator's own day (i.e., Mormon's life). This would account for why Mormon introduces himself so late in the narration. However, given Mormon's tendency to comment on the stories he was abridging, he may have felt it necessary to introduce himself earlier than planned.

7. S. Kent Brown, "Lehi's Personal Record: Quest for a Missing Source," 19–42.

understood his role at the time to be one of restoring Israel through the gathering of the Jews rather than of a restoration of the Church of Christ. The affidavit was published in 1834 and sworn by Hezekiah McKune, a Harmony, Pennsylvania, neighbor to the Smiths and an in-law of Emma. Sometime in the months after his arrival in Harmony near the end of 1827, Joseph is said to have described his divine mission by claiming to be "a prophet sent by God to bring in the Jews." [8]

In line with this reported Hebraic emphasis in Joseph Smith's prophetic consciousness, in early 1828 Martin Harris is said to have characterized the Book of Mormon's purpose more in "Old Testament" terms than in "New Testament" terms. Report of this comes to us from John H. Gilbert, a Palmyra resident and friend of Martin Harris who became the typesetter for the 1830 Book of Mormon. Although recalling the communication with Martin just over five decades later, other verifiable aspects of his recollection (such as his description of the Book of Mormon manuscripts that he had not seen for a half century at the time of his testimony) confirm his memories to a fine level of detail.[9] He writes,

> Late in 1827 or early in '28, was the first I heard Harris speak of Jo's finding the plates. . . . The plates . . . *as represented at the time*, purported to be a history of the lost tribes of Israel—and not establishing a new religion, but *confirming the Old Testament.*[10]

Although the account's broad strokes description of the Book of Mormon as a story of "lost tribes of Israel" was common, even among non-Mormons well-acquainted with the book's contents, his dating of the conversation with Martin as occurring in late 1827 or early 1828 would have placed it at a time when Martin could have only had knowledge of the contents of the lost pages portion of the Book of Mormon and nothing beyond it.

Martin's description of the Book of Mormon's earliest text would be puzzling if applied to its later, published text. While the latter includes many Old Testament elements, such as the making of covenants, the exodus to a promised land, and the building of a temple, it foregrounds at least as

---

8. Hezekiah McKune, "Statement, March 20, 1834," in Vogel, *EMD*, 4:327. McKune was married to Elizabeth Lewis, daughter of Emma's maternal uncle Nathaniel Lewis. He was also the son of Joseph McKune Sr., whose property adjoined Joseph and Emma's. McKune does not date his conversation with Joseph Smith, but a lasting alienation occurring between Joseph and the Lewises in mid–1828 places the conversation around early 1828.

9. On the accuracy of Gilbert's memories of the Book of Mormon manuscripts, see Royal Skousen, "Worthy of Another Look: John Gilbert's 1892 Account of the 1830 Printing of the Book of Mormon," 58–72.

10. John H. Gilbert to James T. Cobb, Feb 10, 1879; emphasis added.

many numerous New Testament elements, including angelic annunciation of Christ's future birth, the institution of baptism, the establishment of a church, Pauline-style missionary work, a new star given as a sign of Christ's birth, post-resurrection appearances of Jesus, a version of the Sermon the Mount, and quasi-Pauline epistles on baptism and on faith, hope, and charity. The completed book, as it would emerge from the 1829 translation effort, was explicit in teaching of Jesus Christ by name and provided a model and detailed plans for a latter-day church built along primitive Christian lines.

Based on these accounts, the two persons primarily engaged in the translation of the lost pages saw both the book's mission and their mission in bringing it forth in profoundly *Hebraic* terms. The book, as they knew it up to this point, had not so much discussed restoring the New Testament church as it had discussed confirming and fulfilling the prophecies of the Hebrew Bible and restoring Jewish nationhood. As will be seen in the remaining chapters, the lost manuscript's focus on the Nephites' multiple connections to Joseph of Egypt, building a tabernacle and later a temple that was modeled on those of Moses and Solomon, dividing Lehi's descendants into tribes, establishing a priesthood alternative to that of Aaron's, and many other details all confirm the Hebraic emphasis described by McKune and Gilbert. In other words, Joseph and Martin described the book they were then translating in such profoundly Hebraic terms because the material they were translating was so profoundly Hebraic, paralleling, extending, and culminating in a new promised land the saga of Israel.

Undoing the Exile: Recreating Israel in the New World

The narrative of the Book of Mormon's lost manuscript begins within that of the Hebrew Bible, recapitulating the saga of Israel and extending it into the New World. Its foundational Book of Lehi narratives of Lehi's family fleeing Jerusalem and of Nephi establishing a kingdom and a new Jerusalem introduce the Hebraic themes of covenant, promised land, exile, and restoration that pervade both the book and the faith that emerged from it. These accounts comprise the narrative bedrock of the Book of Mormon and an important historical foundation for the Restoration. In their overarching narrative, Lehi and Nephi suffer the loss of the Israelite world they had known—and seek to rebuild it.

Lehi's story begins in Jerusalem soon after the reign of the reformist Josiah and in the biblical narratives of Jeremiah, who prophesied of the Jews' exile and the end of David's dynasty. Lehi had a vision and promptly joined with Jeremiah and other prophets, warning Jerusalem of pending exile and destruction. He, like Jeremiah, was rejected and his life threatened. Yet, being warned that the Judean land of promise was soon to become a land of bondage, as Egypt had been for his forebears, Lehi fled to the wilderness.

Lehi's exile was well-timed, with his calling vision occurring "in the commencement of the first year of the reign of Zedekiah" (1 Ne. 1:4). In view of how Zedekiah's reign began, detailed in the next chapter, this places Lehi's vision in the immediate wake of—or even *during*—a Babylonian invasion that installed Zedekiah *as* king and began the first wave of the Babylonian Exile. Lehi's exodus thus occurred immediately after Nebuchadnezzar II's armies plundered the temple, leaving worshippers without their literal touchstones with Deity—the divinely inscribed tablets of the Ark of the Covenant—and without their other touchstones with God, the Urim and Thummim.[11] Nebuchadnezzar II's armies carried the previous king and many of Jerusalem's notables in bondage to Babylon, a small beginning to a vast Exile. During this time, Lehi abandoned Jerusalem in anticipation of the emperor's final invasion and the world-shattering changes it would bring for Jews and Judaism: the destruction of the First Temple, the abolition of the Davidic monarchy by the capture of Zedekiah and execution of his sons, and the exile of much of the population to Babylon. The generations of Jews after the Babylonian Captivity inherited the fractured world of the Diaspora, never restoring the pristine wholeness of living in a single body, ruled by the house of David, and worshipping in a temple with the Ark and its sacred memorials of the Exodus.

Lehi's band escaped this forced exile to Babylon only by undertaking *voluntary* exile in the wilderness. They endured most of the losses that characterized the Exile, with the additional loss of the biblical high priest and the Aaronite priests. Thus, the Book of Mormon exiles, no less than the biblical exiles, were dispossessed of their inherited land, the temple, the divine presence embodied in their sacred relics and enshrined in the Ark of the Covenant, and the sacral rule of the Davidic dynasty. They became "wanderers cast out from Jerusalem" (Jac. 7:26).

The lost pages open with the Book of Lehi's account of their exile, and much of its action is motivated by the problem of such an exile—the loss of the institutions of the Jewish commonwealth. Yet, although the Nephites suffered the same loss of religious and political center as the Babylonian exiles, their interpretation and consequent response differed dramatically. Instead of an exile, their journey became an exodus to a new promised land—the birth of a new Israelite nation. Nephi preserves his people's Israelite identity by establishing institutions like those he knew in the pre-Exilic Israelite commonwealth. Despite

---

11. The loss of the Urim and Thummim is indicated by Ezra 2:63 and Nehemiah 7:65. The Ark of the Covenant would have disappeared from the temple no later than Nebuchadnezzar's earlier capture of Jerusalem when he installed Zedekiah, in which he stripped the temple of its golden treasures (2 Kgs. 24:13). The Ark's fate is not definitely known. Rabbinical lore says Josiah hid the Ark, and the apocryphal 2 Maccabees says it was hidden by Jeremiah.

that commonwealth's destruction, his people were not long bereft of sacred city, temple, relics embodying God's presence, instruments of revelation, and a divinely chosen king. With Lehi as their Moses, they found a new promised land. Under Nephi, they built a new Jerusalem, and in it a temple where they housed the memorials of their exodus and resumed sacrifice to Israel's God.

Most of the clues to the Book of Lehi's contents cluster around this central theme of founding a new nation of Israel and restoring what had been lost as a result of exile. As will become evident in the various bits of the lost manuscript we will identify, it delineated more overtly than the extant account how Lehi and Nephi's lives echo the major events of the founding of Israel. The unifying theme of the Lehi and Nephi narratives is the establishment of a new Israelite nation modeled on the establishment of the biblical Israelite nation.

The Lehi and Nephi chapters of this book thus have an overarching thesis: *In the Book of Lehi's accounts of Lehi and Nephi, they countered their loss of the commonwealth of Israel in the Old World by constructing a smaller but structurally parallel commonwealth of Joseph in the New World.* Lehi and Nephi *re-create in microcosm* the Israel they left behind. Their story thus recapitulates the biblical story of Israel's founding. The stories in these chapters will accordingly be organized around key, biblically modeled events in the establishment of the Nephite commonwealth: division into tribes, exodus, inaugurating worship in a tabernacle, conquest of the promised land, founding a dynasty, and building a temple.[12]

Reconstructing the Missing Stories

Given the likely size of the lost manuscript, from at least 116 pages to as many as 200 to 300 pages, it goes without saying that many stories and details are missing from the published Book of Mormon. While we can't recover all of these narratives and details, we do know that the earliest and lost Book of Mormon manuscript offered far more narrative detail regarding Lehi and his sojourn, as well as the first four and a half centuries of Nephite history, than does the small plates account.

How can we know this? We can still see evidence and references to details that *were* in the lost narrative. These clues reside in three realms of primary source material: (1) large-scale characterizations of the lost manuscript; (2) references within the published text; and (3) historical recollections alluding to the lost pages.

---

12. The ordering of the elements, though similar to that of the Bible, is not identical, and is difficult to order precisely since the beginning of each of these processes may long precede its culmination.

Large-Scale Characterizations of the Lost Manuscript

As discussed in Chapter 5, our best available evidence suggests that the lost manuscript was considerably longer than the traditional count of 116 pages. However, even at only 116 pages, it would have had finer narrative detail than contained in the small plates accounts due to the latter's inclusion of lengthy prophecies, doctrinal exposition, and biblical quotations. Since these non-narrative elements make up much of the small plates, a comparable-sized lost manuscript that omitted such elements would contain much more narrative than the replacement text.

The lost manuscript would then likely provide several times the detail on early Nephite history than we now possess in the extant text. And given that our evidence points to that manuscript being significantly longer than 116 pages, it would have offered a specificity and richness of detail many times over what the present text does for four and a half centuries of Nephite history. And given that the lost manuscript was characterized as more Hebraic and based on the dynastically-linked large plates, it would particularly have offered greater detail on certain themes, such as those linked with the kings in Nephi's dynasty and Hebraic themes like temple, lineage, and the observance of Jewish festivals.

References within Our Book of Mormon

Many passages in our published Book of Mormon contain contextual clues or references to material that is now missing but was once there. For example, in Alma 10 we are told by Amulek that he is a descendent of "Aminadi who interpreted the writing which was upon the wall of the temple, which was written by the finger of God" (v. 2). The way that Mormon shares this account without providing additional information on Aminadi implies that the reader would have already been made aware of this story. By following such clues further to where they lead, and cross-referencing them with other texts and clues, we can connect the dots between references to see outlines of the missing information. (For more on Aminadi and the writing on the wall see Chapter 13.)

Historical Recollections Alluding to the Lost Pages

In addition to large-scale characterizations of the lost manuscript and references within the published Book of Mormon, there are contemporary documents (such as the May 1829 revelation published as Doctrine and Covenants 10) and later recollections that point to content in the lost manuscript. A few recollections utilized in this book are those of Fayette Lapham, Emer Harris, and Francis Gladden Bishop—all of which have already been quoted in previous chapters concerning information on both the translation of the golden plates and the physical manuscript pages. Their comments on the content of the Book of Mormon provide clues to what close insiders Joseph Smith Sr. and Martin Harris said about the narratives in the lost pages. For example, Lapham reports that Nephi's killing of Laban and acquisition of the brass plates occurred during "a great feast"—a detail that is not explicitly given by Nephi in his small plates account.[13]

Given the challenges of time and memory, such details should not be accepted without scrutiny. By checking them against the broader structural aspects of the Book of Mormon and references within it, we can not only gauge the reliability of the recollected details, we can sharpen those details and discover further insights into the lost manuscript. Thus, as will be shown in the following chapter, by examining Lapham's account of a feast in light of the Hebraic emphasis of the missing pages and references within Nephi's small plates account, we can surmise that Laban's drunkenness on the night that Nephi snuck into Jerusalem to acquire the brass plates was connected to the celebration of the Jewish Passover—a festival that both looked back on the Israelites' Exodus from Egypt toward their Promised Land in Canaan and launched the Lehites' exodus from Jerusalem toward their own promised land in the Americas.

Although the very first translation of Mormon's abridgment of the Nephite record has been missing for nearly two centuries, examining large-scale features of the lost manuscript (including its length and Hebraic emphasis), references contained in both the small plates accounts and Mormon's writings, and later recollections can provide us with numerous pieces that we can put together as we seek to reconstruct the Book of Mormon's missing stories.

---

13. Fayette Lapham, "Interview with the Father of Joseph Smith, the Mormon Prophet, Forty Years Ago. His Account of the Finding of the Sacred Plates," in Vogel, *EMD*, 1:465.

CHAPTER 7

A PASSOVER SETTING FOR LEHI'S EXODUS

This chapter examines the narrative of 1 Nephi 1–5 as a series of events occurring at the Passover season, beginning with Lehi's theophany (vision of God) at the start of the Passover month of Nisan and culminating with Nephi's slaying of Laban on the final day of the Jewish Passover celebration.[1] Although this text comprises five chapters in the current Latter-day Saint edition of the Book of Mormon, it constitutes just one chapter—the original 1 Nephi Chapter I— in the first edition of the Book of Mormon and presents a single overarching narrative of the escape of Lehi's family from destruction in Jerusalem and the beginning of their exodus to a new promised land. Read against the backdrop of the Passover season, the narrative of Lehi's exodus is not merely a narrative of one family's deliverance from temporal destruction but also a typological narrative of the redemption of humanity by the divine Lamb of God.

Fayette Lapham's Interview with Joseph Smith Sr.

In early 1830, shortly before the Book of Mormon came off the Grandin press, Palmyra businessman Fayette Lapham and his brother-in-law Jacob Ramsdell called at the Joseph Smith Sr. home in Manchester to get information on the forthcoming book.[2] As Palmyra residents, Lapham and Ramsdell would have heard the considerable buzz in town about the Book of Mormon

---

1. I am grateful to my friends Joe Spencer and Kirk Caudle for helping me link the feast mentioned by Fayette Lapham with the Passover. Kirk also provided valuable assistance in researching the biblical Passover.

2. Lapham dates his interview with Joseph Smith Sr. to 1830 but does not specify a month. However, his narrative enables us to place the interview more precisely. Lapham reports that his curiosity about the Book of Mormon was aroused by the hubbub surrounding its printing in Palmyra. That Lapham journeyed to neighboring Manchester in order to learn more rather than examining one of the five thousand printed copies of the book in Palmyra indicates that such copies were not yet available, as well as the fact that Lapham does not describe Joseph Sr. attempting to sell or show him a copy. In recounting the emergence and contents of the Book of Mormon, Joseph Sr. was fulfilling the instructions of an earlier revelation given for his benefit. As Colby Townsend explains, the February 1829 revelation (D&C 4) that instructed him to thrust in his sickle and reap souls for the Lord "nudged Joseph Sr. to engage in the work of spreading the story about Smith's discovery of the plates and the forthcoming book based on those plates." Colby Townsend, "Rewriting Eden with the Book of Mormon: Joseph Smith and the Reception of Genesis 1–6 in Early America." The connection

but were not yet able to satisfy their curiosity by reading its pages. Instead, the two young men enjoyed the rare privilege of hearing the Prophet's father relate the story of the Book of Mormon's emergence, and they were given an oral sneak preview of its contents. Four decades later, Lapham published an extensive account of this interview in an 1870 issue of *The Historical Magazine*.[3] Despite the lapse of years and the account's occasional garbling of fact, Lapham's narration is filled with firsthand information that demonstrates his reliance on a primary source with knowledge of the actual information and events, indicating that he may have written his newspaper account from detailed notes of his interview with Joseph Sr.[4] Whether Lapham's source was interview notes or an extraordinary memory, his accuracy on many obscure but confirmable details, such as the order in which Joseph Smith translated Mormon's abridgement and Nephi's small plates after the manuscript loss, lends credence to additional, unique details he provides.[5]

In relating Nephite history, Lapham's account largely retells familiar Book of Mormon stories. Yet at key points it also adds to the existing narrative some story elements not found in the published Book of Mormon. These additional pieces of Nephite narrative, though new or unknown, fit remarkably well into the familiar, known narrative, suggesting that they are not errors but echoes of narrative from the lost pages. Surprisingly, the interview account gives nearly five

---

of Doctrine and Covenants 4 with Fayette Lapham's interview with Joseph Sr. was suggested to me by Colby Townsend, personal communication, July 19, 2019.

3. Fayette Lapham, "Interview with the Father of Joseph Smith, the Mormon Prophet, Forty Years Ago. His Account of the Finding of the Sacred Plates," in Vogel, *EMD*, 1:462.

4. The scholar who has given Lapham's interview account the finest level of analysis is Mark Ashurst-McGee, who identifies some errors in Lapham's account but concludes from Lapham's reporting of "remarkable details (several of which can be corroborated) four decades later" that "Lapham must have had some notes of his conversation with Joseph Smith Sr." Mark Ashurst-McGee, personal email message to the author, September 26, 2017.

5. Lapham's account is notable for the detail it provides regarding the emergence of the Book of Mormon and for its surprising accuracy on a number of points in that narrative. For instance, he reports that after the manuscript theft Joseph Smith Jr. resumed translating at the point in the narrative "where they left off," rather than immediately shifting over to replacing the purloined manuscript with the small plates of Nephi. Modern textual criticism confirms Lapham's report—that Joseph Jr. resumed translating where the current Book of Mosiah begins rather than start over with the First Book of Nephi at the head of the small plates. As the earlier of only two historical sources reporting this detail of the translation process order (the other being another member of the family, the Prophet's sister Katharine Smith Salisbury), Lapham's interview with Joseph Sr. appears to have, indeed, been informed by a close insider. Kyle R. Walker, "Katharine Smith Salisbury's Recollections of Joseph's Meetings with Moroni," 16.

times as much space to the period of the narrative covered by the lost pages as it does to the period that follows the lost portion. One wonders if the Prophet's father, realizing his interviewers would not be able to read the fuller Nephite narrative given in the lost manuscript, attempted to provide more of that early narrative than the published book would provide. This seems to be the most probable explanation for the additional Nephite narrative given in Lapham's account.

Despite his intellectual interest, Lapham was never a believer in Joseph Jr. as a prophet and appears to have never even read the Book of Mormon. In fact, Lapham came away from his interview with Joseph Sr. believing the Book of Mormon to be a hoax, which obviated his need to read it. Given this lack of familiarity with the book, and especially its missing pages, it is unlikely that Lapham could have identified what was missing from lost manuscript narrative and constructed elements that fill those gaps and fit the pattern of Book of Mormon narrative.

Fayette Lapham's Account of Nephi's Quest for the Brass Plates

Among the stories Fayette Lapham relates from Joseph Smith Sr.'s narration are those of Lehi's flight from Jerusalem and Nephi's quest for the brass plates. The interview account of these events is as follows:

> In answer to our question as to the subject of the translation, he said it was the record of a certain number of Jews, who, at the time of crossing the Red Sea, left the main body and went away by themselves; finally became a rich and prosperous nation; and, in the course of time, became so wicked that the Lord determined to destroy them from off the face of the earth. But there was one virtuous man among them, whom the Lord warned in a dream to take his family and depart, which he accordingly did; and, after traveling three days, he remembered that he had left some papers, in the office where he had been an officer, which he thought would be of use to him in his journeyings. He sent his son back to the city to get them; and when his son arrived in the city, it was night, and he found the citizens had been having a great feast, and were all drunk. When he went to the office to get his father's papers he was told that the chief clerk was not in, and he must find before he could have the papers. He then went into the street in search of him; but every body being drunk, he could get but little information of his whereabouts, but, after searching a long time, he found him lying in the street, dead drunk, clothed in his official habiliments, his sword having a gold hilt and chain, lying by his side—and this is the same that was found with the gold plates. Finding that he could do nothing with him in that situation, he drew the sword, cut off the officer's head, cast off his own outer garments, and, assuming those of the officer, returned to the office where the papers were readily obtained, with which he returned to where his father was waiting for him. The family then moved on, for several days, when they were directed to stop and get materials to make brass plates upon which to keep a record of their journey.[6]

---

6. Lapham, "Interview," in Vogel, *EMD*, 1:462.

Readers familiar with the opening narratives of the present Book of Mormon will immediately note the several garbled elements of the familiar story: (1) it mistakenly identifies Lehi's family as beginning the narrative already separate from the main body of Jews; (2) while accurately affirming the presence of "brass plates" in the story, it identifies the object of Nephi's quest as "papers" rather than those plates; (3) it describes only one of Lehi's four sons (obviously Nephi) seeking this record; (4) it implies that the record's possessor was the "chief clerk" of an "office"; (5) it implies that Lehi had once worked at this office; and (6) it reports that Laban was absent when Nephi first went to acquire the record from him.

In making the errors he does, Lapham is often responding to authentic features of the story. His first error, identifying the Book of Mormon as the story of a group of Jews who separated from the main body of the Jews at the time of the biblical Exodus, conflates two different exodus narratives. While the Book of Mormon is indeed "the record of a certain number of Jews, who . . . left the main body and went away by themselves," Lapham's timetable is confused because he confuses *Lehi's* exodus near the Red Sea with *Moses's* Exodus across it. Lapham's third error, describing only one son making the quest for the record, is unremarkable given that one son plays the lead role in that story and acquires the record single-handedly. And Lapham's fourth error, making the record's possessor a "chief clerk" is probably not a blatant misidentification but a conflation of the record's two possessors: Laban and Zoram. While Laban, who was the record's *owner*, appears to be an "officer" of a military sort—one who can "command fifty" (1 Ne. 3:31)—Zoram, who was the record's *custodian*, might fittingly be identified as a "clerk."

Even with its demonstrable confusions, the essence of Lapham's account and a number of its details clearly echo an encounter with the accurate story. It and the present Book of Mormon text share this core narrative in common: A wicked Israelite nation is about to be destroyed, but God warns a righteous man in that nation by a dream to take his family and flee into the wilderness. Notably, in both cases there are opening journeys by the Red Sea. They travel three days in the wilderness. God then commands him to send his son, here highlighting the main protagonist Nephi, back to retrieve a document. The son makes multiple attempts to obtain the record and ultimately succeeds when he finds the record's current possessor lying drunk in the street. He draws the man's sword, the fine workmanship and gold hilt of which are noted, and then, out of necessity, beheads the man with it. He then takes the sword and dresses in the man's clothes. In this disguise he obtains the record, which he takes to his father in the wilderness, immediately after which the narrator in each case discusses the "brass plates."

Lapham's account adds a crucial new story element that suggests that the officer who possessed the brass plates was drunk when Nephi found him *because of a feast being celebrated at the time*, one which would fit the characterization of a Jewish festival. While the published Book of Mormon does not mention such a feast being celebrated at the time of Lehi's departure from Jerusalem, it does provide details that would fit naturally in such a festival context:

- Laban had been out that night with *"the elders of the Jews"* prior to Nephi finding him drunk in the street (1 Ne. 4:22).
- Zoram appears to find nothing suspicious in Laban (actually Nephi in Laban's clothing) wanting to go out again late that night, this time with the precious sacred record, to meet with the elders by the city gates (1 Ne. 4:26).
- Lehi offered sacrifice—a requirement for many of the feasts—both before his sons went to retrieve the brass plates and after their return (1 Ne. 2:7; 5:9).

Each of these details would fit well into a festival context reported by Lapham.

Lapham's plausible report of a festival context for the Book of Mormon's opening narrative (1 Nephi 1–5 and its lost pages counterpart) raises the question of which festival best fits that narrative. The evidence presented below will demonstrate that the celebration of *Passover* closely fits this narrative's details, enabling us to draw fresh insights about both the available Book of Mormon text and its lost pages. The value of these new insights will, in turn, confirm one of the central premises of the present book—that mining nineteenth century sources about the content of the lost Book of Mormon text helps illuminate the Book of Mormon text we already have.

At the outset of our examination, a question naturally arises: if the narrative of 1 Nephi 1–5 occurs during the Passover season, why doesn't the text explicitly mention such a celebration? The "great feast" in Lapham's account suggests that the lost manuscript did, in fact, mention this festival. According to Terrence L. Szink and John W. Welch, the extant Book of Mormon possibly omits explicit mentions of Jewish celebrations because of the assumptions its authors have about its readers:

> While the Book of Mormon never mentions Passover, the Feast of Tabernacles, or any other religious holiday specifically by name, several reasons can be suggested to explain this omission. The ancient writers may have assumed that their readers would naturally understand. A person does not have to say the word *Christmas* to refer implicitly to that special day. Even a casual mention of "wise men" or "decorating a tree" is enough. In just the same way, the words *Passover* or *Pentecost* do not need to appear in the Book of Mormon to evoke images alluding to the Israelite holidays.[7]

---

7. Terrence L. Szink and John W. Welch, "King Benjamin's Speech in the Context of Ancient Israelite Festivals," 153.

However, while the extant Lehi and Nephi narrative never mentions the celebration of the Passover festival explicitly, it refers to it implicitly through action in the narrative. Evidence from Nephi's small plates account dovetails perfectly with the lost manuscript having situated Nephi's acquisition of the brass plates in the context of a Jewish festival and helps to identify that festival as Passover. Recognizing this evidence requires having in mind certain features of the Jewish Passover celebration and its origin in the Israelites' Exodus out of Egypt, as described in the Hebrew Bible.

Historical and Biblical Context of Passover

Passover is a spring festival that commemorates Israel's exodus out of Egypt. As prelude to the Exodus, Moses is confronted by God at the burning bush on Mount Sinai and told to go and ask Pharaoh to let the Israelites travel three days into the wilderness to make sacrifices. Moses and Pharaoh repeatedly negotiate on the issue, but Pharaoh refuses to yield despite a series of divine curses on his land (Ex. 8–10). He is at last persuaded by the final curse—the coming of "the angel of death" for each firstborn male in the land. The Israelites were told to protect themselves and their children by offering the divinely commanded sacrifice of an unblemished lamb and marking their door posts with the lamb's blood. Those who complied were "passed over" by the angel of death, but those who did not saw the death of their firstborn. Surrendering to Moses and the Lord, Pharaoh finally gave permission for the Israelites to go (Ex. 11–12).

Before leaving, the Israelites took advantage of the situation and implored their former Egyptian overlords for gold and silver, which the Egyptians, now eager to be rid of them, were willing to give (12:35). The Egyptian surrender was only momentary, however, and when Pharaoh changed his mind and ordered his armies to pursue the Israelites, God parted the Red Sea for the Israelites to pass over on dry ground but closed it on the armies of Pharaoh, swallowing them up (Ex. 12–14).

In commemoration of the Lord redeeming Israel from Egyptian bondage, God commanded that subsequent celebrations of the Passover begin on the fifteenth day of the first calendar month, Nisan, and then last seven days (Ex. 13:3–4). Each family was to collect one unblemished lamb "in the tenth day of [Nisan]" and keep that lamb until it was time to sacrifice it on "the fourteenth day of the same month" (12:3, 6). The lamb was to be killed, the blood was to be put over the door posts, and in turn the angel of death would again pass over Israel (vv. 5–13, 23). Finally, pointing to the urgency of the original Passover, the meal was commanded to be eaten "in haste" so that the participants could be ready to leave in a moment's notice (v. 11), symbolizing an immediate deliverance from sudden destruction.

The Feast of Unleavened Bread

While the Passover feast was to be observed in perpetuity, it was not always observed in the same way. King Josiah (reigned ca. 641–609 BC), who initiated the first stages of the Deuteronomic reform, held a vast Passover celebration that apparently marked an innovation in how the feast was celebrated (2 Chr. 35:1–19). Happening just over two decades before Lehi's family left Jerusalem, Josiah's notable Passover was punctiliously patterned on the Law, centering the celebration on "the word of the Lord by the hand of Moses" (v. 6). Despite so scrupulously focusing on the Law in celebrating Israel's deliverance from Egypt, Josiah tragically did not obtain a similarly miraculous deliverance. In an ironic reversal of Israel's deliverance from the armies of Pharaoh at the Red Sea, Josiah eventually died facing Egyptian armies (vv. 19–27). Josiah's Passover itself, however, was still remembered as an unparalleled success:

> And there was no passover like to that kept in Israel from the days of Samuel the prophet; neither did all the kings of Israel keep such a passover as Josiah kept, and the priests, and the Levites, and all Judah and Israel that were present, and the inhabitants of Jerusalem. (2 Chr. 35:18)

It is this Passover, and the Deuteronomic reforms of which it was part, that comprise the most immediate biblical background for Lehi and Nephi's Passover some twenty years later.

A Passover Setting for Lehi's Exodus

Although a Passover context is never made explicit in our available Book of Mormon, on a close examination of the text of 1 Nephi 1–5 we can see that it already points to Lehi's calling from God having both a Passover *context* and Passover *content*. The chronological context of Lehi's calling vision, disclosed by close reading of the text, is that of the Passover season. And the content Lehi receives in that vision reveals the Book of Mormon's ultimate meaning behind the Passover: the sacrifice of the messianic Lamb of God. After this Passover-themed vision, the narratives of Lehi's exodus and Nephi's brass plates quest continue to reflect their Passover context by reenacting events of the original Passover, reflecting the observance of the festival of Passover, and verbally referencing Passover events in the Bible.

All of these echoes of Passover support Lapham's account that "a great feast" was being celebrated in Jerusalem during early events of this first narrative of the Book of Mormon.

The Passover Context of Lehi's Vision

Close attention to the detail of Lehi's initial calling and theophany in 1 Nephi 1 places that event, and therefore the beginning of the Book of

Mormon itself, early in the Passover month of Nisan, setting Lehi's vision and the events that follow in the Passover season.

The familiar account of Lehi's calling theophany, in the opening verses of the extant Book of Mormon, puts it "in the commencement of the first year of the reign of Zedekiah" (1 Ne. 1:4). This phrase's familiarity to the Book of Mormon's readers may obscure its significance. When was "the commencement of the first year of the reign of Zedekiah," and how, exactly, was his reign commenced? In the biblical narratives, Zedekiah's reign begins during an invasion of Jerusalem by the forces of Babylonian emperor Nebuchadnezzar II, and Jerusalem reportedly fell to Babylon's siege in Adar, the twelfth month in the Jewish calendar. As a result, Jehoiachin, king of Judah at the time of the siege, was dethroned and replaced by the Babylonians at the end of the calendar year. As the Chronicler puts it, "[W]hen the year was expired, king Nebuchadnezzar sent, and brought him [Jehoiachin] to Babylon, with the goodly vessels of the house of the LORD, and made Zedekiah his brother king over Judah and Jerusalem" (2 Chr. 36:10). The inauguration of the first year of Zedekiah's reign was therefore timed to coincide with the ringing in of the new calendar year with the month of Nisan.

The Book of Mormon offers multiple clues for determining when Lehi's warning and prophetic call occurred. The specific meaning of the phrase "in the commencement of the [n^{th}] year" can be gleaned from its use elsewhere in the Book of Mormon, and, in fact, in one instance, the phrase is used in conjunction with an exact calendar date, enabling us to discern how literally "in the commencement" can be taken: Alma 56:1 narrows "the commencement of the . . . year" to a specific date—"the second day in the first month" (i.e., the second day of the entire calendar year)—suggesting that such phrasing is meant to be taken quite literally. When the narrative places Lehi's calling and warning vision "in the commencement of" Zedekiah's first year, this should be taken at face value: it means in the very first days of Zedekiah's reign, which coincidentally were the very first days of the new calendar year (2 Chr. 36:10). Thus, coming "in the commencement" of that year, Lehi's calling theophany should have occurred shortly before Passover, which began on the fourteenth of Nisan.[8]

Additional dating within the Book of Mormon provides further support for such timing. The occurrence of Lehi's exodus during the Passover season is implied by the date on which Jesus was crucified in the Nephite calendar system. According to 3 Nephi 8:5 this happened on "the first month, the

---

8. Given the common dating of Zedekiah's reign as commencing in 597 BC, the relevant Passover would have begun on April 26 of that year, placing the final day of Passover on May 3 or 4, 597 BC, depending on whether the celebration was ended on the biblical seventh day or a later traditional eighth day.

fourth day of the month." What this means can be best understood by pulling together various Book of Mormon data points about the Nephite calendar.

- Nephite calendar dates were marked from when Lehi left Jerusalem (Jacob 1:1; Enos 1:25; Mosiah 6:4, 29:46; 3 Ne. 1:1, 2:6, 5:15).[9]
- The time of Lehi's exodus is also used as a benchmark to predict the coming of the Messiah, and in Passover language that symbolically connects Lehi's exodus to the birth of Jesus, the "Lamb of God" (e.g., 1 Ne. 10:4–10).[10]
- The time of Jesus's crucifixion—at Passover—aligns closely with the beginning of the Nephite calendar year. In the Gospel of John, the Crucifixion occurs on the fourth and final day of the Passover preparatory period (John 19:14); in 3 Nephi it occurs on the fourth day of the Nephite calendar year (3 Ne. 8:5).

Collectively, these three points establish that the Nephite calendar year began with the Passover season: if Jesus's crucifixion was on the fourth day of the preparatory period preceding Passover *and* on the fourth day of the Nephite calendar year, then that would mean that *the Nephite calendar began with the opening of the four-day preparation for Passover*. And given that the Nephite calendar was based on Lehi's departure from Jerusalem, this, in turn, would mean that Lehi and his family began their exodus from Jerusalem at the beginning of the preparation for Passover.[11]

A less technical and more typological reading of scripture and sacred history similarly implies a Passover timing for Lehi's exodus: in a pattern of redemptive events preceding and following Lehi's exodus, Passover is the time at which the Lord redeems His people. Crucial redemptive events in the history of Israel share this same precise timing.

---

9. See Randall P. Spackman, "The Jewish/Nephite Lunar Calendar," 48–59.

10. John P. Pratt, "Passover: Was It Symbolic of His Coming?" 38–45n7; John P. Pratt, "Lehi's 600-year Prophecy of the Birth of Christ"; John P. Pratt, "The Nephite Calendar."

11. This timetable is complicated by the question of whether the Nephite calendar was re-centered on a new initial day when its year count was restarted at the time Jesus' birth was portended by the appearance of a new star. However, 3 Nephi indicates that despite the new year count, time—including time for the purposes of calculating when the Messiah would come—was still being marked "from the time that Lehi left Jerusalem" (3 Ne. 1:1–9; cf. 1 Ne. 10:4; 19:8; 2 Ne. 25:19). It seems remarkable for the purposes of assessing the timing of Lehi's exodus relative to Passover that the 1 Nephi evidence places the beginning of Lehi's narrative "in the commencement" of the traditional Jewish calendar year (i.e., just before Passover) and the Nephite New Year began just days before the Passover at which Jesus was crucified.

- **The Mosaic Exodus.** Lehi's exodus echoes the contours of Moses's Exodus in the Bible. That exodus, *the* Exodus, began with Passover. There is thus no more natural time for Lehi's exodus to begin.
- **The Crucifixion of Christ.** The ultimate redemptive event, the Crucifixion of the Lamb of God, was made at the time of Passover.
- **The Coming of Elijah to the Kirtland Temple.** As pointed out by Stephen Ricks, Elijah's restoration of the sealing keys on April 3, 1836, happened precisely when Jews were inviting Elijah to join their Passover celebration.[12]

The original Passover was the time the Lord set His hand to deliver Israel from bondage in Egypt. The much later Passover following Zedekiah's enthronement would have been, on our argument here, when the Lord set His hand to deliver Israel *again* by leading Lehi's family preemptively from bondage to Babylon. The Passover some six centuries later was when Christ, the Lamb of God, was offered up as *the* Passover lamb. And it was again on Passover in 1836 that the keys to seal and redeem the living and the dead were restored in the Kirtland Temple. Again and again, Passover has been a time at which God delivers His people.

The Passover Content of Lehi's Vision

The visionary *content* of Lehi's theophany carries Passover themes, revealing the divine reality behind the symbols of Passover to be the messianic Lamb of God, further placing Lehi's exodus in the context of the Passover month. The available Book of Mormon text opens with Lehi seeing God sitting on his throne surrounded by angels and being shown the impending destruction of Jerusalem (1 Ne. 1:8–14). Shortly after this vision, Lehi preached to the people that he had seen in his vision not only Jerusalem's coming demise but also "the coming of a Messiah, and also the redemption of the world" (1 Ne. 1:19). Furthermore, there were many other things that Lehi saw that Nephi did not include in his abridgement of his father's vision (v. 16). One of these things that Lehi saw is later discussed in his sermons to his children and almost certainly further detailed in lost Book of Lehi: the Messiah as the Passover lamb.

That the Lamb of God was part of the fuller account of Lehi's vision is subtly revealed later in the narrative when Lehi expounds to his sons the content of his vision and when Nephi seeks to have his own repetition of that

---

12. Stephen D. Ricks, "The Appearance of Elijah and Moses in the Kirtland Temple and the Jewish Passover," 1–4. As suggested in Chapter 3, another major event in the redemption of Israel that may have been timed to coincide with Passover is the beginning of Joseph Smith's work of translating the Book of Mormon in March 1828.

vision. After relating to his sons a dream of the tree of life, Lehi expounds to them again what he learned in his vision, using nearly identical language to that theophany—that Jerusalem would be destroyed and that the Lord would raise up "this *Messiah*, of whom he had spoken, or this *Redeemer of the world*" (10:2–5). While Lehi does not, in the terse extant account of his discourse, identify his calling vision as the source of his information, the vision account itself makes clear that it was the source: "the things which he saw and heard, and also the things which he read in the book, manifested plainly of the coming of a *Messiah*, and also the *redemption of the world*" (1:18–19).

As he continues expounding, Lehi describes to his sons in some detail how a future prophet would "baptize the Messiah with water" and how "after he had baptized the Messiah with water, he should behold and bear record that he had baptized the *Lamb of God*, who should take away the sins of the world" (10:9–10). Given that Lehi could only have learned such detail by a vision or comparable revelation, and that Lehi has to this point used this discourse to expound to his sons the contents of his calling vision, Lehi is probably here continuing to expound contents from his vision—and among these were the Messiah's baptism and his identity as the sacrificial Lamb of God.

That these "Lamb of God" themes were part of Lehi's vision is further confirmed by Nephi's personal reiteration of the vision. Immediately after Lehi concluded teaching his sons about the destruction of Jerusalem, the Redeemer of the world, and the baptism of the Lamb of God, Nephi petitioned God: "I desire to *behold* the things which my father saw" (1 Ne. 11:3). Tellingly, he was answered with, *"Behold the Lamb of God"* (v. 21). He was shown more than merely the destruction of Jerusalem; he was also given a vision of the life of the Messiah, identified explicitly as the Lamb. Nephi's vision, given so he could see "the things which my father had seen" (v. 1) is so thoroughly imbued with Passover themes, referring some fifty-six times to the Lamb, that one author, unaware of the Passover context of these events, has suggested that Nephi's vision "might be called a paschal [i.e., Passover] vision."[13]

If Nephi's echo of his father's visionary experiences could be called a Passover vision, then it seems all the more certain that his father's original experience was itself a Passover vision. And such Passover content best fits in a Passover context. Lehi's visionary identification of the Messiah as "the Lamb of God, who should take away the sins of the world" (1 Ne. 10:10) *belongs* in the context of the Passover month of Nisan. As the inhabitants of Jerusalem, including Lehi's family, made ready to select an unblemished lamb to be sacrificed as their Passover, what was revealed to Lehi was that the Messiah *was* the "Lamb slain from before the foundation of the world" (Rev. 13:8).

---

13. George S. Tate, "The Typology of the Exodus Pattern in the Book of Mormon," 249.

This visionary identification for Lehi of the Messiah as the Lamb of God during Passover season may help explain a puzzling feature of the Lehi narrative. When Lehi teaches his fellow Jerusalem citizens of the coming of a Messiah, they are incongruously angry and seek to kill him (1 Ne. 1:19–20), a strange reaction to the promise of a Messiah and redemption. But if Lehi taught, during the Passover season, that this coming redeemer was *God's lamb*—plainly implying that his role was to be sacrificed rather than to deliver Israel from Babylon—this could account for the anger against him. In the immediate wake of a Babylonian invasion that had humiliated the Jews by dethroning their king, plundering their temple, and carrying their nobles in exile to Babylon, they would have wanted Lehi to promise a liberating conquering Messiah and not a spotless lamb intended for slaughter.

Finally, there is a third way in which Lehi's theophany may have involved the heavenly Lamb of God. Lehi's vision follows the pattern of heavenly-ascent throne theophanies, in which someone sees God sitting on His throne surrounded by singing, worshipping angels—a pattern reported not only by Lehi but also by Enoch, Ezekiel, John the Revelator, and Joseph Smith and Sidney Rigdon. Note the similarity of the visions of Lehi, John, and Joseph Smith:

- **Lehi:** "And being thus overcome with the Spirit, he was carried away in a vision, even that he saw the heavens open, and he thought he saw *God sitting upon his throne, surrounded with numberless concourses of angels* in the attitude of singing and praising their God. And it came to pass that he saw One descending out of the midst of heaven, and he beheld that his luster was above that of the sun at noon-day. And he also saw twelve others . . . and the first came and stood before my father, and gave unto him a book, and bade him that he should read" (1 Nephi 1:8–11).

- **John the Revelator:** "And I beheld, and, lo, *in the midst of the throne* . . . stood *a Lamb* as it had been slain. . . . [A]nd, lo, a great multitude, which no man could number, of all nations, and kindreds, and people, and tongues, stood *before the throne*, and before *the Lamb*, clothed with white robes, and palms in their hands; And cried with a loud voice, saying, Salvation to *our God which sitteth upon the throne*, and unto *the Lamb*. And *all the angels stood round about the throne* . . . and fell before the throne on their faces, and worshipped God, Saying, Amen: Blessing, and glory, and wisdom, and thanksgiving, and honour, and power, and might, be unto our God for ever and ever." (Rev. 5:6, 7:9–12)

- **Joseph Smith:** "And we beheld the glory of the Son, on the right hand of the Father, and received of his fulness; and saw *the holy angels*, and them who are sanctified before *his throne*, worshiping God, and *the Lamb*, who worship him forever and ever." (D&C 76:20–21)

These heavenly-ascent theophanies all follow the same pattern. Each involves seeing God sitting on his throne surrounded by worshipping angels. However, note that Joseph Smith's and both of John the Revelator's theophanies include not only God on this throne and angels but also the Lamb of God, as Lehi's exposition to his sons implies his theophany had as well. Furthermore, Lehi's throne theophany is immediately followed by Lehi seeing "One" descending and carrying a book. This, of course, parallels John's Revelation, wherein he sees in heaven one bearing a book whom he also identifies as the Lamb (Rev. 5:1–9; 21:27). Lehi's calling theophany is thus echoed by three other theophanies that center on the Lamb of God. So when Lehi himself expounds his heavenly-ascent theophany by describing to his sons the Lamb of God, he is not changing to an unrelated subject but is instead recounting one of the aspects of Lehi's experience of which Nephi did "not make a full account" in his abridgement (1 Ne. 1:16).

Passover Themes in Lehi's Exodus

After Lehi's vision, the Book of Mormon's narrative of Lehi, Nephi, and Laban continues to provide evidence for its Passover context by (1) *reenacting the original Passover in their lives*, (2) *reflecting their observance of the Passover festival* under celebration at the time, and (3) *rehearsing words spoken to and by them that evoke Passover*. These various reflections of the Passover, in re-creation, celebration, and reference are spread through the narratives of Lehi's exodus and Nephi's quest for the brass plates.

The story resumes with Lehi's exodus, which promptly begins to echo some of the circumstances of the biblical Passover. Upon Lehi's arrival at his home after witnessing an Exodus-like pillar of fire descend on the rock before him, the Lord came to him in a dream and warned him to get his family out of Jerusalem in order to avoid destruction and those in the city that sought to kill him (1 Ne. 2:1). Lehi did not delay in acting on this commandment, leaving so quickly that they failed to bring their most valuable possessions (3:22). This escape from the city then took them toward the Red Sea (2:2, 5).

Lehi's exodus both recapitulates and reverses the biblical Exodus and the setting for the original Passover. With Lehi as their Moses, his family traveled *away* from the biblical Promised Land rather than toward it. Similarly reversing the Exodus narrative, Lehi and his family did not receive gold and silver as they set out on their journey; rather, leaving in haste and taking only the true essentials, they left behind the gold and silver they already had. Their "three day's journey" in the wilderness then took them toward the Red Sea—the final boundary the Israelites crossed to free themselves from Egypt. After thus evoking the original Exodus narrative, the Lehi narrative then describes him offering a sacrifice to God. The occasion for the sacrifice is not specified, but it is consistent with the observance of Passover. Soon thereafter, Lehi was commanded to send his sons back to Jerusalem to acquire the scriptural brass plates that contained the Hebrew scriptures written in Egyptian script (Mosiah 1:2–4).

In the biblical Exodus narrative, the brothers Moses and Aaron negotiated with Pharaoh to allow them to lead the Israelites into the wilderness, ultimately taking with them the remains of the patriarch Joseph. Mirroring this, Lehi's sons sought to bargain with Laban to allow them to take the brass plates into the wilderness—plates Laban possessed because of his descendancy from Joseph (1 Ne. 5:16). They even offered their gold and silver for trade, reversing the Israelites' Passover request for the Egyptians' riches before leaving Egypt. This failed, however, with Laban seizing their gold and silver, keeping the brass plates, and chasing Nephi and his brothers out of the city. Hiding in a cave outside the walls of Jerusalem, Nephi then exhorted his discouraged brothers by turning to sacred history. In Jewish tradition, the first day of the week-long Passover festival commemorates the "passing over" of the Israelites by the angel of death and the final day of Passover commemorates the "passing over" by the Israelites of the Red Sea.[14] Nephi refers directly to this latter passing over or deliverance at the Red Sea to persuade his brothers that God would deliver them as he had their ancestors:

> [L]et us go up, let us be strong like unto Moses, for he truly spake unto the waters of the Red Sea and they divided hither and thither, and our fathers came through, out of captivity, on dry ground, and the armies of Pharaoh did follow and were drowned in the waters of the Red Sea. Now behold ye know that this is true; and ye also know that an angel hath spoken unto you; wherefore can ye doubt? Let us go up; the Lord is able to deliver us, even as our fathers, and to destroy Laban, even as the Egyptians. (1 Ne. 4:2–3)

As we have seen, the story recounted in 1 Nephi implicitly connects Laban to both Joseph and Egypt by his inheriting the Egyptian brass plates as a descendant of Joseph of Egypt. Laban thus plays a dual role in the story as both Jew and Egyptian.

Likewise, Lehi's exodus has the dual role of recreating yet reversing the ancient exodus, in both particular and thematic elements. The dual passing-overs that are celebrated during the holiday give parallel significance to the sequence of Lehi's sacrifice (possibly the Passover lamb) followed several days later by Nephi comparing Laban to the Egyptians at the Red Sea and then, later that night, slaying him. If Lehi's wilderness sacrifice was a Paschal lamb, then

---

14. Eliyahu Kitov, *The Book of Our Heritage: The Jewish Year and its Days of Significance*, 666–68.

Nephi's comparing Laban to the Egyptians at the Red Sea and then slaying him would have come near the end of the Passover week—the time at which Jews were celebrating the Israelites' deliverance from the Egyptians at the Red Sea.

A Passover Setting for Nephi's Quest for the Brass Plates

After exhorting his brothers, Nephi was "led by the Spirit" as he sneaked into the city to find Laban, who he found passed out drunk in the street. According to Fayette Lapham, this was because of a great feast being celebrated in the city at the time. As Nephi recounted, Laban was "drunken with wine" after being *"out by night among the elders"* (1 Ne. 4:7, 22). Passover was not merely a family celebration but a communal celebration. This was especially the case following the reign of Josiah, who changed the nature of the celebration to place more emphasis on Passover as a community rite with the Law at the center of the celebration (2 Kgs. 23:21–23). As Karen Armstrong summarizes the change, "Passover had been a private, family festival, held in the home. Now it became a national convention."[15] A prominent man like Laban who could "command fifty" (1 Ne. 3:31) would, indeed, have celebrated the Passover with other Jewish elders and elites.

Laban's connection with the Passover in this instance would have extended beyond it merely being an occasion for community socializing and drinking. Laban died at Passover, and this echoes the original, biblical Passover under Moses, when God destroyed those who tried to oppose his people. Laban had been celebrating with the Jerusalem elders, wearing full military dress and carrying a finely crafted sword. In the commandment in the Book of Exodus instituting the celebration of Passover, observance of the feast includes two ceremonial occasions or "holy convocations" (Ex. 12:16). One was on the first day of Passover, related to death passing over Israel's children and landing instead on the Egyptians' firstborn, the other was on the festival's final day, related to passing over the Red Sea and the destruction of the Egyptians.[16] If Lehi's sacrifice before sending his sons for the plates was a Passover observance accompanying the first convocation, commemorating the deliverance of the Israelites' firstborn, then the occasion of Laban celebrating with the elders would have been the final convocation, commemorating the Israelites' deliverance at the Red Sea and the Egyptians' destruction.

Viewed from the perspective of God's chosen faithful, Passover was a miraculous deliverance—being passed over by calamity, by the angel of death. But viewed from the perspective of the Egyptian oppressors, it was an occasion of

15. Karen Armstrong, *The Great Transformation: The Beginning of our Religious Traditions*, 195.

16. Kitov, *The Book of Our Heritage*, 666–68.

destruction. At the biblical Passover under Moses, the families of the Egyptians were not passed over by death at all, but struck squarely and painfully: the first-born of each family was slain. While the firstborn in this biblical narrative will not be envied, being a firstborn was generally an enviable thing in the Bible: the firstborn or birthright son was the special inheritor of family property. As inheritor of the brass plates from "his fathers," Laban himself would have likely been the firstborn son of his family (1 Ne. 5:16). As such, he shared the fate of the Israelites' oppressors' firstborn. As firstborn heir, a military leader, and a symbolic proxy for Pharaoh and the Egyptian armies (1 Ne. 4:3), Laban parallels both sets of Egyptians destroyed at the first Passover: those slain by the angel of death on the first evening and those destroyed at the Red Sea on the last day.

When we read 1 Nephi in a Passover festival context, the Spirit's words to Nephi become clearer: "Behold the Lord slayeth the wicked to bring forth his righteous purposes. It is better that one man should perish than that a nation should dwindle and perish in unbelief" (1 Ne. 4:13). Upon hearing this, Nephi again "remembered the words of the Lord which he spake unto me . . . inasmuch as thy seed shall keep my commandments, they shall prosper in the land of promise" (v. 14). Just as the firstborn of the Egyptians needed to die in order for the Lord's people to be delivered, so now Laban needed to die for Lehi's people to be delivered. Nephi learns that Laban must be destroyed, "even as the Egyptians," and then becomes "the angel of death" to Laban, slaying the firstborn in order to lead God's people out of bondage and to the Promised Land.

A final and crucial clue to a Passover setting for the brass plates narrative comes from words spoken at Nephi's killing of Laban. The Spirit's words to Nephi that it is better "that one man perish than that a nation dwindle and perish in unbelief" are striking because they echo Caiaphas' New Testament words about Jesus at the beginning of the Passover week in which Jesus was crucified. Caiaphas, acting as high priest, "prophesied that Jesus should die for" the nation of the Jews, saying, "[I]t is expedient for us, that one man should die for the people, and that the whole nation perish not" (John 11:50).

The implicit juxtaposition in these parallel phrases of the wicked Laban and humanity's sinless Passover lamb Jesus is perplexing. Yet a clear parallel does exist between the 1 Nephi 4 and John 11 passages. The rationale given for Nephi's beheading of Laban is the same as that given by Caiaphas for the crucifixion of Jesus: it is better that one man perish than that a whole nation perish. So the parallel is in the role of a scapegoat, or one who stands in for all. Although Laban clearly should not be understood as a Passover "sacrifice," he nonetheless plays a role in Lehi and Nephi's Passover that echoes Moses's Passover and may parallel Caiaphas's justification of Jesus's death. If Caiaphas—a skeptic of Jesus's divine mission—intended to compare Jesus to anyone from the Passover narrative, it would not have been the lamb. Rather, it would have been the firstborn among the Egyptians who had to die in order that the nation of Israel might not perish. Similarly to those Egyptian firstborn, here, in the Spirit's words, it is Laban who must die to save a nation.

When Laban's drunkenness, which enables Nephi to acquire the brass plates, is placed in context of a Passover feast, then the Nephite nation can be seen to have been saved from dwindling and perishing because of Passover. *Because* Laban thus celebrated the Passover, Nephi's nation was delivered. The Passover was not only the occasion of the Nephites' deliverance; it also made their deliverance possible.

Additional Insights into Nephi's Quest

Besides the Passover context for Nephi's return to Jerusalem to procure the plates, additional insights into the importance of both Nephi slaying Laban and the two items he acquired by it can be drawn from similar examinations of historical recollections and relevant scripture.

Nephi's Goliath and Kingship

In describing his beheading of Laban, Nephi adopts the language of a parallel moment in the story of David killing Goliath in 1 Samuel:

- Therefore David ran, and stood upon the Philistine, and took *his sword, and drew it out of the sheath thereof,* and slew him, and *cut off his head* therewith. And when the Philistines *saw* their champion was dead, *they fled.* (1 Sam. 17:51)
- And I beheld *his sword, and I drew it forth from the sheath thereof.* . . . [A]nd I *smote off his head* with his own sword. And it came to pass that when Laman *saw* me he was exceedingly frightened, and also Lemuel and Sam. And *they fled* from before my presence; for they supposed it was Laban, and that he had slain me and had sought to take away their lives also. (1 Ne. 4:9, 18, 28)

Here, three actions in the first verse describing David killing Goliath are repeated with the exact or nearly exact language in Nephi's account: David/Nephi drawing the sword of Goliath/Laban from its sheath, the cutting/smiting off of the head—with the victim's own sword—and the Philistines/brothers fleeing after seeing the victor and assuming their ally to be dead.

The near-identical language might not seem intentional if such phrasing were common in the Bible and the Book of Mormon. However, the phrase "the sheath thereof" occurs only two other times in the King James Bible (2 Sam. 20:8; 1 Chr. 21:27), both of which involve narratives about or surrounding David and neither of which involve a sword being drawn to kill another. And the Book of Mormon, despite mentioning swords over 150 times and several times explicitly discussing people drawing swords, has no other mention of sheaths.

This all points to Nephi (and his translator Joseph Smith) intentionally echoing the account of David killing Goliath in order to establish his own narrative of becoming the first Nephite king. According to BYU political scientist Noel Reynolds, the Laban incident is centrally positioned in a larger narrative that promotes and expounds Nephi's right to be "a ruler and a teacher over [his] brethren" (1 Ne. 2:22, 16:37; 2 Ne. 5:19).[17] Val Larsen has extended these insights, showing how the parallels between Nephi's divinely assisted triumph over Laban and David's divinely assisted triumph over Goliath portray Nephi as his people's divinely chosen ruler, their king, their David.[18]

And Benjamin McGuire similarly concludes from his analysis of literary allusion in the Nephi-Laban narrative that "Nephi's intent in including the narrative of his killing Laban has significant implications for his kingship." More explicitly:

> Nephi established his kingship through his narrative, to be passed on to his children, and his children's children. And it was not just Nephi's kingship. Through this narrative we also see the legitimizing of a new dynasty. The Lehite offshoot of Israel no longer has a Davidic king. They have Nephi.[19]

Nephi's encounter with Laban provided precisely what founding such a sacral dynasty would require of him: legitimacy as a new David, a "David" of the tribe of Joseph. And the proof of Nephi's new role was his possession of the fatal sword, by which his Goliath had been slain.

The Sword of Laban and Brass Plates' Egyptian Provenance.

Laban, however, was not the first to possess the sword or plates that Nephi procured by his death—and certainly not the first to possess the plates, which Nephi expressly said Laban had inherited from "his fathers" (1 Nephi 5:16). By examining how Laban came to inherit the brass plates, we can also surmise a similar origin and means of inheritance for Laban's sword.

The Brass Plates. While describing how Lehi found "the genealogy of his fathers" back to Joseph on the brass plates, Nephi's account in the small plates tells us also that "Laban also was a descendant of Joseph, *wherefore he and his fathers had kept the records*" (1 Ne. 5:14–16). This brief description of the plates and the line through which they were passed implies that the brass

---

17. Noel B. Reynolds, "The Political Dimension in Nephi's Small Plates," 15–37; Noel B. Reynolds, "Nephi's Political Testament," 220–29.

18. Val Larsen, "Killing Laban: The Birth of Sovereignty in the Nephite Constitutional Order," 26–41.

19. Ben McGuire, "Nephi and Goliath: A Case Study of Literary Allusion in the Book of Mormon," 26.

plates were a record of the family of Joseph and that possession of this record constituted or accompanied a distinction of status within that family. This and other passages describe several features of the brass plates' transmission, content, and language that distinguish them from the Bible:

- The plates were "kept"—preserved and updated—by successive members of a patriline descending from the Genesis patriarch Joseph (1 Ne. 5:16).
- They contained genealogies of Joseph's descendants that were sufficiently detailed to enable Lehi to trace his line across the eleven centuries separating him from the patriarch (1 Ne. 3:3; 5:14, 16).
- The plates transmit a version of the Hebrew scriptures that particularly focuses on the descendants of Joseph and thus incorporates accounts of the non-biblical prophets Zenos and Zenoch,[20] who are both described in the Book of Mormon as descendants of Joseph (3 Ne. 10:16–17).[21]
- The brass plates' distinctive focus on the line of Joseph of Egypt goes all the way back to the patriarch himself. The record evinces a unique degree of access to Joseph's life and words, presenting details not contained in the familiar biblical text—such as prophecies on his descendants (2 Nephi 3) and narrative about his famously polychromatic coat (Alma 46:23–24).
- The brass plates record was inscribed in Egyptian characters—"the language of the Egyptians" (Mosiah 1:4; cf. 1 Ne. 1:2).

The first four of these distinctive traits of the brass plates are closely related: each explicitly connects the plates to the patriarch Joseph. The fifth, the plates' link to Egypt, is a curious outlier; while the idea of recording Hebrew scripture in Egyptian script is familiar to readers of the Book of Mormon, the idea's familiarity can obscure its oddity.[22]

---

20. On the spelling "Zenoch" rather than "Zenock" for the name of the brass plates prophet, see Royal Skousen, ed., *The Book of Mormon: The Earliest Text*, xli.

21. In 3 Nephi 10:17 the narrator refers to the prophets Zenos and Zenoch and calls the Nephites "a remnant of their seed," and in the following verse he also refers to the Nephites as "a remnant of the seed of Joseph." John L. Sorenson discusses Zenos and Zenoch as Josephite prophets (and therefore presumably part of the Northern Kingdom of Israel). John L Sorenson, "The 'Brass Plates' and Biblical Scholarship," 31–39.

22. One Latter-day Saint interpreter considered the writing of the brass plates in Egyptian "unquestionably" "the most insistent problem for Book-of-Mormon scholarship." Jesse Nile Washburn, *The Contents, Structure and Authorship of the Book of Mormon*, 81.

Altogether, the brass plates' connections to both Joseph and Egypt imply the plates' specific origin. At the head of the Josephite patriline, by definition, stands Joseph himself, who was fluent in Egyptian and the source of the prophecies contained within the plates. Who better than Joseph himself to record his prophecies about his seed, establish the precedent of inscribing them in Egyptian, and begin handing them down through his patriarchal heirs? Although it may seem initially outlandish, Joseph of Egypt should be understood as the brass plates' initial author. And once he is, each of the five distinctive characteristics of the plates becomes natural rather than anomalous.[23]

The brass plates' origination with Joseph of Egypt, implicit in Nephi's small plates account and elsewhere in the Book of Mormon, was likely explicit in the lost manuscript. Nephi's extant record says he intentionally avoided duplicating many things from his father's record, including details of genealogy (1 Ne. 6:1). Since the brass plates contained a detailed genealogy that informed Lehi of his own descent from Joseph (5:26; 6:1), they most assuredly also detailed that of Laban's "fathers [who] had kept the records," back to whatever "father" had established the precedent of keeping the plates in Egyptian and handing them down among his descendants (5:16). Given the advanced prophecies of Joseph (2 Ne. 3) and Zenos (Jacob 5) concerning the necessary role that the Lehites would play in God's plans for Israel and humanity at large, it would seem natural that Lehi would begin his part of this plan by inheriting the records and prophecies that Joseph of Egypt initiated. Though Nephi's brief account fails to transmit all the specifics of Laban's lineage, and thus all the steps by which the brass plates descended to him, the logic of Nephi's statement that Laban "was a descendant of Joseph, *wherefore* he and his fathers had kept the records" reveals that Nephi understood *Laban's* descent from Joseph to account for the *plates'* descent from Joseph to Laban.

The Sword of Laban. This reading of the Book of Mormon's internal evidence on the origin of Laban's brass plates dovetails with a similar explanation for the origin of Laban's sword, this time drawn from outside the text. This explanation was offered by Martin Harris's longtime friend and confidant Francis Gladden Bishop.[24]

---

23. That the brass plates trace back to Joseph of Egypt himself has been argued by John L. Sorenson, who concluded four decades ago that the Egyptian-script brass plates "could have begun . . . certainly no later than the time of Joseph, the Egyptian vizier." Sorenson, "Brass Plates," 36. See also Brett L. Holbrook, "The Sword of Laban as a Symbol of Divine Authority and Kingship," 71; and Daniel N. Rolph, "Prophets, Kings, and Swords: The Sword of Laban and Its Possible Pre-Laban Origin," 73–79.

24. Bishop's relationship with Martin is discussed further in Chapter 5. See also Richard L. Saunders, "Francis Gladden Bishop and Gladdenism: A Study in the Culture of a Mormon Dissenter and his Movement."

As discussed in Chapter 5, Bishop is one of the only people known to have acquired information from Martin about the lost pages. He further demonstrated a pattern of conveying information that he likely acquired from Martin without attribution. Examples include sharing Martin's view that the lost manuscript was taken by an angel (see Chapter 4), describing the stack of golden plates as only four inches high,[25] and describing the plates' engravings as being filled with a black stain.[26] Bishop's writings further suggest unacknowledged reliance on Martin when he lengthily discusses Zechariah's "flying roll" (Zech. 5:1)—a subject of particular interest to Martin, who had for some time adopted a belief in the "flying roll" revelations of the Shaker community.[27]

In his *An Address to the Sons and Daughters of Zion*, Bishop offered further information for which Martin Harris is the likely source—a detailed account of the sword of Laban's origin and its role in earlier, pre-Lehi sacred history:

> The history of this sword is as follows: It was caused to be made by Joseph, of old, in Egypt, by the direction of God, and was in the hand of Joshua when he led the house of Israel into the land of Canaan. And after him it came down in the lineage of Joseph to Laban, from whom it was taken by Nephi, according to the account given in the Book of Mormon; and since the fall of the Nephites it has been preserved with the other sacred things, to come forth into the hand of a descendant of Joseph of old, in the line of Ephraim.[28]

That the information given here by Bishop was consistent with Martin's knowledge about the sword of Laban is implied by the fact that Martin gave his support to Bishop and his publications, such as this, for several years. Martin, as a scribe for the lost manuscript, would have been aware of what was contained or not contained in its narratives. The greater the detail Bishop gave about the sword, the greater his risk of contradicting Martin's prior

---

25. Every witness who examined the golden plates described the thickness of the stack as at least five inches, with one exception—Martin Harris, who repeatedly placed it at four. David B. Dille, "Additional Testimony of Martin Harris (One of the Three Witnesses) to the Coming Forth of the Book of Mormon," 545; "Mormonism--No. II," in Vogel, *EMD*, 1:305. Compare with Francis Gladden Bishop, *An Address to the Sons and Daughters of Zion, Scattered Abroad, Through all the Earth*, 48.

26. For the "black stain" in the golden plates' engravings, see the descriptions in Chapter 1. While Martin is not the only possible source for this description of the engravings, he is the plausible one. The other three Book of Mormon witnesses alive at the time of Bishop's writing had no known connections with Bishop and all lived in Missouri.

27. Brigham Young noted Martin's influence on Bishop: "There is a man named Martin Harris, and he is the one who gave the holy roll to Gladden." Brigham Young, April 17, 1853, *Journal of Discourses*, 2:127. H. Michael Marquardt, "Martin Harris: The Kirtland Years, 1831–1870," 18–19, 28. Francis Gladden Bishop, *A Proclamation from the Lord to His People, Scattered Throughout All the Earth*; Bishop, An Address, 23, 36.

28. Bishop, *An Address*, 2.

knowledge. As such, to safely stay consistent with Martin's knowledge of the sword's history, Bishop would have needed to limit his details on the sword largely to those Martin himself had provided.

Furthermore, while caution should be exercised with such details on their own, we have already noted how the available Book of Mormon text implies a very similar origin for the brass plates. If Laban's paternal lineage made him heir to one important relic of Joseph of Egypt, other such relics could naturally come to him in the same way. Bishop, having access to a privileged source regarding the lost manuscript, thereby made claims about the Laban's sword that harmonize beautifully with the available text.

These claims also harmonize well with modern Book of Mormon scholarship. In Brett Holbrook's analysis of the Nephite regal relics he finds Bishop's report of the sword of Laban's Josephite provenance "not without basis."[29] And Daniel N. Rolph's examination of the sword of Laban's provenance arrives at the same conclusion without reference to Bishop's account, arguing that the relic was a "birthright sword" that descended from Joseph to Laban.[30] Only recently have scholarly readers begun to notice the political role played by these items in Nephi's narrative and how inferences from the Book of Mormon point to Laban's sword and plates descending from Joseph of Egypt—as a confidant of Martin Harris was saying over a century and a half ago. And, as will be shown in the following chapters, these relics play a crucial role as the Lehites seek to replicate the political and religious institutions of Jerusalem in their new promised land.

Implications of a Passover Setting for Lehi's Exodus

Returning to the Passover theme, the clues within 1 Nephi, along with Lapham's account of a "great feast" being celebrated at the time, are strong indications that the lost manuscript story of the Lehite exodus contained more information about its Passover context. Reading the Book of Mormon's opening chapters in light of this Passover festival setting can thus bring greater meaning to those narratives, to the Book of Mormon as a whole, and even to the Passover itself.

The major Passover celebration under King Josiah's rule focused on the Law. The Book of Lehi Passover narrative appears also to have focused on the Law, in the sense that it is primarily about acquiring the Law recorded on the brass plates. Yet the Lehite narrative also introduces some major contrasts to Josiah's Passover. First, Lehi's Passover season begins with a vision equating the Passover lamb with the Messiah, making the latter the "Lamb of God." This would have contrasted with the Josian reform's effort to put down idolatry in Israel and emphasize strict monotheism—something that

---

29. Holbrook, "The Sword of Laban," 71.
30. Rolph, "Prophets, Kings, and Swords," 73–79.

would have disallowed the existence of multiple divine persons, like a divine Son or a messianic Lamb of God. Second, while Lehi's family sought the Law contained in the brass plates, they did not do so because they privileged the Law above all else but because they were commanded to by prophetic revelation through the Spirit and "wisdom in God" (1 Ne. 3:19; 4:10–12). One of the most basic of the Law's commandments was "Thou shalt not kill"; yet the Spirit overrode this, commanding Nephi to violate the Law in order to acquire it for his descendants, so they might retain their covenants with God.

The meaning of the Passover to the reformers under Josiah is thus contrasted greatly with the meaning of the Passover in the Book of Mormon. Josiah's Passover centered tightly and literally on the Law, "the word of the Lord by the hand of Moses" (2 Chr. 35:6), while Lehi and Nephi's Passover centered on acquiring the Law by acknowledging a greater importance of the Spirit, which in this case commanded the Law to be seemingly violated. The Lehite Passover also understood the Law as a system of signs pointing *beyond* itself, to the redemption of the world by a divine Messiah, who was also the sacrificial "Lamb of God."

So while the Josian Passover centered on the divine word—the Law—Lehi and Nephi's Passover centered, not on the divine Law, but on the divine Persons. Heading into the Passover season, Lehi saw God sitting upon His throne—i.e., the Father—and then the Son descending to earth (cf. Acts 7:55–56). And during that Passover, Nephi was commanded to contravene or counter the Law by the Spirit of the Lord. Lehi and Nephi's Passover was not a Passover of the Law of God, but a Passover of the Spirit of God, and, more fully, a Passover of the Father, Son, and Spirit, the persons of the Godhead who "are one God" (2 Ne. 31:21; D&C 20:27–28).

Thus, Lehi and Nephi paradoxically rely upon yet also transcend the Law. This is a pattern we will see repeated later, such as in the building of a temple without a Levitical priesthood (see Chapter 10) and in the narrative of King Mosiah (see Chapter 14)—that the Book of Mormon echoes the Josian pattern in *form* but differs from it in emphasis and substance. This simultaneous embrace and transcendence of Josian law in the Book of Mormon narratives is crucial. It reveals a key pattern and significant contribution of the Book of Mormon as an interpretive lens for the Bible. Perhaps one of the most important features of the Book of Mormon resides here—that as a book of scripture, it both embraces and transcends the Bible. It does this as it magnifies and clarifies, reiterates and complicates, revisits and deepens, and recreates and explains the messages in the Bible—in a complex, sophisticated, and unequalled way.

The Passover context of Lehi's vision also provides a further window into the Book of Mormon itself. Lehi's vision of the Lamb of God in the context of the preparation for Passover provides a narrative bridge from a low Christology—a relatively unexalted view of the Messiah that, rightly or wrongly, can be read out

of the Hebrew Bible—to the Book of Mormon's inarguably high Christology—
its fully divine view of the Messiah, of a Christ who "is THE ETERNAL GOD"
(Title Page). If Lehi and Nephi came from the same context as the Jews just before the Exile, why did they have a precocious conception of a Messiah, and of
a divine Messiah at that? Lehi's vision of Messiah as Lamb at the Passover season
offers an explanation. Given in the context of Passover, Lehi's vision would have
provided Lehi and his family a clear notion of a self-sacrificing, divine Messiah.
The revelation that the Messiah was the divine Lamb of God, the substance of
which the Passover lamb was a mere shadow, would have given the Nephites the
radical understanding of a divine Messiah—and of the Passover and the entire
Law of Moses as symbols pointing to that divine Messiah.

The Passover setting for the Book of Mormon's opening narrative also re-
casts the book's opening message. The Book of Mormon begins with the story
of Lehi's personal temporal deliverance—from potential captivity and death.
Viewed in the context of its Passover setting, this narrative of Lehi's deliverance becomes also an echo or reiteration of Israel's deliverance at the original
Passover. And viewed in context of Lehi's revelation about the messianic Lamb
of God, it becomes still more: a type of the spiritual deliverance to be wrought
by the Messiah. Framed by the festival of Passover and by a revelation of what
that Passover means, the story of the temporal deliverance of a family of pre-
Exilic Jews becomes a representation of the larger deliverance of humankind,
one celebrated in a Passover that points to the Lamb of God.

The Book of Mormon is not just a book about a particular family. Like
the heavenly book Lehi saw in his original theophany, from the beginning the
Book of Mormon manifested "plainly the coming of a Messiah, and also the
redemption of the world" (1 Ne. 1:13–16, 19). Our present brief abridgement of the Book of Mormon's opening events, greatly condensed from the
initial manuscript, may appear to be simply about the family of a certain
Israelite man of the sixth century BC and their deliverance from temporal
destruction. However, when these narratives are placed within their original
context, once offered by Mormon's intended fuller account in the Book of
Lehi, the significance of the events changes dramatically.

Read in light of their Passover context, these narratives prove not to be
merely or even mostly about the temporal deliverance of one man; they are
about the spiritual deliverance of all men, of humanity as a whole, through "the
Lamb slain before the foundation of the world" (Rev. 13:8). The divine Messiah
waits six centuries into Nephite history to make his physical appearance, yet
from its very beginnings "in the commencement of the first year of the reign of
Zedekiah" (1 Ne. 1:4), the Book of Mormon is already a witness of Jesus Christ.

CHAPTER 8

LEHI'S TABERNACLE IN THE WILDERNESS

Just as the beginning of Lehi's exodus echoed that of the original Exodus, events during his family's travels to their promised land similarly point back to the biblical narrative of the Israelites traveling to reach theirs. This chapter will reconstruct portions of the lost Book of Mormon text pertaining to three such echoes of the Mosaic Exodus in the Lehi story: Lehi's construction of a tabernacle; Lehi and Nephi's acquisition, use, and preservation of instruments paralleling the miraculous instruments that facilitated the biblical Exodus; and their eight years wandering in the wilderness.

Lehi's Tabernacle

After returning to his father with the brass plates, Nephi says that Lehi began searching this set of scriptures and learned that they contained not only the books of Moses and records of the Israelite kings, but that they also contained "the prophecies of the holy prophets, from the beginning, even down to the commencement of the reign of Zedekiah; *and also many prophecies which have been spoken by the mouth of Jeremiah*" (1 Ne. 5:13). These prophecies of Jeremiah would have surely included his condemnation of the temple a decade or two earlier when he both called out the temple priests for failing their obligations to the oppressed and prophesied of the temple's destruction:

> Trust ye not in lying words, saying, The temple of the Lord, The temple of the Lord, The temple of the Lord, are these. . . .
>
> Behold, ye trust in lying words, that cannot profit. Will ye steal, murder, and commit adultery, and swear falsely, and burn incense unto Baal, and walk after other gods whom ye know not; And come and stand before me in this house, which is called by my name, and say, We are delivered to do all these abominations? *Is this house, which is called by my name, become a den of robbers in your eyes? Behold, even I have seen it,* saith the Lord. . . . And now, because ye have done all these works, saith the Lord, and I spake unto you, rising up early and speaking, but ye heard not; and I called you, but ye answered not; *Therefore will I do unto this house, which is called by my name, wherein ye trust, and unto the place which I gave to you and to your fathers, as I have done to Shiloh.* . . . Therefore pray not thou for this people, neither lift up cry nor prayer for them, neither make intercession to me: for I will not hear thee. (Jer. 7:4–16)[1]

---

1. Many of these words should be familiar to readers, since they are quoted by Jesus during his ministry when he similarly condemns the temple and prophesies of its destruction. By quoting Jeremiah, it would have been clear to those who heard

This reminder of the temple's corruption and prophesied destruction, combined with Lehi's own knowledge of Jerusalem's pending destruction, may have been what initiated an event reported in Fayette Lapham's account that is not clearly mentioned in Nephi's small plates. According to Lapham, after Nephi obtained Laban's record and returned to his father,

> The family then moved on, for several days, when they were directed to stop and get materials to make brass plates upon which to keep a record of their journey; *also to erect a tabernacle, wherein they could go and inquire whenever they became bewildered or at a loss what to do.* After all things were ready, they started on their journey, in earnest; a gold ball went before them, having two pointers, one pointing steadily the way they should go, the other the way to where they could get provisions and other necessaries.[2]

Comparing this with Nephi's small plates account, it becomes clear that Lapham garbled some of what he heard. Yet even where Lapham has mis-interpreted, the details he gives are, with one exception, known elements of the Lehi narrative. Elements of retrieving the brass plates, acquiring gold for Nephi's own record, and discovering the Liahona are swapped around, but the construction of "a tabernacle, wherein they could go and inquire" is a unique detail and not merely a combination or facile misreading of elements of that narrative. Like Lapham's mention of the great feast at which Laban got drunk (discussed in Chapter 7), the tabernacle detail adds an important interpretive key to understanding other aspects of the Book of Mormon text.

Internal Evidence for Lehi's Tabernacle

Evidence dovetailing with Lapham's report that Lehi constructed a tab-ernacle can be found in the report by Book of Mormon prophets that they tried scrupulously to observe the law of Moses, which required a sanctuary for the fulfillment of its ritual observances (2 Ne. 5:10; 25:24; Jacob 4:5; Mosiah 13:27; Alma 25:15; 3 Ne. 1:24–25). During his exodus Lehi could not meet this requirement with a settled temple, but he could meet it by creating a portable temple like Moses's wilderness sanctuary, the Tabernacle.

Given the way that Lehi's exodus is patterned on the biblical Exodus, his building of a tabernacle also seems a natural fit. It further continues another pattern in the narratives of Lehi and Nephi—their construction of a new commonwealth of Israel. Almost immediately on arriving in the wilderness, Lehi built an altar he could use in place of sacrificing in the Jerusalem temple.

---

him that it was not the moneychangers but the temple priests who were under condemnation. Thus, when "the scribes and chief priests heard it, [they] sought how they might destroy him" (Mark 11:15–18).

2. Lapham, "Interview with the Father of Joseph Smith, the Mormon Prophet, Forty Years Ago. His Account of the Finding of the Sacred Plates," in Vogel, *EMD*, 1:465.

Building a tabernacle during their exodus would go still further in the same direction—that of building parallel institutions to substitute for the Israelite national institutions they had abandoned. Though, of course, any makeshift tabernacle Lehi's family could have constructed on their journey would be small and meager compared to the elaborate biblical Tabernacle.

That the band of travelers would feel authorized and even obligated to construct a replacement for the temple in Jerusalem is made clear by Nephi building a temple modeled on, and functionally replacing, Solomon's in the promised land (2 Ne. 5:16). For the same reason, it would make sense that they would build a tabernacle to accompany their altar and enable the Lehites to live the Mosaic law more scrupulously until they could construct a permanent temple after reaching their destination (1 Ne. 4:15; 2 Ne. 5:10).[3]

Lehite Separatist Worship

Lehi's quick construction of his substitute altar after leaving Jerusalem has implications for understanding why he abandoned the city. In the decades before his flight and construction of temple substitutes, worship at the temple in Jerusalem had undergone sweeping change. Both for better and for worse, the various types of reform initiated by the young King Josiah snowballed until the reformers had altered sacrificial practices (e.g., forbidden families from performing their own Passover sacrifices) and rejected foreign idols and Israelite relics alike. The Babylonian invasion continued this process. When Nebuchadnezzar II subdued Jerusalem just prior to Lehi's departure, his forces plundered the temple and "carried out thence all the treasures of the house of the LORD," leaving the temple desecrated and desacralized (2 Kgs. 24:10–13). If, by chance, the Ark and its relics survived this first siege, they would not have for long when the city again fell and Nebuchadnezzar's forces demolished the temple and carried away the last of its treasures (25:13–17).

For the devout, the loss of a sacred presence as central as that embodied by the relics in the Ark of the Covenant calls not only for mundane explanation (e.g., superior military force) but also for *theological* explanation. And the Book of Mormon provides a theology to explain the desacralization and abandonment of temples. In the published text, the Nephite prophet-king Benjamin explains that a temple can be desacralized when it is polluted by persistent sin and thus rendered unholy. God then withdraws his protective presence from it and has no place there any longer, "for he dwelleth not in

---

3. Potentially dovetailing with the descriptions of Lehi's family constructing progressively more elaborate places of worship on their journey, archaeologist F. Richard Hauck has explored the remains of a small Solomon's-temple-like sanctuary at Khor Kharfot in Oman, a candidate for the Book of Mormon's Bountiful. Scot Proctor and Maurine Proctor, "Archaeological Dig: Was There a Holy Place of Worship at Nephi's Bountiful?"

unholy temples" (Mosiah 2:36–37).[4] Benjamin almost certainly learned this temple theology from his father, Mosiah$_1$, who acted as a second Lehi and led the righteous on an exodus from the land of Nephi to Zarahemla. In doing so, Mosiah$_1$ abandoned the temple of Nephi when its worshippers waxed wicked and polluted it. (See Chapter 14.)

Memorials of the New Exodus

Beyond just the golden Ark of the Covenant and the stone tablets it held, the temple in Jerusalem held other sacred objects that served as memorials of the divine providence that had provided the Israelites aid during the Exodus. Similarly, along the journey to their new promised land Lehi's band acquired objects that would serve as memorials of their own exodus. By the time they decided to construct a tabernacle, they had already come into possession of two such objects to remind them of this divine aid: the brass plates and the sword of Laban, which respectively correspond to the Law of Moses held in the Ark and the sword of Goliath that had been kept in the biblical Tabernacle (1 Sam. 21:8–9)

A third sacred relic that Lehi's family acquired on their exodus adds to our understanding of his tabernacle. Referred to in the small plates as a "ball" (1 Ne. 16:10–30) or "compass" (1 Ne. 18:21, 21; 2 Ne. 5:12), the Book of Mormon later provides a name for it when the prophet Alma$_2$ tells his son Helaman about "the thing which our fathers call a ball, or director—*or our fathers called it Liahona*, which is, being interpreted, a compass; and the Lord prepared it" (Alma 37:38), indicating that the lost manuscript likely used this name as well.

Discovering and Operating the Liahona

After traveling some distance from Jerusalem, Lehi awoke one morning and opened the door of his tent to find the Liahona, a brass orb with two small rods or pins that acted as pointers, lying on the ground:

> And it came to pass that as my father arose in the morning, and went forth to the tent door, to his great astonishment he beheld upon the ground a round ball of curious workmanship; and it was of fine brass. And within the ball were two spindles; and the one pointed the way whither we should go into the wilderness. (1 Ne. 16:10)

Although the small plates say that the pointers in this instrument directed Lehi's band where to go as they traveled through the wilderness and across

---

4. That the divine Spirit preserves the temple from destruction is intimated by King Benjamin's analogy of the temple with the individual soul. The person who disobeys God loses the divine Spirit that has "preserved" him or her. God has "no place" in this desecrated soul just as he has "no place" in a desecrated temple—"he dwelleth not in unholy temples." That soul's "doom" is therefore to be damned (Mosiah 2:36–39).

the ocean, as well as where to find food and other necessities (vv. 30–31), it provides only a minimal description of how the Liahona operated:

> I, Nephi, beheld the pointers which were in the ball, that they did work according to the faith and diligence and heed which we did give unto them. And there was also written upon them a new writing, which plain to be read, which did give us understanding concerning the ways of the Lord; and it was written and changed from time to time, according to the faith and diligence which we gave unto it. (1 Ne. 16:28–29)

We do, however, get additional information on the Liahona from the recollections of Fayette Lapham and Francis Gladden Bishop, both of whom were likely told about content in the lost manuscript. As noted earlier in this chapter, Lapham reports that the Liahona had "two pointers, one pointing steadily the way they should go, the other the way to where they could get provisions and other necessaries."[5]

Bishop, likely being given information from Martin Harris, provides even more details:

> The last of the sacred things to be named, is a curious Ball, spoken of in the Book of Mormon, and called Directors, from the circumstance, of there being in it two steel points, (called spindles, in the Book of Mormon,) which points directed the enquirer by faith the proper course to take. This instrument is composed of a small brass ball, about three inches in diameter, having two steel points coming out of it, in opposite directions. Around each of these points, are 12 squares, and between these 24 squares on the ball, are figures of various descriptions, representing various things on the earth, as vegetation, animals, running streams of water, &c.[6]

While it is difficult to visualize the device precisely as Bishop intended, it is clear that on his model there were pictures around the spindles. So while one spindle pointed a *direction*, the other spindle could point to a *picture*. This detail, if correct, would help fill a gap in the published Book of Mormon's description of the Liahona. Nephi says that "within the ball were *two* spindles; and the *one* pointed the way whither we should go into the wilderness" (1 Ne. 16:10), but he leaves the function of the second spindle unaccounted for. Lapham's report corrected this deficiency, indicating that the second spindle pointed "the way to where they could get provisions and other necessaries." Bishop's account also indicates that the second spindle may have aided in the finding of provisions, but his description implies that the Liahona did so by pointing to a picture rather than by pointing in a direction. A composite of all three descriptions suggests

---

5. Lapham, "Interview," in Vogel, *EMD*, 1 465.

6. Francis Gladden Bishop, *An Address to the Sons and Daughters of Zion, Scattered Abroad, Through All the Earth*, 13. For clarity of reading, I have removed Bishop's numerous italics, which serve no evident purpose.

a possible model for how the Liahona worked: the first spindle mandated the *direction* of travel; the second spindle, by pointing to one of the picture symbols around it, identified the *purpose* of travel. Together, the two spindles could show the Liahona's users where to go and what they would find when they got there.[7]

After guiding the Lehi colonists to their new promised land, the Liahona passed through the line of Nephi's dynasty, perhaps so that future kings could consult it for divine guidance. Yet, curiously, by the time of Mormon's extant record of the Nephite kings (beginning with Benjamin), the device appears to have dropped from use, or at least to have left no further textual evidence of its use. Thus, when Alma$_2$ entrusts his son Helaman with the Nephite relics, he speaks of the Liahona only in terms of its past use by "our fathers" (Mosiah 1:16–17; Alma 37:1, 38–47). No longer functional as an *instrument* of divine power, the Liahona still served as a *memorial*, or *token*, of the divine guidance and sustenance given Lehi's family during their exodus.

The Liahona's Role in Lehi's Exodus

The Liahona served as *the* central instrument of divine power facilitating Lehi's exodus, combining the functions of several miraculous instruments and phenomena of the biblical Exodus that came to serve as memorials either kept *before* the Ark of the Covenant (Ex. 16:33–34; 1 Kgs. 8:9; 2 Chr. 5:10) or actually *in* the Ark (Heb. 9:4). These were the pot of manna, Aaron's rod that budded, and, for most of the Israelite nation's history, Moses's brazen serpent (Heb. 9:4; Ex. 16:33–34).

Manna. In the biblical Exodus narrative, Manna was a strange edible substance in the form of a ball that the Israelites found on the ground in the mornings:

> [I]n the morning the dew lay round about the host. And when the dew that lay was gone up, behold, upon the face of the wilderness there lay *a small round thing.* . . . And when the children of Israel saw it, they said one to another, It is manna: for they wist not what it was. And Moses said unto them, This is the bread which the Lord hath given you to eat. (Ex. 16:13–14)

The pot of manna kept in the Tabernacle and temple was thus a token of divine providence to the Israelites during their Exodus: it was through the manna they had been given sustenance.

Aaron's rod that budded. This was a branch or staff used to settle the dispute over which tribe of Israel had right to act as priests in the Tabernacle. Each tribe was to leave a staff with its name written on it overnight in front of the Ark

---

7. For an intriguing analysis of the Book of Mormon's Liahona passages from another angle that compares some of its described workings to that of an astrolabe, see Timothy Gervais and John L. Joyce, "'By Small Means': Rethinking the Liahona," 207–32.

in the Tabernacle. The tribe whose rod grew blossoms by morning would be the one chosen by God as Israel's priests. Aaron's rod (representing the tribe of Levi) first "brought forth buds," then "bloomed blossoms," and finally "yielded almonds" (Num. 17:8). Thus, Aaron's rod was used to divine the will of God.

The rod was afterward enshrined in front of the Ark in the Tabernacle, where it was "to be kept for a token against the rebels"—a perpetual sign that God had chosen the tribe of Levi to administer in the priesthood (v. 10).

The brazen serpent. During the Exodus, the children of Israel began to complain, despite their daily miraculous rations of manna, "there is no bread, neither is there any water." In response, "the LORD sent fiery serpents among the people, and they bit the people; and much people of Israel died" (Num. 21:4–6). After some pleading by Moses, God told him to construct a brass serpent to cure those who were bitten:

> And the LORD said unto Moses, Make thee a fiery serpent, and set it upon a pole: and it shall come to pass, that every one that is bitten, when he looketh upon it, shall live. And Moses made a serpent of brass, and put it upon a pole, and it came to pass, that if a serpent had bitten any man, when he beheld the serpent of brass, he lived. (vv. 7–9)

After its creation, the serpent pole was preserved among Israel's Tabernacle and temple relics for several centuries until it was destroyed by Hezekiah as part of his reformist goals to eliminate idolatry from Israel (2 Kgs. 18:4). Called *Nehushtan* by Hezekiah, the brazen serpent may have functioned as more than just a memorial of the Exodus. The name is often thought to have been coined by Hezekiah as a dismissive reference to the relic as a mere "thing of brass." However, the name likely signifies more than this by evoking an earlier root: *nahash*—Hebrew for "snake"—that also functions as a verb meaning "to divine." This would indicate that the brass snake in Solomon's temple was possibly employed (in some way) as an instrument for divining the will of God.[8]

Exactly where in Solomon's temple this pole was kept is not specified. The proto-Israelite temple at Hazor, built on a parallel plan to Solomon's temple, enshrined a bronze serpent in its Holy of Holies.[9] Because the other Exodus memorials of Solomon's temple were in the Holy of Holies (either in or near the Ark), it seems likely that the serpent pole was also enshrined there.[10]

---

8. Shawna Dolansky, "A Goddess in the Garden? The Fall of Eve," 16n57.

9. Two bronze serpents have been excavated in the Holy of Holies of the Hazor temple, one from Stratum I B, which is dated to 1400–1300 BCE, the other from Stratum I A, dated to 1300–1200 BCE. Maciej Münnich, "The Cult of Bronze Serpents in Ancient Canaan and Israel," 40.

10. The Nehushtan could have been kept within, atop, or beside, or the Ark.

The Liahona and the Memorials of Moses's Exodus

Rather than just being a mere analogue to the Israelite Temple relics, the Liahona served parallel functions to each of the three miraculous instruments of the Exodus. First, the Liahona provided sustenance. Just as manna had been the divine means of providing sustenance to the Israelites in the wilderness, the Liahona was the divine means of providing it to the Lehites. Through it Lehi and Nephi could access the will of God and be led to their sustenance in the wilderness. Making the connection between the Liahona and pot of manna even stronger, the language Nephi uses to describe the discovery of the Liahona directly evokes the Hebrew Bible's description of the Israelites discovering manna:

> And it came to pass, that at even the quails came up, and covered the camp: and *in the morning* the dew lay round about the host. And when the dew that lay was gone up, behold, *upon the face of the wilderness there lay a small round thing.* (Ex 16:13–14)

> And it came to pass that as my father arose *in the morning*, and went forth to the tent door, to his great astonishment he beheld *upon the ground a round ball of curious workmanship.* (1 Ne. 16:10)

Second, the Liahona served a revelatory or divinatory function, with its pointers supernaturally providing directions similar to the way divining rods are used and echoing the divinatory use of Aaron's rod. As suggested by Hugh Nibley, the pointing of the rods or pins in the Liahona also constitutes a form of rod divination.[11] While Aaron's rod divined the will of God by budding leaves, the connection between it and traditional divining rods is made clear by Joseph Smith's revelations identifying Oliver Cowdery's use of a rod or "the gift of working with the rod" as "the gift of Aaron" (D&C 8:6–8).[12]

Third, the Liahona, like the *Nehushtan* or brazen serpent, served as an instrument of deliverance. This parallel is implicit in the narrative of Lehi's exodus and in the teachings of Book of Mormon prophets, particularly Alma₂—who used identical language to describe both the brazen serpent and the Liahona. During his ministry Alma preached to the Zoramites regarding the use of the brazen serpent in Moses's Exodus: "a type was raised up in the wilderness, that *whosoever would look upon it might live.* And many did look and live" (Alma 33:19). Shortly afterward, Alma₂ echoed his words about the brazen serpent in his words about the use of the Liahona in Lehi's exodus: "it prepared for them, that *if they would*

---

11. Hugh Nibley discussed the Liahona in the context of rod or arrow divination in Hugh Nibley, *Since Cumorah*, 251–59.

12. The phrase of "the gift of working with the rod" is used in the first printing of the revelation. "Book of Commandments, 1833," 19 (7:3). The earliest version of the revelation referred to the rod as a "sprout." Revelation, April 1829–B [D&C 8], 12.

look they might live (Alma 37:46). Thus, again we see how the Liahona played yet another parallel role to the miraculous instruments of the Exodus.

The Liahona and the Tabernacle

According to Fayette Lapham, Lehi and family "were directed to stop and . . . erect a tabernacle, wherein they could go and inquire whenever they became bewildered or at a loss what to do," after which they were guided through the wilderness by the ball "having two pointers, one pointing steadily the way they should go, the other the way to where they could get provisions and other necessaries."[13]

This account connects the Liahona and Lehi's tabernacle in multiple ways. First, it connects them temporally, placing the finding of the Liahona in the narrative immediately after the erection of Lehi's tabernacle.

Second, it connects them functionally. According to Lapham, Lehi's tabernacle was a *place* to "go and inquire whenever they became bewildered or at a loss what to do," and the Liahona a *means* by which to inquire. Thus, the tabernacle was the most natural place to use the Liahona.

Third, true to the larger pattern of Lehi's exodus mirroring the biblical Exodus, the Liahona is related to Lehi's tabernacle in the same way that the biblical Urim and Thummim is related to Moses's Tabernacle. During this time the Liahona served as Lehi's stand-in for the Urim and Thummim, and its discovery is connected to the construction of his tabernacle. In a similar way, the Urim and Thummim are first mentioned just after and in connection with the commandments to build the Israelite Tabernacle (Ex. 25:9; 28:30, 43), and they first physically appear in the narrative within the Tabernacle at Aaron's consecration as high priest (Lev. 8:3–8). Likewise, just as the Liahona was the instrument by which the Lehites inquired of God, so too was the Urim and Thummim the instrument by which the Israelites inquired of God, each in their respective tabernacles. By doing so, Lehi stepped into the shoes of the high priest, signaling his rejection and purposeful replacement, not only of a desecrated Jerusalem temple, but also of a corrupt Aaronite priestly class.

Fourth, Nephi's description of the Liahona as being "of curious workmanship; and . . . of fine brass." (1 Ne. 16:10) utilizes a term tied to the construction of the Israelites' Tabernacle. The word "curious" appears nine times in the King James Translation of the Hebrew Bible. One use broadly describes "curious works . . . in gold, and in silver, and in brass" that would adorn the Tabernacle (Ex. 35:32), and the other eight uses all describe the "curious girdle of the ephod" that would be worn by the High Priest when performing his sacred duties in the Tabernacle (Ex. 28:8, 27–28; 29:5; 39:5, 20–21; Lev. 8:7).

---

13. Lapham, "Interview," in Vogel, *EMD*, 1:465.

Fifth, Lehi's finding of the Liahona echoes Moses's inauguration of the Tabernacle. When describing Lehi's discovery of the Liahona, Nephi writes: "as my father arose in the morning, and went forth to the *tent door*, to his great astonishment he beheld upon the ground a round ball of curious workmanship" (1 Ne. 16:10). Like Nephi's use of "curious," his referring to Lehi finding it at the "tent door" again connects his narrative to that of the Tabernacle. While this may initially seem to just be simply referring to Lehi rising and finding the Liahona upon opening the door of his personal tent, the specific phrasing may point to this being the door of Lehi's tabernacle.

Reference to the doors of tents may be found in several narratives of the King James Bible. However, the specific phrase "tent door" is found in only two, both of which describe theophanic encounters with God. The first is when "the *Lord appeared unto [Abraham]* in the plains of Mamre [as] he sat in the *tent door* in the heat of the day" (Gen. 18:1), and the second occurs during Moses's inauguration of the Tabernacle:

> And it came to pass, that *every one which sought the Lord* went out unto the tabernacle . . . and stood every man at his *tent door*, and looked after Moses, until he was gone into the tabernacle. And it came to pass, as Moses entered into the tabernacle, the cloudy pillar descended, and stood at the door of the tabernacle, and *the Lord talked with Moses*. And all the people saw the cloudy pillar stand at the tabernacle door: and all the people rose up and worshipped, every man in his *tent door*. And *the Lord spake unto Moses face to face*, as a man speaketh unto his friend. (Ex. 33:7–10)

Even in its terse extant form, the narrative of Lehi finding the Liahona evokes this Exodus narrative. Just as the Israelites' pillar of cloud that would "lead them the way" (Ex. 13:21) appeared at the door of the Moses's Tabernacle, so too does the Lehites' Liahona—which Nephi said "led us" and "pointed the way" (1 Ne. 16:10)—appear at the door of Lehi's tabernacle.

That the use of the phrase "tent door" in the Liahona story is an intentional rather than accidental echo of the Tabernacle story is suggested by Book of Mormon echoes of the narrative of the Israelites pitching their tents around the Tabernacle during its own narrative of King Benjamin's sermon. When Benjamin addressed his people from a tower erected by the temple, the people "pitched their tents round about the temple, every man having his tent with the door thereof towards the temple, that thereby they might remain in their tents and hear the words which king Benjamin should speak unto them" (Mosiah 2:6).

Lapham's account of Lehi acquiring the Liahona in connection with building a tabernacle not only fits elegantly into the extant Lehi story, it also has both biblical Exodus models and later Book of Mormon exodus echoes. This account illuminates how Lehi used the Liahona and how he began reconstructing temple worship as it had previously existed in the Jerusalem temple.

The narrative of Lehi building a tabernacle, acquiring the Liahona, and consulting the Liahona in his tabernacle *belongs* with the rest of the Lehi saga.

And the whole narrative of the Liahona—how it was found like the manna, filled the functions of the sacred instruments of the biblical Exodus, was used in the Tabernacle, and was preserved like the memorials of the biblical Exodus—helped give the Nephites an origin story like that of the biblical Israelite nation and laid the foundation for the Nephites to restore or reconstruct temple worship like what had been practiced in Solomon's temple.

Wandering in the Wilderness

In both the biblical and Book of Mormon exoduses, the people pitched their tabernacle at the various encampments they were led to along their journey. However, despite their divine guidance, both groups moved toward their respective promised lands with painful sluggishness. The Israelites wandered forty years to traverse the distance between Egypt and Palestine. The Lehites made better time, yet they still managed to take eight years to go from Jerusalem to the bottom of the Arabian Peninsula—a pace of about 5 miles per *week*.

Based on Nephi's description of Lehi's record and of Nephi's own large plates—sources behind the lost manuscript—that manuscript would have detailed "the more part of all our proceedings in the wilderness" (1 Ne. 19:2)."[14] Such narrative detailing the Lehi colony's slow progress is missing from the extant Book of Mormon account of Lehi's journey. However, the cause of their sluggishness was given in the earliest part of the Book of Mormon manuscript Joseph Smith dictated after resuming his translation, beginning with the Book of Mosiah:

> And moreover, [King Benjamin] also gave [Mosiah$_2$] charge concerning . . . the ball or director, which led our fathers through the wilderness, which was prepared by the hand of the Lord that thereby they might be led, every one according to the heed and diligence which they gave unto him. Therefore, as they were unfaithful they did not prosper nor progress in their journey, but were driven back, and incurred the displeasure of God upon them; and therefore they were smitten with famine and sore afflictions, to stir them up in remembrance of their duty. (Mosiah 1:16–17)

Lehi's band failed to progress in their journey when they failed to give "heed and diligence" to God. In particular, Alma$_2$ tells us that the Lehites failed to progress due to the Liahona ceasing to work when their "faith and diligence" waned:

---

14. John Tvedtnes first suggested that the lost manuscript might detail Lehi's wandering in the wilderness in John A. Tvedtnes, *The Most Correct Book: Insights from a Book of Mormon Scholar*, 37–52.

And behold, [the Liahona] was prepared to show unto our fathers the course which they should travel in the wilderness. And it did work for them according to their faith in God; therefore, if they had faith to believe that God could cause that those spindles should point the way they should go, behold, it was done. . . .

Nevertheless . . . [t]hey were slothful, and forgot to exercise their faith and diligence and then those marvelous works ceased, and they did not progress in their journey; therefore, they tarried in the wilderness, or did not travel a direct course, and were afflicted with hunger and thirst, because of their transgressions. (Alma 37:38–42)

The stories hinted at here, of the Lehi colonists being afflicted and driven back, are, for the time being, largely unavailable. However, the published Book of Mormon does offer one instance in which either the Liahona failed to provide the needed guidance or Lehi failed to diligently consult it. After traveling for many days, the group found themselves without food and with Nephi's bow broken, causing his brothers and even his father to despair. It was at this point, when Nephi demonstrated his faith by constructing a new bow and sling and asking his father for guidance, that Lehi humbled himself and "did inquire of the Lord." Lehi was then told by the voice of the Lord, "Look upon the ball" (1 Ne. 16:18–26). Nephi writes:

And it came to pass that I, Nephi, beheld the pointers which were in the ball, that they did work according to the faith and diligence and heed which we did give unto them. . . . And it came to pass that I, Nephi, did go forth up into the top of the mountain, according to the directions which were given upon the ball. . . . And it came to pass that I did slay wild beasts, insomuch that I did obtain food for our families. (vv. 28–31)

Despite not being the eldest son, Nephi's successful use of the instrument bolstered his right to possess it after his father's death. The incident again also creates a parallel between Lehi and his family to the biblical Jacob and his family. In the Genesis narrative of Jacob and his sons, during an extended period of hunger there was one son who saved the entire family from starvation: Joseph (Gen. 41–46). In saving his own family, Nephi stepped into his forebearer's shoes. The Lehites' journey to the promised land continued to echo the Israelite wandering in the wilderness, even while they crossed the ocean, and Nephi, for his part, continued to take the role of the family's Joseph.

In the new promised land, Lehi would take up the roles of Jacob and Moses once more, blessing his family and dividing them into tribes as Jacob had and giving them a valedictory modeled on that of Moses in Deuteronomy. And as Lehi's part in the new Israel's sacred drama ended, Nephi took on a new role in leading the work of resettlement.

CHAPTER 9

THE SEVEN TRIBES OF LEHI

The published Book of Mormon narrates Lehi building his family and a nation of several tribes with little detail. However, clues discussed in this chapter point to a far richer version of this story in which Lehi dividing his family into distinct tribes was part of building up an American miniature of the house of Israel.

The Lineages of Laban, Ishmael, and Zoram

A revelation to Lehi identifies his family as "a branch from the fruit of the loins of Joseph" (Jacob 2:25; cf. 2 Ne. 3:5), echoing the biblical Jacob's deathbed blessing on the head of his beloved son: "Joseph is a fruitful bough, even a fruitful bough by a well; whose branches run over the wall" (Gen. 49:22). The core of this new, American Israelite commonwealth was to be formed by the intertwining lineages of Lehi, Ishmael, Zoram, and the tribes from which they descended. While the Book of Mormon traces Lehi's lineage to Manasseh, son of Joseph (Alma 10:3; cf. 1 Ne. 3:2–4; 5:14–16), it says nothing of Ishmael's or Zoram's lineages—though it does identify Zoram's master Laban as also being a descendant of Joseph (1 Ne. 5:16).

Tribal Genealogies in the Lost Pages

Multiple recollections report that the Book of Mormon's lost text identified Ishmael as belonging to the tribe of Ephraim. For example, in 1896 Elder Franklin D. Richards recalled hearing Joseph Smith explaining how the Book of Mormon could fulfill Ezekiel's prophecy of "the stick of Ephraim" or "stick of Joseph, which is in the hand of Ephraim" (Ezek. 37:16, 19):

> Away back in 1843 . . . [at Joseph Smith's Mansion House] I ventured to walk in, and scarcely had more than time to exchange usual civilities, when this brother said: "Brother Joseph, how is it that we call the Book of Mormon the Stick of Joseph in the hands of Ephraim, when the book itself tells us [in Alma 10:3] that Lehi was of the lineage of Manasseh? I cannot find in it about the seed of Ephraim dwelling on this land at all." Joseph replied:
> "You will recollect that when Lehi and his family had gone from Jerusalem out into the wilderness, he sent his son Nephi back to the city to get the plates which contained the law of Moses and many prophecies of the prophets, and that he also brought out Ishmael and his family, which were mostly daughters. This Ishmael and his family were of the lineage of Ephraim, and Lehi's sons took Ishmael's daughters for wives, and this is how they have grown together, 'a mul-

titude of nations in the midst of the earth' [Gen. 48:16, 19 – Jacob's prophecy about Ephraim].

"If we had those one hundred and sixteen pages of manuscript which Martin Harris got away with, you would know all about it, for Ishmael's ancestry is made very plain therein. The Lord told me not to translate it over again, but to take from Nephi' s other plates until I came to the period of time where the other translation was broken off, and then go on with Mormon's abridgment again. That is how it came about that Ishmael's lineage was not given in the Book of Mormon, as well as Lehi's."

This explanation from the Prophet himself made a deep and abiding impression upon my mind, as I had but recently been reading the passage referred to in the third verse of the tenth chapter of Alma, and was pondering over the same thing with anxious desire to know how this could be, if the ancestry of the race were all of Manasseh.[1]

Richard's firsthand recollection is supported by earlier statements from two other Latter-day Saint apostles, Orson Pratt and Erastus Snow.

In a tract he published nearly a half century earlier in England, Pratt reported:

The records of Manasseh in the hands of Ephraim shall gather out the Lord's elect from the four winds, from one end of the earth to the other The Book of Mormon is the record of Manasseh; it is now in the hands of Ephraim. . . . The American Indians are partly of the children of Manasseh; though many of them are of Ephraim, through the two sons of Ishmael.[2]

While Pratt failed to identify this information as coming from the lost manuscript, Snow, speaking in 1882, did name it as the source:

The Prophet Joseph Smith informed us that the record of Lehi was contained on the one hundred sixteen pages that were first translated and subsequently stolen, and of which an abridgment is given us in the First Book of Nephi, which is the record of Nephi individually, he himself being of the lineage of Manasseh; but that Ishmael was of the lineage of Ephraim, and that his sons married into Lehi's family, and Lehi's sons married Ishmael's daughters, thus fulfilling the words of Jacob upon Ephraim and Manasseh in the 48th chapter of Genesis [verse 16] which says: "And let my name be named on them, and the name of my fathers Abraham and Isaac; and let them grow into a multitude in the midst of the earth." Thus these descendants of Manasseh and Ephraim grew together upon this American continent.[3]

One last source comes to us from Charles B. Thompson, an 1835 convert who reported Ishmael's Ephraimite lineage in the March 1852 issue of his

---

1. Franklin D. Richards, "Origin of American Aborigines," 425.

2. Orson Pratt, *Divine Authenticity of the Book of Mormon*, 1:91–92.

3. Erastus Snow, May 6, 1882, *Journal of Discourses*, 23:184–85.

Zion's Harbinger. Like Richards and Snow, Thompson attributed this information to the Book of Mormon's lost pages:

> We are in possession of information that Ishmael, whose daughters were wives of Lehi's sons, was of the tribe of Ephraim; and that the servant of Laban was of the same tribe; and Ishmael had two sons also; and when Laman and Lemuel, the sons of Lehi, revolted from Nephi, the whole family of Ishmael revolted with them except the wives of Nephi and Sam. Hence the Lamanites were principally Ephraimites. . . . It may be proper to state, that our information of the origin of this family of Ishmael is derived from the 116 pages of the Book of Mormon, that were stolen from the possession, in Manchester, New York.[4]

While Thompson does not explain how he knows this information was in the lost pages, his earlier writings demonstrate that he knew it prior to, and therefore independent of, Joseph Smith's 1843 explanation overheard by Franklin D. Richards. In 1841, Thompson had published his lengthily titled *Evidences in Proof of the Book of Mormon Being a Divinely Inspired Record, Written by the Forefathers of the Natives whom We Call Indians (Who are a Remnant of the Tribe of Joseph)*. Much of Thompson's book is an argument that Native Americans, as Lamanites, were descendants of Joseph—particularly of *Ephraim*—and thus heirs to the biblical promises and prophecies regarding that tribe.[5] Since the extant Book of Mormon explicitly identifies Lehi as a member of the tribe of Manasseh (Alma 10:3), Thompson appears to have already understood the Lamanites' other founding progenitor, Ishmael, to be the source of their Ephraimite heritage.

Thompson's 1841 information, while not contained in the extant Book of Mormon text, is consistent with it and agrees with what Joseph Smith would later say was in in the Book of Lehi. The Lamanite nation, which early Latter-day Saints straightforwardly equated with all Native Americans, was comprised of three intermixed Lehite tribes: Lamanites, Lemuelites, and Ishmaelites (D&C 3:18). Laman and Lemuel, founders of two of the tribes, both married Ishmael's Ephraimite daughters. And the Ishmaelites, male-line descendants of Ishmael's two sons, shared his patrilineal descent from Ephraim. Thus, the resulting Lamanite nation was as genealogically identified with the tribe of Ephraim as with the tribe of Manasseh.

Not only does Thompson's early account lend weight to the later accounts from Richards, Snow, and Pratt, it also goes beyond them. Thompson additionally reports that "the servant of Laban," Zoram, was also of Ephraim, giving him the same tribal origin implied for his master Laban by the account

---

4. Charles B. Thompson, "A Correspondent Writes," 22

5. Charles Blancher Thompson, *Evidence in Proof of the Book of Mormon Being a Divinely Inspired Record, Written by the Forefathers of the Natives whom We Call Indians (Who are a Remnant of the Tribe of Joseph)*, 31, 37–38.

that Laban inherited Joshua's sword (see Chapter 7). Together, everyone traveling to the promised land with Lehi was from either the tribe of Manasseh or that of Ephraim.

Did Lehi Have Daughters Who Married Ishmael's Sons?

Erastus Snow's 1882 recollection reported that the sons of Ishmael "married into Lehi's family."[6] While Snow does not specify just how this occurred, the most obvious explanation would be that Lehi had unmentioned daughters who married Ishmael's sons.

This does not appear to have been the case. When Ishmael's group traveled from Jerusalem to Lehi's camp, Nephi refers to "the two sons of Ishmael and their families," indicating that Ishmael's sons were married prior to joining Lehi's group (1 Ne. 7:2–6).[7] If these wives were daughters of Lehi, then that would mean their father left them in Jerusalem for its destruction and only had them join him when he was told that his own sons would need wives to establish themselves in their promised land (v. 1). That the Book of Mormon mentions these women only in reference to Ishmael's sons, with Nephi calling them "their families" (v. 6) and "their wives" (18:9), and Mormon calling them merely "Ishmaelitish women" (Alma 3:7), similarly implies that they were not Lehi's daughters.

Nothing in the published Book of Mormon text explicitly rules out Ishmael's sons marrying Lehi's daughters. Nothing supports it either, and the textual evidence weighs against it. If Ishmael's sons somehow married into Lehi's family, discovering how may have to await the identification of new evidence about the Book of Mormon's lost narratives.[8]

Taking the Crown from "the Drunkards of Ephraim"

The interplay of Lehi, Ishmael, Nephi, and Laban and their lineages reflects the complex relationship between the two tribes of Joseph, Ephraim

---

6. Erastus Snow, May 6, 1882, *Journal of Discourses*, 23:184–85.

7. Nephi mentions sisters in 2 Nephi 5:6, but these do not seem to have been married to Ishmael's sons. Unlike the wives of Ishmael's sons, who became part of the Lamanite nation and took on them the Lamanite curse" (Alma 3:7), these sisters followed Nephi. Furthermore, Nephi lists them, like his younger brothers, without husbands or children (2 Ne. 5:6). Since these sisters were not listed by Nephi in his introduction to1 Nephi, it is likely that they, like Jacob and Joseph, were born during the family's sojourn in the wilderness.

8. The possibility that Lehi had daughters in addition to those Nephi cursorily mentions in 2 Nephi 5:6 is very real. The Genesis narration on Jacob's family implies that he had twenty-one daughters in addition to his twelve sons, yet only one of these daughters (Dinah) is mentioned by name (Gen. 46:15).

and Manasseh. Joseph's father Jacob passed over the older Manasseh for the birthright. In blessing Manasseh and Ephraim, Jacob crossed his hands, placing his right hand, used to bestow the birthright, on the younger Ephraim (Gen. 48:13–20).

As noted, while Nephi was from the older, but birthright-less, Manasseh, Laban inherited Joseph's sword through the younger, birthright son Ephraim. Laban also epitomizes the pride of the once-dominant tribe of Ephraim, bewailed by Isaiah:

> Woe to the crown of pride, to the drunkards of Ephraim, whose glorious beauty is a fading flower, which are on the head of the fat valleys of them that are overcome with wine! . . . The crown of pride, the drunkards of Ephraim, shall be trodden under feet. (Isa. 28:1, 3)

Nephi seized Joseph's birthright from this archetypal "drunkard of Ephraim," for himself and his tribe (Gen. 25:29–34; 27:1–41). In supplanting Laban as Joseph's heir, Nephi shifted dominance within the house of Joseph temporarily from the Ephraim to Manasseh. Nephi's interplay with Laban here echoes David's with Saul. In supplanting Saul, David removed leadership over Israel from Saul's tribe, Benjamin, and acquired it for his own tribe, Judah (Gen. 49:10; 1 Sam. 9:1; 17:12). By "delivering" Laban, and thus also the sword with which he would be slain, into Nephi's hands, God effectively crossed his own hands *back*, taking Joseph's birthright relics and blessings from Laban— and Ephraim—and bestowing them on Nephi—and thus Manasseh. Much later, the collapse of the Nephite nation and the recovery of Joseph's relics by Joseph Smith, identified as an Ephraimite, would complete the circle.[9] The relics, and the birthright of which they were symbolic and part, thus crossed from Manasseh back to Ephraim.

This dynamic resembles the Pauline and Book of Mormon theology in which Israel's apostasy opens the door of salvation to the Gentiles, who, in turn, bring salvation once again to Israel. The pattern in each case is chiastic and reflects a divine master plan whereby one group's temporary fortunate "fall" (Rom. 11:11; 25) opens doorways that ultimately make salvation "free for all men" (2 Ne. 26:27; 3 Ne. 16:4).[10]

---

9. The Book of Mormon and Joseph Smith's revision of the Bible identify him as a descendant of the biblical Joseph (2 Ne. 3:4–7; JST Gen. 50:27, 33). His later revelations identify Latter-day Saints in general and him in particular as descendants of Ephraim (D&C 64:36; 113:4; 133:30, 32, 34). He is similarly identified as an Ephraimite in blessings given to him by Joseph Smith Sr. (December 9, 1834) and Oliver Cowdery (September 22, 1835). See "Blessing from Joseph Smith Sr., 9 December 1834," 9; "Blessing from Oliver Cowdery, 22 September 1835," 15.

10. For a close and insightful reading of Paul's theology of Israel and the Gentiles in Romans, and corresponding understandings in the Book of Mormon, see Joseph

Implications of Ephraimite Lineage

The Ephraimite lineage shared by Laban, Zoram, and Ishmael has significant implications. First, it helps account for the Book of Mormon's heavy emphasis on the Lehites as a Josephite nation. Rather than being exclusively Ephraimite or Manassehite, as an admixture of Ephraim and Manasseh the Lehites could claim both lines of Joseph and be recipients of the blessings pronounced by Jacob on each of those lines (Gen. 48–49).

Second, the Ephraimite descent of Ishmael and Zoram, and also of Laban, would make the golden plates partly and the brass plates thoroughly Ephraimite records. Thus, Joseph Smith's revelatory description of the plates in Moroni's charge as "the record of the stick of Ephraim" (D&C 27:5) is illuminated by this genealogy he had previously dictated in the lost manuscript. This description is drawn from a prophecy of Ezekiel, in which sticks representing the peoples of Judah and Joseph (through Ephraim) are written on and then brought together in one hand to represent their joining into a single nation.

Although he was one of the exiles taken during the siege of Jerusalem that deposed Jehoiachin and installed Zedekiah, Ezekiel's prophetic ministry did not begin until several years later in Babylon after Lehi's family had already departed. His prophecies, then, would not have been included in the brass plates. From his exile, Ezekiel wrote:

> The word of the LORD came again unto me, saying, moreover thou son of man, take thee one stick, and write upon it, For Judah, and for the children of Israel his companions: then take another stick, and write upon it, For Joseph, the stick of Ephraim, and for all the house of Israel his companions: And join them one to another into one stick; and they shall become one in thine hand. And when the children of thy people shall speak unto thee, saying, Wilt thou not shew us what thou meanest by these? Say unto them, Thus saith the Lord God; Behold, I will take the stick of Joseph, which is in the hand of Ephraim, and the tribes of Israel his fellows, and will put them with him, even with the stick of Judah, and make them one stick, and they shall be one in mine hand. And the sticks whereon thou writest shall be in thine hand before their eyes. And say unto them, Thus saith the Lord God; Behold, I will take the children of Israel from among the heathen, whither they be gone, and will gather them on every side, and bring them into their own land: And I will make them one nation in the land upon the mountains of Israel; and one king shall be king to them all: and they shall be no more two nations, neither shall they be divided into two kingdoms any more at all. (Ezek. 37:15–22)

Although this prophecy could not have been known to Lehi or Nephi, the Book of Mormon has Lehi presenting a parallel prophecy from Joseph of Egypt found in the brass plates:

M. Spencer, *For Zion: A Mormon Theology of Hope.*

[T]he fruit of thy loins shall write; and the fruit of the loins Judah shall write; and that which shall be written by the fruit of thy loins, and also that which shall be written by the fruit of the loins of Judah, shall grow together, unto the confounding of false doctrines and laying down of contentions, and establishing peace among the fruit of thy loins, and bringing them to the knowledge of their fathers in the latter days, and also to the knowledge of my covenants, saith the Lord. (2 Ne. 3:12)

Latter-day Saint interpreters have naturally seen the implicit connection between Ezekiel's prophecy and that spoken of by Lehi. Joseph Smith's revelation describing the golden plates as "the record of the stick of Ephraim" (D&C 27:5) makes the link explicit.[11] However, the Book of Mormon's own metaphor for the writings of Joseph and Judah, while paralleling Ezekiel's prophecy, also differs from it. Joseph's prophecy in 2 Nephi 3 does not speak of dead "sticks" to be moved about by human hands. For him the writings of Joseph and Judah are *live branches* that will organically "grow together" (2 Ne. 3:12; cf. 29:8, 13). In this way they resemble Lehi's nation itself. While it might be identified with Ezekiel's "stick of Ephraim" or "stick of Joseph," this nation grows into "a fruitful bough" like the one foreseen by the biblical Jacob (Gen. 49:22) and into "a righteous branch unto the house of Israel," as foretold by Joseph (2 Ne. 3:5). The destiny of that nation, as also foretold in the Book of Mormon, is to grow and intertwine with the other branches of Israel (2 Ne. 29:13–14; 3 Ne. 15:17–21; 16:3).

The Seven Tribes of Lehi

In his role as a new Moses, Lehi brought together and led members of the tribes of Ephraim and Manasseh to a Josephite promised land. That he named his two sons born during this time Jacob and Joseph may point to him looking back to these Patriarchs as he considered the implications of establishing a new nation in their own promised land. Thus, in his role as a Jacob to the new nation, he founded his own Josephite tribes by demarcating tribal divisions within his own nation, in much the same way Jacob had when he gave deathbed patriarchal blessings to his children and grandchildren.

In an 1828 revelation responding to the manuscript loss, the Lord promises that the record would still go to the descendants of the Lehites, dividing them up into seven distinct tribes: "the Nephites, and the Jacobites, and the Josephites, and the Zoramites," and also "the Lamanites, and the Lemuelites, and the Ishmaelites" (D&C 3:17–18).[12] Dictated soon after the manuscript's

---

11. The term "stick" in Joseph's revelation appears to refer to the *people* of Ephraim rather than to the book. The book is referred to as the *record of* the stick of Ephraim.

12. In the earliest surviving copy of this manuscript, this list was copied such that "Zoramites" and "Lemuelites" were each replaced with "Lamanites," rendering

loss, this revelation would almost certainly reflect the tribal divisions observed within it, and subsequent Book of Mormon texts seem to confirm this by enumerating the tribes in the same way and the same order (Jacob 1:13; 4 Ne. 1:36–37; Morm. 1:8).

The Lehite Tribes in the Lost Manuscript

In his own narration in the small plates, Nephi's younger brother Jacob reports Nephi commanding him to limit the subject matter about which he wrote:

> Nephi gave me, Jacob, a commandment concerning the small plates . . . ; that I should not touch, save it were lightly, concerning the history of this people. . . . For he said that the history of his people should be engraven upon his other plates. . . . And if there were preaching which was sacred, or revelation which was great, or prophesying, that I should engraven the heads of them upon these plates, and touch upon them as much as it were possible, for Christ's sake, and for the sake of our people. (Jacob 1:2–4)

In keeping with this injunction Jacob declares his intention to elide certain distinctions that might be important to a more detailed account of the Lehites' early history but are not important to his account focused on prophecy, testimony, and doctrine. He thus lumps the various Lehite tribes together into two national groupings or meta-tribes: the Nephites and the Lamanites—a precedent followed for the remainder of the small plates. However, Jacob is careful to indicate that this narratorial convention does *not* express the practices of those whose story he is narrating. The people who lived during this period were still "*called* Nephites, Jacobites, Josephites, Zoramites, Lamanites, Lemuelites, and Ishmaelites" (Jacob 1:13). "But," he explains, "*I, Jacob,* shall not hereafter distinguish them by these names, but I shall call them Lamanites that seek to destroy the people of Nephi, and those who are friendly to Nephi I shall call Nephites" (v. 14).

That Jacob needed to explain this aspect of his narration reveals that it could not be assumed to be a standard convention. The practice was presumably *not* followed in the contemporaneous history kept in the other plates— of which the lost manuscript was an abridgment. In such an account, which takes the perspective of the kings, issues of lineage and the shifting political alliances and conflicts between the individual tribes would have been more important than in Jacob's narrative (1 Ne. 6:1–3, 19:2).

---

a triple repetition of "Lamanites." The redactors who published this revelation in the *Book of Commandments* interpreted this as a mistaken attempt to render the list as given in the paragraph above, and I accept their emendation as reflecting the revelation's intent and original text. Compare "Revelation, July 1828 [D&C 3]," 2; and "Book of Commandments, 1833," 8 (2:6).

Later in the Book of Mormon, these tribal affiliations are mentioned only occasionally. Thus, any information we can uncover on the origin, meaning, and enduring significance of these tribal distinctions will give us a window onto this lost history. The natural beginning place for such inquiry would be Lehi's blessings on his posterity, by which he divided them into tribes.

Constructing the Seven-Branched Nation

According to John W. Welch, the roots of the Lehite tribal structure are in Lehi's deathbed blessings to his posterity:

> One of the most enduring legacies of Lehi's last will and testament appears to be the organization of his descendants into tribes. Just as the ancient patriarch Jacob left the House of Israel with a family structure composed of twelve tribes, Lehi addressed his posterity in seven groups. . . . Lehi spoke (1) to Zoram in 2 Nephi 1:30–32, (2) to Jacob in 2 Nephi 2, (3) to Joseph in 2 Nephi 3, (4) to the children of Laman in 2 Nephi 4:3–7, (5) to the children of Lemuel in 2 Nephi 4:8–9, (6) to the sons of Ishmael in 2 Nephi 4:10, and (7) to Sam together with Nephi in 2 Nephi 4:11. The seven groups recognizable here are exactly the same as the seven tribes mentioned three other times in the Book of Mormon, each time in the rigid order of "Nephites, Jacobites, Josephites, Zoramites, Lamanites, Lemuelites, and Ishmaelites" (Jacob 1:13; 4 Nephi 38; Mormon 1:8; see also D&C 3:17–18). . . . Even in the final days of the Nephite demise, Mormon still saw the general population divided along this precise seven-part line (Mormon 1:8). . . .
>
> I see Lehi here acting like Jacob of old. Both Jacob and Lehi pronounced their blessings to "all [their] household" who were gathered around them shortly before they died to organize a household of God in a new land of promise (2 Nephi 4:12; cf. Gen. 49).[13]

Curiously, the seven patrilineal tribes Lehi established do not correspond exactly to the nation's founding male figures. The Lehite nation had tribes named for Nephi, his wilderness-born younger brothers Jacob and Joseph, his difficult older brothers Laman and Lemuel, and even his erstwhile captive and later friend Zoram. However, there is no tribe named for Nephi's cooperative older brother Sam. Similarly, neither of Ishmael's sons had their own tribe and are instead grouped together under their father's name.

The small plates offer a reason for the unevenness of these tribal divisions. They were not made on an abstract principle but by the will of Lehi. In the house of Israel, as in that of Lehi, the tribes did not map one-to-one onto the founding patriarch's sons. Jacob/Israel adopted his grandsons through Joseph—Manasseh and Ephraim—as his own, making two tribes from his favored son (Gen. 48:5). Furthermore, the Levites, entrusted with priestly powers and responsibilities, were not given their own territory. Instead, they were

---

13. John W. Welch, "Lehi's Last Will and Testament: A Legal Approach," 68–69.

expected to leaven the whole Israelite lump by spreading out and performing their sacred functions for all the other tribes. They were thus not a politically and geographically distinct tribe but a priestly caste within the twelve tribes.

One effect of this gerrymandering of the tribal system is that it kept the number of tribes to the culturally meaningful number twelve that is the product of two other numbers sacred to the Hebrews: three and four.[14] Lehi's tinkering with the tribal boundaries within his group had a similar effect. By custom tailoring the boundaries of his family and using apparently arbitrary criteria to determine who got their own tribe and who did not, Lehi created the seven tribes that included Ishmael's now fatherless children and Zoram, who had married one of Ishmael's daughters and had proven his loyalty to Nephi (2 Ne. 1:30).

Seven, the most sacred number to the Hebrews, was also a combination of the sacred numbers three and four—in this case not their product, but their *sum*. That Lehi's nation of seven tribes was conceptualized as the sum of four tribes and three tribes is evident from how these tribes are listed in the Book of Mormon and Joseph Smith's revelations. As noted, the tribes are rigidly listed in the order of (1) Nephites, (2) Jacobites, (3) Josephites, (4) Zoramites, (5) Lamanites, (6) Lemuelites, and (7) Ishmaelites. This ordering flouts both age ordering and family in favor of political and religious alliances. The list first groups together the majority four tribes that followed Nephi and comprised the "Nephite" polity, beginning with Nephi's own eponymous tribe. It then groups together the minority three tribes that followed Laman and comprised the "Lamanite" polity, placing Laman's own tribe at the head of this group. With one exception, the tribal lists are arranged in two groupings separated by a break in the text, with the four tribes that followed Nephi comprising one group, and the three that followed Laman comprising the other. For example:

> And it came to pass in this year there began to be a war between the Nephites, who consisted of the Nephites and the Jacobites and the Josephites and the

---

14. Three and four both appear in the Hebrew Bible as symbols of completeness. Three corresponds to the three known regions of the universe (heaven, earth, water), is the number of primary Hebrew patriarchs (Abraham, Isaac, Jacob), etc. Four corresponds to the number compass points and thus the "corners" of the earth, and reflects the number of letters in the sacred name of God, the Tetragrammaton. Seven is the most sacred number in the Hebrew Bible, representing perfection. It is sacred because it is the sum of three and four, and because it corresponded to the seven planets and to the Sabbath as the seventh day. Twelve "derived its sacred character from the fact that it is the product of three and four and is the number of the months of the year." Caspar Levias, "Number and Numerals," 9:348–50.

Zoramites; *and this war was between the Nephites,* and the Lamanites and the Lemuelites and the Ishmaelites (Morm. 1:8; cf. 4 Ne. 1:36–38; D&C 3:17–18).[15]

In Hebraic culture and in myriad instances from Genesis to Revelation, the number seven symbolizes fullness, completeness, or perfection. Lehi grouped his people into two distinct sets of tribes—the Nephite set and the Lamanites—each of which might, and frequently did, fancy itself a full Israelite nation, with no need of the other. Their founding patriarch, Lehi, was wiser than his offspring; he had strategically divided them into a set of four tribes and a set of three tribes that could only be *complete* when joined together in their intended fullness as a nation of seven tribes.

---

15. The exception to the pattern of listing the four Nephite tribes separately from the three Lamanite tribes is found in Jacob 1:13, which lists the seven tribes in the same order but without distinct groupings: "Now the people which were not Lamanites were Nephites; nevertheless, they were called Nephites, Jacobites, Josephites, Zoramites, Lamanites, Lemuelites, and Ishmaelites."

CHAPTER 10

NEPHI'S CONQUEST

After the Israelite Exodus, the Hebrew Bible narrates the long, difficult, and often violent work of the Conquest that was initiated by Moses and directed by Joshua. The Conquest is presented as a process of first sending spies to scout out the promised land and then, jarringly, of clearing out those who already lived there to make geographical and cultural space for the nation of Israel. The biblical rationales for the Conquest are those of giving the Israelites land on which to live and of keeping them from religious and moral influences dissonant with their religion.

The Book of Mormon also narrates a drama of resettlement that entailed exploration of a new land, the opening of geographical space, and the struggle to maintain cultural and religious purity. The narrative of the Nephites' settlement of the promised land, particularly with the details that can be recovered about the lost pages, framed their inheritance of the land and their relationship to its previous inhabitants (the Jaredites) and other concurrent inhabitants (the Lamanites) as a second conquest. This Conquest framing, present beneath the surface of the extant text's narratives of Lehite exploration and of the Lamanite curse, is brought to the surface by recovering elements of the lost pages narrative using internal evidence and external sources.

The Biblical Conquest

As the Israelites approached Canaan, Moses sent Joshua and others "to spy out the land" (Num. 13:1–17). When they returned, the spies reported that the land flowed "with milk and honey" (v. 27) but was already inhabited by other peoples, including the Amalekites, the Canaanites, and, worst of all, the fearsome Rephaim and "sons of Anak" (vv. 28–29). The spies described this last group as "giants" that made the Israelites "in our own sight as grasshoppers" (v. 33). The Israelites, under Joshua, would eventually make room for themselves by killing and sweeping these inhabitants from the land. The Anakim and Rephaim were exterminated from all but a few strongholds: Ashdod, Gaza, and Gath—the birthplace of the most famous biblical giant, Goliath (Josh. 11:21–22; 1 Sam. 17:4). The Canaanites were more entrenched and became persistent enemies of the Israelites as they fought over the cherished territories. They were further looked down on by the Israelites as incorrigible idolaters and heirs to a curse that went back to when Noah cursed the descendants of Ham (beginning with Ham's son Canaan) to be servants of Ham's brother Shem, ancestor of the Israelites (Gen. 9:25–27).

The land claimed by Israel was also peopled by others who would long remain as thorns in their side, such as the Philistines, from whom Palestine would take its name (Josh. 13:3). The biblical books of Numbers and Joshua narrate the Israelites' extensive campaigns, led by Joshua, to clear the land of these competitors. Much of the Hebrew Bible dwells at length on these and other challenges of settling the Israelite Promised Land—dividing the land among the twelve tribes, governing the new nation, and preventing the contamination of Israelite religion by the surrounding cultures.

Lehi's Scouts

By contrast, the extant Book of Mormon says relatively little of the challenges Lehi's people confronted in establishing themselves in their new promised land. The small plates account describes their landing in the New World laconically: "after we had sailed for the space of many days we did arrive at the promised land; and we went forth upon the land, and we did pitch our tents; and we did call it the promised land" (1 Ne. 18:23). From there, they began to "till the earth," "plant seeds," and encounter various types of "beasts" and "all manner of ore" (vv. 24–25). These discoveries are mentioned matter-of-factly, as if the immigrants merely tripped over goat herds and gold mines. Only by close attention to the narrative's asides about these discoveries occurring "in the forests" and "as we journeyed in the wilderness" (v. 25) does one realize the discoveries were made during active scouting missions. Nephi's participation in these explorations is indicated by his use of the inclusive first-person plural "*we* journeyed" (v. 25).

Taking a less active role in the new land is Lehi. Despite all the pains he had taken in leading his family's exodus to the new promised land, Lehi does not get to enjoy the new home. Though allowed to enter his promised land, he is not permitted to tarry. A mere ten verses of narrative action in the small plates separate Lehi's landing in the New World from his deathbed sermons and blessings. Indeed, speaking from his deathbed is the first action attributed to Lehi after he arrived in his promised land (2 Ne. 1:1). Lehi thus fared slightly better than Moses, who, after leading the Israelites forty years in the wilderness, was not permitted to enter.

A hint that Nephi's initial settlement of the land of Nephi was viewed as a conquest on the biblical model is that Zeniff's attempted reiteration of his settlement of the land of Nephi four centuries later was done in conscious imitation of Nephi *and* was clearly modeled on the biblical Conquest. In their first attempt to retake the land, the settlers sent out spies and considered utterly annihilating the Lamanites—clear echoing Joshua's Conquest (Moses.

9:1). Yet, Zeniff, a participant in this conquest effort, takes on himself the role of a new Nephi by urging a more peaceful approach to the Lamanites and echoing Nephi in the opening words of his own record:

> I, Zeniff, having been taught in all the language of the Nephites, and having had a knowledge of the land of Nephi, or of the land of our fathers' first inheritance, and having been sent as a spy among the Lamanites . . . being over-zealous to inherit the land of our fathers, collected as many as were desirous to go up to possess the land, and started again on our journey. (Mosiah 9:1)

Zeniff seeing himself as undertaking a Conquest-like resettlement of the promised land in the spirit of Nephi suggests he understood Nephi's original settlement of the land as just such a conquest.

The Nephite-Lamanite Split

Before closing the book of his life, Lehi borrowed a final chapter from the biblical Jacob. Lehi, as we have seen, blessed his children and grandchildren, dividing them into seven tribes and warning of the perpetual conflict that could break out between the nation of Nephi, who was chosen to rule, and the descendants of Laman and Lemuel, who would bring upon themselves a curse if they rebelled against their brother. However, despite Lehi's view of the tribes that sprang from him as one Israelite nation, the idea that the Lamanite tribes were cursed made them parallel, in the Nephite mind, to the Israelites' enemies in the wars of the Conquest—particularly the Canaanites who they understood as having a similar curse to that which divided their sibling ancestors.

"Cut Off from the Presence of the Lord"

Despite Lehi's warning, Laman, Lemuel, and the sons of Ishmael do, in fact, rebel against Nephi by refusing to follow his religious and political lead and even plotting his murder:

> Yea, they did murmur against me, saying: Our younger brother thinks to rule over us; and we have had much trial because of him; wherefore, now let us slay him, that we may not be afflicted more because of his words. For behold, we will not have him to be our ruler; for it belongs unto us, who are the elder brethren, to rule over this people. (2 Ne. 5:3)

Just as his father, Nephi was warned by God to "flee into the wilderness" (2 Ne. 5:5; cf. 1 Ne. 5:8). Thus, walking in his father's footsteps, Nephi led those who would follow him on an exodus from the land he shared with his brothers to a land where his people would be separated from the Lamanites, taking with him the sword of Laban, brass plates, and Liahona. There, they would establish a new nation in what they would call the land of Nephi, with Nephi serving as their first king. Angry at Nephi for taking what they believed to be theirs as Lehi's eldest sons, Nephi's brothers and their descendants would ever after dispute his possession of the throne, the regalia, and the land.

According to Nephi, after his departure, Laman, Lemuel, and their followers were cursed for rebelling against him and enacting their fratricidal plot:

> I had been their ruler and their teacher . . . until the time they sought to take away my life. *Wherefore*, the word of the Lord was fulfilled which he spake unto me, saying that: Inasmuch as they will not hearken unto thy words they shall be cut off from the presence of the Lord. . . . And he had caused the cursing to come upon them, yea, even a sore cursing, because of their iniquity. (2 Ne. 5:19–21).

Laman and Lemuel rejected Nephi and forced him to flee. The implication may be that their curse was largely self-inflicted by depriving themselves and their families of God's word in the brass plates and through Nephi, and depriving themselves of God's physical presence embodied in the sacred relics Nephi took and in the temple he built. In this case, their being cut off would not be the result of supernatural intervention but a more direct consequence of their actions.[1]

Nephi attributed to the curse several secondary effects on the Lamanites: "because of their cursing which was upon them they did become an idle people, full of mischief and subtlety, and did seek in the wilderness for beasts of prey" (2 Ne. 5:21–24). To keep his own people from this curse, Nephi prophetically prohibits the Nephites from marrying Lamanites, claiming that the Lamanites were marked with "a skin of blackness" to discourage such intermarriage (vv. 21–23).

However, despite their genetic and geographical isolation, the Lamanites were to fulfill an important function in the Nephites' covenant. If Nephi's people failed to keep God's commandments—a condition for their prospering in their land of promise—then:

> [The Lamanites] shall be a scourge unto [Nephi's] seed, to stir them up in remembrance of me; and inasmuch as they will not remember me, and hearken unto my words, they shall scourge them even unto destruction. (2 Ne. 5:25)

This threat and promise would shape much of the rest of Nephite history.

---

1. The understanding of this consequence of Laman and Lemuel's plot as a "curse" almost certainly has some roots in the biblical narrative of Cain. In Genesis, Cain's killing of his brother Abel leads to his being cursed. In consequence of this, he would be hid from God's face and socially shunned, he would wander as a fugitive and a vagabond, and the land would not yield its strength to him (Gen. 4:11–14). Nephi and his successors viewed Laman and Lemuel as following in Cain's footsteps, committing the sin of fratricide—at least in their hearts—and thus taking on a similar divine curse. The consequences they report as part of this curse evoke those of Cain's curse: the Lamanites are described as having been cut off from God's presence, isolated from the Nephites, and fated to "wander about in the wilderness" and live off the capture of "beasts of prey" rather than off the strength of the land (2 Ne. 5:20–24; Enos 1:20).

Previous Inhabitants of the Promised Land

The division of Lehi's house into warring factions is a crucial element of the Lehite settlement and conquest of the new promised land, but other important events of this settlement and conquest occurred before the split and even before Lehi's death. While information about the early stages of Lehite settlement is scarce in the small plates, it was more abundant in the lost manuscript. The omitted narrative of settlement and conquest belongs to the Nephites' political history, a subject skimped on in the small plates but reported by Nephi to be detailed explicitly in the lost manuscript's source, Nephi's large plates (2 Ne. 5:29–33).

Fortunately, some of the lost fragments of the Book of Mormon peoples' settlement narrative survive in information passed on by familiar sources—Joseph Smith Sr. and Martin Harris.

Lehite Spies and Jaredite Giants

The first of these narratives is about the scouts or spies Lehi sent out to the promised land and what they found. In his report of what the elder Smith told him, Fayette Lapham writes:

> After sailing a long time, they came to land, went on shore, and thence they traveled through boundless forests. . . . When they . . . first beheld this country, they sent out spies to see what manner of country it was, who reported that the country appeared to have been settled by a very large race of men, and had been, to all appearances, a very rich agricultural and manufacturing nation.[2]

This description dovetails with Nephi's extant small plates description of discoveries he and his brothers made "in the forests" and "as we journeyed in the wilderness" (1 Ne. 18:25). However, Lapham's account fills voids in the published text, making it explicit that when Lehi's colony arrived in their new land and encountered its forests, they recapitulated the pattern of the Exodus and the Conquest by sending spies to scout out the land and look for other inhabitants. Like the spies sent by Moses into Canaan, Lehi's advance scouts encountered prior inhabitants of formidable size—but with a crucial difference. These people, next to whom the Lehites might have felt like grasshoppers, would offer no resistance. There was no need to clear the land of them to make room—they had already done it themselves. While the land's "very large" inhabitants "*had* been" a great nation, they were now gone. Lehi's spies found only their remains.

---

2. Fayette Lapham, "Interview with the Father of Joseph Smith, the Mormon Prophet, Forty Years Ago. His Account of the Finding of the Sacred Plates," in Vogel, *EMD*, 1:465–66.

That the extinct Jaredites seemed very large or even giant to the Lehites is indicated in the published Book of Mormon, where the Book of Ether's narrator, Moroni, describes the Jaredites as "large and mighty" from their founding prophet, the brother of Jared (Ether 1:34), down to the last survivors of their civilization (15:26). Additionally, the breastplates the Jaredites left behind after their civil war were notably "large" to the Nephites (Mosiah 8:10).

Lucy Mack Smith similarly characterized the breastplate her son Joseph found with the brother of Jared's interpreters as extending "from the neck downwards as far as the center of the stomach of a man of extraordinary size."[3] The interpreters or "spectacles" themselves were reportedly described by Martin Harris as "enormous,"[4] by Joseph Smith's father as "a pair of spectacles, about one and a half inches longer than those used at the present day,"[5] by his brother William as "too wide for his [Joseph's] eyes" and designed to be "used by much larger men,"[6] and by David Whitmer as constructed with a bridge between the lenses that was "longer apart . . . than we usually find in spectacles."[7]

These various indications of the Jaredites' unusual size were not lost on early Latter-day Saints. In 1832 the Church periodical *The Evening and the Morning Star* editorialized on the Jaredites, curiously characterizing them with the exact phrase used by Lapham—"a very large race of men." The editorial further linked the Jaredites with occasional sensational findings of what appeared to be oversized human bones: "[A]s they were a very large race of men, whenever we hear that uncommon large bones have been dug up from the earth, we may conclude, That was the skeleton of a Jaredite."[8]

Encountering the remains of people who appeared to be much larger than themselves, Lehi's spies, like the spies sent to Canaan by Moses, returned with the report of giants. The very large Jaredites therefore took a role in the Nephite conquest of other inhabitants who had to be cleared from the land, echoing the biblical giants in the Israelites' Promised Land at the time of their Conquest.

Covenant Curses and the Destruction of Giants

In this narrative of the Lehites succeeding the Jaredites as possessors of the promised land, we get our first glimpse of a theme that will characterize

---

3. Lavina Fielding Anderson, ed., *Lucy's Book: A Critical Edition of Lucy Mack Smith's Family Memoir*, 389–90.

4. Charles Anthon to E. D. Howe, February 17, 1834.

5. Lapham, "Interview," in Vogel, *EMD*, 1:462.

6. William Smith interview with J. W. Peterson and W. S. Pender, July 1891 in J. W. Peterson, "The Urim and Thummim," 7.

7. David Whitmer, interview, April 1878, in P. Wilhelm Poulson, "Correspondence. Interview with David Whitmer," 2.

8. W. W. Phelps, "The Book of Ether," 22.

the Book of Mormon narrative of Conquest: that of covenant blessings and curses. The peoples led by Lehi and Nephi did not need to vie with the Jaredite giants for their promised land because the Jaredites had already been removed by their own violence, in consequence of breaking their national covenant with God. This land of promise had been covenanted to the Jaredites for their inheritance, but as part of this covenant and his larger covenant on or with the land, the Lord had

> sworn . . . that whoso should possess this land of promise, from that time hence-forth and forever, should serve him, the true and only God, or they should be swept off when the fulness of his wrath should come upon them. (Ether 2:7–8)

In narrating the story of the brother of Jared, Moroni expounds on God's commandments to whoever would inhabit the land:

> [I]t is a land of promise; and whatsoever nation shall possess it shall serve God, or they shall be swept off when the fulness of his wrath shall come upon them. And the fulness of his wrath cometh upon them when they are ripened in iniq-uity. For behold, this is a land which is choice above all other lands; wherefore he that doth possess it shall serve God or shall be swept off; for it is the everlasting decree of God. And it is not until the fulness of iniquity among the children of the land, that they are swept off. (Ether 2:9–10)

God similarly tells the brother of Jared: "[R]emember that my Spirit will not always strive with man; wherefore, if ye will sin until ye are fully ripe ye shall be cut off from the presence of the Lord" (Ether 2:15; cf. Gen 6:3).

The rationale here for why the Jaredites were swept from the land and Lehi and Nephi's people were brought to it is the same rationale Nephi gives for the destruction of the Israelites' adversaries:

> And after [the Israelites] had crossed the river Jordan he did make them mighty unto the driving out of the children of the land, yea, unto the scattering them to destruction. And now, do ye suppose that the children of this land, who were in the land of promise, who were driven out by our fathers, do ye suppose that they were righteous? Behold, I say unto you, Nay. . . . [T]his people had rejected every word of God, and they were ripe in iniquity; and the fulness of the wrath of God was upon them; and the Lord did curse the land against them, and bless it unto our fathers; yea, he did curse it against them unto their destruction, and he did bless it unto our fathers unto their obtaining power over it. . . . And he leadeth away the righteous into precious lands, and the wicked he destroyeth, and curseth the land unto them for their sakes. (1 Ne. 17:32–38)

Here, Nephi employs the same ideas as Moroni and even uses some of the same phrasing, speaking of "the children of the land" becoming "ripe in iniquity" and thereby provoking "the fullness of the wrath of God" (or "the fullness of his wrath") and causing their destruction.[9]

Furthermore, the Book of Ether is explicit about the self-inflicted curse that caused the Jaredites' destruction. Their prophets warned them repeatedly of their possible fate:

> [T]hey had testified that a great curse should come upon the land, and also upon the people, and that there should be a great destruction among them, such an one as never had been upon the face of the earth, and their bones should become as heaps of earth upon the face of the land except they should repent of their wickedness. (Ether 11:6)

The Jaredites were also warned that if they brought on covenant curses to the point of their own destruction, "the Lord God would send or bring forth another people to possess the land" (11:21) and this new chosen people would then "receive the land for their inheritance" (13:21).

The Sword of Joshua

While it was Lehi who led his people to the promised land, it was Nephi who assisted him as a man of action. Once in the promised land, Lehi's role as shepherd of the exodus ended and Nephi culminated the work of relocation by overseeing settlement. As a spy and the designated leader of the group under Lehi, Nephi's efforts paralleled those of Joshua, the most prominent of the spies Moses sent into Canaan who later became Moses's second in command.

This Nephi-Joshua parallel bears fuller exploration. Joshua was one of the leading figures in the Conquest from the initial scouting mission through the Israelites' successful rout of the giants and Canaanites. Under Moses's prophetic direction, he served as Israel's military commander and was second only to Moses in political authority during the former's lifetime. Since Moses had been forbidden by God to enter the Promised Land, it was Joshua who succeeded him and oversaw the Israelites' wars of conquest and eventual settlement of the land.

Throughout these war narratives, Joshua's sword is featured prominently as the Hebrew Bible again and again declares what Joshua accomplished "with the edge of the sword." By the sword's edge, he "discomfited Amalek" (Ex. 17:13), and he "utterly destroyed Makkedah "and all the souls therein; he let none remain" (Josh. 10:28), as also Libnah (v. 30), Lachish (v. 32), Eglon (v. 35), Hebron (v. 37), and Debir (v. 39). By his sword and those of the hosts under his command he also "smote" Hazor, "utterly destroying" it

---

9. Heightening the connection, these two passages—1 Nephi 17:3 and Ether 2:10—are the only two in the Latter-day Saint canon that use the phrase "the children of the land."

so "there was not any left to breathe . . . as Moses the servant of the LORD commanded" (11:10–12). Joshua's sword was thus both the Conquest's literal leading edge and one of its chief symbols.

The Sword of Laban as the Sword of the Conquest

It is thus significant that Francis Gladden Bishop, while in Martin Harris's confidence, identified Nephi's sword as not only the sword of Joseph, forged in Egypt, but also as the sword of Joshua, by which he led the work of the Conquest. As we saw in Chapter 7, Bishop offered the following ancient provenance of the sword of Laban:

> The history of this sword is as follows: It was caused to be made by Joseph, of old, in Egypt, by the direction of God, and *was in the hand of Joshua when he led the house of Israel into the land of Canaan.* And after him it came down in the lineage of Joseph to Laban.[10]

This identification of Nephi's sword as the sword of Joshua befits Nephi's crucial role echoing that of Joshua over his people's settlement of their new promised land

Wielding a sword that was simultaneously that of Joseph, Joshua, and Laban was ideal for establishing Nephi as heir of Joseph, possessor of the new promised land, and rightful king over the land's seven tribes. The provenance narrative that Nephi's sword was forged by Joseph and handed down through Joshua to Laban implies that Joshua, and therefore Laban, should be understood as inheritors of Jacob's birthright, passed down through Jacob's birthright son Joseph and *his* birthright son Ephraim. In inheriting through divinely authorized expropriation the sword that had been passed down as *part* of the birthright of Joseph (and thus of Jacob as well), Nephi could claim the privileges of that birthright. Joseph Smith, similarly, would have been the inheritor of that birthright as he inherited the sword, plates, and other relics from the fallen Nephites.

But from whence did Bishop derive the identification of Nephi's sword with Joshua's? We have seen that Bishop was in Martin Harris's confidence regarding the lost manuscript. If Martin informed Bishop that Laban's sword had been forged at the behest of Joseph of Egypt, it seems likely that Bishop is also correct in conveying information from Martin that the sword had descended from Joseph to Joshua.[11]

---

10. Gladden Bishop, *A Proclamation from the Lord to His People, Scattered Throughout All the Earth*, 1–2; emphasis added.

11. While what is important here is that the Nephites *understood* Laban's sword to descend from Joseph, not that the sword literally did so, it is not unheard of for ancient swords to have been preserved intact across millennia. The Frankish sword

Joseph's Anticipation of the Exodus and Conquest

Further supporting Bishop's account, Joshua's reported inheritance of a sword forged by Joseph in Egypt also coheres with the narratives given about each of these men in the Latter-day Saint canon. The biblical text itself offers a plausible context for the narrative of Joshua inheriting Joseph's sword, since it identifies Joshua as Joseph's descendant through his birthright son Ephraim (Num. 13:8, 16). Furthermore, other elements of the biblical Joseph narrative—particularly as extended in the brass plates account of Joseph in the Book of Mormon—give the Josephite provenance for Joshua's sword more than plausibility by providing it with a compelling narrative logic.

According to this narrative, Joseph forged the sword by which his descendant Joshua would lead the Conquest because Joseph *foresaw* the Exodus, the Conquest, and Joshua's leading role in both. In the Hebrew Bible, Joseph foresees and prophesies the Exodus and Conquest and makes preparations for them, and Moses and Joshua follow up on Joseph's intentions for these events. The Book of Mormon enhances this narrative by presenting expanded brass plates prophecies of Joseph in which he also foreknows major figures of the Exodus and Conquest and receives promises from God about these events. Finally, in Joseph Smith's prophetic expansion of Genesis, Joseph of Egypt further prophesies additional figures of the Exodus-Conquest cycle, identifies one of the sacred relics to be used by Moses during the Exodus, predicts Lehi's exodus, and reinforces preparations for his own remains to be carried to the promised land by Moses and buried there by Joshua.

Collectively, these texts portray the Egyptian Joseph as aware of the persons and even objects to be used in his people's return to the Promised Land, the Exodus-Conquest, and of the Lehites who would maintain his lineage. It is in this light that Joseph's reported creation of Joshua's sword of Conquest is to be understood.

Joseph's Anticipation in the Bible

In the Genesis narrative, Joseph is a diviner and dreamer who predicts that God would lead the Israelites out of Egypt and back to their own land, and he thus puts his family members under oath to "carry up my bones" with them when they go (Gen. 50:25; Ex. 13:19). Furthermore, the Hebrew Bible gives this prediction and oath surprising prominence. The coffin in which Joseph's remains are placed is implicitly juxtaposed in the Exodus narrative with the Ark of the Covenant. According to Jerome Segal, "in the Bible, the

---

of Joyeuse, the Japanese seven-branched sword, the Chinese Goujian, and scores of Viking Ulfberht swords have lasted longer than the time that would have elapsed between Joseph and Nephi, given the biblical and Book of Mormon chronologies.

same Hebrew word, *aron*, is used to refer both to Joseph's coffin and the Ark of the Covenant." He then observes, "From the texts about Joseph's bones, we can infer that alongside the Ark carried by the Israelites, there was a second similar structure carried: the sarcophagus of Joseph, a second Ark."[12] Thus, Segal notes,

> There is not just one Ark carried by the Israelites, there are two, one created according to God's instructions, symbolizing his presence and carrying his words, his law for how mankind should live, and the other carrying Joseph himself, a figure of mercy.[13]

Bringing the narratives of Joseph and Joshua further together, Joseph's oath and its ultimate fulfillment are positioned, respectively, at the conclusion of two major books—Genesis and Joshua:

> And Joseph said unto his brethren, I die: and God will surely visit you, and bring you out of this land unto the land which he sware to Abraham, to Isaac, and to Jacob. And Joseph took an oath of the children of Israel, saying, *God will surely visit you, and ye shall carry up my bones from hence.* So Joseph died, *being an hundred and ten years old*: and they embalmed him, and he was put in a coffin in Egypt. (Gen. 50:24–26)

> So Joshua made a covenant with the people that day, and set them a statute and an ordinance in Shechem.
>
> And Joshua wrote these words in the book of the law of God, and took a great stone, and set it up there under an oak, that was by the sanctuary of the Lord. And Joshua said unto all the people, Behold, this stone shall be a witness unto us; for it hath heard all the words of the Lord which he spake unto us: it shall be therefore a witness unto you, lest ye deny your God. . . .
>
> And it came to pass after these things, that Joshua the son of Nun, the servant of the Lord, died, *being an hundred and ten years old*. . . .
>
> *And the bones of Joseph, which the children of Israel brought up out of Egypt, buried they in Shechem, in a parcel of ground which Jacob bought* . . . and it became the inheritance of the children of Joseph. (Josh. 24:25–32)

This intriguing story of a promise made at the end of Genesis and fulfilled, four centuries later, at the end of Joshua, invites analysis and reflection. According Segal,

> [E]ndings are critical to any story, and in making Joseph's bones the common subject matter of both the ending of Genesis and the ending of Joshua, the Bible appears to be signaling the reader to pay attention to a story of a significance, one that opens with a promise about Joseph's bones and ends with the fulfillment of that promise. The tale that proceeds immediately after Joseph's death

---

12. Jerome M. Segal, *Joseph's Bones: Understanding the Struggle between God and Mankind in the Bible*, 9, 28.

13. Segal, 9.

and through the next several books of the Bible runs from the birth of Moses, through the forty years the Israelites wander in the desert, plus the period of the conquest of Canaan. In setting this story between these two references to Joseph's bones, the Bible hints that in some way Joseph and the fate of his bones are central to the meaning of this larger narrative of God and the Israelites.[14]

At minimum, the placement of this oath at the end of Genesis and its fulfillment at the end of Joshua serves the following functions: First, as Segal notes, it establishes the story of Joseph's oath as a context in which the narrative of Israel's relocation to Canaan is intended to be read. The Exodus-Conquest narrative that comprises the biblical books from Exodus through Joshua is carefully bookended with the stories of Joseph administering the oath about his burial and his people's fulfillment of that oath. The narratives of Joseph's oath thus, by authorial design, *frame* the narrative of the Exodus and Conquest, creating an inclusio.

Second, the placement of this oath and its fulfillment at the respective ends of the books of Genesis and Joshua highlights the parallels and connections between Joseph and Joshua. At the end of Genesis, Joseph, having settled the Israelites in Egypt, puts them under covenant about their return to the Promised Land. He then dies at the age of 110. Likewise, at the end of the book named after Joseph's descendant, Joshua, having settled the Israelites in the Promised Land, put them under covenant about their life in that land. He too then dies at the age of 110. The parallel placement of events involving Joseph's bones at the conclusions of Genesis and Joshua calls attention to the parallel covenants Joseph and Joshua administered in connection with those events. Occurring at opposite bookends of the Exodus-Conquest cycle and at the literal book-ends, or conclusions, of Genesis and Joshua, these covenants stand in literary juxtaposition: the Israelites' covenant to Joseph to carry his bones to the Promised Land is put into a narrative relationship with the Israelites' covenant under Joshua to serve the Lord in the Promised Land. Joseph's covenant had looked forward to the Israelites' return to their promised land. That accomplished, Joshua's covenant now laid out the terms they must fulfill in order to remain on the land and prosper in it.

Third, the parallel placement of these narratives makes Joshua's Conquest a continuation of Joseph's saga. Only when Joshua's work is done can the covenant that Joseph exacted of the Israelites on his deathbed be finally fulfilled. It was Joseph who had led the Israelites into Egypt, as an act of temporal deliverance, and, though he was dead, his story was not complete until

14. Segal, 3.

Joshua, as his heir and proxy, led the Israelites and his remains back into their covenant land of Canaan, a second act of temporal deliverance.[15]

In sum, the Hebrew Bible connects the story of Joseph's mortal remains with the story of Israel's return to and resettlement of Canaan. Joseph, in the biblical narrative, anticipates the Exodus and the Conquest. Joseph's descendant Joshua is in several ways a parallel figure, and his work of conquest and settlement is a continuation of the story of Joseph and his mortal remains. Joseph does not rest in peace until Joshua rests in peace after successfully concluding the Conquest, intimately tying together Joseph's vision for the fate of his bones and the work of Joshua's sword.

Joseph's Anticipation in the Brass Plates

The Book of Mormon and Joseph Smith's prophetic revision of Genesis greatly expand the narrative of Joseph's covenant, deathbed prophecies, and post-mortem legacy by enlarging the story of Joseph's death and providing an epilogue to the burial of his bones. While nearing his own death in his own promised land, Lehi tells his son Joseph about prophecies made by his son's namesake that he had discovered in the brass plates:

> For behold, thou art the fruit of my loins; and I am a descendant of Joseph who was carried captive into Egypt. And great were the covenants of the Lord which he made unto Joseph. . . .
>
> Yea, thus prophesied Joseph: I am sure of this thing, even as I am sure of the promise of Moses; for the Lord hath said unto me, I will preserve thy seed forever. And the Lord hath said: I will raise up a Moses; and I will give power unto him in a rod; and I will give judgment unto him in writing. Yet I will not loose his tongue, that he shall speak much, for I will not make him mighty in speaking. But I will write unto him my law, by the finger of mine own hand; and I will make a spokesman for him. (2 Ne. 3:4, 16–17)

The theme of covenant, prominent in the Joseph story at the end of Genesis, is further elaborated here. In the Genesis account Joseph bound his family to return his bones to the Promised Land because of his certainty that God would lead them back to that land. In the brass plates, Joseph's certainty is given a divine grounding: he put *the Israelites* under covenant to take him back to the Promised Land because *he* had received a covenant that God would lead them back to that land. "Great were the covenants of the Lord which he made unto Joseph," says Lehi. And among the covenant promises Joseph received was "the promise of Moses" and the Exodus. (2 Ne. 3:4, 16).

---

15. It will be recalled that although Moses led the Israelites in their wandering through the wilderness he was not allowed to enter the Promised Land. Instead, it was Joshua who led them into the land.

Joseph's Anticipation in Joseph Smith's Translation of the Bible

Joseph Smith's prophetic expansion of the Bible places Joseph's detailed prophecies of the Exodus firmly in the context of the deathbed scene in Genesis 50. Here Joseph prophesies of Israel's deliverance from bondage through Moses immediately after he acknowledges his imminent death. From his familiar "I die," Joseph's words in the expanded text continue:

> . . . and go unto my fathers; and I go down to my grave with joy. The God of my father Jacob be with you, to deliver you out of affliction in the days of your bondage; for the Lord hath visited me, and I have obtained a promise of the Lord, that out of the fruit of my loins, the Lord God will raise up a righteous branch out of my loins; and unto thee, whom my father Jacob hath named Israel, a prophet. . . . And this prophet shall deliver my people out of Egypt in the days of thy bondage. (JST Gen. 50:24)

Joseph Smith's revised Genesis also adds greater detail to the biblical Joseph's prophecies of the Exodus and strengthens the link between the Lord's covenants with Joseph and the covenant Joseph exacts from his family:

> And the Lord sware unto Joseph that he would preserve his seed forever, saying, I will raise up Moses, and a rod shall be in his hand, and he shall gather together my people, and he shall lead them as a flock, and he shall smite the waters of the Red Sea with his rod. . . . And I will make a spokesman for him, and his name shall be called Aaron. And it shall be done unto thee in the last days also, even as I have sworn. *Therefore*, Joseph said unto his brethren, God will surely visit you, and bring you out of this land, unto the land which he sware unto Abraham, and unto Isaac, and to Jacob. And Joseph . . . took an oath of the children of Israel, saying unto them, God will surely visit you, and ye shall carry up my bones from hence. (JST Gen. 50:34–37)

The oath God swore to Joseph became the basis on which Joseph asked his family to swear an oath to him. Joseph's confidence in the future thus rested on covenants made to him by both God and his people.

The Hebrew Bible, we have seen, takes some pains to emphasize that the Israelites fulfilled the covenant they had made with Joseph. In Joseph Smith's prophetic expansion of Genesis, this theme is stressed still more, explaining that the Israelites never buried Joseph's body but kept it ready to be carried to the Promised Land:

> So Joseph died when he was an hundred and ten years old; and they embalmed him, and they put him in a coffin in Egypt; and he was kept from burial by the children of Israel, that he might be carried up and laid in the sepulchre with his father. And thus they remembered the oath which they sware unto him. (JST Gen. 50:38)

Extending themes present in the Hebrew Bible, Latter-day Saint scriptures emphasize the fulfillment of the deathbed covenant between Joseph and the Israelites, and they show Joseph anticipating explicitly and in detail the Exodus and the Conquest, the events by which God would fulfill his covenant to Joseph that the Israelites would again live in their promised land.

Joseph Foresees Joshua

While sharing the prophesies of Joseph contained in the brass plates with his son Joseph, Lehi begins by telling his son that "great were the covenants of the Lord which he made unto Joseph [of Egypt]" and describes Joseph as a "seer" who could foresee his descendants thousands of years in the future—namely, Lehi, Nephi, Nephi's brother Joseph, and even the latter-day Joseph Smith and his scribe Oliver Cowdery (2 Ne. 3:4–21). If Joseph, as described by Lehi, foresaw the activities of his millennia-distant descendants and the roles his brother Levi's descendants would play in retaking the Israelites' Promised Land, there is no obvious reason why his detailed knowledge of the Israel's return to Canaan and of his future descendants would omit the central role his own descendant Joshua would play in the Conquest and in returning his remains to his homeland. A seer who could foresee that Moses would use a rod in leading the Exodus would also be able to see that his own descendant would complete Moses's work with a sword—and forge him one for that very purpose.

When writing about what his father had discovered in the brass plates, Nephi places the most emphasis on Joseph's time in Egypt and his descendants later Exodus out of Egypt:

> And after they had given thanks unto the God of Israel, my father, Lehi, took the records which were engraven upon the plates of brass, and he did search them from the beginning. And he beheld that they did contain the five books of Moses, which gave an account of the creation of the world, and also of Adam and Eve, who were our first parents; And also a record of the Jews from the beginning, even down to the commencement of the reign of Zedekiah, king of Judah; And also the prophecies of the holy prophets, from the beginning, even down to the commencement of the reign of Zedekiah; and also many prophecies which have been spoken by the mouth of Jeremiah.
>
> And it came to pass that my father, Lehi, also found upon the plates of brass a genealogy of his fathers; *wherefore he knew that he was a descendant of Joseph; yea, even that Joseph who was the son of Jacob, who was sold into Egypt, and who was preserved by the hand of the Lord, that he might preserve his father, Jacob, and all his household from perishing with famine. And they were also led out of captivity and out of the land of Egypt, by that same God who had preserved them.*
>
> And thus my father, Lehi, did discover the genealogy of his fathers. *And Laban also was a descendant of Joseph, wherefore he and his fathers had kept the records.* (1 Ne. 5:10–16)

Just as the Book of Mormon reports that Joseph received many covenant promises from God regarding his seed without enumerating those promises, Joseph Smith's expanded Genesis indicates that the patriarch knew much more about the events he prophesied than is recorded there or in the Book of Mormon. When Joseph told his family about how God would bring their descendants back to "the land which he sware unto Abraham, and unto Isaac, and to Jacob," he also "confirmed many other things unto" them that are not detailed in that account (JST Gen.50:37).

Using the account of Joseph of Egypt in the published Book of Mormon and Francis Gladden Bishop's synergistic account, we can posit the likelihood that the lost manuscript recounted one such detail not included in the scriptural canon—a story explaining the origin of Laban's sword. In this story, Joseph, foreseeing the Conquest and Joshua's role in it, instructed that a sword be forged for Joshua, with which he would lead the Israelites into battle. On this narrative, Joseph's coffin and the bones it bore were not to be his only material legacy. With Joseph's coffin/ark on the Exodus and into the Promised Land would go both the brass plates on which he inscribed his own covenant and prophecies and the sword of conquest he had forged for Joshua. The sword's journey, however, would not end there—and perhaps neither would the purposes for which Joseph had forged it. Joseph had not only foreseen the biblical Exodus to the Promised Land, he also, according to Lehi, foresaw the exodus of his Lehite descendants to the new promised land and received divine covenants about these descendants (2 Ne. 3:4–5)—making Joseph's descendants' exodus to the Americas a central part of his even larger story.

So Joseph, foreseeing among his descendants Nephi—a *new* Joseph and the Joshua of a new conquest, might well have forged his sword not only for Joshua but also for Nephi.

The Lamanites as Canaanites

As Joshua to Lehi's Moses, and heir to Joshua's sword, Nephi stepped into Joshua's shoes as conqueror of giants and Canaanites. Stepping, less enviably, into the shoes of the peoples whose land Joshua had conquered were the Jaredites and the Lamanites.

Although the Jaredites did not require any conquering, their description by Fayette Lapham and others as a very large race discovered by Lehi's spies parallels them with the biblical giants discovered by Joshua and his fellow spies in the land of Canaan. For the Nephites, the role of the Canaanites against whom Joshua had taken up the sword of conquest was filled by the Lamanites, against whom Nephi took up the sword of Laban (Jacob 1:10)— and therefore, reportedly, the sword of Joshua. This Nephite identification of the Lamanites with the Canaanites is admittedly ironic and theologically

problematic, since the Book of Mormon identifies the Lamanites as genealogical Israelites, and Lehi, in constructing a seven-branched Israelite nation,
made the Lamanites an integral part of it. Despite the paradox, the Nephites
framed the Lamanites as analogous to the biblical Canaanites while framing
themselves, in contrast, as analogous to the biblical Israelites.

It is under this framing of the Lamanites as Canaanites that much of what
the Nephite narrators in the Book of Mormon say on race and the Lamanite
curse can be understood. Signs of this framing occur in (1) the Lamanites'
role as "scourge," (2) the characterization of Lamanites as idolatrous, (3) the
part assigned the Lamanites in the Nephite re-conquest of the land of Nephi,
(4) the name the Nephites gave to one of their most significant places, the
river Sidon, and (5) their description of the Lamanite curse.

Lamanites as the Nephites' Scourge

A first indication that the Lamanites were analogized to Canaanites in
the Nephite cultural narrative is the role they are assigned as the Nephites'
"scourge." In the biblical narrative, the role of scourge to the chosen nation
was assigned to the indigenous Canaanites. Warning his people away from
mixing with the Canaanites and thereby taking on their idolatry, Joshua
declared:

> Know for a certainty that the Lord your God will no more drive out any of these
> nations from before you; but they shall be snares and traps unto you, *and scourges*
> *in your sides*, and thorns in your eyes, until ye perish from off this good land
> which the Lord your God hath given you. (Josh. 23:13)

Although the Nephites were the bearers of the Israelite faith and of the
divine promises of God's covenant with Nephi, these privileges came at a cost:
disobedience could mean destruction. This promise was given to Nephi in
one of his early revelatory experiences. After telling his brothers of the divine
confirmation of what his father had told him, Nephi writes:

> And it came to pass that the Lord spake unto me, saying: Blessed art thou,
> Nephi, because of thy faith, for thou hast sought me diligently, with lowliness of
> heart. And inasmuch as ye shall keep my commandments, ye shall prosper, and
> shall be led to a land of promise; yea, even a land which I have prepared for you;
> yea, a land which is choice above all other lands. *And inasmuch as thy brethren*
> *shall rebel against thee, they shall be cut off from the presence of the Lord.* And inas-
> much as thou shalt keep my commandments, thou shalt be made a ruler and a
> teacher over thy brethren.
>
> For behold, in that day that they shall rebel against me, I will curse them
> even with a sore curse, and they shall have no power over thy seed except they
> shall rebel against me also. And if it so be that they rebel against me, *they shall be a*
> *scourge unto thy seed*, to stir them up in the ways of remembrance. (1 Ne. 2:19–34)

Years later, after fleeing from his threatening brothers, Nephi again points out how although the Lamanites were cursed by being shut out from God's presence, they would play a divinely assigned role of a scourge in enacting the covenant curse of destruction on the Nephites:

> Wherefore, the word of the Lord was fulfilled which he spake unto me, saying that: *Inasmuch as they will not hearken unto thy words they shall be cut off from the presence of the Lord. And behold, they were cut off from his presence.* . . .
>
> And thus saith the Lord God: . . . cursed shall be the seed of him that mixeth with their seed; for they shall be cursed even with the same cursing. And the Lord spake it, and it was done. . . .
>
> And the Lord God said unto me: *They shall be a scourge unto thy seed*, to stir them up in remembrance of me; and inasmuch as they will not remember me, and hearken unto my words, they shall scourge them even unto destruction. (2 Ne. 5:20–25)

Lamanite Idolatry

A second way the Lamanites are implicitly paralleled with the Canaanites is in the description of their religious practices. Within a generation after the separation of the Nephites from the Lamanites, Nephi's nephew Enos described the latter as being "full of idolatry" (Enos 1:20), a characterization that continues throughout the Book of Mormon (Alma 17:15; Morm. 4:14, 21). Idolatry was also the characteristic sin of the Canaanites and a primary reason the Israelites were forbidden from mixing with them:

> Neither shalt thou make marriages with them; thy daughter thou shalt not give unto his son, nor his daughter shalt thou take unto thy son. For they will turn away thy son from following me, that they may serve other gods: so will the anger of the Lord be kindled against you, and destroy thee suddenly. (Deut. 7: 3–4; cf. Josh. 23:6–12, 1 Kgs. 11:1–4).

Zeniff's Canaanites

A third way the Lamanites parallel the Canaanites comes in the story of the Nephite expeditions to reclaim the land of Nephi. Some four centuries after Nephi, the leader of the first expedition played out a new conquest narrative in which he cast the Nephites in the role of the Israelites and the Lamanites in the role of Canaanites: he first sent out spies to watch the Lamanites, and then, like the leaders of the biblical Conquest, ordered that these indigenous competitors for the land be exterminated (Omni 1:27–29; Mosiah 9:1–2). Though one of their leaders, Zeniff, was hesitant due to his observation of "that which was good among them" (Mosiah 9:1), after being overtaken by the Lamanites he reinstates their Canaanite description of being "lazy and idolatrous" (v. 12).

The River Sidon

Fourth, that this framing of Lamanites as Canaanites was wide and enduring is indicated by the name the Nephites gave to one of their promised land's most prominent geographical features. The river whose headwaters marked part of the boundary between Nephite territory and Lamanite territory was given the name "Sidon" (Alma 22:27–29). In the Hebrew Bible the place Sidon takes its name from the firstborn son of Canaan, who was cursed by Noah. This place's significance is that it marks the boundary between the Israelite and Canaanite territories (Gen. 10:15–19). The choice of this same name for the boundary separating the Nephites from the Lamanites seems hardly coincidental, and it identifies the Nephites with the Israelites and the Lamanites with the Canaanites.

The Lamanite Curse

Another boundary separating the Lamanites from the Nephites was the Lamanite curse. It was this—the idea that the Lamanites, like the Canaanites, were divinely cursed—that defined the Lamanites for the Book of Mormon's Nephite narrators. In connection with their curse, the Lamanites were segregated from the Nephites, paralleling the outsider treatment of the Canaanites during the Israelites' Conquest narrative. The isolation of the Canaanites and the Lamanites is particularly evident in the Israelite and Nephite marriage laws, respectively. John M. Lundquist and John W. Welch observe:

> A new law was then issued that no Nephite should intermarry with the Lamanites. The penalty for anyone who might break this law was affliction with a curse (see 2 Nephi 5:23). This New World prohibition compares to the similar law given to the Israelites at the time of their conquest in the Old World: it prohibited them from intermarrying with the Canaanites (see Deuteronomy 7:3–4).[16]

The rationale for this prohibition against Nephites marrying Lamanites is similar to that of the Israelites who were prohibited from marrying Canaanites in order to keep them from adopting the Canaanites' religious practices, particularly their idolatry:

> Neither shalt thou make marriages with them; thy daughter thou shalt not give unto his son, nor his daughter shalt thou take unto thy son. For they will turn away thy son from following me, that they may serve other gods: so will the anger of the Lord be kindled against you, and destroy thee suddenly. (Deut. 7:3–4)

---

16. John M. Lundquist and John W. Welch, "Kingship and Temple in 2 Nephi 5–10," 67. Abraham and Isaac similarly prohibit their sons from marrying Canaanites, though without offering a specific rationale (Gen. 24:1–4; 28:1).

Since the Nephites were proscribed from marrying Lamanites "that they might not mix and believe in incorrect traditions which would prove their destruction" (Alma 3:8), both marital prohibitions were intended to prevent the chosen nation from adopting the false religious ideas and idolatrous practices of the cursed nation and thereby bringing themselves to destruction. Thus, according to Mormon, the "mark" accompanying the Lamanite curse was imposed to prevent such intermixing:

> And their brethren sought to destroy them, therefore they were cursed; and the Lord God set a mark upon them, yea, upon Laman and Lemuel, and also the sons of Ishmael, and Ishmaelitish women. And this was done that their seed might be distinguished from the seed of their brethren, that thereby the Lord God might preserve his people, that they might not mix and believe in incorrect traditions which would prove their destruction. (Alma 3:7–8)

The various parallels are clear. The Book of Mormon narrators' descriptions of the Lamanite curse and the injunction forbidding intermarriage cast the Lamanites in the role of the Canaanites of the new promised land.

When we understand that the Book of Mormon narrators fit the Lamanites into the Nephite conquest narrative by making them its Canaanites, the roots of their notion of the Lamanite curse become clearer. The view that the Lamanites carried a curse patterned on that of the Canaanites arose out of the narrative that the Nephites were the new Israelites, carrying out a new conquest of their promised land patterned on the biblical Conquest of the land of Canaan.

As if looking through a backward Urim and Thummim that projected darkness onto light, the Nephites viewed the Lamanites through the lens of biblical stories of Canaanites rather than through the lens of God's covenant with Lehi. Forgetting Lehi's lesson that they were a single seven-branched nation, incomplete without their lost tribes, the Nephites most often saw the Lamanites not as Israelites and brothers but as strangers and foreigners, imagining themselves alone to be God's chosen.

Nephi's Laws of War

While the legacy of the Nephite conquest with respect to race is disquieting its legacy with respect to violence is far easier to affirm than that of the biblical Conquest. Nephi classed the Lamanites as Canaanites in order to protect his people from adverse Lamanite cultural influences. He also felt the need to protect them from the Lamanites militarily. As his people's "great protector," he "wielded the sword of Laban in their defense" (Jacob 1:10). As a military leader, in addition to a warrior, he equipped them for battle: "I, Nephi, did take the sword of Laban, and after the manner of it did make many swords, lest by any means the people who were now called Lamanites should come upon us and destroy us" (2 Ne. 5:14). The Nephites thus had not merely one sword of Laban—or of Joseph or Joshua—but many, all to be used to defend themselves against the Lamanites.

The defensive nature of Nephi's military activities is consistent both with his generally peaceable character and with a revelation on warfare we are told he received but which is not available in our extant text. In an 1833 revelation to Joseph Smith, a law of defensive warfare is laid out that describes "the law I gave unto my servant Nephi" (D&C 98:32). This Nephite law, or set of laws, regarding warfare was almost certainly given in the context of the only wars Nephi ever fought: those with the Lamanites.[17] And the revelation of this law or laws was almost certainly described in the historically and politically rich and dynastically-linked lost manuscript.

What was "the law I gave unto my servant Nephi"? The revelation commands that God's people must "bear patiently" the first, second, and third acts of aggression against them by their enemies. However, after the enemies have established "three testimonies" against themselves in the sight of God, then

> thine enemy is in thine hands; and if thou rewardest him according to his works thou art justified; if he has sought thy life, and thy life is endangered by him, thine enemy is in thine hands and thou art justified. (D&C 98:23–31)

It is here that the revelation adds, "Behold, this is the law I gave unto my servant Nephi, and thy fathers, Joseph, and Jacob, and Isaac, and Abraham, and all mine ancient prophets and apostles" (D&C 98:32).

That such a law had been given in the fuller account of Nephi's reign is also implied in a later Book of Mormon war narrative. When the Lamanites opened up a string of attacks on the Nephite republic, the Nephites, under their captain Moroni, saw their defense of their families, faith, and liberties, as

> the duty which they owed to their God; for the Lord had said unto them, *and also unto their fathers*, that: Inasmuch as ye are not guilty of the first offense, neither the second, ye shall not suffer yourselves to be slain by the hands of your enemies. And again, the Lord has said that: Ye shall defend your families even unto bloodshed. (Alma 43:45–47)[18]

The requirement here to defend oneself and one's family, though only after multiple offenses by the enemy, is very similar to the commandment given in Joseph's 1833 revelation but with a telling difference. Where the revelation

---

17. Nephi reported that prior to his encounter with Laban he had never shed blood and that he was loath to do so even in Laban's case (1 Ne. 4:10).

18. The connection of Doctrine and Covenants 98:32 to Alma 43:46 was first made by John Tvedtnes, who argued that Nephi received rules of battle that were recorded in his "large plates" and possibly in the lost 116 pages. See John A. Tvedtnes, *The Most Correct Book: Insights from a Book of Mormon Scholar*, 55.

asks the Saints to "bear patiently" with *three* offenses and fight back only after a fourth, the law given to the Nephite fathers stipulated that they could fight after only *two* unprovoked offenses.

While the principle embodied in them is the same, the respective laws reflect the different contexts from which they emerged. Joseph's revelation was intended to encourage patience on the part of the Missouri Mormons who were then under threat of violence. The Nephite laws of warfare grow out of Nephi's experience with Laban, who had made two attempts on the lives of Lehi's family members: first on the life of Laman (1 Ne. 3:13), then on the lives of Nephi and all his brothers (v. 25). Nephi's first-person account describes him as nonetheless loath to shed blood, doing so only after being reminded by the Spirit of the Lord that Laban had tried to kill them and that his death was necessary for the salvation of an entire nation. As in Joseph's revelation, the enemy was placed "in thine hands" after multiple attacks in which "he has sought thy life"; thus, Nephi was told of Laban, "Behold the Lord hath delivered him into thy hands" because "he had sought to take away" Nephi's life (D&C 98:31; 1 Ne. 4:11).[19]

The wording of the Nephite law of warfare presupposes a broad context and multiple enemies: "Inasmuch as ye are not guilty of the first offense, neither the second, ye shall not suffer yourselves to be slain by the hands of your enemies." The context of Nephi killing Laban seems too narrow to have given rise to this general law about destructive enemies, but the experience provided the groundwork for a more general revelation to guide him in warfare—one that would guide him in his conflict with the very brothers he had once stood side by side with against Laban.

Assessing Nephi's Conquest

The sword Nephi acquired at the beginning of the Book of Lehi perfectly symbolized his role as the leader of a new conquest and the founder and defender of a new Israelite kingdom. As the sword of Joseph, it was perfect for conquering the land of Joseph and for marking its possessor as Joseph's heir—and thus as the land's rightful ruler. As the sword of Joshua, it was ideal for the new conquest, marking Nephi also as the new Joshua. Finally, as the sword of Laban—Nephi's Goliath—it further evoked the sword of Goliath used by David to behead the giant, rout the Philistines, and set him on the path of becoming the king of Israel.

---

19. Nephi's revelation also justified Laban's demise on the grounds that he had stolen Nephi's property. It may also implicitly appeal to Laban's breaking of the Deuteronomic covenant, on which life in the Promised Land depended: he "would not hearken unto the commandments of the Lord (1 Ne. 4:11).

The identification of Nephi's sword as the sword of Joshua not only creates continuity between his conquest and Joshua's, it affirms the important role of the Nephites in God's divine plan for Israel and humanity. These were not people who merely happened to leave Jerusalem; they were specifically chosen—just like Joseph and Joshua—to play roles in God's "work and glory—to bring to pass the immortality and eternal life of man" (Moses 1:39).

However, although Nephi's conquest symbolically continues Joshua's, it materially diverges from it in its relationship to violence. Nephi and Joshua, as we have seen, are presented in their respective narratives as putting the sword to quite different use. Nephi does not use it in wars of offense, much less of extermination, against giants and idolators. Rather, his people's conquest consists, first, in peaceably inheriting their covenanted land after the giant Jaredites clear themselves from the land by their covenant-breaking and military suicide. Second, it consists in living in harmony with God's Spirit, each other, and their land such that they would prosper and be strong enough to defend themselves by the sword against those they saw as their Canaanites—the Lamanites who had cursed themselves from God's presence. Yet while he identifies his brothers' families as under a curse like that of the Canaanites, neither Nephi nor his successors take this as license to subjugate them and put them into servitude, as the biblical Israelites did to the Canaanites. The relatively pacific nature of the Nephite conquest implies an ambiguity toward, if not an aversion to, warfare that one does not find in the biblical Conquest narrative. The Nephites' settlement of their new promised land was framed as a conquest in order to recapitulate the creation of biblical Israel. However, theirs was a conquest in concept only. It was not about taking over the land of Israel but about taking on an identity *as* a new Israel. Their conquest was about the fulfillment of covenant—Joseph's covenant that his posterity would be a righteous branch in a new land, Lehi's covenant of a promised land for his family, and Nephi's covenant that his people would be protected and prospered as they kept God's commandments.

War was useful to the Nephites only as a defense, and even then it was only effective as a defense when they lived the terms of their covenant. The Book of Mormon explains the Nephites' comparatively greater military strength over the Lamanites as a result of the Nephites enjoying the presence of God. When God began to withdraw his presence from them, as he would withdraw it from "unholy temples," they faltered became "weak, like unto their brethren, the Lamanites" (Hel. 4:24–26; Morm. 2:26). And when God at last fully withdrew his presence from them, their vastly superior military technology—swords modeled on the sword of the Conquest—could not save them (Moro. 8:28–29).

The Book of Mormon's attitude toward military conquest and toward the effectiveness of violence is represented perfectly in the fate of the relics the Nephites traced to Joseph of Egypt and which Nephi acquired from Laban. By Joseph Smith's time, the sword that the ancient Joseph forged reportedly "had rusted away and become useless," leaving only the hilt for the young prophet to find.[20] However, the brass plates containing God's covenants with Joseph would, Lehi declared, "never perish; neither should they be dimmed any more by time" (1 Ne. 5:19). They "will retain their brightness," prophesied Alma, "yea, and also shall all the plates which do contain that which is holy writ" (Alma 37:3–5). The sword by which Joshua led the Conquest is long gone, but, millennia later, the words of "holy writ" and divine covenant endure, a testament to Mormon's declaration that "the word" has a "more powerful effect upon the minds of the people than the sword, or anything else" (Alma 31:5).[21]

---

20. Lapham, "Interview," in Vogel, *EMD*, 1:462

21. The texts indicating that the brass plates would never be "dimmed" or "lose their brightness" intimate that they are kept untarnished by supernatural agency, while the sword apparently receives no such divine protection from the vicissitudes of time.

CHAPTER 11

NEPHI'S TEMPLE

Among the losses entailed by both the Jewish Exile and Lehi's self-imposed exile were those of the Jerusalem temple, the Levitical priests who functioned in the temple, and the sacred relics kept within. Yet, despite these losses the Book of Mormon tells us that the Nephites lived the Law of Moses scrupulously—something only possible if they constructed religious institutions that paralleled and replaced those they had lost. Just as Nephi established a commonwealth of Joseph with political institutions modeled on those of the original commonwealth of Israel, he also built a temple city in which both the monarchy and the priesthood centered. In their new temple, Nephi reestablished Israelite worship with its requisite priests and sacred relics.

Details of the Nephite temple system are likely to have appeared in the lost manuscript, which had a distinctively Hebraic emphasis, offered a narrative of the loss and restoration of Israelite institutions, closely described the Nephite relics, and told Nephite history from closer to its religious and political center—the monarchy—than do the small plates accounts by the descendants of Jacob. The latter small plates narrative raises more questions about the details of Nephite temple worship than it answers, including questions on the name of Nephi's temple, the relationship of Nephi's temple to Solomon's, and the relationship of Nephite priesthood to the priesthood of Aaron's line. How should the reader envision temple worship in the world of the Book of Mormon? How did it replicate and replace, even as it differed from, temple worship in the world of the Bible? How, for instance, could its temple worship function without the Levitical high priest and the Ark of the Covenant, which were key to the central Day of Atonement ritual?

Behind the published Book of Mormon text we can glimpse a carefully constructed system of temple worship that included substitutes for the Aaronic high priest, the priestly Urim and Thummim, the relics associated with the Ark of the Covenant, and even the ark itself that were likely detailed more clearly and completely in the lost manuscript.

The City of Nephi and the Temple of Nephi

As seat of both the dynasty and the temple, Nephi's city served as another Jerusalem. It is fitting then that just as Jerusalem had been poetically termed "the city of David," Nephi's Jerusalem was straightforwardly named "the city of Nephi" (Mosiah 9:15, 20:3, 21:1; Alma 47:20).

The lost pages would presumably have correspondingly referred to the temple that Nephi built within the city of Nephi as "the temple of Nephi." This Nephite model of naming temples for the one who built them, a pattern not seen in the Bible, is documented early in the Book of Mormon, which refers to the Jerusalem temple by the non-biblical name "temple of Solomon" (2 Ne. 5:16). That this name "the temple of Nephi" was used in the lost pages is evidenced by one of the earliest newspaper articles on the Book of Mormon and the emerging Restoration.

In the summer of 1829 Martin Harris visited newspaper printers in the Palmyra area to persuade them to print the Book of Mormon. Martin told them about the book's content and that its publication was to result in the establishment of a New Jerusalem. Soon thereafter, Jonathan A. Hadley published articles on the Book of Mormon in *The Palmyra Freeman*, reporting what he had learned from Martin. One article relayed that believers in the Book of Mormon intended to construct a New Jerusalem with a temple within it.[1] Hadley thus provided the earliest glimpse of intentions to build a city of Zion and a temple—one referred to as the "temple of Nephi."[2]

Martin calling the anticipated New Jerusalem temple the "temple of Nephi" has two vital implications. First, it intimates that the phrase "temple of Nephi" was used in the lost pages as the name for the Nephites' first temple. Second, it indicates that the earliest believers in the Book of Mormon either used Nephi's new Jerusalem and temple as a model for the New Jerusalem and temple they intended to build or anticipated actually re-building Nephi's city and temple.

For his part, Nephi described his temple as "like unto the temple of Solomon," indicating that the new temple was patterned on the one in Jerusalem that his people had lost. That the new temple of Nephi was *not* like Solomon's in opulence and grandeur (2 Ne. 5:16) presumably means that it was instead similar to Solomon's temple in structure and function, enabling the Nephite priests to fulfill the same ritual obligations the Aaronic priests had in Jerusalem.

---

1. Hadley's *Palmyra Freeman* article, now lost, was echoed in another Palmyra paper, *The Reflector*, printed at the E. B. Grandin press by Abner Cole. For reconstruction of what Martin told Hadley about the New Jerusalem, see Don Bradley, "Building the Temple of Nephi: Early Mormon Perceptions of Cumorah and the New Jerusalem," 264–77.

2. The *Palmyra Reflector* stated that "the building of the TEMPLE OF NEPHI is to be commenced." This August 1829 account almost certainly reflects Martin Harris's own ideas and words. Other accounts confirm Martin telling printers he visited about the coming New Jerusalem. Also details such as the name "Nephi" and even the expectation of a temple could only have been gleaned from insiders like Martin. See Bradley, "Building the Temple of Nephi."

How was the Nephite temple system constructed toward these ends? Who was the high priest in charge, and what was the basis of his authority? And how could the Nephites fulfill the Law of Moses with exactness without the Ark of the Covenant and its divinely imbued sacred tablets, the touchstones from which holiness radiated out to the rest of the temple?

The Nephite High Priest

The biblical high priest had central roles in the religion of ancient Israel. Three of the most crucial were his leadership over the priesthood, his performance of the Day of Atonement rituals, and his use of sacred implements to divine God's will. The Aaronic high priest was, at least after the Exile, exactly what his title signifies—highest in the Israelite priestly order, supreme leader over the priests. He also, as specified in the Pentateuch, had unique access to the Ark of the Covenant and used this access to perform one of the most crucial rituals of the year: the Day of Atonement (Yom Kippur) sacrifice that would secure forgiveness for Israel's sins. In this ritual, the high priest sacrificed a bull for the nation's sins and entered the Holy of Holies to sprinkle its blood on the lid of the Ark of the Covenant. Expanding his role beyond that of ritual and into prophecy, the high priest also possessed and used the Urim and Thummim to make judgments of truth and divine God's will.

While the published Book of Mormon says the Nephites observed the various sacrifices required by the Mosaic Law, it does not identify who performed key ritual functions assigned in the Bible to the high priest. It does, however, identify who in Nephite society took the role of leading the priests as well as who took the role of divining the will of God.

The Nephite King as Chief Priest

In Israelite kingship, as reflected in the Bible, "military, religious, and civil offices were . . . combined in the person of the king."[3] These three responsibilities defined "the king's role in the protection of society as warrior, the guarantor of justice as judge and the right ordering of worship as priest."[4] As first noted by Daniel C. Peterson, during the period of the Nephite monarchy it is overwhelmingly the *kings* who consecrate priests.[5] Nephi, Benjamin, Mosiah$_2$, Zeniff, and Noah are each described as doing so. (The first high priest over the temple of Nephi was thus fittingly *Nephi* himself.) The one

---

3. Brett L. Holbrook, "The Sword of Laban as a Symbol of Divine Authority and Kingship," 42.

4. Keith W. Whitelam, "Israelite Kingship: The Royal Ideology and Its Opponents," 130; as cited in Holbrook, "The Sword of Laban," 42. I also paraphrase Holbrook in introducing this quotation.

5. Daniel C. Peterson, "Authority in the Book of Mosiah," 149–85.

non-king who consecrates priests during this period is Alma₁. However, the text makes clear that Alma$_1$'s authority is *derived* from that of the king, he having been made a priest by King Noah (Mosiah 11:5; 17:1–2). And even though Alma$_1$, as leader of the church in the land of Zarahemla, was a higher priest than those he presided over (23:16–17), he was not the highest priest. His authority to preside over the church was explicitly derived from the still greater authority of Mosiah$_2$ who "had *given* Alma$_1$ the authority over the church" (26:8) and "gave him power to ordain priests and teachers over every church" (25:19). Mosiah$_2$'s authority was intrinsic; Alma$_1$'s was derivative. While Alma$_1$ was a high priest in the sense of being the immediate presiding figure running the church, Mosiah$_2$ was the high priest in the sense of being the highest priestly authority among the Nephites.[6]

The Nephite King as Revelator

The king's position as high priest is also revealed by his role in divining God's will for his people using a physical instrument of revelation. This role was originally taken among Lehi's people by Lehi himself, who consulted the Liahona to guide his family on their exodus. Nephi also consulted this oracle on the journey, and, after his father's death, absconded with it, along with the sword of Laban and brass plates, and passed these treasures from generation to generation in the line of kings that sprang from him.

The Liahona served Lehi and then Nephi's dynasty as a stand-in for the Urim and Thummim, making it vital to early Nephite temple worship. In the biblical books of Ezra and Nehemiah, Zerubbabel (builder of the Second Temple that replaced Solomon's) told the priests to "not eat of the most holy things, till there stood up a priest with Urim and with Thummim" (Ezra 2:63; Neh. 7:65), indicating that Israelite temple worship *required* a high priest with the Urim and Thummim. A Nephite high priest having the Urim and Thummim or a substitute would have thus been crucial to re-establishing credible temple worship in the new promised land.

The Nephite Urim and Thummim

While the Liahona served as a decent stand-in for the Urim and Thummim, the Nephites later acquired an instrument for divining God's will that much more precisely paralleled the one used by the biblical high priest. Aaron and his successors had consulted the stones collectively known as the Urim and

---

6. An analogy from Latter-day Saint religious practice may prove useful here. While the designated "President of the Quorum of Twelve" presides over this quorum directly, he is, in turn, presided over by a still more senior apostle, the President of the Church.

Thummim, which they stored in the pocket of the sacerdotal breastplate. The Nephite equivalent "interpreters" also attach to a breastplate and are called in later revelation "the Urim and Thummim" (D&C 17:1). Intriguingly, this Nephite counterpart to the Jerusalem high priest's most important relic was not the possession of a separate set of prophets or temple priests but rather of the Nephite *kings*—three of whom are said or implied to have had this instrument: Mosiah$_2$, his father Benjamin, and his grandfather Mosiah$_1$.

Mosiah$_2$, last in the line of kings, passed the instrument to Alma$_1$'s son Alma$_2$, who succeeded his father and Mosiah$_2$ as the Nephites' supreme priestly and political leader. And Mosiah$_2$ used the interpreters to translate Ether's twenty-four plates recovered by Limhi's people (Mosiah 28:11–17). How did he acquire the interpreters? Although Mormon narrates Mosiah$_2$'s entire reign (Mosiah 7–29), he makes no mention of the momentous recovery of the interpreters. The interpreters are *already* with the Nephite monarchy early in Mosiah$_2$'s reign when his people encounter Limhi's people, who had found Ether's plates. We are left to understand that Mosiah$_2$ received the interpreters in the transfer of relics from his father (1:16).

That Benjamin had the interpreters was similarly signaled in the Book of Ether and stated outright in the Book of Mosiah. The Book of Ether says the brother of Jared's record was "sealed up with" the interpreters by which it would be translated, then it says that Benjamin had this record and the capacity to translate it—i.e., he had the interpreters.[7] The Book of Mosiah is more explicit, quoting Ammon$_1$ telling Limhi: "[T]he king of the people who are in the land of Zarahemla is the man that . . . has this high gift from God," which gift it equates with "the things . . . called interpreters" (Mosiah 8:13–14). We are also given Limhi's response: "Limhi was again filled with joy on learning from the mouth of Ammon that king Benjamin had a gift from God, whereby he could interpret such engravings" (21:28).[8]

Benjamin's possession of the interpreters and sealed plates has often gone unrecognized because although it is reported in the Book of Mormon's earliest text, as quoted above, later editions of the Book of Mormon have his name changed to "Mosiah" to preempt criticism of a perceived discrepancy in the text. This is due to some seeing Limhi's rejoicing of Benjamin's possession of the interpreters as a chronological error, though it is not clearly so.[9] Similarly,

---

7. See Ether 4:1 in Royal Skousen, ed., *The Printer's Manuscript of the Book of Mormon: Typographical Facsimile of the Entire Text in Two Parts*, 2:918.

8. See Skousen, 2:353. Note that this reading differs from that of the second printing and later editions of the Book of Mormon.

9. See Benjamin McGuire, "Benjamin or Mosiah? Resolving an Anomaly in Mosiah 21:28." The order in which Benjamin's death is mentioned relative to the sending of the Ammon$_1$ expedition need not require that the events occurred in that order.

Benjamin's possession of the brother of Jared's sealed record has been rejected by critics who confuse *the brother of Jared's* record on the sealed plates accompanying the interpreters with *Ether's* record on the twenty-four plates found by Limhi's people.

The Book of Mormon's earliest text thus twice places the interpreters in Benjamin's hands. Nothing is said in the extant text of how Benjamin gets the interpreters, which may imply simply that he received them from his own father. That Mosiah₁, whose reign was detailed in the lost manuscript, possessed, and used, the interpreters is also implied in the small plates. The Book of Omni records:

> And it came to pass in the days of Mosiah, there was a large stone brought unto him with engravings on it; and *he did interpret the engravings by the gift and power of God*. And they gave an account of one Coriantumr, and the slain of his people. (1:20–21)

The means by which Mosiah₁ "interpreted" the engravings on the Jaredite stone record are not specified, but elsewhere where languages are interpreted it is, fittingly, by means of the *interpreters*. Mosiah₂ translated Ether's twenty-four plates "by the means of those two stones which were . . . prepared from the beginning, and *were handed down from generation to generation, for the purpose of interpreting languages*" (Mosiah 28:13–14). Mosiah₁'s own "interpret[ing] the engravings" implies his similar possession of the interpreters.

The declaration that Mosiah₁ interpreted the engravings "by the gift and power of God" indicates this even more strongly. Two subsequent passages use nearly identical language to indicate that Mosiah₁'s successors used the Jaredite interpreters to translate or "interpret such engravings" by "the gift of God" or "a gift from God" (Mosiah 8:11–14; 21:28). In these passages the translational gift from God *is* the interpreters: "[H]e has wherewith that he can look, and translate all records that are of ancient date; and *it* is a gift from God. And the things are called interpreters" (8:13). Since this "gift" from God is the revelatory *object*, use of this phrase to describe how Mosiah₁ translated identifies him as having that tangible gift. Thus, as Sidney B. Sperry concluded, "[T]hese sacred 'interpreters' were certainly in the possession of the Nephites as early as the days of the elder Mosiah, who must have used them in translating engravings on a large stone which had been brought to him."[10] (A question left open in the Book of Mormon's published text is, where did Mosiah₁ get the interpreters? For an examination of this see Chapter 14.)

Tellingly, the interpreters appear to have not been handed down through the line of prophet-record keepers who held the small plates; instead they were handed down through the line of kings. Mosiah₁'s use of them to trans-

---

10. Sidney B. Sperry, *Book of Mormon Compendium*, 27.

late the Jaredite stone record would place the interpreters in the hands of the Nephite kings even while the prophetic small plates record was still being passed through Jacob's lineage. Aligning with this, the prophet-narrators of the small plates report receiving and passing on the plates, but they say nothing of doing the same with the interpreters or other temple relics. Thus, when the last small plates author Amaleki turns the plates over to King Benjamin, he says nothing of turning over the interpreters (Omni 1:25). Benjamin did not need to be given the interpreters by Jacob's heir; he already had them. With the interpreters being equivalent to the biblical high priest's Urim and Thummim, Benjamin was already the equivalent to the biblical high priest. In other words, the Nephite king *was* the high priest.

Melchizedek as the Nephites' High Priestly Model

Prior to the separation of temple and state under the reign of the judges, the symbols of regal power and the sacred implements of the high priest were one and the same, because the king and the high priest were one and the same. The model for Nephite priesthood is thus very different from that of the Levitical priesthood, in which the priests comprised a distinct class and lineage. Lacking Levites, the Nephites had to appeal to a different precedent than Aaron to ground the authority of their high priest. The model they chose was the archetypal priest-king—"Melchizedec, king of Salem, priest of the most high God" (Heb. 7:1). It was he on whom the author of the Epistle to the Hebrews modeled both Jesus's role as high priest and the priesthood of the Davidic kings, declaring, "Thou art a priest after the order of Melchizedec" (v. 17).

Rather than being a Levitical priesthood "after the order of Aaron," Nephite priesthood was modeled primarily on Israelite royal priesthood "after the order of Melchizedek."[11] Thus when Alma$_2$ discusses his own priesthood authority "being after the order of his Son, which order was from the foundation of the world," he notes that "Melchizedek . . . was also a high priest *after this same order* which I have spoken" (Alma 13:7, 14). In Nephite society both political and priestly authority flowed from the ruler, who, like Melchizedek, was both a king and "a priest of the Most High God" (Gen. 14:18). The original model for such rulers in Nephite society was Nephi himself, who was

---

11. While the biblical model for the Nephite priesthood structure is evidently the royal priesthood of Melchizedek, this model does not account for all distinctive features of priesthood in the Book of Mormon. For instance, when Lehi first goes into the desert, he offers sacrifice although he is clearly not a priest of Levitical lineage. (He is explicitly said in Alma 10:3 to be of the tribe of Manasseh.) Possible roots of Lehi's priesthood in a Josephite/Northern Kingdom of Israel tradition are explored in Richley Crapo, "Lehi, Joseph, and the Kingdom of Israel," 289–304.

a prophet, a priest, and a king. Yet the ultimate model for such rulers was the Messiah, whom the Nephite rulers prefigured. As prophets, priests, and kings, they symbolized *the* Prophet, Priest, and King of Israel and were thus "ordained after the order of his Son, in a manner that thereby the people might know in what manner to look forward to his Son for redemption" (Alma 13:2).

The Nephite Relics and Ark

Where it was not possible for the Nephites to reconstitute the biblical temple system with exactness, substitutions were made. We have seen that the Nephites, lacking Aaronic priests, followed the biblical model of Melchizedek and made their king their high priest. Likewise, since they lacked Solomon's temple, their high priest oversaw worship in *Nephi's* temple, which replicated Solomon's in function but without its elaborate ornateness. As Kevin Christensen has observed, while substitutes for key features of Jerusalem temple worship were had by the Nephites, they lacked the most important "of the specific temple artifacts kept in the holy of holies, the ark of the covenant . . . and the cherubim [which adorned the ark's lid]."[12] The ark, with the relics it held—from which the divine presence was believed to emanate—was literally central to the Jerusalem temple. Indeed, the temple was, in one sense, a house for the Ark of the Covenant, which in turn housed Moses's stone tablets that God touched with His finger on Sinai during the Exodus and provided Israel with an embodiment of His presence. The First Temple was structured in concentric zones of sacredness, around the Ark, with the chamber that contained the Ark being the holiest place of all, "the Holy of Holies." There, the Ark served as the temple's holiest altar, where on the Day of Atonement the high priest sprinkled sacrificial blood to secure forgiveness for his people's sins (Lev. 16).

Nephite Substitutes for the Treasures of the Ark

The Nephite sacred relics handed down from king to king included the sword of Laban, brass plates, Liahona, Jaredite breastplate, and the interpreters. As discussed in Chapter 7, each of these Nephite high priestly heirlooms parallels relics associated with the biblical Ark of the Covenant, including both the implements used by the Ark's custodian (the high priest) and the objects placed in or near the Ark. The Nephite high priest-king used divining instruments parallel to the biblical high priest's Urim and Thummim—first the Liahona, which paralleled it in function, and then the interpreters, which paralleled it in both function and form. This parallel was not lost on early Mormons, who quickly began calling the interpreters "the Urim and

---

12. Kevin Christensen, "Paradigms Regained: A Survey of Margaret Barker's Scholarship and its Significance for Mormon Studies," 18.

Thummim" (cf. D&C 17:1) and conflated the Nephite high priestly breast-plate with that of Aaron.[13] Similarly, the Nephites' cache of regal and high priestly treasures included at least one relic parallel to those kept in or with the biblical ark. The Liahona paralleled aspects of both Aaron's rod and the pot of manna. It paralleled Aaron's budding rod in function and paralleled the preserved manna in its function (sustenance), in its form (a round ball), and in the way it was introduced into the narrative (being found on the ground in the morning).

Likewise, the two sets of metal plates (brass and gold) inscribed with the sacred word parallel the two sets of stone tablets housed in the Ark of the Covenant. The later golden plates of the Nephites have an additional connection to the Bible's Ark-related heirlooms. The Ark was built of acacia wood but covered in gold plates (Ex. 37:1–2). The Ark's custodian, the high priest, wore a gold plate on his crown engraved with the sacred words: "Holiness to the LORD" (Ex. 39:30). Indeed, the plate on the high priest's miter is the only engraved golden plate in the entire Bible, making it the biblical object most similar to the Nephite golden plates.

The final relic passed down in the Nephite regal and high priestly cache of treasures is the sword of Laban. The story of Nephi killing Laban is of great political importance for the narrative of Nephi's dynasty. It highlights the superior faithfulness that marked Nephi as ruler over his brothers, and, perhaps more importantly, connects Nephi's ascension to the Nephite throne with David's ascent to being the Israelite king. As discussed in Chapter 7, observing Nephi narrate his encounter with Laban in language sometimes identical to the account of David slaying Goliath, we are able to watch Nephi follow precisely in the footprints and sword strokes of King David with this first and symbolic victory.

Laban's sword became a relic Nephi passed on to his priest-king successors. According to the First Book of Samuel, after David's anointing by Samuel and rise to prominence, he becomes a rival to Saul for the throne. At one point David, bereft of wherewithal to defend himself, took refuge in the Tabernacle (at that point still the residence of the Ark of the Covenant) and asked the high priest Ahimelech for a weapon:

> And David said unto Ahimelech, And is there not here under thine hand spear or sword? for I have neither brought my sword nor my weapons with me, because the king's business required haste. And the priest said, The sword of Goliath the Philistine, whom thou slewest in the valley of Elah, behold, it is here wrapped in a cloth behind the ephod: if thou wilt take that, take it: for there is no other save that here. And David said, There is none like that; give it me. (1 Sam. 21:8–9)

---

13. W. W. Phelps in particular conflated the Nephite breastplate with the breastplate of the biblical high priest. See, for example, William H. Dame Journal, January 14, 1855.

The sword's location and custodian are telling. It is kept by the high priest, in the Tabernacle, behind the ephod—one of the sacred garments the high priest wore when performing rites, and to which he attached the breastplate with the Urim and Thummim. In other words, Goliath's sword was kept with the high priestly vestments. It was *a temple relic.*

The sword of Laban may also parallel the Ark of the Covenant in its battle function. The Israelites took the ark out to battle with them, believing that the presence of God that went with it would ensure their victory (1 Sam. 4:3). The Nephite kings who fight against the Lamanites are similarly described as wielding the heirloom sword in battle, possibly with the idea that employing this sacred implement in battle would similarly ensure victory (2 Ne. 5:14; Jacob 1:10; W of M 1:13). In any case, it is significant that one of the artifacts in the Nephite reliquary that paralleled the Ark of the Covenant was, like the Ark itself, taken to battle.

One by one, *each* of the heirlooms in the sacred cache of the Nephite high priest-kings parallels relics housed in the Ark of the Covenant or held by the high priest. The systematic parallels manifest that *the Book of Mormon's sacred treasury was gathered to deliberately parallel that of the biblical high priest and Solomon's temple.* Thus, the Nephite king, who acted as custodian of these relics and consulted his own Urim and Thummim, possessed the revelatory power and authority over the temple that in the Bible belongs to the high priest.

That the Nephite kings possessed both temporal and spiritual authority, and that the relics they passed down were *priestly* relics rather than merely symbols of state power, is confirmed by the relics' fate after the end of the monarchy. With that end came an eventual separation of temple and state, and a division of priestly and political powers. Before his death, Mosiah$_2$ designated Alma$_2$, who had already been made the high priest over the church by his father to be the first chief judge (Mosiah 29:42). However, after roughly eight years Alma$_2$ designated a new chief judge so that he could focus on his ministry as the high priest:

> And he selected a wise man who was among the elders of the church, and gave him power according to the voice of the people. . . . Now this man's name was Nephihah, and he was appointed chief judge; and he sat in the judgment-seat to judge and to govern the people. Now *Alma did not grant unto him the office of being high priest over the church, but he retained the office of high priest unto himself; but he delivered the judgment-seat unto Nephihah.* And this he did that he himself might go forth among his people, or among the people of Nephi, that he might preach the word of God unto them. (Alma 4:16–19)

Before Alma$_2$'s death, he handed the relics to his son who was also a high priest rather than the chief judge (Alma 37:1–47), demonstrating the relics' *priestly* rather than political significance.

The Nephite Sacred Treasures as Temple Relics

The published Book of Mormon omits where the high priestly relics—what Alma₂ would call the "sacred things"—were kept (Alma 37:47). The natural location, and also the one that would continue the Book of Mormon's echoing of the biblical pattern, would have been the high priest's own domain, the temple. Storing these objects in the Book of Mormon temple would reinforce that temple's likeness to and claim to equal sacredness with the Jerusalem temple. It would further underscore a key purpose of the Nephite temple, like the Jerusalem temple, of housing the divine presence. Just as the Israelite temple held the two stone tablets touched by the Lord on Mount Sinai (Ex. 31:18), the Nephite temple would have held the two stone interpreters that were touched by the premortal Christ on Mount Shelem (Ether 3:6, 23–24). With these sacred objects at its center, the Nephite temple could be held as sacred as Solomon's.

Point by point, the Nephites replaced the relics lost with the plundering and destruction of Solomon's temple. However, this description of the Nephite temple system is only completed after the time of Mosiah₁, who (as will be discussed in Chapter 15) acquired the interpreters that the extinct Jaredite nation had left behind. Prior to this discovery, the instrument of revelation used by the Nephite priest-kings in their tabernacle and then their first temple was the Liahona.

The Liahona as an Embodiment of God's Presence

While the Liahona paralleled the interpreters in being an instrument of revelation, it is less obvious how and why the Liahona could embody the divine presence in the same way the stone tablets and stone interpreters could. This is in part because, unlike both the stone tablets and the interpreters, the Liahona has a limited explanatory narrative. We know how Lehi found it but not how it came to exist and have power to communicate the divine will.

The Liahona having been touched by the finger of God is instead implied by its function. The Liahona worked *like* a divine finger in pointing the way. The idea of attributing miracles to the touch of God's finger may be unfamiliar in modern culture, including to modern Latter-day Saints, but it had greater currency both in the biblical world (Ex. 8:17–19) and among the early Latter-day Saints. For example, Doctrine and Covenants 84 tells us that the future site of the New Jerusalem temple in Missouri was "appointed by the finger of the Lord" (D&C 84:3).

Dovetailing with this, an 1832 revelation describes the Book of Mormon and other revelations as "that which I have written" (D&C 84:57). Also, as discussed in Chapter 3, Joseph and others appear to have understood the

English text of the Book of Mormon Joseph saw and read to his scribes to have been written by God in a very strong sense—spelled out by His finger.

With the Book of Mormon describing "Aminadi who interpreted the writing which was upon the wall of the temple, *which was written by the finger of God*" (Alma 10:2), it would be surprising if the miraculous writing appearing on the Liahona (1 Ne. 16:29) were not similarly explained. A Liahona that was "prepared by *the hand* of the Lord" (2 Ne. 5:12; Mosiah 1:16) and whose operations were attributed to the finger of God would have made a fitting substitute for Moses's stone tablets, filling their function as a physical embodiment of God's presence.

The importance of the Liahona in early Nephite religion has probably been underestimated. Serving as a stand-in for several relics of the Jerusalem temple and probably embodying for the Nephites God's presence in their temple, the Liahona played a central role in Nephite religion, particularly in temple worship. When the Liahona was later replaced by the interpreters (see Chapter 15), its functions and significance were transferred to them, making these also a central and heretofore underestimated sacred object in Nephite religion.

A Nephite Ark

For all the similarities of the Nephite high priestly treasures to those of the Jerusalem temple, there is an obvious difference. While the published Book of Mormon repeatedly mentions the sacred objects that comprise the Nephite temple relics, it never explicitly mentions the container that housed them. The omission likely results in part from the available text's general lack of emphasis on Nephite temple worship. The lost manuscript, which offered greater detail on the Nephite temple system that is mostly just hinted at in the published text, would have likely described the Nephites' parallel to the Israelites' Ark.

As discussed in Chapter 1, Martin Harris referred to the stone box that contained the golden plates and Nephite relics as an "ark."[14] Further clues suggest this may have been or been modeled on the Nephite ark. Just as Nephi's temple was built to serve the ritual purposes of Solomon's temple "save it were

---

14. John A. Clark, reporting on detailed 1828–29 narrations by Martin Harris wrote of Joseph Smith's discovery of the plates, "This book . . . was contained in a chest, *or ark.*" John A. Clark, Letter to "Dear Brethren," in Vogel, *EMD* 2:264, emphasis added. The primary definition at this time for "ark" in the Webster's dictionary was "a small close vessel, chest or coffer, such as that which was the repository of the tables of the covenant among the Jews" and another was "a depository." The stone vessel in which the plates had been deposited fits both. Noah Webster, *An American Dictionary of the English Language*, s.v. "ark."

not built of so many precious things" (2 Ne. 5:16), it would make sense for the Nephite ark to share its temple's utility and lack of ornateness.

Joseph Smith described the box in which he found the Nephite relics as a stone box of simple construction held together by a kind of cement. With the golden plates contained within, it would have poetically inverted the pattern of the biblical ark: in place of stone tablets in a golden ark, the Nephite sacred cache consisted of golden tablets in an ark of stone.

The Ark of Joseph

Unlike the biblical high priestly and Ark relics, which were associated with Moses and Aaron, the relics of the sacred cache for Nephi's temple had a distinctively Josephite provenance: a sword and brass plates forged by Joseph in Egypt; golden plates modeled on the brass plates, forged by Joseph's heir Nephi and engraved in Egyptian; the Liahona a token of God's mercy in the founding of a new, Josephite nation of Israel. The Nephite ark might thus be identified as an "ark of Joseph," one bearing relics from Joseph himself and from a nation that sprang from him.

As noted in Chapter 10, the idea of a second sacred ark, one that memorializes Joseph of Egypt and may be juxtaposed with the Ark of the Covenant, does not first emerge among the Nephites but among the biblical Israelites. That the relatively unique Hebrew term *aron* is used for both the Ark of the Covenant and for the coffin of Joseph has led one biblical scholar, Jerome Segal, to refer to Joseph's coffin as the "second Ark, the Ark of Joseph."[15] The existence of a second ark was also not lost on ancient rabbis reading the Genesis and Exodus texts. The Mekilta de-Rabbi Ishmael, a midrash dating to the early centuries after Christ, notes that there were two arks of the Exodus and describes them being carried side: "the coffin of Joseph went alongside the ark of the Eternal."[16] Segal relates more of Rabbi Ishmael's narrative:

> Joseph has been placed in a coffin by the Egyptians and the coffin was sunk in the Nile. Moses succeeds in getting the coffin to rise by throwing into the river a tablet of gold on which the name of God is engraved, and then calling on Joseph to come up. In response, the coffin, or Ark, rises to the surface. Once possession of the coffin is attained, the Mekilta links Joseph's coffin to the Ark of the Covenant.[17]

The parallel is striking: the rabbinic narrative of Joseph's coffin associates it with an engraved gold plate while Joseph Smith's accounts and the Book of

---

15. Jerome M. Segal, *Joseph's Bones: Understanding the Struggle between God and Mankind in the Bible*, 9, 28.

16. Segal, 30.

17. Segal, 30.

Mormon describe the Nephite repository of Josephite relics housing a book of engraved gold plates. Among both the Jews and the Nephites, an ark of Joseph stands parallel to the Ark of the Covenant.

Nephite Temple Worship

The use of a stone ark to house relics in a temple that was like Solomon's but without many "precious things" reveals the values in Nephite temple worship. The emphasis of Nephite temple worship was not on the *container*—the material value of the building or the ark—but on its sacred *contents*, the divine presence and the instruments through which God was revealed.

While many details of the Nephite temple system can be teased out of the published Book of Mormon, there are reasons to believe the lost manuscript said much more about the structure of Nephite temple worship. First, the lost text provided more detail of the early period of Nephite history, when worship at the temple of Nephi and then the temple of Mosiah was first established. As a more detailed historical record in general, it was likely to convey more regarding the history of the Nephite temples in particular, including their construction, the identity and actions of their high priests, and the establishment of worship in these temples—just as the earlier texts of the Hebrew Bible during and surrounding the Exodus provide much more detail on Israelite temple worship than do the later books.[18]

Second, the lost manuscript covered nearly the entire period during which Nephite worship centered on temple rather than on church. A shift in emphasis from temple to church occurs in the middle of the book that picks up where the lost manuscript left off: the Book of Mosiah. While the temple appears as a sacred center in the first chapters Joseph dictated after resuming translation (Mosiah 1–6), emphasis on the church—and even the word "church"—first appears well into the Book of Mosiah, when Alma$_1$ (the founder of the Nephite church [Mosiah 23:16]) performs the first baptisms and establishes the first "church of Christ" at the waters of Mormon (18:7–17). So, the first book we have of Mormon's abridgment is the one that bridges the religious and political changes that occurred just after the lost-pages period—the transition from the reigns of the kings to the reigns of the judges, and from the dominance of the temple to that of the church. From half way into the Book of Mosiah, and

---

18. The lost text also covered the period when Lehite temple worship was conducted in their tabernacle, and it almost certainly said something of how they established worship there. By way of parallel, the record of the biblical Exodus lays out in tremendous detail the functioning of the Israelite priesthood, how the Ark of the Covenant was to be constructed, and how worship in the Tabernacle was to be conducted. The corresponding portion of the Book of Mormon would have appeared early in the lost manuscript.

from there through the end of the Book of Mormon, Nephite religious life is chronicled as a history of *the church*, with Mormon noting that "they were called the church of God, or the church of Christ, *from that time forward*" (v. 17). Covering as they did the pre-church period, the lost pages could not have framed Nephite worship as a history of the church and would have instead framed it in terms of other Nephite religious institutions, the most consistent and notable of which was the temple.

A third factor also gives reason to believe the lost pages included more about Nephite temple worship, including the details of the king's priestly role and the royal treasures' dual function as temple relics. Unlike the published text, the lost text was a sacred history of the Nephite line of *kings*, and it was, as we have seen, the kings, who played the central role in Nephite temple worship. Given the kings' role as guardians and priestly users of the temple relics, a narrative focused on the kings and abridging the record kept *by* the kings would have almost certainly featured more centrally these relics and their place in Nephite temple worship.[19]

The Nephite Temple and the Restoration

The narrative of Lehi and Nephi was one of loss and restoration—loss of the sacred institutions of the Israelite commonwealth of Judah and the restoration or re-creation of those institutions in a new Israelite commonwealth of Joseph. Lehi and Nephi recapitulate the founding of the biblical nation of twelve tribes in the founding of their own, seven-branched nation. By successively recapitulating the history of the biblical patriarchs, the Exodus, the Conquest, the monarchy, and the like, they progressively restored elements of the biblical commonwealth. With the establishment of worship in Nephi's temple, that process reaches its fruition.

In light of how worship is established in Nephi's temple, earlier incidents in Nephite sacred history seem to occur primarily to make this worship possible by enabling Nephi to acquire the appropriate sacred relics by which to bring the divine presence into the temple and to acquire with them authority as Joseph's heir and the Josephite "David," making Nephi the legitimate king—and thus the legitimate high priest over the new temple.

Looking back over the story of Lehi and Nephi from its end, a fully functioning system of temple worship is the goal toward which the early events of their history tend, the culmination to which they build. This centrality of temple worship to Lehi's and Nephi's New World dispensation forecast the

---

19. Only one small portion of the extant text, the Book of Mosiah chapters on Benjamin and Mosiah₂, gives any substantive narrative on the line of kings, making it unlikely that it would detail their roles vis-à-vis the temple.

centrality of temple worship to the Restoration. That Latter-day Saints early on believed they would rebuild the temple of Nephi is fitting. Figuratively, they have.

While the lost manuscript narratives of Lehi and Nephi and others never had an audience outside of Joseph Smith and his scribes, the understanding of temple worship presented there likely had a great impact on Joseph Smith's own early understanding of temple worship, providing him with important insights for the later work of the Restoration. Still more, Lehi and Nephi's work of restoration provided a model for the work of restoration Joseph and the Saints would undertake. So the more we are able to flesh out the details of the lost manuscript over time and understand worship in Nephite temples, the better we will be able to understand worship in our latter-day temples.

CHAPTER 12

THE LOST MIDDLE PERIOD

For all the surprising things we can know about what was in the Book of Mormon's lost manuscript, there is a great deal we do not yet know. Indeed, most of the lost pages' contents remain unknown, particularly the middle period of the "reign of the kings," a lost period comprising over two centuries between Jacob and the destruction occurring in the year 320 (Omni 1:5). While little detail of the period is known—for instance, no personal names, and no complete narratives—the lost period's geographical setting and chronological arc can be reconstructed from our available Book of Mormon text.[1]

What We are Missing

The Book of Mormon's lost manuscript consisted of a more detailed narrative of Nephite history from Lehi down to the middle of King Benjamin's reign. Although the small plates cover this same period, they provide far less detail of its events, focusing instead on prophecy and doctrinal discourse (Jacob 1:2–4). Even the reasonably rich narrative of Lehi's exodus, presented in Nephi's first-person experience, omits many of the details of his father's experience and teachings. However, after Lehi's exodus—and particularly after the deaths of Nephi and his siblings—the level of detail in the small plates drops precipitously. Entire centuries can be covered in just a few pages or even a few verses. For example, the nine verses of Omni 1:3–11 cover about 120

---

1. It has been suggested that we do know a personal name from this period. Mosiah 18:4 introduces the reader to "to a place which was called Mormon, having received its name from the king, being in the borders of the land having been infested, by times or at seasons, by wild beasts." Several interpreters—Charles G. Eads, Daniel H. Ludlow, John Tvedtnes, Alan C. Miner, and Anita Wells—have read this to mean that the place was named *after* a king named Mormon. Context suggests it means the place was named *by* the king, and that "the king" was Noah. "The king" is used seven other times in this chapter and 42 times in the larger Noah narrative, always as a term for Noah. The phrase "having received its name from" frequently appears in books of Joseph's time to introduce an etymology, explaining who named something, and why. For example, the 1847 *The Nautical Magazine and Naval Chronicle* reports: "Of the derivation of the Nore, and *its having received its name from the Romans*, there is little doubt—Ora Mouth, Ore Mouths. N'Ore, or an addition of an Ore, in or by the mouths of the Thames and Medway." If Mosiah 18:4 uses the phrase in the same way, it would be saying that the waters were given the name Mormon by King Noah because of its "being in the borders of the land having been infested, by times or at seasons, by wild beasts."

years, and four of those verses fail to offer any narrative of Nephite history, reporting solely the transmission of the plates between record keepers and leaving the remaining five verses to cover the entire history of this period. For perspective on how little narration this provides for that period we can note that if the entire Nephite experience from Lehi to Moroni were given this same rate—one verse for every twenty-four years, the Book of Mormon would consist of only twenty-seven verses.

The period between the death of Nephi's brother Jacob and the destructions of the year 320 after Lehi's exodus (likely associated with the prophet Aminadi, mentioned in Alma 10:2 and discussed in Chapter 13), a period of about 230 years—half of the lost manuscript—is covered especially scantly. For the history of the Nephite nation during this period we have only some twenty verses of Enos, Jarom, and Omni and one external source that *may* refer to Lehite burial customs during this period (discussed later in this chapter).[2]

For the early history of the Nephites, we have both a rich record in the small plates and external sources, including accounts by those who have learned about the contents of the lost manuscript from Joseph Smith Sr. and Martin Harris, to guide us in reconstructing the narratives of the period. For the end of the lost manuscript, we have some of the same external sources to flesh out the details, as well as a skeletal narrative in the Book of Omni and the Words of Mormon. In the Book of Omni, Amaleki covers the career of Mosiah₁ and the early reign of his son Benjamin in nineteen verses (1:12–30). While this is extraordinarily brief, these nineteen verses provide much denser coverage of this period than the twenty verses that cover the roughly 230-year lost period between Jacob and the destructions of 320. Within his summary of Mosiah₁'s career and Benjamin's early reign, Amaleki introduces four new proper names that become important to the Book of Mormon narrative (Mosiah, Benjamin, Coriantumr, and the land of Zarahemla). In comparison, the summary coverage of the earlier 230 years in the books of Enos and Jarom and Omni mentions *no one* by name aside from those who kept the records of the period.

What Can We Say about the Lost Period?

The twenty verses of historical narrative in the small plates provide only a glimpse of the lost period. What can be known of this period beyond what we are straightforwardly told in those verses? Fortunately, although the informa-

---

2. I am counting verses that narrate the general history of the Nephites during this period, rather than just the personal experience of the record keeper and the transmission of the record itself. I enumerate qualifying verses as follows: Enos 1:14, 20–25; Jarom 1:3–13; Omni 1:2–3.

tion on the surface of the available text is scant, there *is* information from a few sources, including (1) close readings of the small plates text, which can tell us things not evident on the surface of the twenty verses; (2) close readings of Mormon's post-lost manuscript abridgment, which echoes and builds on the lost portion of his abridgment; and (3) a sermon of Joseph Smith which refers to an otherwise unknown Book of Mormon text, likely from this period.

200 Years of Ascent and 200 Years of Decline

Though the small plates say only a little about the lost period on their surface, there is more that can be mined from their depths. One observation we can make about early Nephite history through close reading of the small plates text is that the original Nephite nation in the land of Nephi went through an extended period of ascent—spiritual progress and material prosperity—followed by a slow decline and ultimate destruction.

The term "original Nephite nation" here merits unpacking. When Nephi first established his people as a nation, he set them up in the land of Nephi as their promised land and there established his dynasty and built the temple of Nephi. Some four centuries later, as discussed in detail in Chapter 14, Mosiah$_1$ warned the people of this nation of impending destruction and took those few in the land of Nephi who would listen and led them on an exodus to the land of Zarahemla (Omni 1:12–13). There they established a *new* joint nation with the Mulochites, in a new promised land, under a new dynasty (that of Mosiah$_1$), and worshipping at a new temple. Mosiah$_1$'s exodus created a cleavage, a major discontinuity, between the original nation and its successor nation. Rather than the same people living in the same place under the same rule, Mosiah$_1$'s nation consisted of a small minority of the original Nephites joined to a much larger body of Mulochites in a new, previously unknown land (Zarahemla) and under a new king and polity. With Mosiah$_1$'s exodus and the subsequent destruction of the body of Nephites in the land of Nephi, the old Nephite nation died and a new nation was born in Zarahemla.

A close reading of the small plates account of the first Nephite nation in the land of Nephi reveals the arc of this nation's rise and fall: two centuries of rise followed by two centuries of fall. In this arc the early Nephite nation paralleled the rise and fall of the later Nephite nation chronicled in Mormon's abridgement in 4 Nephi, where the Nephites' pattern of progress culminates in the 200th year after the birth of Jesus and begins to lapse in the 201st year. Describing a Zionic period following Jesus Christ's post-mortal ministry among the Nephites, Mormon notes that when "two hundred years had passed away," the Nephites achieved peak prosperity:

> And it came to pass that *two hundred years had passed away*; and the second gen-
> eration had all passed away save it were a few. And now I, Mormon, would that
> ye should know that the people had multiplied, insomuch that they were *spread*
> *upon all the face of the land*, and that they had *become exceedingly rich*, because of
> their prosperity in Christ. (4 Ne. 1:22–23)

It would not last. Having reached their zenith, the post-Christ Nephites began their decline. Mormon identifies the beginnings of decline with the year
201, again reinforcing the idea of the year 200 as the apex:

> And now, in this two hundred and first year there began to be among them those
> who were lifted up in pride, such as the wearing of costly apparel, and all manner
> of fine pearls, and of the fine things of the world. And from that time forth they
> did have their goods and their substance no more common among them. And they
> began to be divided into classes; and they began to build up churches unto them-
> selves to get gain, and began to deny the true church of Christ. (4 Ne. 1:24–26)

Mormon's account of the earlier Nephite nation in the land of Nephi is
lost with the initial manuscript, but the small plates account of this period
identifies the *other* Nephite year 200—two hundred years from Lehi's exodus
out of Jerusalem—as the zenith of *that* nation's spiritual progress and material
prosperity. In this account, Jarom, using the exact verbal formula Mormon
would of the later Nephite nation two centuries after Christ, notes that the
original Nephite nation achieved its apex two hundred years after Lehi's family left Jerusalem:

> And now, behold, *two hundred years had passed away*, and the people of Nephi
> had waxed strong in the land. They observed to keep the law of Moses and the
> sabbath day holy unto the Lord. And they profaned not; neither did they blas-
> pheme. And the laws of the land were exceedingly strict. And they were scattered
> upon much of the face of the land. . . . [O]ur kings and our leaders were mighty
> men in the faith of the Lord; and they taught the people the ways of the Lord;
> wherefore, we withstood the Lamanites and swept them away out of our lands,
> and began to fortify our cities, or whatsoever place of our inheritance. And we
> multiplied exceedingly, and *spread upon the face of the land*, and *became exceed-*
> *ingly rich* in gold, and in silver, and in precious things, and in fine workmanship
> of wood, in buildings, and in machinery, and also in iron and copper, and brass
> and steel, making all manner of tools of every kind to till the ground, and weap-
> ons of war. . . . And thus being prepared to meet the Lamanites, they did not
> prosper against us. But the word of the Lord was verified, which he spake unto
> our fathers, saying that: Inasmuch as ye will keep my commandments ye shall
> prosper in the land. (Jarom 1:5–9)

Thus the chronologies of the first Nephite nation and the second Nephite
nation, with their respective "after Lehi" and "after Christ" calendars, coincide at this point, using identical verbal formulas and in each case placing
their nation's apex in the year 200. Having reached its apex in the year 200,

each Nephite nation then begins its decline. Mormon makes explicit in his account of the second Nephite nation that the apex at the year 200 means that decline begins in the year 201. It seems likely that Mormon's missing account of the *first* Nephite nation and its apex and decline did the same in that nation's chronology. Jarom, in the small plates, leaves it implicit, noting the apex in the year 200 and a subsequent trajectory of descent into "wars, and contentions, and dissensions" when he again takes his nation's spiritual temperature, but he fails to highlight the post-apex year as the pivot on which the nation's progress or regress turned (Jarom 1:13).

Intriguingly, the chronologies of these two nations appear to correspond not only at the point of their common apex but at two other significant points as well. A second evident chronological parallel between the two nations occurs in the timing of their respective destructions. For the later, post-Christ Nephite nation, its decline toward destruction would take two hundred years. Exactly two hundred years from that nation's apex, Moroni writes in the year 400 to describe the final battle at Cumorah and to report that the Nephites are no more:

> Behold, *four hundred years have passed away* since the coming of our Lord and Savior. And behold, the Lamanites have hunted my people, the Nephites, down from city to city and from place to place, *even until they are no more*; and great has been their fall; yea, great and marvelous is the destruction of my people, the Nephites. (Morm. 8:6–7)

The exact year when the earlier Nephite nation had reached this point of destruction, likely given in Mormon's detailed account in the lost pages, is not specified in the small plates account. However, the chronological information about the surrounding events places Mosiah₁'s exodus around four hundred years after Lehi's exodus from Jerusalem.[3] The destruction of the first Nephite nation at or very close to the year 400 of its calendar—the same point at which the later Nephite nation was destroyed—suggests a purposeful typological parallel between the accounts of the two Nephite nations.

That the two chronologies are purposely presented with a parallel in mind is further suggested by the appearance of yet another common date in the two chronologies: the year 320. In the summary record of the decline of the early Nephite nation given in the small plates, the record keeper Amaron reports a watershed event in his nation's decline toward total destruction:

> And now I, Amaron, write the things whatsoever I write, which are few, in the book of my father. Behold, *it came to pass that three hundred and twenty years had passed away*, and the more wicked part of the Nephites were destroyed. (Omni 1:4–5)

---

3. John P. Pratt, "Book of Mormon Chronology," 169–171. See also the dates provided for Mosiah 9–12 in modern official Latter-day Saint editions of the Book of Mormon.

Amaron accounts for this destruction in precisely the opposite way that Jarom had accounted for Nephite prosperity in the year 200:

> For the Lord would not suffer, after he had led them out of the land of Jerusalem and kept and preserved them from falling into the hands of their enemies, yea, he would not suffer that the words should not be verified, which he spake unto our fathers, saying that: Inasmuch as ye will not keep my commandments ye shall not prosper in the land. (v. 6)

Having inherited the record from his father, Amaron then passes it to his brother Chemish.

In the summary record of the decline of the later Nephite nation given in 4 Nephi, the same year is called out, with the exact same phrasing—"it came to pass that three hundred and twenty years had passed away"—to note a watershed event in this nation's decline toward total destruction. The record keeper Amos, having received the record from his father, passed it to his brother, Ammaron (4 Ne. 1:47) who is forced to respond to his people's growing wickedness with drastic measures:

> And *it came to pass that when three hundred and twenty years had passed away,* Ammaron, being constrained by the Holy Ghost, did hide up the records which were sacred—yea, even all the sacred records which had been handed down from generation to generation, which were sacred—even until the three hundred and twentieth year from the coming of Christ. And he did hide them up unto the Lord, that they might come again unto the remnant of the house of Jacob, according to the prophecies and the promises of the Lord. And thus is the end of the record of Ammaron. (4 Ne. 1:48–49)

Given how few specific years are noted in the 4 Nephi chronology of the late Nephite nation and all the more so in the small plates chronology of the early Nephite nation, it seems more than coincidental that in both chronologies the year 200 is used to describe the nation's apex, that the nation is destroyed in approximately if not exactly the year 400, and that the year 320 is in each nation the precise year of a watershed moment in that terminal decline, with the event being recorded in each case by a record keeper named Am(m)aron whose father and brother were record keepers as well. An authorial hand appears to be at work in shaping these chronologies to make them so tightly parallel—whether that author is the human author of the text or the divine Author of history.

One possibility is that in his account of the apex, downturn, and decline of the late Nephite nation in 4 Nephi, Mormon presents these events so as to echo his account of the apex, downturn, and decline of the *early* Nephite nation, *which he had given in the lost pages.* Since, in Mormon's original, complete account of Nephite history, the lost manuscript and 4 Nephi were part of the same work, readers would then be able to see that the later Nephite nation's decline mirrored or followed the pattern of the earlier nation's decline.

While the small plates account is not structured by Mormon, it is implied to have been created for the purpose of filling the gap that would occur in Mormon's abridgement due to the manuscript loss, and it is perhaps thus also structured in places to mirror Mormon's later abridgement.

Regardless of whether the small plates account is cohesive with Mormon's abridgement, Mormon's abridgement should be cohesive with itself. Recognizing the intended cohesiveness of Mormon's full account of Nephite history, we can use his account of the later Nephite nation in the available part of his abridgement to shed light on what he had written in his lost account of the earlier Nephite nation.

Seen in this light, various passages in the Book of Mormon take on a new significance. For instance, if the early Nephite nation had been destroyed 400 years after Lehi left Jerusalem, then Samuel the Lamanite's prophecy that the later Nephite nation would be destroyed 400 years after Christ (Hel. 13:5, 9) was not the introduction of a new theme but the reintroduction of an old one. In the context of that earlier history, Samuel was warning that the same consequence would follow on the same cause—breaking the commandments would lead to the destruction of the second Nephite nation just as it had led to the first. Only this time the destruction would not be partial but absolute. This time there would be no Mosiah to lead a few away on an exodus to yet another promised land.

Textual Clues on the Geography of the Lost Period

In addition to revealing the chronology of the lost manuscript's narrative, clues in the extant text reveal the *geography* of that narrative as well. A pattern of Mormon's abridgement is that when he first mentions a new geographical location in the text, he orients the reader by noting the name of the place and identifying where it stands in relation to other, already familiar places in the text. As Anita Wells has noted, because of this pattern we can infer from how places are first mentioned in Mormon's extant abridgement whether those places had already been mentioned in the earlier, lost portion of his abridgement.[4] In other words, if Mormon takes care to introduce a location, then it is the first time he is referencing the location; on the other hand, if Mormon fails to introduce a location where we first see it mentioned in his available abridgement, then it was likely already introduced in the lost manuscript. We might expect this inference to hold particularly for places that are mentioned *early* in Mormon's extant abridgement and *frequently* or *centrally* there. So, for instance, when Mormon mentions "the land of Zarahemla" without in-

---

4. Anita Cramer Wells, "Lost—But Not Forgotten—116 Pages: What the Book of Mormon Might Have Included," unpublished manuscript in possession of author.

troduction in the very first verse of his extant abridgement (Mosiah 1:1) and this place is mentioned frequently thereafter and mentioned as the central location in the narrative, we are safe in assuming that Zarahemla appeared in Mormon's lost abridgement as well.

When we note what places Mormon does and does not introduce in his extant abridgement, the results imply that the lost pages surprisingly omitted some locations that are vital to the later narrative. Several important geographical features of the later Book of Mormon narratives are introduced apparently for the first time well into the extant text. Among these features that were thus likely absent from Mormon's lost abridgement—and noticeably absent even from the early part of his extant abridgement—are the River Sidon, the narrow neck of land, and the distinctions between the land northward and the land southward, all of which are not introduced until the Book of Alma (Alma 2:15; 22:31; 63:5), and the land Bountiful, which is not introduced until Alma 22:29.

Although Mormon takes care to introduce these locations in his remaining abridgment, there are other locations that he does not bother to introduce when first mentioning them, implying that he had already introduced them in the lost manuscript. These are listed here in the order in which they appear in Mormon's extant abridgement, an order which likely also reflects their probability of having appeared in his lost abridgement:

- **The land of Zarahemla** (Mosiah 1:1) – This location would have appeared in the lost manuscript. (Also indicated to have been in the lost pages in Omni 1:12.)
- **The land of Lehi-Nephi** (Mosiah 7:1) – This location (also called "the land of Nephi" [Mosiah 7:6]) would have appeared in the lost manuscript. (Also indicated to have been in the lost pages in Words of Mormon 1:13.)
- **The city of Lehi-Nephi** (Mosiah 7:1) – This location (also called "the city of Nephi" [Mosiah 9:15]) would have appeared in the lost manuscript.
- **The land of Shilom** (Mosiah 7:5) – This location would have appeared in the lost manuscript, likely in connection with the land of Nephi, to which it was near.
- **The hill that was north of the land Shilom** (Mosiah 7:5) – This location probably also appeared in the lost manuscript based on its mention in Mosiah 11:13. As discussed in Chapter 13, this hill likely appeared in the lost narrative in association with the exodus of Mosiah₁.
- **The hill Manti** (Alma 1:15) – This location probably appeared in the lost manuscript, in connection with the land of Zarahemla.

- **The city of Zarahemla** (Alma 2:26) – This location would have appeared in the lost manuscript.
- **The land of Sidom** (Alma 15:1) – This location is likely to have appeared in the lost manuscript. If it did, then its apparent position north of Zarahemla means it could have appeared in the lost narrative only after Mosiah I's exodus from the land of Nephi in the south to the land of Zarahemla to the north.
- **The land of Midian** (Alma 24:5) – This location likely appeared in the lost manuscript, in narratives occurring in proximity to the land of Nephi, and thus probably prior to the exodus of Mosiah I.
- **The hill Onidah** (Alma 32:4) – This location may have appeared in the lost manuscript.
- **On the south of the hill Riplah** (Alma 43:31) – This location may have appeared in the lost manuscript.

In summary, the lost pages appear to have mentioned up to eleven locations that appear in Mormon's later abridgement: five lands, four hills, and a mere *two* cities—only the city of Nephi (or Lehi-Nephi) and Zarahemla! Since we know that the city and land of Zarahemla entered the lost narrative near its end—when Mosiah₁ made his exodus to Zarahemla and first encountered the Mulochites there (Omni 1:14)—it appears that Mormon's pre-Mosian exodus narrative included only *one* city that is found in his extant narrative: the city of Nephi or Lehi-Nephi. Quite possibly, then, the original Nephite nation in the land of Nephi was centered on a single city.

While mention of cities appears to have been scarce in Mormon's lost abridgement, the mention of hills seems relatively abundant—with four hills from the extant narrative having likely appeared in the lost narrative. This raises a question: Why would a narrative so poor in cities be so rich in hills? Quite possibly these hills were accorded sacred significance, as will be argued for one hill particularly—the hill north of the land Shilom—in the discussion of Mosiah₁'s exodus in Chapter 14.

Furthermore, the places apparently mentioned in the lost pages group naturally into different narrative sets. Some of these places, for instance, are described to be near the land of Nephi and thus almost certainly appeared in narratives connected with the earlier, pre-Zarahemla phase of the lost pages. These places include the land of Shilom and the land of Midian. Other locations include some that are described as in the vicinity of Zarahemla and thus almost certainly would have been introduced later in the narrative after Mosiah₁'s exodus. These include the hill Manti and the land of Sidom. The remaining locations that may have appeared in the lost pages—the hills Riplah and Onidah—are not clearly close to either the land of Nephi or the land of

Zarahemla, so it is uncertain how they would have entered in the lost narrative. However, since the hill Riplah appears to have been intermediate between the lands of Nephi and Zarahemla, it is not implausible that it, like the hill north of the land Shilom, appeared in the narrative of Mosiah₁'s exodus.

Of course our list of eleven locations likely present in the lost manuscript does not mean that these were the only places mentioned there. Indeed, it is possible, and even likely, that the lost pages mentioned some locations not present in the extant text. However, judging from present evidence it appears that on the whole the action occurring in the lost manuscript took place within a much more restricted range than that of the published text and that the lost manuscript presented a simpler version of the Lehite promised land's geography.

Using the information above about the geography of the action in the lost manuscript may facilitate further reconstruction of the lost manuscript's narratives, enabling us to better infer what occurred in the lost manuscript—and where.

Sacred Burial Places

Additional content in the lost manuscript that is likely (though not certainly) connected with its extensive lost period comes from a Nauvoo sermon by the prophet Joseph Smith. While memorializing Elder Lorenzo Barnes on April 16, 1843, Joseph made reference to a detail from the Book of Mormon text:

> [T]he place where a man is buried has been sacred to me.—this subject is made mention of In Book of Mormon & Scriptures. to the aborigines regard the burying places of their fathers is more sacred than any thing else.[5]

Joseph appears to refer to a description from the Book of Mormon that its peoples regarded the burial places of their fathers as sacred. Noting that the published Book of Mormon text does not describe this or appear to make any mention of the subject, Grant Hardy and Heather Hardy have raised the question of what the Prophet is referring to. One possibility they suggest is that although Joseph translated the Book of Mormon, he may not have been intimately familiar with its text. After all, Joseph tended far more often to preach from the Bible than from the Book of Mormon. Another possibility, also raised by the Hardys, is that Joseph's reference to an otherwise unknown Book of Mormon text harks back to a text we no longer have from the lost pages.[6] My own work in understanding Joseph Smith's relationship to the Book of Mormon text strongly suggests to me that although he did

---

5. Joseph Smith, April 16, 1843, in Andrew F. Ehat and Lyndon W. Cook, ed., *Words of Joseph Smith: The Contemporary Accounts of the Nauvoo Discourses of the Prophet Joseph*, 195.

6. Personal communication from Grant Hardy and Heather Hardy, email, November 13, 2019.

not typically preach from the Book of Mormon, he knew its contents closely. I thus side with the Hardys' second interpretation: if Joseph Smith cited an unknown Book of Mormon text, he was not speaking from inferior knowledge to ours but from superior knowledge. The Book of Mormon text he was familiar with was more extensive than ours, so his allusion to a passage we do not know is almost certainly to part of that larger text—a manuscript that is lost to us but was still present for him in memory.

What remains unclear is exactly *where* in the lost manuscript the passage to which Joseph refers was located and in *what context* the notion of sacred burial sites was had. Since the lost period between Jacob and Aminadi constitutes almost exactly half of the entire lost manuscript, it is as probable as not to be the location of this particular passage. Based on its themes, I would argue that this text is *more* probable to have appeared in the lost period. A reference to the burial sites of the fathers being sacred to the Book of Mormon peoples seems particularly unlikely to have occurred early in the lost manuscript's narrative, since they would probably not yet have established distinctive traditions regarding burial and would not yet have buried many *fathers* in their new promised land. Furthermore, the very late narratives of the lost manuscript—those of Mosiah$_1$ and Benjamin—occur primarily in the land of Zarahemla, after the Nephites had abandoned the original homeland (the land of Nephi), where such burials of their fathers would have been. If a lost manuscript narrative mentioned a tradition of honoring the burial places of the fathers as sacred, this narrative most likely occurred after at least a few generations of Nephite settlement in the promised land but before their exodus to Zarahemla—i.e., in the manuscript's lost middle period.

Without more information about this period, the narrative context in which sacred burial sites appeared in the lost manuscript is difficult to surmise. Hopefully, further sources about the lost manuscript's contents emerging over time may shed additional light on this interesting question.

Evidence providing hints to the contents of the middle 230 or so years of the lost manuscript's narrative is scant, but the available evidence does enable us to sketch this period in very broad strokes. Its narrative appears to have occurred within a restricted geographical framework and to have been structured around a gradual arc of ascent and descent as the Nephites first honored and later flouted God's covenant with Nephi that they would prosper as they kept the commandments.

Despite this relatively simple meta-narrative, the lost manuscript almost certainly offered a wealth of narrative detail for this period—detail that will await the discovery or identification of further evidence to flesh it out.

CHAPTER 13

GOD AND AMINADI IN THE TEMPLE

As the Nephites' deviations from the commandments grew more extreme, God's covenant curse on the land for violating the commandments became more threatening and the time for the exodus of the righteous and the destruction of the city of Nephi loomed nearer.

Two centuries after Lehi left his first land of inheritance in quest of a new one, the blessing clause of the covenant had been strikingly fulfilled, with the Lord verifying his promise to the Nephites that if they would keep the commandments they would prosper in the land. The Lord had "preserved them from falling into the hands of their enemies" (Omni 1:6). Yet by the late 200s, a generation before the destruction of "the more wicked part" of the Nephites in the year 320, even Jacob's heir in keeping the prophetic record, Omni, was by his own account "a wicked man" who had not kept the commandments (v. 2). Another measure of the people's spiritual state in Omni's day is how much responsibility he attributes to God in ensuring their security. When Omni reports that he had "fought much with the sword to preserve my people, the Nephites, from falling into the hands of their enemies, the Lamanites" (v. 2), he uses language that elsewhere ascribes *God* to having "kept and preserved them from falling into the hands of their enemies" (v. 6; cf. Mosiah 1:14, 2:31). As the Nephites continued their slide into wickedness, the burden of preserving them in safety progressively shifted from God's shoulders onto their own.

In Omni's generation, the Nephites succeeded at self-preservation. He fathered two sons who also survived the destruction of 320 and, in succession, kept the small plates. The second of these sons he named "Chemish," a slight variation on the name of the god Chemosh, to whose idolatrous worship the children of Israel were tempted, perhaps reflecting an amalgamation in Omni's day of the monotheistic faith of Israel with idolatrous traditions (1 Kgs. 11:7, 33; 2 Kgs. 23:13).

The first son, Amaron, inscribed on the plates a brief overview of the divine judgment visited on the Nephites 320 years after the Lord led Lehi out of Jerusalem:

> Behold, it came to pass that three hundred and twenty years had passed away, and the more wicked part of the Nephites were destroyed, for the Lord would not suffer, after he had led them out of the land of Jerusalem and kept and preserved them from falling into the hands of their enemies, yea, he would not suffer that the words should not be verified, which he spake unto our fathers, saying

that: Inasmuch as ye will not keep my commandments ye shall not prosper in the land; wherefore, the Lord did visit them in great judgment; nevertheless, he did spare the righteous that they should not perish, but did deliver them out of the hands of their enemies. (Omni 1:5–7)

Though Amaron's brief account does not specifically identify how or from whom the righteous were delivered, it hints at the larger course of events. In other places where the Book of Mormon speaks of people being delivered "out of the hands of" their enemies, those delivered had either been in bondage to their enemies or threatened with annihilation by a much more formidable enemy force (e.g. Mosiah 7:15; 3 Ne. 4:8).

The usual enemies from whom the Nephites required deliverance were the Lamanites. But marauding Lamanite armies, ever equal-opportunity destroyers, may not have discriminated between "the righteous" and "the more wicked part" of the inhabitants of the land of Nephi. Other possible scenarios of destruction may include Nephite civil war, in which the righteous either do not participate, or they heed prophetic warning and temporarily relocate to beyond the city while destructions occur. The author's spare description of the event leaves the temporal details of this destruction ambiguous, allowing for these and other possible military scenarios. However, it makes its spiritual cause crystal clear. Amaron explicitly ascribes the destruction to his people's refusal to keep the commandments:

Inasmuch as ye will not keep my [the Lord's] commandments ye shall not prosper in the land; wherefore, the Lord did visit them in great judgment. (Omni 1:7)

The lesson of this destruction, for those who did not die demonstrating it, is that God's *punitive* clause in the prosperity covenant, like His positive promises, was in earnest. Having fulfilled His blessing to Nephi, that if the Nephites kept the commandments they would prosper, God would not allow the accompanying curse He had spoken to go unfulfilled but would write it in stone and verify it in deed.

Based on Book of Mormon precedent and principle, the people of the land of Nephi should have been warned repeatedly, and then with urgent finality, that in resisting the commandments they were ripening for destruction (cf. Alma 45:16; Hel. 8:26; Ether 2:9, 15). The pattern of God first sending prophets to warn His people, intensifying the warning as the end draws near, and sometimes also sending a deliverer to lead the righteous to safety are played out in the destruction of the city of Ammonihah, the destruction following the crucifixion of Christ, and the final destructions of both the Jaredites and the Nephites. Nephi, the son of Lehi, even raised these patterns to the level of general principles:

And as one generation hath been destroyed among the Jews because of iniquity, even so have they been destroyed from generation to generation according to their iniquities; and never hath any of them been destroyed save it were foretold them by the prophets of the Lord. (2 Ne. 25:9; cf. Amos 3:7)

And he raiseth up a righteous nation, and destroyeth the nations of the wicked. And he leadeth away the righteous into precious lands, and the wicked he destroyeth, and curseth the land unto them for their sakes. (1 Ne. 17: 37–38)

We are told in the small plates of warnings to the people of Nephi a century in advance of the year 320 (Jarom 1:10), but we are not specifically informed on how and by whom they were warned on the eve of their destruction. Mormon's later abridgment, however, gives us a strong candidate for a prophet on whom the burden of this final warning fell: Aminadi.

Amulek's Forefather Aminadi

A man of commerce who became a prophet, Amulek had been a long-time inhabitant of the city of Ammonihah before Alma$_2$, high priest over the church, arrived to preach repentance. Amulek and Alma$_2$ were the two prophets who gave a final warning of destruction to Ammonihah, an American sister city to Sodom and Gomorrah, sharing both their wickedness and their fate. In introducing himself as a preacher of repentance to his fellow citizens, Amulek emphasized his stature in the community as "a man of no small reputation" who had "acquired much riches by the hand of my industry" and had "many kindreds and friends" (Alma 10:4). But before appealing to his individual merits he grounded his status in a recitation of his lineage, highlighting his descent from Aminadi:[1]

I am Amulek; I am the son of Gidanah, who was the son of Ishmael, who was a descendant of Aminadi; and it was that same Aminadi who interpreted the writing which was upon the wall of the temple, which was written by the finger of God. And Aminadi was a descendant of Nephi, who was the son of Lehi, who came out of the land of Jerusalem, who was a descendant of Manasseh, who was the son of Joseph who was sold into Egypt by the hands of his brethren. (Alma 10:2–3)

Amulek's emphasis on his ancestor Aminadi and explanation that his Aminadi was "that same Aminadi" who interpreted the writing on the wall show that the story was a familiar one and that Aminadi was a man of stature in Nephite history—as Brant Gardner put it, "an illustrious ancestor (Aminadi) known by name to all those present." Despite having known but little of religion previous to Alma$_2$'s arrival, Amulek was keenly aware of his ancestor's role in the writing-on-the-wall incident (Alma 10:5). Aminadi's

1. Brant Gardner, *Second Witness: Analytical and Contextual Commentary on the Book of Mormon*, 4:164.

role in the incident was also sufficiently renowned that even the citizens of Ammonihah, an irreligious people on whose hearts "Satan had gotten great hold" and who rejected as "foolish traditions" the tenets of the church, could be assumed to know it (Alma 8:9, 11).

Just what is the story of Aminadi that was familiar to the Nephites but only touched on in our surviving Book of Mormon text? As scant as the mention of Aminadi's story is in our text, even this brief allusion provides information with which we can begin to place Aminadi in his proper time, place, and circumstance to recover his prophetic message.

The Time of Aminadi

Commentators on Alma 10 who have attempted to locate the Aminadi story chronologically and geographically have placed it at the temple in the city of Nephi prior to Mosiah$_1$'s exodus to Zarahemla. Nineteenth-century Book of Mormon scholar George Reynolds argued that although Amulek's story gives no record of when Aminadi lived, "it must have been in the land of Nephi before the Nephites migrated to Zarahemla as he was at least four generations separated from Amulek."[2] Brant Gardner suggests that this event may have "occurred before Mosiah$_1$ led his people of out the city of Nephi."[3] And Verneil Simmons places it in the city of Nephi at a time when "destruction was imminent."[4]

The text provides clues by which we can judge these surmises. First, Aminadi's role in the writing-on-the-wall incident logically places it in the land of Nephi before the exodus to Zarahemla and the subsequent reign of Mosiah$_1$. Given Mosiah$_1$ and his successors' prophetic ability to interpret sacred writings, there would have been no need for Aminadi to interpret the writing on the temple wall during their reigns.

Second, Amulek's personal and genealogical self-revelations imply a chronology that would put his ancestor Aminadi in the land of Nephi before Mosiah's exodus. When he describes himself as having children (Alma 10:11) and as "a man of no small reputation," with "many kindreds and friends," and having "acquired much riches by the hand of my industry" (v. 4), Amulek implies his age. A family, an extensive social network, and acquired wealth are products of time, and Amulek's possession of all these make him likely not less than forty at the time of his preaching (around year 508 from Lehi's exodus, or 82 BC), placing his likely time of birth before year 479.

---

2. George Reynolds, *A Dictionary of the Book of Mormon, Comprising its Biographical, Geographical and other Proper Names*, 54.

3. Gardner, *Second Witness*, 4:164.

4. Verneil Simmons, *Peoples, Places and Prophecies: A Study of the Book of Mormon*, 161

The next chronological clue Amulek provides is that Aminadi is a paternal-line ancestor four or more generations distant. After stating that he is the son of Gidanah,[5] who was the son of Ishmael, Amulek reports that Ishmael was a "descendant" of Aminadi, placing Aminadi at least two generations prior to Ishmael and at least four generations prior to Amulek. Without a specific number for the length of each of these generations, the best proxy is the *average* length of a paternal generation, which several recent studies in anthropology and population genetics have put at about thirty-five years.[6]

Taking the average as our guide, an Aminadi living four or more generations before Amulek would have been born before the mid–300s in the Nephite calendar and thus prior to Mosiah$_1$'s exodus from Nephi to Zarahemla at about Nephite year 400 (ca. 200 BC). Thus, George Reynolds was correct when estimating that Aminadi's generational distance from Amulek placed his ministry "in the land of Nephi before the migration to Zarahemla."

Aminadi as a Wisdom Figure

The prominence accorded to Aminadi for giving the interpretation of the writing on the wall marks it as an extraordinary achievement, one identifying him and establishing his reputation as a prophet. He interpreted the writing on the wall for the people of Nephi when others, like the priests in whose domain it appeared, could not. However, his revelatory act was not entirely unique and is part of a broader pattern of incidents in which Hebrew prophets, biblical and Nephite, acted as wisdom figures or as interpreters of the hidden meanings of divine manifestations. Identifying this pattern of wisdom figures and situating Aminadi in it will help flesh out his story.

We can discern this wisdom-figure pattern in the narratives of the biblical prophet Daniel, the patriarch Joseph, and of the Book of Mormon prophet Abinadi. While varying in their details, these narratives share a common core: a captive prophet displays divine wisdom before the king by interpreting what the king's "wise" men cannot and accurately forewarning of calamity. Looking at the specific instances of prophetic interpretation allows us to draw connections between each of these three warning prophets and Aminadi.

The strongest and most obvious scriptural parallel to Aminadi's interpretation of the writing on the wall of the temple is the story of Daniel interpreting the writing on the wall of the palace of Belshazzar, king of Babylon. During a great feast Belshazzar brought out the gold and silver vessels that his father Nebuchadnezzar had plundered from Solomon's temple for his revelers

---

5. Although the name of Amulek's father is given as "Giddonah" in printed editions of the Book of Mormon since 1830, it appears in manuscript as spelled here.

6. Donn Devine, "How Long Is a Generation?"

to drink wine from while they praised "gods of gold, and of silver, of brass, of iron, of wood, and of stone" (Dan. 5:1–4). In an untimely crashing of the sacrilegious merriment, there "came forth fingers of a man's hand, and wrote over against the candlestick upon the plaister of the wall of the king's palace: and the king saw the part of the hand that wrote" (v. 5). At the appearance of the hand, the king cried out for "the wise men of Babylon." "But," the author tells us, "they could not read the writing, nor make known to the king the interpretation thereof" (vv. 6–8). The king sent for Daniel, a Jew taken captive from Jerusalem during the Babylonian conquest who had established his reputation with Nebuchadnezzar for the "interpreting of dreams, and shewing of hard sentences, and dissolving of doubts" (v. 12). Daniel then interpreted the writing to portend Belshazzar's death and the fall of his kingdom, both of which occurred immediately "in that night" (vv. 13–31).[7] This successful prophecy, along with his previous interpretation of Nebuchadnezzar's dream, established Daniel as a prophet of God and the "revealer of secrets," resulting in him receiving a high political rank (2:47; 5:29).

The parallels between Daniel's story and even the small amount we know of Aminadi's are substantial. In each, a supernatural hand appears and writes on the wall with its finger or fingers. This writing cannot be understood by ordinary persons or even the learned wise men and priests but must be interpreted by the prophet. These two appearances of supernatural writing, despite their differing locations, also share a temple theme with one of them occurring in the temple and the other being prompted by the profaning of temple relics.

Although Aminadi's reported New World experience as a wisdom figure strongly parallels Daniel's experience in the Old World, both hark back to much earlier biblical precedent established by Aminadi's patriarchal ancestor Joseph of Egypt.[8] Joseph, who interpreted Pharaoh's dream of seven fat cattle and seven lean cattle to predict seven years of plenty followed by seven years of famine, provided the earliest model of the prophet-interpreter (Gen. 41). Aminadi's story, even in the broad strokes with which it is sketched in our Book of Mormon, follows Joseph's blueprint. In each, a prophet is interpreting for others a divine manifestation they could not interpret for themselves. This parallel may account for Amulek's decision to emphasize Joseph among Aminadi's ancestors, rather than patriarchs such as Abraham, Isaac, and Jacob.

---

7. The penalty of death follows naturally from the profaning of the temple relics. Under the Law of Moses the priests were told that none but they were to have contact with the temple vessels "that neither they, nor ye also, die" (Num. 18:3).

8. Although Daniel's experience likely preceded Aminadi's by some two and a half centuries, neither Aminadi nor the audience of his prophetic warnings would have been familiar with that earlier event, since it occurred after Lehi and his colony set out from Palestine for the New World.

Joseph's experience also established a model for Daniel's. Anticipating Daniel by well over a millennium, Joseph too was an exile from Palestine and a captive who was called upon to interpret a revelatory experience for the king that his wise men could not, who interpreted that experience as a harbinger of calamity, and whose reputation as a prophet and position as the king's advisor was established by this incident (Gen. 41:37–45).[9]

Finally, a Book of Mormon wisdom figure on the pattern of both Joseph and Daniel is Abinadi, who prophesied some generations after Aminadi. Abinadi, like Daniel, stood in opposition to a wicked king and in competition with his priests. He foretold the downfall and death of King Noah, who "did not keep the commandments of God, but . . . did walk after the desires of his own heart" (Mosiah 11:2). When captured, Abinadi was tried by the king and priests for prophesying against Noah and preaching of Christ.[10] In the course of the trial, Noah's priests asked Abinadi to interpret prophecies of Isaiah (Isa. 52:7–10). He obliged but not without seizing the opportunity to contrast the learned priests' ignorance of spiritual things with his own divinely given wisdom:

> Are you priests, and pretend to teach this people, and to understand the spirit of prophesying, and yet desire to know of me what these things mean? . . . Ye have not applied your hearts to understanding; therefore, ye have not been wise. (Mosiah 12:25, 27)

Abinadi also read and expounded other scripture to the priests—laying peculiar stress on the Ten Commandments. Throughout his trial, Abinadi preached, acted, and even displayed divine power in ways that evoke the writing of the commandments by the finger of God on Mount Sinai—a theme to which we will return in our discussion of Aminadi's message.

While demonstrating that the priests misunderstood the law of Moses rather than Christ to be the source of salvation, Abinadi nonetheless affirmed the necessity of keeping "the commandments which the Lord delivered unto Moses in the mount of Sinai," and he rebuked them for neither keeping these commandments nor teaching them (Mosiah 12:33, 37). When the enraged priests tried to interrupt his reading of the Ten Commandments, he was transfigured before them so that "his face shone with exceeding luster, even as Moses' did while in the mount of Sinai, while speaking with the Lord" (13:5). Under divine protection, Abinadi announced that he would "read unto you the remainder of the commandments of God, for I perceive that

---

9. Paralleling Joseph, as an interpreter Daniel did not limit his work to walls but also read the meaning of dreams.

10. Abinadi's trial was likely held either in King Noah's palace or in the temple, both potential gathering places for the king and priests. (See Mosiah 11:9–11.)

they are not written in your hearts," alluding again to God writing the Ten Commandments on the tablets of Sinai by his finger (v. 11).[11] Completing the commandments, Abinadi preached the redemptive work of Christ and predicted the king's death. His burden of prophecy delivered, Abinadi was burned to death "because he would not deny the commandments of God" (17:20).

Though Abinadi diverged from the messages of the biblical wisdom figures Joseph and Daniel in that the divine manifestations he interpreted and expounded were in *scripture*—that is, the prophecies of Isaiah and the commandments given on Sinai—his story shares the structure of theirs. He, like them, is a captive prophet displaying his revelatory power before the king, interpreting what the king's wise men cannot, and forewarning of catastrophe—including in this case, as in Daniel's, the king's death.

Abinadi also echoes his near-namesake predecessor among the Nephite prophets, Aminadi. As Aminadi had prophesied in the original city of Nephi before its destruction, Abinadi prophesied in the rebuilt city of Nephi (Mosiah 11:10–11). Also like Aminadi, Abinadi acts as a wisdom figure and a prophetic interpreter. But the strongest links between Aminadi and Abinadi—how their prophetic messages build on the giving of the Ten Commandments on Sinai—will have to await full development later in this chapter.

That Aminadi strongly parallels each of these three other wisdom figures individually suggests that he also fits their shared narrative template. The core narrative of all these other instances of interpretation by divine wisdom would also be the narrative in which his interpretation of the writing on the wall belongs: Aminadi was a captive who interpreted a divine manifestation that the king's wise men could not, and from this he forewarned of calamity.

Noting that Daniel's writing on the wall "spelled doom and destruction to the king of Babylon and his kingdom," Book of Mormon commentator Verneil Simmons perceptively asked, "Did the Lord warn the Nephites at the temple in the City of Nephi by a similar method, that destruction was imminent?"[12] The unique parallel between the Aminadi and Daniel incidents suggests that their warning experiences were given in similar circumstances and for similar purposes; that is, Aminadi's interpretation of the writing on the wall gave a final warning of imminent doom to his king regarding both the king's fate and that of his kingdom.[13]

---

11. Grant Hardy, *Understanding the Book of Mormon: A Reader's Guide*, 157–60.

12. Simmons, *Peoples, Places and Prophecies*, 161.

13. An even more forceful warning of destruction, in this case complete annihilation, is given in the story of Amulek's preaching in Ammonihah, where the surviving reference to Aminadi is introduced. Alan C. Miner notes the parallel "between the *sudden* destruction of the kingdom of Babylon" warned of by Daniel's interpretation of the writing on the wall "and the prophecies of Alma and Amulek

Interpreting the Writing on the Wall

The repeated prophetic narrative that Aminadi appears to share and his particular parallel with Daniel's warning prophecy to Belshazzar suggest that the writing Aminadi interpreted from the wall of the temple warned his king and people of imminent destruction. But this does not tell us the reasons behind this rebuke and threatened destruction. What provoked God to set his hand to write on the wall of Nephi's temple? To put flesh on our skeletal story of Aminadi, we, like him, must discern the meaning of the writing on the wall.

Thus far we have identified how Aminadi's experience, encapsulated by his descendant Amulek, parallels that of Daniel and other prophets. But to accurately "read" the import of the writing on the wall, we must also examine how Aminadi's experience *diverges* from the other instances of prophetic interpretation. These differences are as instructive as the similarities and reveal in broad strokes the divine message Aminadi read from the wall of the temple.

The fundamental differences between Aminadi's incident of reading the writing on the wall and Daniel's are in where the writing appears and to whom it is attributed. In Daniel's case, the writing appears on the wall of Belshazzar's palace, while in Aminadi's it appears on the wall of the temple of Nephi. In the Daniel event, the profaning of temple sacredness (through the sanctuary relics) had been the impetus and implicit subject for the writing on the wall of Belshazzar's palace. There, temple sacredness was (again) profaned as a result of the destruction of Jerusalem and its temple, from which these relics had been plundered. In the Aminadi event, one natural subject for writing appearing on the temple would be the temple itself. God's writing would affirm the temple's sacredness and might warn of the consequences that were to follow for profaning it—judgments on the wicked and the withdrawal of his presence—leading to the temple's destruction (Hel. 4:24–25; cf. 1 Cor. 3:16–17), and the ultimate destruction of the people of the land of Nephi with their temple. Rather than condemning the people for past actions, in Aminadi's case the writing on the wall could *forewarn* that such destruction was coming if the people, who have ignored God's commandments and begun to pollute his temple, continued to do so.[14]

---

concerning the sudden destruction of the city of Ammonihah (Alma 10:20–27; 16:1–11)," drawing the implication that Aminadi's writing on the wall also warned of imminent destruction. Alan C. Miner, "The Lord Redeems His Covenant Children: Alma 1 -- Alma 44"; emphasis in original.

14. A message about the reverencing or pollution of the temple would most naturally be addressed to the very audience we have posited for Aminadi—the king and priests. Priests are the functionaries of the temple, and in the Book of Mormon kings are the caretakers and high priests over the temples. (See Chapter 11.)

A message *about* the temple in the writing read by Aminadi would account for the place of its appearance (the temple wall) but not for its reported source (the finger of God). This is the other significant difference between Daniel's interpreted text and Aminadi's: what is said of the supernatural scribe. In the Daniel incident, the writer's identity is indefinite: the writing was done by the miraculously appearing "fingers of a man's hand," with no indication whether the hand belonged to God, an angel, another supernatural being, or perhaps something more illusory. For the author of Daniel, it did not matter to whom the hand belonged, only what it wrote. In the Aminadi incident, however, the owner of the hand was unequivocally identified. The writing on the wall was not made merely by "the fingers of a man's hand" but "by the finger of *God*."

Why was the message interpreted by Aminadi given in such a distinctive way, written on the wall of the temple, and specifically by God's finger? There are numerous modes of revelation that could have been employed, such as dreams, tongues, visionary symbolism, by one of the many gifts of the Spirit, or by *speaking* God's words: "Thus saith the Lord." Instead it was delivered through a visual message that Aminadi had to interpret and read out. Such an unusual medium of prophecy might be resorted to when other methods (like the spoken word) have not succeeded in getting the people's attention before the destroying armies or angels begin their work. This would account for the *drama* of the experience but still not for its specific form. Why employ writing by God's finger instead of giving a sign in the heavens, speaking out of a whirlwind (as God did to Job), sending an angel with a drawn sword (as God did to Balaam), or any other distinctive medium?

The reason for using one medium over another is often that the medium chosen to communicate a message can become part of the message itself that sharpens, reinforces, and carries part of its content. In the case of God speaking to Job out of a whirlwind, the form through which the message is presented is tailored to the message itself. God demands to know of Job by what right he questions God's understanding and will as nature's creator and master, demonstrating the power of nature of which he speaks—and his own mastery of it—by clothing himself in the whirlwind. In the case of the Lord's message to Balaam also, the medium—an angel with a drawn sword—reinforces the message that Balaam must act in the role of prophet only as the Lord commands or he will be destroyed (Num. 22:21–35). After later using his prophetic role to mislead the Midianites and Israelites into offering sacrifices to Baal at Peor (25:1–5; 31:8, 16) and thus ignoring the sword in the hand of the angel, Balaam dies by a sword in the hand of an Israelite (31:1–8).

As the medium was carefully tailored to the message in the cases of Job and Balaam, so it was also in that of Aminadi. Writing by the finger of God was not a neutral medium through which to communicate (if any ever is), but it was one laden with symbolic meaning and historical connections that the audience would have recognized and that comprised part of the message itself. To a pious Israelite, or anyone familiar with the Bible, the medium of writing by the finger of God evokes the giving of the Ten Commandments, which God inscribed in this way on stone tablets (Ex. 31:18; Deut. 9:10). The use of the same medium to give this message as God had used to give the Ten Commandments on Sinai has several functions or effects. First, it confirms the story of the Ten Commandments having been given in that way, reinforcing their divine authority. Second, it imparts to the new message the same authority held by the Ten Commandments. Third, it connects the new revelation to the theme of commandments, implying that it almost certainly reiterated the perennial message of the prophets to the Nephites: keep the commandments, because your spiritual well-being, material prosperity, and ultimate survival depend on it.

The writing of this covenant on the temple wall by the finger of God would have demonstrated that it was as divine in origin and immutable as the God-inscribed commandments themselves. The temple of Nephi, which lacked the actual stone tablets inscribed by God's finger and held in the temple of Solomon, would now possess an equivalent reminder of the commandments' divine authorship and of God's presence in the temple—a presence granted conditionally, so long as his people did not pollute the temple and themselves to the point that He would have to withdraw his Spirit and thus leave them to destruction. Removing all room for doubt, these and other consequences of breaking the commandments would have been literally spelled out and written in stone—God's word assuring that the Nephites could not prosper if they did not keep his commandments would have been mercifully verified by this miraculous message of warning before it was verified in their destruction.[15]

Aminadi, like Abinadi, delivered his message in a way that evoked (as strongly as any could) the inscribing of the commandments on the stone tablets of Sinai, because the purpose of Aminadi's prophetic mission was the same as Abinadi's—to demonstrate to the king, priests, and people of the land of Nephi the literal divine origin of the commandments and the necessity to salvation and survival of keeping them. The people comprising the original Nephite nation in the land of Nephi, however, did not heed this message, and they were eventually destroyed for continued disobedience to the command-ments—except for those led away by Mosiah₁.

---

15. In the strongest reiteration of the Ten Commandments and God's covenant with the Nephites, his finger would have written *both* on the temple wall, along with a specific warning that without repentance destruction was imminent.

Aminadi and the Destruction of the Year 320

That Aminadi's interpretation of the writing on the wall warned of the destruction of "the more wicked part" in the year 320 is manifested by three distinct lines of evidence. First, Aminadi foretelling the catastrophe of 320 would account for his enduring cultural fame. Few events could be expected to produce such broad post-mortem fame as that enjoyed by Aminadi, and predicting the near-destruction of the nation is surely one of those few.

Second, what we know of the period and place of Aminadi's interpretive prophecy fits the context of the destruction in the year 320. As discussed earlier, when Amulek discusses his genealogy from Aminadi, he skips at least one generation. This requires Aminadi to have lived at least four generations prior to Amulek. However, if there was only one intervening generation between Amulek's grandfather Ishmael and Aminadi, it is difficult to see why Amulek described Ishmael as Aminadi's descendant rather than just naming that person. Amulek thus likely abbreviated his geneaology to avoid the cumbersome need to enumerate *multiple* intervening generations. Two omitted generations (five total generations) would push Aminadi's birth back to a range around the year 303, making him a young man at the time of the destruction; and a third (giving six in total) would make him middle-aged.

The third reason to associate Aminadi's prophecy with the 320 destruction is the way that the two events pair together so perfectly. Both events built on the pattern of repeated prophetic warning that the Nephites must keep the commandments or, in accordance with God's covenant, they would no longer prosper in the land and ultimately be destroyed. The catastrophe of 320, which verified this covenant oath of destruction, would have been heralded by a final prophetic repetition of the oath it was to verify—an ultimatum to repent and keep the commandments immediately or face present destruction. Aminadi's message written by the same divine finger that had written the Ten Commandments on the stone tablets on Sinai would reiterate that oath powerfully and make a fitting final warning before the onslaught of destruction.

A warning of this magnitude through Aminadi could have been fulfilled by only one of a handful of events in early Nephite history, and the only calamitous destructions in evidence for the period are the final destruction of the city of Nephi in about the year 400, warned of by Mosiah₁, and that of 320, doubtless also preceded by a final prophetic warning. Thus, Aminadi's prophetic warning and the destruction of "the more wicked part" belong together. As the destruction of 320 approached for the unrepentant people of Nephi, truly the writing was on the wall.

Aminadi in the Lost Manuscript

The story of Aminadi interpreting the writing on the wall and of the associated destruction of "the more wicked part" of the nation is a substantive part of Nephite political and religious history and, as Brant Gardner posits, would have been included in the comprehensive large plates of Nephi, of which the lost manuscript was an abridgment.[16] For our purposes here we must also ask, did Mormon select this story for inclusion in his abridgment of them in the lost manuscript? The evidence of the text with regard to this narrative is that Mormon should have included it, would have included it, and in fact did include it.

Given the importance and prominence of the event, Mormon *should* have included it in his abridgment from the large plates. The incident of Aminadi interpreting the writing on the wall occurred in a central institution of Nephite society (the temple), was miraculously dramatic, and, as we have seen, evidently provided a warning on which the survival of the Nephite nation hinged, enabling the righteous to escape the destruction of the year 320.

Furthermore, Mormon *would* have included it in his abridgment because of his demonstrated editorial purposes. The story of the 320 destruction in general, and of Aminadi's warning in particular, fulfill one of the basic didactic purposes of Mormon's record—to demonstrate that the people's survival on the land depends on keeping God's commandments. For Mormon to have omitted crucial material of Nephite history that so perfectly advanced his authorial purposes would be baffling.

Finally, given how Mormon deals with Amulek's allusion to this story, it seems evident that Mormon *had* included it earlier in his record. Amulek's account gives evidence that the story was extremely well known among the Nephites. Not only did Amulek himself know of his forebearer's story despite having only recently begun to take an interest in religion (Alma 10:5), he could assume that the people of Ammonihah, better known to us as scriptural book *burners* than as scripture readers (14:8), would also know of Aminadi and the writing on the wall. Mormon, like Amulek, felt no need to explain

---

16. Gardner, *Second Witness*, 4:164. Commentator Daniel H. Ludlow has said of Amulek's mention of Aminadi: "This is the only time Aminadi is mentioned, and our present Book of Mormon gives no further details concerning the writing upon the wall of the temple written by the finger of God. Evidently an account of this incident was recorded on the large plates of Nephi, but Mormon did not include it in his abridgment." Daniel H. Ludlow, *A Companion to Your Study of the Book of Mormon*, 198. Ludlow's conclusion that the story of Aminadi, although on the large plates of Nephi, must not have been included in Mormon's abridgment since it is not in the extant text fails to take into account that much of Mormon's abridgment is lost.

Aminadi's identity beyond this brief mention, apparently assuming his readers would know the significance of the writing on wall incident.[17] Royal Skousen notes the "abruptness" with which this name, like the name Muloch (Mulek) in Mosiah 25:2, is introduced, and he posits that Aminadi therefore "may have been mentioned" in the lost manuscript. Anita Wells similarly reasons that Mormon had introduced Aminadi earlier in his abridgment, "otherwise one might suppose he would have either explained the reference or not included it." I concur: given that Mormon was writing for an audience whose only knowledge of the Nephites would be through his book, he could only assume the reader's familiarity with the story if he had included it earlier in his record.[18] Mormon's quotation of Amulek's cryptic allusion to Aminadi without further explanation thus attests that he had included the fuller story in the early, lost portion of his abridgment.

Aminadi and the Nephite Temple

The most striking thing about the story of Aminadi and the writing on the wall is what it reveals about the function of temples among the Nephites. The temple, as seen here, is much more than a house of sacrifice. For the Nephites, as it functions in the story of Aminadi, the temple is where God's presence resides and may be entered, where covenant relationship with God is established or reaffirmed, and where hidden knowledge can be acquired.

The writing on the wall by God's finger at the temple of Nephi demonstrated his presence there, the sacredness of the place, and that it was to be kept holy. In the temple manifestation for which Aminadi acted as divine interpreter, the Lord affirmed the oaths he had spoken to Lehi and Nephi blessing the land to those who keep the commandments and cursing it to those who break them, and He did so by writing this covenant with his finger just as He had Israel's covenant at Sinai. Here, the temple is also a place for inquiring after and receiving hidden knowledge. While a distinctive feature of the narrative is the medium employed to deliver the divine message—namely, the finger of God writing on the temple wall—the most distinctive aspect of this revelation is that while its message was delivered publicly, the content of the message remained hidden until interpreted by Aminadi. Thus, the revelation was unfolded in two stages: first a presentation of symbols, and only

---

17. Verneil W. Simmons similarly observed, "When Mormon wrote the words of Amulek he apparently felt no further need to explain them." Simmons, *Peoples, Places and Prophecies*, 161.

18. Royal Skousen, *Analysis of Textual Variants of the Book of Mormon*, 3:1465. Anita Cramer Wells, "Lost—But Not Forgotten—116 Pages: What the Book of Mormon Might Have Included," 8.

later, and upon inquiry, an interpretation of those symbols.[19] If the medium is part of the message, then there is an implicit message to the two-stage process of revelation employed in this event that may tell something about both the Nephite temple and God's expectations of the people of Nephi.

The functions of the temple in the story of Aminadi come into sharper focus when that story is viewed in the context of the other sacred events in which God touches earthly objects with his finger. One such event that we have already encountered, in a sacred, temple-like context, is the translation through the interpreters of the Book of Mormon's lost pages. In that process Joseph use the sacred instrument to interpret words written on the veil or curtain in front of him, words the Lord later described as "that which I have written" (D&C 84:57), suggesting the scriptural motif of words being written by his finger (see Chapter 3). Other accounts of God touching objects with his finger appear in scripture. The Aminadi story is one of three narratives in Restoration scripture of God physically touching with his finger, the others being the story of the brother of Jared from the Book of Mormon and the familiar story of Moses at Mount Sinai. Significantly, each of the three "finger of God" stories in the body of Restoration scripture occurs in a temple context. The temple context of the Aminadi story is self-evident. Less evident, though still abundantly clear, is the temple context of the writing of the commandments on the tablets at Mount Sinai.

Sinai was the original and paradigmatic Israelite temple. God declared the sacredness of Sinai when he told Moses through the burning bush: "Put off thy shoes from off thy feet, for the place whereon thou standest is holy ground" (Ex. 3:5). High places, like mountains, often have sacred significance in the scriptures that could both symbolically represent and serve as natural temples.[20] Joseph Smith would later teach that when God's people are unable to build temples, God uses mountains in place of temples:

> The keys are certain signs & words by which false spirits & personages may be detected from true.— which cannot be revealed to the Elders till the Temple is completed.— The rich can only get them in the Temple . The poor may get them on the Mountain top as did moses.[21]

It was at Sinai that the Tabernacle, the portable temple the Israelites carried with them through the Exodus, was first constructed, enabling them to carry with them the mountain's sacred functions, and—in the form of the God-

---

19. A similar revelatory pattern may be found in the corresponding gifts of tongues and the interpretation of tongues, the two requiring each other, in sequence, to impart a full divine revelation (1 Cor. 12:10, 30; 14:5, 13–15, 26–28).

20. Donald W. Parry, "Sinai as Sanctuary and Mountain of God," 482–500.

21. "Discourse, 1 May 1842, as Reported by Willard Richards."

touched stone tablets—a portion of the divine presence manifested there, even when leaving it physically behind (Ex. 31–34). The Ark of the Covenant, created to house Sinai's stone tablets and ultimately rest in Solomon's temple, was constructed there (Ex.37; 2 Chr. 5:10). Indeed, the temple was built to a great extent to house the presence of God brought from Sinai and borne in the Ark (2 Sam. 7:1–6).

An event not known to Aminadi or his contemporaries but preceding the giving of the law on Sinai and sharing these themes occurred on Mount Shelem and is narrated in the Book of Ether. On this mountain, the cryptically named "brother of Jared," while in exodus from the tower of Babel to the New World, spoke with God and saw his finger. As Moses went to Sinai to encounter God, so the brother of Jared went to Shelem—presumably because the cloud in which the Lord had been going before the Jaredites had rested on this mountain, just as the cloud of the biblical Exodus rested on Sinai (Ether 2:4–5, 14; 3:1; Ex. 14:19, 16:10, 24:15–16).

On Shelem, as on Sinai, the Lord appeared veiled in the cloud but then also appeared outside the cloud, unveiling his glory (Ether 3:13–20). And, just as the Lord touched two stone tablets with his fingers to engrave the Law upon them, on Shelem the Lord touched two sets of stones—one set provided by the prophet (v. 1), the other by the Lord (v. 23). The first of these sets of stones would shine physical light for the Jaredites on their journey, as the pillar of fire later would for the Israelites; the second set, the stones of the interpreters used by Nephite prophets and Joseph Smith to translate sacred texts, would shine spiritual light, revealing "secret things" and "hidden things" (Mosiah 8:17, Alma 37:23). Finally, Shelem's temple function is visible in the interaction there between the brother of Jared and the Lord. As M. Catherine Thomas and P. Scott Ferguson have argued, the experience of the brother of Jared on Shelem—with its elements of divine testing, communication through the veil, the granting of greater light in return for obedience, and entering God's presence—can readily be identified by Latter-day Saints as temple endowment worship.[22]

The stories of the natural mountain temples, Sinai and Shelem, share the temple themes identified above from the Aminadi narrative—divine presence, covenant, and hidden knowledge. In the story of Moses on Mount Sinai, God was present on the mount; though Moses first encountered Him in the burning bush (Ex. 3) and later in a cloud (24:16), God eventually admitted Moses into his unveiled presence (33:20–23). The Lord and Moses then desired to similarly bring all the Israelites into His presence on the mountain, but to their

---

22. M. Catherine Thomas, "The Brother of Jared at the Veil," 388–98; P. Scott Ferguson, "Mahonri's Model for Temple Worship: Rending the Veil of Unbelief," 37–45.

displeasure the people would have none of it (Ex. 19:10, 20:18–21). Instead, the Lord touched the stone tablets, transmitting something of Himself—both a symbolic presence and an actual holiness—into them. These tablets then not only *represented* His presence, they *embodied* it, as if a portion of divinity inhered in the grooved stone so that He was understood to be near when the Ark of the Covenant bearing those tablets was at hand. The temple was built to be a house for God by housing the stone tablets of the Law that He had touched. It was this presence through the stone tablets that made the Ark the site of the mercy seat, God's throne on earth (Ex. 25:22).

The giving of the commandments by the finger of God on Sinai was regarded as a binding covenant on the children of Israel (Deut. 5:2, 29:1; 1 Kgs. 8:9; 2 Chr. 5:10; Gal. 4:24). Before giving the commandments, the Lord pledged to them, "if ye will obey my voice indeed, and keep my covenant, then ye shall be a peculiar treasure unto me above all people . . . and ye shall be unto me a kingdom of priests, and an holy nation." In response, "all the people answered together, and said, All that the Lord hath spoken we will do" (Ex. 19:5–8; Deut. 26:16–19). Contingent on their obedience to this covenant at Sinai to keep the Lord's commandments was their prosperity and prolonged life on the land of their inheritance (Deut. 5:2, 30–33).

In the traditional biblical story of the Ten Commandments, Moses broke the tablets in his wrath over his people's worship of the golden calf. God then provided a replacement, writing the same words again on new tablets (Ex. 34:1–2; Deut. 10:1–2). However, in Joseph Smith's prophetic revision of Deuteronomy 10:2, the passage instead has God withholding from the second set of tablets things that had been written on the first but for which the Israelites had shown themselves unworthy: "And I will write on the tables the words that were in the first tables which thou brakest, *save the words of the everlasting covenant of the holy priesthood*" (JST Deut. 10:2).[23]

These same themes that play out in the story of Aminadi at the temple of Nephi and that of Moses on Mount Sinai appear again in the story of the brother of Jared on Mount Shelem. Just as Moses took the second set of stone tablets that he had hewn to Mount Sinai for inscription by God's touch, the brother of Jared took the stones he manufactured up Mount Shelem for illumination by his touch. At Shelem, as in the temple of Nephi in Aminadi's day, the Lord reached His hand through the veil. He then touched the stones one by one with his finger, imparting holiness and power to them as he had to Moses's stone tablets. In the process, the brother of Jared saw the Lord's hand, provoking a dialogue with the Lord that tested the brother of Jared's

---

23. The italicized words are those added in the Joseph Smith Translation.

knowledge and faith; he was then admitted into the Lord's presence and thus redeemed from the Fall.

Shelem is also associated with covenant in the brother of Jared story. The Jaredites are described as having a covenant similar to that of the Nephites, through which the Lord promises that they will prosper if they serve him but threatening their destruction if they take the opposite course (Ether 2:15).[24] It is unclear in the narrative when this covenant was made, though Moroni's abridgement of the Jaredite record first introduces the covenant in the passages immediately preceding the Jaredites' arrival at the place they called Moriancumer that adjoined Mount Shelem (v. 15).

One of the strongest themes of the story of the brother of Jared at Mount Shelem is that of hidden knowledge. There is a public portion of his revelation and a hidden one. Correspondingly, the Book of Ether tells of two records of his experience on the mountain: the one we read *in* the Book of Ether, and the one withheld from us and contained only in the sealed portion of the golden plates. The brother of Jared was told to write and seal up the panoramic vision he was given of the full story of humankind, past, present, and future (Ether 3:22, 27). Moroni, though granting his reader a particle of that world-encompassing revelation in his record, was similarly told to seal up the full account of this vision, which he had transcribed onto the golden plates (4:5).

Moroni's plates, containing the sealed record, were to be hidden up and withheld because of unbelief (Ether 4:3). If the sealed plates could be found today, they would still be in an unreadable script lost after the tower of Babel to all but the now extinct Jaredites, an esoteric language originally "given by the finger of God" (Moses 6:46) and comprehensible only to the few who can read it through the interpreters given to the brother of Jared (Ether 3:22). There are thus two types of plates, or tablets, containing material from the brother of Jared—unsealed and sealed, paralleling the two sets of tablets given at Sinai: one manifest, one hidden. The unsealed plates parallel the second, unbroken set of stone tablets, which contained only the lesser law. The sealed plates parallel the broken (and therefore perhaps unreadable) tablets containing the higher law, the texts of each unavailable because of the collective unrighteousness of their intended audiences.

Yet even for the reader who cannot read a sealed book, a book hid up and conveyed in an unknown tongue, Moroni promises that its content can someday be made available through repentance and faith like that demonstrated by the brother of Jared (4:6–7, 13–15). Until then the reader must

---

24. On the Jaredite covenant, see Lee L. Donaldson, "The Plates of Ether and the Covenant of the Book of Mormon," 69–79.

abide the lesser portion of the revelation, in hope of obtaining those "greater things" (4:4–14; 3 Ne. 26:9–10).

With this review of these temple-related narratives of the finger of God, we can better discern the temple's functions in the story of Aminadi and other Restoration scriptures as a place of entering the divine presence, making covenants, and acquiring hidden knowledge. The writing on the wall of the temple in the Aminadi story by the finger of God symbolizes and actualizes his presence in the temple and further imbues it with divinity. By this writing he signifies that he had been there, was there yet, and would remain unless or until forced by the sanctuary's pollution to withdraw his presence. It further demonstrates that the temple was to be kept holy in how it was treated and by those who entered there keeping themselves holy by keeping his commandments and thus abiding their end of the covenant.

God's intention for Israel, as revealed at Sinai, was to bring all his people into his presence. This did not happen to them collectively, but in the parallel story of the brother of Jared we see it happen to him *individually* through a temple ordeal or test by which he obtained a sure knowledge of God and was redeemed out of the human condition of separation from God. By the light of the Sinai story, the writing by the finger of God on the wall of the temple of Nephi can be seen to recreate the covenant context in which the Law was given and to reaffirm both the Lord's covenant with Lehi and Nephi and also his original covenant with Israel that if they kept the commandments, they would prosper and see their days prolonged on the promised land (Deut. 5:30–33).

Placing the Aminadi temple incident in the context of the other events in which the finger of God plays a role, we can see that it involved both lower and higher levels of revelation. The lower-level (but vital) message to all was essentially that God was present—that the temple of Nephi, like Sinai, was a sacred place and must be treated as such, giving implicit warning against anything or anyone impure entering the temple. The higher-level message was the specific content of God's word as revealed through Aminadi's interpretation thereof—his affirmation of his covenant with their fathers and whatever other meaning he chose to convey.

In *each* of the three incidents in Latter-day Saint scripture involving the finger of God, there is a temple context and revelatory knowledge given in lower and higher levels or degrees, the lesser things, which are available to all, and the greater things, which are esoteric—withheld from those, including the mass of the people, who are unprepared for them. The lesser portions of these revelations point to and require further revelation, either inspired interpretation plumbing their deep or hidden, meanings, or additional revelation supplementing and completing them. Such deeper meanings and higher truths, though hidden from world, are potentially available to those who purify themselves and inquire—like Lehi, the brother of Jared, and Aminadi—at a temple and in faith.

Sadly, the example of Aminadi was lost on the generations that followed after him. These did not grow in spiritual light, but ripened in iniquity. But before the harvest, the Lord would send another messenger into the vineyard, one who like Aminadi would warn, like Moses would deliver, and the like the brother of Jared would attain to the presence of God: Mosiah$_1$.

CHAPTER 14

THE MOSIAN REFORM

Mosiah₁ is one of the most important and powerful kings in the Book of Mormon. With a name evoking Moses who led the Israelites to their Promised Land, Josiah who initiated a reformation in Jerusalem to rid his people of idolatry[1], and the Messiah who would redeem humankind,[2] Mosiah₁ was a truly transformational leader—a prophet, priest, king—who would guide his people to a *new* promised land, steer them away from idolatry, and prepare them for the promised Messiah revealed to their father Lehi in the opening narrative of their history. Not to be confused with his grandson Mosiah₂, the central king in our extant Book of Mosiah, Mosiah₁ marked a pivotal point in the early history of the Nephites, and yet the explicit detail of his life and reign given in Mormon's abridgement have been lost with the manuscript that contained them.

Despite the loss of the Mosiah₁'s detailed narrative, we can piece together a surprising amount of information to reconstruct his prophetic and royal career that served as a bridge between peoples, times, lands, temples, nations, dynasties, and even modes of revelation from God. These include leading an exodus of the remaining righteous in the land of Nephi to a new home in the land of Zarahemla, establishing the temple of Mosiah following the corruption of the temple of Nephi, initiating a new dynastic monarchy no longer led by Nephi's patrilineal heir, founding a new nation comprised of both Lehites and Mulochites (or Mulekites), and receiving revelation as a seer through the Jaredite stone interpreters rather than the Liahona. In all of this, Mosiah₁ can be regarded as the head of a new Nephite dispensation inaugurated by the apostasy of the original Nephite religious and political system established by Lehi and Nephi. Mosiah₁ arrived at a key point in Nephite history, culminating and reversing a lengthy pattern of decline.

---

1. Hugh Nibley noted that the name "Mosiah" evoked "both the early reform of Moses and its later imitation by Josiah." Hugh W. Nibley, *The Prophetic Book of Mormon*, 388.

2. Book of Mormon Critical Text director Royal Skousen notes that Joseph Smith pronounced the name "Mosiah" identically to "Messiah" and that "Mosiah" was "his spelling for Messiah." Royal Skousen, *Analysis of Textual Variants of the Book of Mormon*, 1:259. Joseph's handwritten emendation of 1 Nephi 12:18 to add "Mosiah" (Messiah) is visible on the Book of Mormon Printer's Manuscript. "Printer's Manuscript of the Book of Mormon, circa August 1829–circa January 1830."

The Land of Nephi Before and After Mosiah₁

Mosiah₁'s life occurs within the larger narratives of the Nephites keeping
and breaking covenants with God, including a cycle of rising righteous prosperity followed by declining righteousness and destruction. Following Nephi's
death in the land of Nephi, his younger brother Jacob saw the wickedness
that had begun to grow among the Nephites and prophetically warned them
of the destruction that awaited them if they failed to turn to righteousness:

> But, wo, wo, unto you that are not pure in heart, that are filthy this day before
> God; for except ye repent the land is cursed for your sakes; and the Lamanites,
> which are not filthy like unto you, nevertheless they are cursed with a sore curs-
> ing, shall scourge you even unto destruction. And the time speedily cometh, that
> except ye repent they shall possess the land of your inheritance, and *the Lord God
> will lead away the righteous out from among you.* (Jacob 3:2–3)

Jacob's preaching succeeded in avoiding a "speedily" coming destruction,
with repentance leading the Nephites to the promised blessing of prosperity
at their 200th year (Jarom 1:9), but the subsequent 120 years saw them sink
into sin until the "more wicked part" were destroyed (Omni 1:5) after reject-
ing Aminadi's warnings in the temple. Subsequent to that *partial* destruction
at the time of Aminadi, came a fuller destruction that ultimately fulfilled
Jacob's words of warning.

Between that partial destruction and the reign of Mosiah₁, little Nephite
history is recorded. Abinadom, father of Amaleki, wrote of this period:

> Behold, it came to pass that I saw much war and contention between my people,
> the Nephites, and the Lamanites; and I, with my own sword, have taken the lives
> of many of the Lamanites in the defence of my brethren. (Omni 1:10)

This set the stage for the Nephites' complete extermination from the land of
Nephi. While Mormon's abridgement of that destruction is now lost, evidence of it remains in our published Book of Mormon. From the Record of
Zeniff (Mosiah 9–22) we know that total destruction came to the *people* of
the land of Nephi—as evidenced by the land's complete take over by the
Lamanites (9:1); to their capital *city* of Nephi—as evidenced by some settlers
needing to rebuild it (v. 8); and to the *temple* of Nephi—as evidenced by
Zeniff's son Noah needing to restore it (v. 10). With a land void of Nephite
people or religion, Zeniff's attempt to reclaim "the land of our fathers' first
inheritance" required his own conquest mirroring that of Joshua and Nephi
ahead of him, one initiated with spies and concluded by clearing out the
land's previous inhabitants (vv. 1, 18). (For more on Nephi's and Joshua's
parallel conquests, see Chapter 10.) The people's ripening in iniquity, which
triggered total destruction, also resulted in the final part of Jacob's prophecy

being fulfilled, with "the Lord God" having Mosiah₁, like Lehi before him, "lead away the righteous out from among" the wicked (Jacob 3:4).

What calamity overtook and destroyed this first Nephite nation? Jacob's prophecy offers clues. The Nephites' failure to repent allowed the Lamanites "scourging" of them, "even unto destruction," so their land of inheritance would be "possessed" by the Lamanites (Jacob 3:4).

The Life of Mosiah₁

Most of the few clear details of Mosiah₁'s formal spiritual and political career are narrated near the end of the small plates in Omni 1:12–23 by Amaleki, who "was born in the days of Mosiah; and . . . lived to see his death" (v. 23). From Amaleki's account we are provided with three natural divisions in Mosiah₁'s life: his mission as a prophet, his exodus, and his kingship.

A Warning Prophet

Amaleki begins his narrative with Mosiah₁ being warned by God to flee before some great danger, evidently the pending destruction of the Nephite nation:

> Behold, I will speak unto you somewhat concerning Mosiah, who was made king over the land of Zarahemla; for behold, he being warned of the Lord that he should flee out of the land of Nephi, and as many as would hearken unto the voice of the Lord should also depart out of the land with him, into the wilderness—And it came to pass that he did according as the Lord had commanded him (Omni 1:12–13)

The actual revelation given to Mosiah₁ is not described, yet Amaleki's account shares strong similarities to the accounts of Lehi and Nephi being warned to flee into the wilderness with those who would follow:

> And it came to pass that the Lord commanded my father, even in a dream, that he should take his family and depart into the wilderness. And it came to pass that he was obedient unto the word of the Lord, wherefore he did as the Lord commanded him. (1 Ne. 2:2–3)

> And it came to pass that the Lord did warn me, that I, Nephi, should depart from them and *flee into the wilderness, and all those who would go with me*. Wherefore, it came to pass that I, Nephi, did take my family . . . and all those who would go with me. And all those who would go with me were those who believed in the warnings and the revelations of God; wherefore, *they did hearken* unto my words. (2 Ne. 5:5–6)

In each of these three accounts, we are presented with a prophetic figure being warned by God to take those who would listen away from their lands and into the wilderness, followed by a recognition of his obedience to God for doing so. Assuming that the similarities did not end there, we can surmise that like Lehi and Nephi, Mosiah₁'s prophetic career began with a theophany

(1 Ne. 1:8–14; 11:1–36) and threats on his life (1 Ne. 2:1; 2 Ne. 5:2)—just as it did with Mosiah$_1$'s partial namesake, Moses (Ex. 3:2–6; 10:28).

A Shepherd Leading an Exodus

Like Moses, Lehi, and Nephi before him, Mosiah$_1$ also led his people on an exodus into the wilderness and eventually to a new home. Amaleki summarizes this exodus succinctly:

> And they departed out of the land into the wilderness, as many as would hearken unto the voice of the Lord; and they were led by many preachings and prophesyings. And they were admonished continually by the word of God; and they were led by the power of his arm, through the wilderness until they came down into the land which is called the land of Zarahemla. And they discovered a people, who were called the people of Zarahemla. (Omni 1:13)

The language here of hearkening to a voice and being led to safety away from threats evokes images of a shepherd leading his flock away from dangerous wolves. For example, Alma$_1$, after reminding his listeners how "the Lord did deliver them out of bondage by the power of his word; and we were brought into this land" (Alma 5:5), launches into a sermon describing Christ as "the good shepherd" and repeatedly instructs them to "hearken unto the voice" of that shepherd so that they might be protected (5:37–60):

> And now I say unto you that the good shepherd doth call after you; and if you will hearken unto his voice he will bring you into his fold, and ye are his sheep; and he commandeth you that ye suffer no ravenous wolf to enter among you, that ye may not be destroyed. (v. 60)

We see similar shepherd imagery evoked earlier in the Book of Mormon when Ammon$_1$ tells Zeniff's grandson Limhi about the Jaredite interpreters that were in possession of Mosiah$_1$'s successor but, as we will see, were first discovered by Mosiah$_1$ (Mosiah 8:13–18). Limhi responded by characterizing seers like Mosiah$_1$ and Mosiah$_2$ as shepherds whose people, "blind and impenetrable," were inclined to flee like an unruly flock:

> [T]hese interpreters were doubtless prepared for the purpose of unfolding all such mysteries to the children of men. O how marvelous are the works of the Lord, and how long doth he suffer with his people; yea, and how blind and impenetrable are the understandings of the children of men; for they will not seek wisdom, neither do they desire that she should rule over them! Yea, they are as a wild flock which fleeth from the shepherd, and scattereth, and are driven, and are devoured by the beasts of the forest. (vv. 19–21)

Mosiah$_1$'s story was likely well known to Limhi, and it intersected with his own. Limhi made his mournful observation in the storied city of Nephi, site of the destruction of the first Nephite nation who refused to follow the prophet Mosiah$_1$ as their shepherd. Limhi's imagery of lost sheep, "scattered," "driven," and "devoured" suggests the destruction in the time of Mosiah$_1$.

Mosiah$_1$'s role as shepherd is also suggested typologically. Shepherding, figurative and literal, runs across the lives of biblical figures Mosiah$_1$ reflects—Moses and David—and that of a Book of Mormon figure who reflects him—his great-grandson Ammon$_2$. Prior to serving as a shepherd to God's *people* in the Exodus (Isa. 63:11–12), Moses was a literal shepherd (Ex. 3:1). Similarly, David, who the Lord referred to as "one shepherd over" Israel (Ezek. 37:23–24), was a shepherd before he acceded to the throne and founded a dynasty (1 Sam. 17:15, 34). Ammon$_2$, in many ways a typological inversion of both David and Mosiah$_1$, was a shepherd after *abdicating* his hereditary right to the throne. He tended a spiritual flock and Lamoni's literal flocks (Alma 17:35).[3] Mosiah$_1$, judging by those in whose footsteps he followed, and the descendant who followed in his footsteps, was a shepherd, perhaps literally at some early point in life, and certainly figuratively as he shepherded his people on their exodus and later led them as their king. In this way, as in many others, Mosiah$_1$ prefigured Israel's "good shepherd."

A New King

Mosiah$_1$'s leadership before and during his exodus out of the land of Nephi was that of a prophetic shepherd guiding "as many as would hearken unto the voice of the Lord" to "depart out of the land with him, into the wilderness" (Omni 1:12), rather than of a kingly authority that could demand it. However, once established in their new home, Omni says that "Mosiah . . . *was made king* over the land of Zarahemla" (vv. 12). Rather than asserting any political authority over those he had led to Zarahemla, the language here implies that it was they who had requested that he be king—just as Nephi and Zeniff had been made king by "the voice of the people" after settling a new land (2 Ne. 5:18; Mosiah 7:9). That Mosiah$_1$ was not the heir of Nephi's dynasty is also, as Brant Gardner notes, indicated by the report that each king in Nephi's dynasty bore the throne name "Nephi," a name Mosiah$_1$ *did* not bear (Jacob 1:11).[4] Mosiah$_1$ was thus, like Nephi and the biblical David, not the continuer of a previous dynasty but the founder of a new one.

A Fallen Nephite Dynasty

If Mosiah$_1$ was not a king in the land of Nephi, then what happened to the last in the line of Nephi's dynasty? The published Book of Mormon doesn't

---

3. Ammon$_2$'s inversion of Mosiah$_1$ is further developed later in this chapter.

4. Brant Gardner, *Second Witness: Analytical and Contextual Commentary on the Book of Mormon*, 3:50

describe this ill-fated king or his relationship with Mosiah₁, but given that the record of the kings was recorded on the large plates (Jarom 1:14; Omni 1:11), his identity and story were surely included in Mormon's abridgment in the lost pages. We may, however, see this fallen king implied or referred to in another text issued by Joseph Smith a few weeks after his translation of that lost manuscript story—in Doctrine and Covenants 3. The relationship between the young Mosiah₁ and the king in the land of Nephi offers a context or explanation for an otherwise cryptic allusion to a fallen figure.

This revelation, given in July 1828 in response to the manuscript loss, chastises Joseph:

> [A]lthough a man may have many revelations, and have power to do many mighty works, yet if he boasts in his own strength, and sets at naught the coun-sels of God, and follows after the dictates of his own will and carnal desires, he must fall and incur the vengeance of a just God upon him. (D&C 3:4)

This warning seems to refer to Joseph setting aside God's counsels in asking to lend Martin Harris the manuscript, but its earliest version includes additional words, emphasized below:

> [A]lthough a man may have many Revelations & have power to do many Mighty works yet if he boast in his own strength & Sets at naught the councils of God & follows after the dictates of his will & carnal desires he must fall *to the Earth* & incur the vengence of a Just God upon him.[5]

Throughout the Book of Mormon, the phrase "fall to the earth" is used to describe buildings or structures that have collapsed (Alma 14:29; 3 Ne. 8:14) and persons who have been killed (Alma 44:14; 47:24; 56:56; Hel. 9:3) or made "as if . . . dead" (Alma 18:42) by becoming unconscious (1 Ne. 4:7; Alma 14:27–28; Hel. 9:4–5, 7, 14) or spiritually overcome (Jacob 7:15, 21; Mosiah 4:1; 27:12, 18; Alma 19:16–17; 27:17, 36:7, 10–11; Hel. 14:7; 3 Ne. 1:16–17; 11:12). Even more applicable to the revelation, a *threat* of "falling to the earth" is given by Captain Moroni in his battle against Zerahemnah. After Moroni "smote Zerahemnah that he took off his scalp and it fell to the earth," Moroni holds up that scalp and issues a warning to the Lamanites:

> Even as this scalp has fallen to the earth, which is the scalp of your chief, *so shall ye fall to the earth* except ye will deliver up your weapons of war and depart with a covenant of peace. (Alma 44:14)

The threat, then, in the original phrasing of the revelation seems to be of destruction or death, and thus does not seem to be abstractly referring to Joseph Smith in the context of the revelation.

---

5. "Revelation, July 1828 [D&C 3]."

The original phrase "fall to the earth" does, however, make sense in the context in which the revelation was given—that is, in July 1828, to an audience familiar with the narratives of the lost manuscript: particularly Joseph Smith and Martin Harris. Later readers of the revelation had no such context, and perhaps it was for this reason that the deadly variation was not included in published versions.

In the immediate background of the July 1828 revelation stood the lost manuscript, which concluded with the full narrative of Mosiah₁ and the beginning of Benjamin's narrative. Joseph Smith's revelations have a pattern of building on one another, with each new revelation alluding back to previous revelations. For example, Doctrine and Covenants 89, the Word of Wisdom, builds extensively on the phrasing and concepts of a revelation from two years earlier, Doctrine and Covenants 27, regarding the use of sacramental wine of the saints' own make and not purchased from conspiring enemies.[6] The July 1828 revelation's mention of a seemingly generic "man [who] may have many revelations, and have power to do many mighty works" but turns away from God and is destroyed appears to similarly allude to a person or story the original readers of the revelation would have recognized.

Having recently translated a portion of Mormon's abridgment that narrated the rise of a new king who took the place of a once-righteous but now-fallen dynasty, Joseph and Martin may have easily recognized the story of the last of Nephi's dynasty who, like David's predecessor Saul (1 Sam. 28:20; 31:4–8), turned away from God and was thus felled to the earth by the hands of Lamanites. Given these Book of Mormon images, the phrase "fall to earth" would have been meaningful to Joseph—warning him not to follow in the steps of this ill-fated king.

Teachings of Mosiah₁

Amaleki describes Mosiah₁'s exodus as one rife with divine directives and instruction: "they were led by many preachings and prophesyings. And they were admonished continually by the word of God" (Omni 1:13); however, he does not convey the content of Mosiah₁'s powerful teachings (ironically, considering the specified purpose of the small plates that he was writing on). Despite direct accounts of Mosiah₁'s own sermons, we can glean some of what he taught through an examination of his son Benjamin's final sermon in Zarahemla (Mosiah 2–6).

After a brief opening, Benjamin begins his sermon with an appeal to his father's teachings: "O my people, beware lest there shall arise contentions among you, and ye list to obey *the evil spirit, which was spoken of by my father*

---

6. Clyde Ford, "The Origin of the Word of Wisdom," 134.

Mosiah" (Mosiah 2:32). This "evil spirit" is alluded to again later in the same sermon, without mentioning Mosiah₁ explicitly:

> And ye will not suffer your children that they go hungry, or naked; neither will ye suffer that they transgress the laws of God, and fight and quarrel one with another, and serve the devil, who is the master of sin, or *who is the evil spirit which hath been spoken of by our fathers*, he being an enemy to all righteousness. (4:14)

Here, "the evil spirit which hath been spoken of by our fathers" clearly parallels "the evil spirit, which was spoken of by my father Mosiah." Both teachings also connect the evil spirit with disobedience and contention.

Benjamin's retelling may communicate the original context, wording, and meaning of his father's "evil spirit" warnings: Mosiah₁ warned his people of an evil spirit who would displace their obedience to God and incite them to contend with one another. By looking closer at the context in which Benjamin shared his father's teachings, we can see further evidence that Benjamin did include additional details given by Mosiah₁:

> O my people, beware lest there shall arise contentions among you, and ye list to obey the evil spirit, which was spoken of by my father Mosiah. For behold, there is a wo pronounced upon him who listeth to obey that spirit. . . . And now, I say unto you, my brethren, that after ye have known and have been taught all these things, if ye should transgress and go contrary to that which has been spoken, that ye do withdraw yourselves from the Spirit of the Lord, that it may have no place in you to guide you in wisdom's paths that ye may be blessed, prospered, and preserved—I say unto you, that the man that doeth this, the same cometh out in open rebellion against God; therefore he listeth to obey the evil spirit, and becometh an enemy to all righteousness; therefore, the Lord has no place in him, for he dwelleth not in unholy temples. (Mosiah 2:32, 36–37)

This wider context conveys additional ideas that seem to confirm Benjamin's use of his father's teachings and points us to the context of their probable origins.

Several of the distinct teachings are:

- Following the evil spirit is antithetical to following the Spirit of the Lord; to obey one is to withdraw from the other.
- Persons destroy themselves by withdrawing from God's Spirit.
- Persons are akin to temples, making one who follows the evil spirit an unholy temple.
- The Lord's Spirit cannot dwell in such unholy temples.
- The fate of an unholy temple is destruction (Hel. 4:24–25; cf. 1 Cor. 3:17).

It is here in Benjamin's allusion to "unholy temples" that we get a clue to Mosiah₁'s teachings about "the evil spirit."

When Mosiah₁ left on his exodus, he abandoned Nephi's temple in the hands of the wicked Nephites who remained and the invading Lamanites who would destroy it. Nephi's temple was the original and to this point *only* temple. How could Mosiah₁ justify abandoning God's temple to the wicked? Benjamin's teachings about the evil spirit offer a rationale for leaving behind something sacred. When a temple is defiled it is made unholy, causing the Spirit of the Lord to withdraw from it. Benjamin is speaking figuratively, comparing *people* to temples, but his father was speaking *literally*. The temple that Nephi had consecrated to the Lord, where the Lord had written a warning for His prophet Aminadi, had become the temple of a people who ceased to hearken to the Lord. It was no longer the Lord's temple. (See Chapter 13.)

The ways in which Nephi's temple was defiled are not spelled out, but idolatry among the Nephites before Mosiah₁'s exodus is implied in the Book of Omni by one of its narrators. Omni writes: "[B]ehold, I of myself am a wicked man, and I have not kept the statutes and the commandments of the Lord as I ought to have done" (Omni 1:2). He passed the record to his son Amaron who passed it to Omni's next son Chemish (vv. 8–9), whose name resembles one of the false gods that the biblical Israelites erred in worshipping: Chemosh. Worship of Chemosh was established in Israel, ironically, by the temple builder Solomon (1 Kgs. 11:7), leading God to decry the Israelites: "[T]hey have forsaken me, and have worshipped . . . Chemosh the god of the Moabites . . . and have not walked in my ways" (v. 33). That Omni gave his son a name closely reproducing that of one of the idolatrous gods suggests both his own struggle with God's commandments and idolatry being one of the sins of Omni's generation—all of this happening just before Aminadi gave his warning in the temple. Indeed, this warning occurring in the temple itself may point to commandments broken: false gods being worshipped in God's own house.

So, by the time Mosiah₁ and his followers abandoned the temple it was no longer the Lord's temple. Wickedness and idolatry had invited the evil spirit into the temple, and the Lord's Spirit had to be withdrawn. Without God's presence, such a temple was fit only for destruction. Thus, Benjamin's figurative teachings about the desecration and destruction of temples were for Mosiah₁ and his band of refugees, quite literal, suggesting that this teaching originated with Mosiah₁.

Mosiah₁'s Exodus

In Chapter 8, we saw how Lehi's exodus into the wilderness followed a pattern set by Moses's, including building a tabernacle and acquiring divine objects to aid their travel. That divine aid was also provided for Mosiah₁ is implied by Amaleki's brief description of his exodus being assisted "by the power of [God's] arm" (Omni 1:13). From two key sources (clues in the published Book of Mormon and Fayette Lapham's recollection) we can see that Mosiah₁ also followed a pattern set by Moses and Lehi as he led his own people on an exodus to yet another promised land—one that began with taking refuge at a mountain or hill, building a tabernacle, and discovering a miraculous instrument for divining God's will.

"The Hill North of the Land Shilom"

The Record of Zeniff contained in the Book of Mosiah reports that the wicked king Noah "caused a great tower to be built on the hill north of the land Shilom, *which had been a resort for the children of Nephi at the time they fled out of the land*" (Mosiah 11:13). This story of the "resort" or refuge at the hill north of the land Shilom is not mentioned in the Book of Mormon prior to this point, but the callback heavily implies that the reader should already be aware of it. What more can we learn about this missing narrative? Our published Book of Mosiah gives us enough information to reconstruct the context of the Shilom hill events.

First, we can see from geographical clues in the text that the land the children of Nephi fled was the land that Nephi founded and where the main body of Nephites dwelt until Mosiah₁ led them to Zarahemla—the land of Nephi (2 Ne. 5:7–28; Mosiah 9:1, 10:13; Alma 22:28, 54:12–13; Omni 1:12–14). The land of Shilom and its hill were close enough to the land of Nephi that King Noah had a watchtower built in Nephi that enabled him to "overlook the land of Shilom" (Mosiah 11:12). He also built a tower on the hill of Shilom itself, apparently a watchtower for the protection of the land of Nephi (v. 13). That it was somewhere between the lands of Nephi and Zarahemla is made clear by the additional references to Shilom connected with travels between the two lands. In Mosiah 7, we are told of Ammon₁ who was directed by Mosiah₂ to travel from the land of Zarahemla to the land of Nephi in order to discover what had become of Zeniff and his people. En route, he and his entourage camped at this "hill, which was north of the land Shilom" (Mosiah 7:5, 7, 16). Similarly, after Ammon₁ discovered Zeniff's descendants (now led by his grandson Limhi), he helped them flee from their Lamanite oppressors, this time traveling from Nephi to Zarahemla. In making that journey "they went round about the land of Shilom in the wilderness, and bent their course towards the land of Zarahemla" (Mosiah 22:8, 11).[7]

---

7. In relating Ammon₁'s journey, Mormon provides seemingly needless genealogical information on Ammon₁ that reveals him to be a typological mirror of Mosiah₁. Mosiah₁, a descendant of Nephi whose line will accede to kingship, leads an exodus from the land of Nephi to the land of Zarahemla. Ammon₁, a descendant of Zarahemla whose line has abdicated kingship, leads an expedition from the land of Zarahemla

What these two journeys tell us is that the course between the lands of Nephi and Zarahemla winds around the edges of the land of Shilom, with the hill north of Shilom serving as a suitable encampment along the path. When Ammon$_1$'s party searched for the land of Nephi and reached this hill, they knew they were near their destination and encamped there, then sent a small advance party "down into the land of Nephi" (Mosiah 7:4–6). Thus the Shilom hill was a place where any group "fleeing out of the land" of Nephi could have taken refuge.

Second, we know from the callback that the fleeing occurred in the lost pages period and prior to Mosiah$_1$'s arrival in the land of Zarahemla. The people fled out of the land *of Nephi*, the locus of the original, pre-Mosian-exodus Nephite nation. This occurred prior to the reign of Noah, contemporary with King Benjamin—whose reign occurred almost entirely before Mormon's extant abridgment (see Mosiah 1:1). The callback thus refers to an incident in the early Nephite nation in the lost manuscript period, accounting for why the mentioned incident is otherwise unfamiliar to readers. In a larger Book of Mormon context, variations of the phrase "fleeing out of the land" are used in two small plates narratives: Lehi's exodus from Jerusalem (1 Ne. 3:18; 2 Ne. 1:3) and Mosiah$_1$'s exodus from the land of Nephi (Omni 1:12). Since, the former is clearly not being referred to, it seems that Mosiah$_1$'s exodus beginning with the divine instruction that he should "flee out of the land of Nephi" (v. 12) is the likely event referenced in Mosiah 11:13. Thus, we can see that near the beginning of Mosiah$_1$'s exodus, he led the children of Nephi to seek refuge at the hill north of Shilom, outside of but within view from the land of Nephi.

Third, the phrase "children of Nephi" is patterned on a distinct usage of the phrase "children of Israel" appearing hundreds of times in the Hebrew Bible. While the phrase is primarily used there as a generic term for the biblical Israelites, a similar usage occurs only twice in the Book of Mormon in 3 Nephi 29:1–2. The remaining six occurrences are specifically referring to the Israelites *of the Exodus*: their captivity preceding the Exodus (1 Ne. 17:25), the flight from Egypt (v. 23), the parting of the Red Sea (Mosiah 7:19), the smiting of the rock (1 Ne. 17:29), the "provocation" in the wilderness (Jacob 1:7), and the giving of the Law (Mosiah 13:29). Since the Book of Mormon uses "children of Israel" to evoke the Exodus led by Moses, the

---

to the land of Nephi (Mosiah 7:1–3). Ammon$_1$ thus reverses Mosiah$_1$'s movement to/from kingship, transposes Nephi and Zarahemla in his journey's geography, and similarly exchanges Nephi for Zarahemla in his genealogy. When Ammon$_1$'s journey is understood as a mirror image of Mosiah$_1$'s journey, Ammon$_1$'s encampment at the Shilom hill traveling south from Zarahemla to Nephi would then reflect Mosiah$_1$'s encampment at the hill traveling north from Nephi to Zarahemla.

parallel "the children of Nephi" in Mosiah 11:13 is likely meant to evoke the exodus led by Mosiah$_1$.[8]

Bringing these three points together, we can reconstruct a sequence of events recorded in the lost pages: *under Mosiah$_1$'s prophetic leadership the remaining righteous Nephites fled from the land of Nephi and camped at the hill north of Shilom en route to Zarahemla.*

Mosiah$_1$ in Fayette Lapham's Account

In his report on the interview he had with Joseph Smith Sr. prior to the publication of the Book of Mormon, Fayette Lapham recounts a narrative of the Nephites that occurred after they had settled the promised land:

> They . . . found something of which they did not know the use, but when they went into the tabernacle, a voice said, "What have you got in your hand, there?" They replied that they did not know, but had come to inquire; when the voice said, "Put it on your face, and put your face in a skin, and you will see what it is." They did so, and could see everything of the past, present, and future; and it was the same spectacles that Joseph found with the gold plates. The gold ball stopped here and ceased to direct them any further.[9]

Lapham describes the interpreters' finder using a tabernacle, the temple's portable counterpart, indicating a period between stationary temples. This narrows the incident Lapham describes to one of two periods, because there are only two gaps between temples in the Book of Mormon—after Lehi leaves Jerusalem but before Nephi builds his temple, and during Mosiah$_1$'s exodus.

The account also narrows to these two possible contexts by giving three indications that the interpreters were found on an exodus. First, the finder of the interpreters echoes Moses in that he has a Sinai-like encounter with God, who asks him, "What have you got in your hand there?" This evokes God, from out of the burning bush, asking Moses about his rod: "What is

---

8. Notably, the phrase is used elsewhere four times: twice as a generic reference to Nephites (Mosiah 10:17; 4 Ne. 1:39); as non-Nephites adopting a Nephite identity (Mosiah 25:12); and Mosiah1's people at the end of their exodus (Mosiah 25:2). While "the children of Nephi" in Mosiah 11:13 could be an unusual generic reference to Nephites, the context of their "fleeing out of the land" suggests that Mosiah1's exodus is evoked.

9. Fayette Lapham, "Interview with the Father of Joseph Smith, the Mormon Prophet, Forty Years Ago. His Account of the Finding of the Sacred Plates," in Vogel, *EMD*, 1:466. The emphasis on the spectacles in Lapham's abbreviated account of the Book of Mormon's narrative is likely due to both Joseph Smith Sr.'s own interest in seer stones and that fact that he had already discussed his son's discovery of the stones with the plates and their use in translation. Green Mountain Boys to Thomas Sharp, February 15, 1844, in Vogel, *EMD*, 1:597.

that in thine hand?" (Ex. 4:2). Second, the seer's covering of his face after an encounter with God is also part of the Exodus. When Moses comes down from Sinai after communing with God, he has to cover his face with a cloth because it is still shining from God's glory (34:29–35). (In assessing the validity of Lapham's account, it is also useful to note its parallel here with Joseph Smith's own practice as a seer or scyer of covering his face with an animal skin, his beaver-skin top hat, while using his seer stone.[10]) Third, the seer has these experiences in a tabernacle his people have erected in imitation of the biblical Tabernacle that was first erected at Mount Sinai (33:7). Again, only the early narrative of Lehi and Nephi and the later narrative of Mosiah₁ fit the context described by Lapham.

The small plates accounts of Lehi's and Mosiah₁'s distinct exoduses, however, do not describe the finding of the interpreters. The narrative of Lehi and Nephi prior to Nephi's building of a temple is allotted some twenty-four chapters (1 Ne. 1–19; 2 Ne. 1–5), while the narrative of Mosiah₁ is allotted only eleven verses (Omni 1:12–22), with Mosiah₁'s actual exodus given only two verses (vv. 12–13). Had the interpreters been found during Lehi and Nephi's exodus, we would expect it to be narrated there with the accounts of their acquisition of the other relics. Given that Mosiah₁ is also the first person implied to have possessed and used the interpreters (Chapter 11), all available evidence points to Mosiah₁ finding this relic during his exodus.

A Nephite Moses

As just noted, Lapham's account of Mosiah₁ and the Hebrew Bible's account of Moses at Sinai both have God inquiring what these men are holding in their hands.[11] For Moses, this was his rod that would miraculously transform into a snake and then back into a rod. For the Nephite Moses, it was the Jaredite interpreters that would miraculously transform an indecipherable script into legible text.

In light of Mosiah₁'s role as a Moses leading the righteous Nephites away from the land of Nephi and into a new promised land, it becomes clear that

---

10. For Joseph's hat as a beaver-skin hat, see "Manchester in the Early Days," in Vogel, *EMD*, 3:229. For further discussion relating this to the use of animal skins for wrapping Israelite temple relics during the Exodus see Don Bradley, "American Proto-Zionism and the 'Book of Lehi': Recontextualizing the Rise of Mormonism," 156–58. See also Meg Stout, "The Beaver Skin Hat: How Joseph Interpreted the Plates."

11. The Lord's questions to Moses and Mosiah₁ strikingly echo the question asked by the Israelites when they first encountered manna: "When the Israelites saw it, they said to each other, 'What is it?' For they did not know what it was" (NIV Ex. 16:15). "Manna" is a Hebrew word meaning "What is it?" For the Liahona as an analogue to Aaron's rod and the pot of manna, see Chapter 11.

Lapham is here recounting a significant event that occurred during this exodus: the discovery of the Jaredite interpreters that would provide the Nephites with a new mode of revelation—and ultimately initiate the translation of the Book of Mormon's golden plates.

Replacing the Liahona

Notably, Lapham's account also explains why the Liahona, which guided travels during the lost-manuscript period, is never used again in Mormon's extent abridgment and seems to instead be handed down as a relic of the past.[12] While Nephi implies that he also utilized the "compass, which was prepared for my father by the hand of the Lord" after Lehi's death (2 Ne. 5:12) and handed it on to be used by his successors, by the time of Mosiah$_2$'s reign it seems that it was no longer functioning. Thus, when his people needed to find the land of Nephi (also called "the land of Lehi-Nephi"), "they knew not the course they should travel in the wilderness to go up to the land of Lehi-Nephi; therefore they wandered many days in the wilderness" (Mosiah 7:4). If the Nephites still possessed the "directors," why were they without *direction*?

Lapham offers an answer to this question: the Liahona stopped working. After Mosiah$_1$ acquired the interpreters—presented as a superior instrument: "a gift which is greater can no man have" (Mosiah 8:13–16)—the inferior Liahona was no longer needed and was, for the lack of better term, retired by God. Although this may seem like a small detail, it explains why the Liahona is never again used in Mormon's abridgment—even during its extensive wars and journeys—while continuing, like the parallel relics of the Exodus in the Ark of the Covenant, to stand as a "token of the covenant" handed down among the Nephite kings and high priests.[13] That Lapham offered a detail with such explanatory power without ever having read the Book of Mormon gives weight to his having been given this content from the lost pages by Joseph Smith Sr.

Finding the Jaredite Interpreters

With Mosiah$_1$ echoing the Exodus pattern of his partial namesake Moses and ancestor Lehi, we can surmise that his acquisition of the interpreters

---

12. The Liahona is handed down from Benjamin to Mosiah$_2$ in Mosiah 1:16. Alma$_2$ discusses the Liahona's symbolic meanings in the context of delivering Nephite sacred relics to his son Helaman. He immediately follows this with the charge, "And now, my son, see that ye take care of these sacred things," suggesting that the Liahona was among the relics being delivered (Alma 37:1, 38–47). For more on the Liahona as a sacred relic, see Chapter 11.

13. For the sacred relics with the Ark as "tokens of the covenant," see Exodus 25:16, especially as translated in Harold W. Attridge and Helmut Koester, eds. *Hebrews: A Commentary on the Epistle to the Hebrews*, 239.

also followed a pattern set by them. Just as Moses acquired the stone tablets touched by the finger of God (Ex. 31:18) and Lehi acquired the Liahona prepared by the hand of God (2 Ne. 5:12) during their respective exoduses, we might expect Mosiah₁'s acquisition of the Jaredite stones touched by the finger of the Lord (Ether 3:6) to also happen during his exodus.[14]

The name of the hill Shilom bears a similarity to the biblical high place Shiloh where the Tabernacle and its relics—including the Urim and Thummim—were kept until the building of Solomon's temple (Josh. 18:1; 19:51; Judg. 18:31; 1 Sam. 1:3; 4:3; 14:3; Ps. 78:60; Jer. 7:12–14), making Shilom a fitting place for Mosiah₁ to have found the interpreters—*his* Urim and Thummim—and brought them into his tabernacle.[15] If the land was named or renamed in connection with this event, it may well be that Shilom was named after Shiloh for this very reason.[16]

Shilom bears similarity to two other exodus events as well. The place where the brother of Jared took his molten stones to be touched by the finger of God during his exodus was Shelem, named so "because of its exceeding height" (Ether 3:1), and another mountain—Mount Sinai—was where Moses first erected his Tabernacle and where he received the Ten Commandments written on two stone tablets by God's finger.

With Shiloh, Shelem, and Sinai as antecedent models for encountering God during a divinely led exodus to a new land, the hill at Shilom is the obvious candidate for where Mosiah₁ acquired the interpreters, with no significant alternatives between the lands of Nephi and Zarahemla. The hill is the only landmark or encampment between the place of departure and their destination with a role in their exodus significant enough to garner mention. As a known high place and resort on Mosiah₁'s exodus, the Shilom hill perfectly parallels Mount Sinai of Moses' Exodus and Shelem of the brother of

---

14. The interpreters' first possessor—the brother of Jared—also acquired them during his exodus (Ether 2–3).

15. Shiloh was also identified in literature of Joseph Smith's time as a place of "resort," perhaps illuminating Joseph's use of this term in translating the description of the Shilom hill in Mosiah 11:13: "Israel were ever accustomed to hills and high places for their resort to transact important concerns as well as acts of devotion. . . . Shiloh, a noted place of such resort, was on a high hill." Ethan Smith, *View of the Hebrews; or the Tribes of Israel in America*, 201.

16. This explanation holds whether the name is understood to have been assigned by the contemporaneous Nephites or by a much later literary author of the narrative. Note that if the hill north of Shilom was the setting for Mosiah₁ bringing the interpreters into the tabernacle, then this hill was also where the Nephite sacred relics were completed.

Jared's exodus, in each of which two stones were touched by the finger of God to give guidance to His people.[17]

Acquiring the Jaredite Interpreters

The origin of the interpreters occurs when the brother of Jared created clear white stones from molten rock, took them to the top of Mount Shelem, and requested that the Lord touch them with His finger. In return, the Lord spoke to him from a cloud through the veil and then reached through the veil to touch the stones. As he did so, the brother of Jared saw the Lord's finger. The Lord then asked him a series of questions, beginning with what he saw, to test the brother of Jared's faith and knowledge. When he passed the test, the Lord then brought him into his presence and declared him redeemed from the primordial fall of Adam and Eve. In this process, the Lord also gave the brother of Jared two white stones—the interpreters (Ether 3:23).[18]

This account shares several elements with Lapham's narrative of a Nephite acquiring the interpreters. Each is the story of a man's initiation as a seer in which the incipient seer approaches the divine presence at the veil in a holy place (whether the metaphysical veil on Mount Shelem or the physical veil of the Nephite tabernacle on the hill north of Shilom). In each case, the man brings stones to God and God makes inquiries, in one case about his own hand and in the other about what's in the man's hand.[19] And in each, the man seeks wisdom by revelation from the other side of the veil. The Nephite seer makes this explicit, responding, when asked what the sacred object in his hand is that "he did not know but had come to inquire."[20] Thus, both narratives relate parallel episodes in the history of the interpreters and the

---

17. Like Sinai and Shelem, the Shilom hill provided a temple-like context for theophany and giving of "keys" (Joseph Smith's term for the interpreters—see Chapter 2), evoking his teaching on the giving of keys: "The rich can only get them in the Temple. The poor may get them on the Mountain top as did moses." "Discourse, 1 May 1842, as Reported by Willard Richards."

18. The brother of Jared receiving white stones from Christ evokes the promise of Christ in Revelation 2:17: "To him that overcometh will I give to eat of the hidden manna, and will give him a white stone, and in the stone a new name written, which no man knoweth saving he that receiveth it." See also Doctrine and Covenants 130:10–11.

19. The next event in the brother of Jared's account is that he sees God, which seems a likely next event in the Mosiah₁ account as well, based on context, parallel with the brother of Jared account, and a statement by Harris linking looking into the interpreters with seeing God. For the Martin Harris statement, see "Martin Harris, Joel Tiffany interview," in *Early Mormon Documents*, 2:305. For fuller discussion of this text, see Bradley, "American Proto-Zionism and the Book of Lehi," 134–159.

20. Lapham, "Interview," in Vogel, *EMD*, 1:466.

New World seers who have used them. Together, they read naturally as two installments in the same larger narrative.

The Jaredite Plates

Given that the Jaredite interpreters were to be sealed with the brother of Jared's record, one would assume that when Mosiah₁ recovered the interpreters he also recovered the brother of Jared's golden plates. This assumption, however, is complicated with there being one passage in our present Book of Mormon that potentially refutes this idea and another that supports it.

In the Book of Mosiah, Limhi tells Ammon₁ of his people finding twenty-four plates from which Moroni would eventually abridge the Book of Ether (Mosiah 8:7–9; Ether 1:1–2; 15:33). If the brother of Jared's record is understood to be part of those plates found by Limhi's people, this would indicate that Mosiah₁ could not have found the brother of Jared's record with the interpreters. However, the twenty-four plates are explicitly said to have been the record kept by the *final* Jaredite prophet, Ether, and not the *sealed* record created by the *first* Jaredite prophet, the brother of Jared. Thus, in the final chapter of the Book of Ether, Moroni writes:

> And the Lord spake unto Ether, and said unto him: Go forth. And he went forth, . . . and he finished *his* record; (and the hundredth part I have not written) and he hid them in a manner that the people of Limhi did find them. (Ether 15:33)

And in the opening chapter of his abridgement of that record, Moroni begins:

> And now I, Moroni, proceed to give an account of those ancient inhabitants who were destroyed by the hand of the Lord upon the face of this north country. And I take mine account from the twenty and four plates which were found by the people of Limhi, which is called the Book of Ether. . . . *He that wrote this record was Ether*, and he was a descendant of Coriantor. (Ether 1:1–2, 6)

While Moroni had access to both the interpreters and the brother of Jared's record (Ether 4:4–5), it is clear from the passages above that they were distinct from Ether's twenty-four plates found by Limhi's people. No indication is made of Ether's record being sealed or of Ether having the interpreters; however, it is made clear that the brother of Jared's record was not only sealed but that the interpreters were sealed with them so that the record could be translated at some point:

> And behold, these two stones will I give unto thee, and ye shall seal them up also with the things which ye shall write. For behold, the language which ye shall write I have confounded; wherefore *I will cause in my own due time that these stones shall magnify to the eyes of men these things which ye shall write.* . . . And the Lord said unto him: Write these things and seal them up; and I will show them in mine own due time unto the children of men. And it came to pass that the

Lord commanded him that he should seal up the two stones which he had received, and show them not, until the Lord should show them unto the children of men. (Ether 3:23–24; 27–28)

When the twenty-four plates of Ether were recovered by Limhi's people, the interpreters were not with those plates. They had *already* been recovered and were held by the Nephite king in Zarahemla (Mosiah 8:13–19). Given that the interpreters were sealed up with the brother of Jared's record with the express purpose of translating that record, it should be clear that Mosiah₁ acquired the brother of Jared's record along with the interpreters that were sealed with it.

The People of Muloch

The destination of Mosiah₁'s exodus was another promised land north of the original land of Nephi—the land of Zarahemla. There, Mosiah₁ encountered the Mulochites or "people of Zarahemla," named after their last king. Who were the Mulochites and how did they get there? Amaleki gives the tiniest thumbnail sketch of their history:

> [They] were called the people of Zarahemla. . . . Behold, it came to pass that Mosiah discovered that the people of Zarahemla came out from Jerusalem at the time that Zedekiah, king of Judah, was carried away captive into Babylon. And they journeyed in the wilderness, and were brought by the hand of the Lord across the great waters, into the land where Mosiah discovered them; and they had dwelt there from that time forth. (Omni 1:14–16)

Amaleki notes that Zarahemla's people, like the Nephites, had come out of Jerusalem at the time of Zedekiah, but he doesn't mention their founder or his connection with Zedekiah. Only later in the Book of Mormon is it reported that King Zarahemla was "a descendant of Mulek," who is a *son* of Zedekiah, and the only one of "the sons of Zedekiah" to have survived the second Babylonian invasion by Nebuchadnezzar II (Mosiah 25:2; Hel. 8:21). Muloch is mentioned abruptly and without explanation for the first time in Mosiah 25:2. Royal Skousen has posited that this "sudden reference to Muloch" may indicate that the "now-lost portions of the original text mentioned this Muloch."[21] Fortunately, there is further information on Muloch. First, there is the correct spelling of his name, which has implications for understanding Muloch's relationship with Zedekiah. Second, there is a Muloch narrative from the lost pages reported by Martin Harris's brother Emer.

Muloch

According to Royal Skousen, based on his analysis of the Book of Mormon manuscripts:

---

21. Skousen, *Analysis of Textual Variants*, 3:1465.

[T]he actual name for the surviving son of king Zedekiah was *Muloch*, not *Mulek*, the implication being that Zedekiah named this son after the pagan god Moloch that they sacrificed children to, thus suggesting a rather ominous aspect to king Zedekiah's character.[22]

With Muloch's name so closely resembling the name of an idolatrous god forbidden to the Israelites—and virtually identical in Hebrew script—why would Zedekiah, the Jewish king, give his child that name?

Idolatry in Jerusalem

Zedekiah's punishment by the invading Nebuchadnezzar II included making him witness the murder of his children before having his own eyes removed (2 Kgs. 25:7). This, of course, raises the question of how one of his sons would have survived. A solution to this problem from the lost pages comes to us in a sermon by Martin Harris's brother Emer Harris.

Emer delivered this narrative in the conference of the Utah Stake in Provo on April 6, 1856, when he was asked to speak on the founding of the Church and the coming forth of the Book of Mormon. His account is recorded in the Utah Stake Minutes, a portion of which is published here for the first time:

> Now I will tell you of the history of those that were lost. When the king from Jerusalem [Zedekiah] had his eyes put out but his son Mulek with some others of the royal family hid themselves, and on coming out of their hiding place they found 4 females of the royal family who also had hid themselves from the wrath of the king, they were married together, there being 4 males and 4 females—they were found in this country in the south part. When they were found they had become a small tribe. Consequently when I compared the saying of the Bible and the Book of Mormon I found them to agree, for the things spoken of in the Bible I found more fully spoken of in the Book of Mormon.[23]

Emer implies that he acquired this detailed information from Martin, the person who scribed for and last possessed the lost pages. Indeed, it is possible that Emer Harris *read the story from the lost manuscript itself.* When his brother Martin borrowed the manuscript, he pledged to show it only to five members of his immediate family. Yet Martin actually showed the manuscript to a wider audience, which likely included his own brother since he showed it to various friends and neighbors. Even if Emer did not read the manuscript himself, he could have heard its contents from his brother Martin and other close family members who had seen the manuscript: his parents Nathan and

---

22. Royal Skousen, "The Original Text of the Book of Mormon and Its Publication by Yale University Press," 82; emphasis in original.

23. "General Minutes, April 6, 1856, Provo Utah Central Stake"; spelling and punctuation updated for clarity.

Rhoda Lapham Harris, his brother Preserved, his sister-in-law Lucy Harris, and his first cousin Polly Harris Cobb.

While Emer gives only a few details of the Muloch story from the lost manuscript, these are more than we have in the published Book of Mormon. While the Book of Mormon makes clear that Muloch was not killed by the Babylonians, it is not clear how he, unlike his siblings, avoided this fate. Emer places Muloch in Jerusalem at the time his father was captured by the Babylonian Nebuchadnezzar II but says that Muloch escaped by hiding with others of the royal family. Providentially, four males of David's line found four females of the royal family as they hid "from the wrath of the king"—presumably Nebuchadnezzar II. However, another possibility is that Emer was saying that Muloch and the other seven royals had hidden from King Zedekiah. While this is a less obvious reading, it has intriguing possibilities for how Muloch escaped while his siblings were slaughtered. After Zedekiah imprisoned Jeremiah, the latter issued an oracle addressed explicitly to Zedekiah that holds the king blameworthy for Jewish worship of Moloch. Chillingly portending the soon-to-be-blinded Zedekiah's encounter with king of Babylon, "his eyes shall behold his eyes," Jeremiah thunders:

> [T]hey, their kings, their princes, their priests, and their prophets, and the men of Judah, and the inhabitants of Jerusalem. . . . [T]hey built the high places of Baal . . . to cause their sons and their daughters to pass through the fire unto Molech; which I commanded them not, neither came it into my mind, that they should do this abomination, to cause Judah to sin. (Jer. 32:4; 32, 35)

Taking up the negative implication of Zedekiah naming a child Muloch—like the god who demanded the sacrifice of one's children—anyone named after Moloch might have been marked for sacrifice to the blood-thirsty deity. If King Zedekiah was desperate to petition divine aid from Israel's god or any other god, then Muloch might have been chosen as an offering to stop the impending threat of Nebuchadnezzar. Furthermore, if Muloch hid himself to avoid sacrifice by either Nebuchadnezzar or by his own father, he would not have been present with his family when Nebuchadnezzar had Zedekiah's children put to death. Adding to the drama, this might also suggest dissension in the royal household—with some members siding with the prophet Jeremiah, who advocated that Zedekiah keep his covenant with Nebuchadnezzar, and others who supported Zedekiah's conspiracy against the Babylonian king.

Regardless of the reason for their hiding, four male royals and four female royals provide the etiological narrative for the Mulochite people. The Mulochites were thus a regal people, a nation raised up to the lineage of King David. Emer's account also tacitly communicates an image echoing the story of Noah: eight souls on a boat, four men and four women, whose role will be to populate the land after a divine destruction (Gen. 8:15–18; cf. 1 Pet. 3:20).

Uniting the Nephites and Mulochites

Among the more significant elements of the Mosiah₁ and Mulochite narratives in the lost manuscript is an explanation of how the Nephite and Mulochite peoples joined together under Mosiah₁'s reign to form a combined Nephite-Mulochite nation. Amaleki tells us:

> And they discovered a people, who were called the people of Zarahemla. Now, there was great rejoicing among the people of Zarahemla; and also Zarahemla did rejoice exceedingly, because the Lord had sent the people of Mosiah with the plates of brass which contained the record of the Jews. . . . And at the time that Mosiah discovered them, they had become exceedingly numerous. Nevertheless, they had had many wars and serious contentions, and had fallen by the sword from time to time; and their language had become corrupted; and they had brought no records with them; and they denied the being of their Creator; and Mosiah, nor the people of Mosiah, could understand them. But it came to pass that Mosiah caused that they should be taught in his language. And it came to pass that after they were taught in the language of Mosiah, Zarahemla gave a genealogy of his fathers, according to his memory; and they are written, but not in these plates. And it came to pass that the people of Zarahemla, and of Mosiah, did unite together; and Mosiah was appointed to be their king. (Omni 1:14, 17–19)

How did the leader of a wandering Nephite band ascend the throne over a foreign nation? Mosiah₁ and the Nephites came to the land of Zarahemla as refugees from the land of Nephi, and King Zarahemla is the established monarch over a settled people much more numerous than Mosiah₁'s group in a land that bears his name (Mosiah 25:2–3). Yet, when Mosiah₁'s and Zarahemla's peoples unite, it is Mosiah₁, the leader of the refugees, not Zarahemla, the sitting king, who ends up as king over the combined nation in Zarahemla's land. The selection of Mosiah₁ as king becomes more puzzling if King Zarahemla is the scion of the house of David, the Hebrew Bible's "everlasting" and divinely ordained dynasty (2 Chr. 13:5). The four founding fathers and four founding mothers of the Mulochite nation, identified by Emer Harris as "of the royal family," were thus *all* members of David's royal house, hereditary kings and queens, making Zarahemla *the* heir of David ruling over other heirs of David. The Mulochites were a royal nation, ruled by one who could claim to be a king of kings. So why does it happen "that the people of Zarahemla, and of Mosiah, did unite together; and Mosiah was appointed to be their king" (Omni 1:19)?[24] Without more of the lost Mosiah₁ narrative, we can only guess at partial and provisional insights and answers.

---

24. The dominance of the incoming, literate monotheistic group suggests colonialism. However, the dominance of the *less powerful* group suggests a kind of reverse-colonialism.

Three likely factors are Mosiah₁'s lineage, his supernatural power, and the Nephites' maintenance of their language and scripture.

First, while King Zarahemla is a descendant of Judah through David, Mosiah₁ is a descendant of Joseph through Nephi (the "David" of Joseph's line) and possessor of Joseph's heirloom sword. In the new promised land this is the superior qualification. On one hand, the Hebrew Bible presents the tribe of Judah as the tribe from which the king would come (cf. Gen. 49:10) and David as the divinely appointed king over Israel's Promised Land (1 Sam. 16:1–13). On the other hand, the Book of Mormon presents the Americas as a promised land for the seed of Joseph, just as Judea was for the seed of Judah (Jacob 2:25). Thus, the resurrected Jesus tells his twelve Nephite disciples that the Nephites are "a remnant of the house of Joseph" and "this is the land of *your* inheritance" (3 Ne. 15:12). The new promised land had been given by divine covenant to Lehi and Nephi (1 Ne. 2:20; 4:14; 5:5). So, while Zarahemla had lineal claim to kingship in the *old* Promised Land, the Nephites had lineal claim to rule in the *new* promised land, inherited by Mosiah₁.

Second, even before his exodus, Mosiah₁ had already proven his prophetic abilities (Omni 1:12–13). With his acquisition of the divine interpreters, he now possessed a "high gift from God . . . a gift which is greater can no man have, except he should possess the power of God" (Mosiah 8:16, 20). Perhaps it was this gift that enabled him to reach out and eventually understand the Mulochites in a way that they could not in return.

Finally, immediately preceding Amaleki's report of Mosiah₁ being made king over the united people, he provides the reason why these two kingdoms that came out of Jerusalem were unable to easily communicate:

> [A]t the time that Mosiah discovered them, . . . their language had become corrupted; and they had brought no records with them; and they denied the being of their Creator; and Mosiah, nor the people of Mosiah, could understand them. (Omni 1:17)

With this barrier in place, it was Mosiah₁ who had the wisdom to teach the Mulochites the Nephites' language so they could better associate one with another (v. 18). Now having a shared language, they "did unite together, and Mosiah was appointed to be their king" (v. 19)—no longer separate tribes of Joseph and Judah but one fold under one shepherd (Ezek. 37:15–24).

Mosiah and Messiah

The Book of Mormon (both our present text and the lost pages) opens up with a vision of a singular Messiah that all others would prefigure (1 Ne. 1:19). With this founding vision, a primary theme throughout the Book of Mormon is the anticipation of such a Messiah. In fact, as Moroni wrote on

the very last leaf of the golden plates, one of the central purposes of the record was "to the convincing of the Jew and Gentile that JESUS is the CHRIST
[MESSIAH]" (Title Page). Thus, there is nary a story or element in the Book
of Mormon that does not pursue Nephi's goal "to write, to persuade our
children, and also our brethren to believe in Christ" (2 Ne. 25:23).

With this Nephite tradition of anticipating the Messiah, it would make
sense then that religious leaders among them would see themselves as model-
ing Christ in one way or another. Thus, we see Alma preach that high priests
after the order of Melchizedek were signposts pointing to a Messiah or Christ.
These priests were ordained "in a manner that thereby the people might know
in what manner to look forward to his Son for redemption" (Alma 13:2). It
is within this tradition of messianic typology that Mosiah₁'s prefiguring of
Christ becomes clear.

Prophet, Priest, and King

Mosiah₁ began, not as a king, but as a *prophet*. Like Lehi and Jeremiah,
he was one warned by God of a coming destruction and who warned others.
Upon acquisition of the Jaredite interpreters, Mosiah₁ added the role of *priest*.
Like the biblical high priests, he utilized the Nephite "Urim and Thummim"
in the tabernacle to divine the will of God. Although a parallel figure to
Aaron, Mosiah₁ was not a Levitical priest. Rather he was a high priest after
the order of the Son of God (or after the order of Melchizedek [JST Heb.
7:3; D&C 107:2–4])—thus adding an additional layer pointing to Christ as
the Great High Priest. Finally, in addition to prophet and priest, Mosiah₁ was
chosen as *king*. Thus, perhaps for the first time since Nephi, the people of the
promised land had a righteous leader serving them as *prophet, priest*, and *king*.

Anointed One

Following the precedent of Nephi anointing his successor, Mosiah₁ would
have been anointed king (Jacob 1:19). This Nephite practice of constituting
kings by anointing echoes the Hebraic practice and prefigures Christ by evoking the very meaning of "messiah": the Hebrew word *mashiach* and Greek
christos both mean "anointed." As a prophet like Jeremiah, a priest like Aaron
and Melchizedek, and an anointed king like the dynastic founder David and
temple-builder Solomon, Mosiah₁ joins such greats as Moses, Nephi, and
Joseph Smith in *combining* these roles and thereby typologically prefiguring
the divine Prophet, Priest, King, and Anointed, Jesus.[25]

---

25. Joseph Smith's diary, kept by his private secretary Willard Richards, describes
his own advance through these offices: "we lea[r]n in a priesthood after th[e] order
of Melchisedek—Propht Priest & king—&I will advance from prophet to priest

True to its meaning "anointed," the Hebrew word *mashiach* is used in the Bible with surprisingly wide application to people and objects anointed with sacred oil, including prophets, priests, and kings, and also "the holy things" of the temple—the altar, the sacred vessels, and the shew-bread. As an anointed prophet, priest, and king who saved his people from destruction and brought another people back to remembrance of their God, Mosiah$_1$ pointed to the Messiah, who would save all from eternal death. It is fitting then, and perhaps intentional, that his name would bear such similarity to that of the anticipated Messiah Lehi learned of in vision and who his own son Benjamin would learn of by an angel (Mosiah 3:2–11). The name "Mosiah" was seen by Joseph Smith as similar to "Messiah" to the point that he pronounced and spelled them identically.[26] Mosiah$_1$'s son Benjamin used that similarity at his own son Mosiah$_2$'s anointing as king to teach his people. It is here that Benjamin, son and father of Mosiahs, urged the Nephites, "the people of Mosiah" (Mosiah 1:10), to take on a name that *is* Messiah in translation—Christ:

> And now, these are the words which king Benjamin desired of them; and therefore he said unto them: Ye have spoken the words that I desired; and the covenant which ye have made is a righteous covenant. And now, because of the covenant which ye have made ye shall be called the children of Christ, his sons, and his daughters. (Mosiah 5:6–7)

Following this request, "there was not one soul, except it were little children, but who had entered into the covenant and had taken upon them the name of Christ." (Mosiah 6:2)

Acquiring the Relics

While Mosiah$_1$ apparently acquired the interpreters himself and made these part of the Nephite regalia, it is unclear how he obtained the relics that had belonged to previous kings of Nephi's dynasty—namely, the brass plates, plates of Nephi, sword of Laban, and Liahona. As Donald Cazier asked, "If Mosiah was not the king when he left the land of Nephi, the question arises as to how he happened to get the large plates of Nephi, which obviously accompanied him to Zarahemla."[27]

& then to King not to the kingdoms of this earth but of the most high god." See "Journal, December 1842–June 1844; Book 3, 15 July 1843–29 February 1844." For exposition of this sermon in the context of Joseph Smith's Nauvoo "reformation," modeled on those of Josiah and Mosiah$_1$, see Don Bradley, "'The Grand Fundamental Principles of Mormonism,' Joseph Smith's Unfinished Reformation," 32–41.

26. See the source and discussion in note 2 of this chapter.

27. Donald Arthur Cazier, "A Study of Nephite, Lamanite, and Jaredite Governmental Institutions and Policies as Portrayed in the Book of Mormon," 72.

The most immediate answer would be that Mosiah₁ was guided to take them from those unworthy to retain them in their now unholy temple. This had precedent. We know from Nephi—first of his dynasty—that he was led by God to steal the Josephite relics (brass plates and sword of Laban) from their otherwise lawful possessor, "that a nation should [not] dwindle and perish in unbelief" (1 Ne. 4:13). Though Nephi is silent on how he took the brass plates and the Liahona when fleeing from his brothers (2 Ne. 5:12), the Lamanites from then on are "wroth with him because he departed into the wilderness . . . and took the records which were engraven on the plates of brass, for they said that he robbed them" (Mosiah 10:17; Alma 20:13; 54:17).

If Mosiah₁ had similarly taken the temple relics to protect them from destruction and prevent his own people from perishing from unbelief, he would have had Nephi as an exemplar. Strengthening the parallel to Nephi even further, Mosiah₁ would have then brought the relics—particularly the brass plates—to the Mulochites, who offer us a perfect counterexample of what would have happened if Nephi had not taken the brass plates from Laban or if Mosiah₁ did not take them from the previous king. The Mulochites, unlike Lehi and Nephi who left Jerusalem at the same time, "had brought no records with them," and therefore "they denied the being of their Creator" (Omni 1:17). By following in the footsteps of his ancient father Nephi, Mosiah₁ not only ensured that his own people would have the scriptures to maintain their beliefs, he was able to restore the beliefs of another people who had long lived without them.

No fewer than three commentators have raised the question of how Mosiah₁ had access to the royal treasury and perceived legitimacy in taking the relics, each suggesting it may have been through kinship.[28] Yet, as we have seen, Mosiah₁ was not the dynastic heir. A possible explanation, one that has also been used to account for Mosiah₁'s unusual non-inherited rise to kingship, is that Mosiah₁ was linked to the previous dynasty by *marriage*.[29] The Book of Mormon offers at least one case of becoming king by marriage—Amalickiah "obtained the kingdom" of the Lamanites, among whom he had no standing by blood, and "was acknowledged king throughout" by marrying the Lamanite queen (Alma 47:35). While Lehite *dynasties*

28. Cazier, 72. Gardner, *Second Witness*, 3:50; Miner, "Out of Bondage through Covenants: Jarom -- Mosiah."

29. Since Mosiah₁ rose to non-inherited kingship over both the Nephites and the Mulochites, marriage to the daughter of the Nephite king or the Mulochite king could help account for his rule of either of those groups, respectively. Val Larsen, "In His Footsteps: Ammon₁ and Ammon₂," 85–113. Personal communication from Brant Gardner, email, November 12, 2019.

are patrilineal, this case suggests that when there is no male heir, men may become kings through marriage.[30]

If Mosiah$_1$ did accede to kingship by marriage, he had good biblical precedent. David legitimated his dynasty by marrying Saul's daughter Michal and linking into the previous dynasty. A Mosian replay of these events would be particularly apropos in the context of Mosiah$_1$'s David-like rise accompanying the old king's Saul-like decline.[31]

Further suggesting Mosiah$_1$'s possible marriage to the daughter of a king is the multifaceted inversion of Mosiah$_1$'s life in that of his great-grandson Ammon$_2$. Mosiah$_1$ (like David) founded his family's dynasty; Ammon$_2$ ended it. Mosiah$_1$ left the land of Nephi to save the Nephites by traveling northward to the land of Zarahemla. Ammon$_2$ left the land of Zarahemla to save the Lamanites by traveling southward to the lands adjoining Nephi. There Ammon$_2$ was invited to marry a king's daughter (Alma 17:24). If the inversion continues, then Ammon$_2$ *not* marrying the king's daughter would inversely point to his great-grandfather Mosiah$_1$ marrying a king's daughter. While such a marriage is hypothetical pending further evidence, it would have explanatory power in understanding Ammon$_2$ as his typological inversion and in helping to account for Mosiah$_1$'s access to the relics of Nephi's dynasty, his accepted legitimacy in acquiring those relics, and his success in establishing his own dynasty.[32]

Translations

Despite likely discovering the brother of Jared's encrypted record along with the Jaredite interpreters, it does not seem that Mosiah$_1$ undertook the effort to interpret them. As Ammon$_1$ told Limhi, the interpreters were to be used only

---

30. The presentation within Mosiah$_1$'s story of the story of the eight Davidic royals, in essence four kings and four queens, may have intertwined with the role of Mosiah$_1$'s wife as queen in the founding of Nephi's own dynasty.

31. David's wife Michal and brother-in-law Jonathan deceived Saul to protect David and assist his rise to kingship by clothing David with Jonathan's own garments and sword, representing a transfer of power from Saul's line to David's—an incident Alan Goff finds echoed in Nephi's account of clothing himself in Laban's garments as he takes Laban's birthright relics (1 Sam. 18:4; 19:11–13). Alan Goff, "How Should We Then Read? Reading Mormon Scripture After the Fall," 137–178. With Mosiah$_1$'s ancestor Nephi disguising himself to acquire the brass plates, it is possible that Mosiah$_1$ followed Nephi's example to get access to the relics.

32. A latter-day parallel to Mosiah$_1$'s marriage to the king's daughter enabling him to acquire the Nephite dynastic relics, and possibly later the interpreters, would be Joseph Smith's marriage to Emma Hale reportedly enabling him to acquire these same relics. (See Chapter 1.)

by divine command (Mosiah 8:13); thus, the mere possession of the interpreters and the Jaredite record was no guarantee that Mosiah$_1$ would have translated that record. Furthermore, Ether 4:1 says that Benjamin (or his son Mosiah$_2$, depending on the printing of the Book of Mormon) specifically withheld the brother of Jared's account from his people—an odd assertion if Mosiah$_1$ had already translated and withheld it from them a generation or two earlier.

While Mosiah$_1$ may not have read the brother of Jared's record, there was another Jaredite record that he did read through the interpreters. Amaleki writes:

> And it came to pass in the days of Mosiah, there was a large stone brought unto him with engravings on it; and he did interpret the engravings by the gift and power of God. And they gave an account of one Coriantumr, and the slain of his people. . . . It also spake a few words concerning his fathers. And his first parents came out from the tower, at the time the Lord confounded the language of the people; and the severity of the Lord fell upon them according to his judgments, which are just; and their bones lay scattered in the land northward. (Omni 1:20–22)

The record found and brought to King Mosiah$_1$ echoes a biblical account of the Book of the Law found in the temple and brought to young King Josiah, the father of Zedekiah. Upon reading the book, Josiah lamented that God's wrath was kindled against Israel "because our fathers have not hearkened unto the words of this book, to do according unto all that which is written." (2 Kgs. 22:13). Acting as his people's proxy, Josiah covenanted in the temple that they would "walk after the Lord, and to keep his commandments and his testimonies and his statutes with all their heart and all their soul, to perform the words of this covenant that were written in this book" (23:3). Josiah's resulting reputation in the Bible was as one who walked a straight path, turning "neither to the right hand, nor to the left" (2 Chr. 34:2), a zeal he displayed most notably in putting down the worship of idols. While the content of the Jaredite stone and Josiah's book might have differed significantly, the warning was the same: failure to live up to God's covenants in the promised land would result in "the severity of the Lord [falling] upon them according to his judgments, which are just" (Omni 1:22). The Jaredite remains scattered about ominously testified of this.

The Mosian Reform

Echoing Josiah, Mosiah$_1$ led his people away from false worship in a defiled temple in the land of Nephi and taught the Mulochites the worship of their forgotten God. As a reformer like Josiah, Mosiah$_1$ reclaimed worship of the one true God for the Nephites and the Mulochites. This reformation of Nephite and Mulochite religion may help explain one of the more curious passages among Joseph Smith's early revelations and the curious fate of that passage.

The revelation that became Doctrine and Covenants 5 had an entire paragraph about a reformation omitted from publication. While Joseph Smith frequently and openly edited his revelations before publishing them in the 1835 Doctrine and Covenants, such editing involved minor tweaks and the occasional *addition* of further revelation. Rarely did it involve the *removal* of revelatory content, and in only one case did it mean the removal of a substantial and substantive text—this portion of section 5.

Originally directed at Martin Harris in March 1829, the revelation came a year after the loss of the initial Book of Mormon manuscript and just as he and Joseph were beginning to resume the work of translation. To understand the portion that was removed, it may help to contextualize it with an adjoining portion that was retained in the published revelation: "Behold, I tell you these things, even as I also told the people of the destruction of Jerusalem, and my word shall be verified at this time as it hath hitherto been verified" (D&C 5:20). No further explanation was given to Joseph and Martin to understand the warning given to "the people" prior to "the destruction of Jerusalem," likely because no further explanation was needed. To the translator and scribe of the lost manuscript, this evoked Lehi's warning's to the people of Jerusalem that stood at the head of the now-lost pages. It would have also recalled the warning on the wall interpreted by Aminadi and Mosiah$_1$'s voice of warning to the people of the land of Nephi that came at near the end of the lost manuscript.

Keeping in mind this narrative context from the lost manuscript, we can better understand the paragraph not included in the published revelation. That portion reads as follows:

> [I]f the People of this Generation harden not their hearts I will work a reformation among them & I will put down all lieings & deceivings & Priest Craft & envyings & strifes & Idolatries and sorceries & all maner of Iniquities & I will establish my Church yea even the church which was taught by my Desiples.[33]

This content is not trivial and is instead quite substantive. It is also distinctive. Not merely repeating what is stated in other scripture, this revelatory text announces that God's work in the last days will enact a reformation and put down many specific forms of evil. So why was it removed from the published Doctrine and Covenants?

The mystery of the removed passage is wrapped up with that of the stolen text of the Book of Mormon. The only scriptural text revealed to Joseph prior to this revelation that could have provided any context for it and its talk of reformation was the lost manuscript of the Book of Mormon. By this

---

33. "Revelation, March 1829 [D&C 5]."

point, the only scriptural texts revealed to Joseph were two brief revelations (D&C 3 and 4) that lack a reformation and the lost pages that ended with the complete story of King Mosiah₁ who reformed the religious practice of both the Nephites and Mulochites. Without the Mosian context, the reformation that would come to the mind of readers of the revelation would be the Protestant Reformation—which does not align with the reformation in the revelation. The Book of Mormon was not intended to be a revision of existing Christianity like that of Martin Luther and John Calvin; it was meant to present a sea change in religion like the reform of Lehi leaving Jerusalem and Mosiah₁ among the corrupt Nephites and apostate Mulochites—departure and restoration. However, with Mosiah₁'s reformation absent from the Book of Mormon, it would have been prudent to remove the allusion to his reformation from the Doctrine and Covenants to avoid evoking the Protestant Reformation as the model for God's latter-day work.

The remainder of the removed paragraph coheres well with this explanation. The reformation to be worked would put down a variety of evils—just like the reformations of Mosiah₁ and Josiah. Four centuries before Mosiah₁, King Josiah put down the idolatrous priests (2 Kgs. 23:5). Mosiah₁'s reformation similarly put down the idolatry of the Nephites and the Mulochites' denial of Israel's God. Assuming that the revelation was pointing to Mosiah₁'s efforts, then it offers another glimpse into the world of the lost pages, wherein the spiritual state of the people of Nephi before Mosiah₁ was one of "lying, deceiving, priestcraft, envying, strife, idolatry, and sorcery, and all manner of iniquities."

Mosiah₁'s Reform and Covenant

The Nephites' sins constituted a breaking of Lehi and Nephi's covenant, in which the Lord had promised prosperity and protection in return for his people keeping his commandments. When the Nephite nation broke the covenant completely, it was revoked and the nation destroyed. Yet, why, when, and how was the Nephites' covenant with the Lord re-made?

Intriguingly, Mosiah₁'s two biblical namesakes, Moses and Josiah, were covenant-makers who put their people under covenant to keep God's law. Moses placed the children of Israel under covenant to keep the Law at Sinai, and Josiah entered a covenant in the temple that his people would keep the commandments in the newfound Book of the Law. As a bearer of *both* these covenant legacies, it seems Mosiah₁ entered his people into a covenant with the Lord that stood at the center of his reformation.

Although any account of such covenant was lost with his story in the initial manuscript, echoes still survive. When Benjamin perpetuated the legacy of "my father Mosiah" by appointing as king "my son Mosiah" and reiterated his father's teachings, the people responded in a coordinated way: "they all cried with one voice," declaring their willingness to "enter a covenant . . . to be obedient to his [God's] commandments" (Mosiah 5:2–5). Far from a spontaneous outburst, "these are the words which king Benjamin desired of them; and therefore he said unto them: Ye have spoken the words that I desired; and the covenant which ye have made is a righteous covenant" (v. 6).

The people's ability to respond with the covenant Benjamin was seeking makes sense if there was a known precedent for such a covenant—that is, if Mosiah₁ had previously placed the people under covenant. Benjamin noted the people's obedience to the commandments given through his father Mosiah₁ as a covenant under which they had prospered, so he exhorted them to similar obedience to the commandments under his son, the new Mosiah:

> I would that ye should do *as ye have hitherto done.* As ye have kept my commandments, *and also the commandments of my father,* and have prospered, and have been kept from falling into the hands of your enemies, even so if ye shall keep the commandments of my son, or the commandments of God which shall be delivered unto you by him, ye shall prosper in the land, and your enemies shall have no power over you. (Mosiah 2:31)

As they came under the rule of a new Mosiah, the people recognized the renewal of a covenant they had made under the first Mosiah.

Further echoes of a covenant initiated by King Mosiah₁ appear in Joseph Smith's early revelations. Joseph's very first revelation after the manuscript loss—and his first known revelation given in the divine voice ("thus saith the Lord")—came in response to the manuscript loss in July 1828 and opens with phrasing that echoes Josiah and his reform:

> The works, and the designs, and the purposes of God cannot be frustrated, neither can they come to naught. For God doth not walk in crooked paths, *neither doth he turn to the right hand nor to the left,* neither doth he vary from that which he hath said, therefore his paths are straight, and his course is one eternal round. (D&C 3:1–2.)

It was Josiah who covenanted to "walk" with integrity to God's commandments, and who, accordingly, walked straight, veering "neither to the right hand, nor to the left" (2 Chr. 34:2),

Why does Joseph Smith's very first revelation, received immediately after the translation of the now-lost narratives of Mosiah₁, begin by evoking the narrative of Josiah and his reform? Again, the only earlier written revelation to Joseph was the lost manuscript itself, culminating with the narrative of Mosiah₁. Section 3 evidently alludes to the covenant walk of Josiah and his reform because those Josian themes had appeared powerfully in the Mosian reform.

Yet another echo of Josian reform in connection with the Book of Mormon appears in D&C 84. This revelation, given on the five-year anniversary of Joseph receiving the plates, declares the saints "under condemnation" for treating lightly "*the new covenant*, even the Book of Mormon." When this revelation exhorts the saints "not only to say, but *to do according to that which I have written*" (D&C 84:57), it quotes Josiah's explanation why *his* people were under condemnation for having not kept the commandments of the recently found Book of the Law: "great is the wrath of the Lord that is kindled against us, because our fathers have not hearkened unto the words of this book, *to do according unto all that which is written.*" (2 Kgs. 22:13).

The Book of Mormon is thus paralleled with the Book of the Law. Both these works of scripture were found-books appearing after having been long missing; and each found-book stood at the center of a reformation—the Book of the Law initiating Josiah's reformation; the Book of Mormon initiating the reformation or restoration announced in the earliest version of Doctrine and Covenants 5. The Book of Mormon also connects with Josiah's Book of the Law by presenting in the account of Mosiah$_1$ and his reformation and covenant a model for the latter-day reformation or restoration it was to bring about. *The Latter-day Saints were to be a covenant people on the model of the people of Mosiah$_1$.* As John W. Welch has shown, Benjamin and Mosiah$_2$'s covenant—and therefore their predecessor in Mosiah$_1$'s covenant—provided early forms of our sacrament covenant.[34] In the sacrament we covenant to keep Christ's commandments and to take on his name—just as Benjamin had called his people to take on the name of Christ. Thus, as Welch further drives home in his essay "Our Nephite Sacrament Prayers," our latter-day sacrament prayers are *Nephite* prayers, with roots in the events of the reign of Benjamin and thus of Mosiah$_1$ before him.[35]

In this light, God fulfilled his promise in the March 1829 revelation. *Through* the Book of Mormon he enacted the reformation described *in* the Book of Mormon—restoring covenant faith as practiced by Mosiah$_1$, Benjamin, Mosiah$_2$, and others. The reformation of Mosiah$_1$ is thus not merely a matter of obscure history. While we do not know all the detail of how it started, it has *never* ended. As Latter-day Saints we are continuers of Mosiah$_1$'s reformation.[36]

Mosiah's Reform vs. Josiah's Reform

The glimpses we can catch in our published Book of Mormon about Mosiah$_1$'s reformation offer contrasts with that led by Josiah. Mosiah$_1$'s ref-

---

34. John W. Welch, "Benjamin's Covenant as a Precursor of the Sacrament Prayers," 295–314

35. John W. Welch, "Our Nephite Sacrament Prayers," 286-89

36. For Joseph Smith's continuing reformation in Nauvoo, see Bradley, "'The Grand Fundamental Principles of Mormonism': Joseph Smith's Unfinished Reformation," 32–41.

ormation echoed Josiah's, yet it also differed from it. In the Josian reform, the Book of the Law was everything. Mosiah$_1$'s reformation focused not on the book of scripture but on the means of revelation. More important to Mosiah$_1$'s reign than finding a book, which he apparently did not translate, was finding the interpreters—an instrument of revelation. This is important, because Mosiah$_1$ was remembered not for his teachings on the Law or a book but for his teachings on the Spirit of God.

This contrast between the Josian reform and the Mosian reform parallels a distinction between biblical Judaism as it emerges out of Josiah's reform and the Restoration faith taught by Joseph Smith. "Mormonism" begins in the *Book* of Mormon with Mosiah$_1$'s reform. Biblical Jews are "people of the Book," grounding their faith in God's revelations contained in sacred texts. Latter-day Saints, like Mosiah$_1$ and the Brother of Jared, are also a people of the book, but they are more fundamentally a people of living revelation—the *process* by which sacred books are revealed.

Knowing Mosiah$_1$ Again

The picture of Mosiah$_1$'s life that emerges from our available evidence is as follows:

In the land of Nephi, under the reign of the final king of Nephi's dynasty, Mosiah$_1$ was called by God as a prophet to warn, like Lehi and Jeremiah, of coming destruction. He led the few who would listen on an exodus before the decisive Lamanite invasion. At the Lord's behest he also rescued Nephi's relics, presumably taking them from the royal treasury by stratagem and likely assisted from within the royal family. Mosiah$_1$ used one of these relics, the Liahona, to guide his people through the wilderness and find refuge nearby at the hill north of Shilom. Here they constructed a tabernacle to worship God outside the polluted temple of Nephi. Mosiah$_1$ preached and prophesied to his people, explaining why they had to abandon what had once been the Lord's temple, teaching them to resist the evil spirit that had come to inhabit that temple and could inhabit them, pointing them to the Messiah, and placing them under personal covenant to keep the commandments. While encamped here, their Sinai, Mosiah$_1$ was led by the Liahona to the interpreters, which the Lord instructed him how to use in the tabernacle. Now replaced, the Liahona ceased functioning, and Mosiah$_1$ guided his people through the wilderness by the interpreters.

Arriving in the land of Zarahemla, they encountered the Mulochites, descendants of David who had no scriptures and had largely lost their Israelite identity. Mosiah$_1$ restored them to knowledge of their Hebrew tongue and Israel's God. Although the Mulochites had been ruled by Zarahemla, the heir of David, they saw in Mosiah$_1$ a seer, the rightful heir of Joseph—in whose promised land they lived—and a forerunner to the Messiah; thus, they embraced him as their new ruler. The people of Nephi and the people of Zarahemla became, together, the people of Mosiah$_1$. Mosiah$_1$ reformed the faith of both the Nephites and the Mulochites, restoring them from apostasy. Serving his people as a prophet, as a priest, and as a king, Mosiah$_1$ constructed a new temple in which to worship Israel's God and receive higher truths, pointing them always toward their Messiah.

What can be gleaned from Mosiah$_1$'s story is both strikingly new and intimately familiar. As a story of apostasy and restoration, of covenant, of repentance, and of looking forward to the coming of Christ, it is also our story of the latter-day Restoration. Though the full story of Mosiah$_1$'s great work is partly lost to us, its spirit is embodied in the faith of the Latter-day Saints. Typologically, we are the people of the ancient Mosiah, and theologically we are the people of the living Messiah.

CHAPTER 15

THE BOOK OF BENJAMIN

The son and heir of King Mosiah₁ is the better-known King Benjamin, whose final sermon is presented in great detail in the opening chapters of our Book of Mosiah and the first pages of the renewed translation of the Book of Mormon. Despite the prominence he holds in the Book of Mormon, what we readily know of Benjamin's early life is described only skeletally in the small plates' Book of Omni and Words of Mormon.

Benjamin's story is in some ways an extension of his father's story. Changes that Mosiah₁ initiated, Benjamin perpetuated. Mosiah₁ relocated the center of Nephite life from Nephi to Zarahemla; Benjamin continued to live in Zarahemla. Mosiah₁ united the Nephites and the Mulochites under the rule of a new dynasty; Benjamin ruled over that united kingdom as his father's successor in that dynasty. Mosiah₁ initiated a reformation of Nephite religion; Benjamin continued this reformation—and extended it.

One reflection of that legacy of religious reformation may be in Benjamin's name, which derives, ultimately, from the son of Jacob (Israel) and Rachel, the younger brother of the biblical Joseph to whom the Nephites traced their genealogy, and which means "son of the right hand."[1] With this meaning, the name Benjamin connected back in various ways to how the motif of the "right hand" had appeared in the Hebrew Bible and reached forward to how it would appear in the New Testament, in the Restoration, and in Benjamin's own late-life teachings. In the story of Jacob/Israel blessing Joseph's sons, being the "right hand" son was associated with being a chosen birthright heir (Gen. 48:13–18). In Stephen's vision in the New Testament (Acts 7:55–56) and in Joseph Smith's theophanies at the head of the Restoration (e.g., D&C 76:24), Jesus the Christ (Messiah) stood at the Father's right hand as his Son.[2] As his father's name had anticipated the Messiah and pointed to him, Benjamin's own name also anticipated the Christ. In giving his people a name before his death and teaching them the meaning of that name, Benjamin built on the meaning of the name he had been given at birth. Not only was Benjamin a "son of the right hand" in similitude of the Christ, the Only Begotten Son (cf. Moses 1:6), all who would live fully in covenant relationship with the Lord would bear the name Christ and stand at his right hand as his chosen sons and daughters:

---

1. For the biblical Benjamin's birth, see Genesis 35:16–20.

2. Note that the motif of the right hand was also significant in the Josian reform and in the echoes of that reform in the latter-day Restoration (2 Chr. 34:2; D&C 3:1–2.)

And now, because of the covenant which ye have made ye shall be called the children of Christ, his sons, and his daughters. . . . [T]herefore, I would that ye should take upon you the name of Christ, all you that have entered into the covenant with God that ye should be obedient unto the end of your lives. And it shall come to pass that whosoever doeth this shall be found at the right hand of God, for he shall know the name by which he is called; for he shall be called by the name of Christ. (Mosiah 5:7–9)

In giving his son this name, Mosiah₁ continued to point his people toward Christ long after his own death. Benjamin would then extend this further by naming *his* son "Mosiah."

The Incomplete Book of Mosiah

Clues in the published Book of Mormon indicate that our Book of Mosiah is missing its original first two chapters that likely contained early narratives of Benjamin's reign. The clue to the existence of these missing chapters is located where Mormon's abridgement resumes—right after the lost pages end—in the opening verse of the Book of Mosiah. This chapter begins with Benjamin's reign *already in progress*, thus catching the narrative in mid-stream:

And now there was no more contention in all the land of Zarahemla, among all the people who belonged to king Benjamin, so that king Benjamin had continual peace all the remainder of his days. (Mosiah 1:1)

This present opening of the Book of Mosiah even begins *grammatically* in mid-stream, starting with the word "And." It refers back to earlier narratives of "contention in all the land" during Benjamin's reign, noting that while Benjamin's people had conflicts early on, this was followed by a substantial period of "continual peace"—during which there was "no more contention." This abrupt entry into the detailed story of Benjamin's reign after only quick references in Omni and the Words of Mormon indicates that the Book of Mosiah's true beginning, containing the earlier narrative and conflicts of Benjamin's reign, is missing.

There are further clues pointing to the published Book of Mormon missing the original opening chapters of Mosiah. First, the Book of Mosiah in the Printer's Manuscript initially lacked a title. Instead, just prior to its publication, Oliver Cowdery inserted one for the book labeling it "The Book of Mosiah."[3] The reason for this can be identified from the chapter's position in the translation sequence. Although Mosiah follows the small plates in the Printer's Manuscript and published Book of Mormon, the first chapter of

---

3. Oliver Cowdery's supralinear addition of the title "The Book of Mosiah" and his associated change of the chapter number, discussed below, are visible "Printer's Manuscript of the Book of Mormon, circa August 1829–circa January 1830," 117.

the present Book of Mosiah is the point at which Joseph Smith resumed the translation after the manuscript loss. (The small plates portion that replaced the lost manuscript would not be translated until the end.) The lack of a title and need for Oliver to later add one suggests that Joseph Smith and Martin Harris had already translated the beginning of the book, including the original title, and that it was almost certainly in the lost manuscript.

Second, the Book of Mosiah not only lacked a title, it also lacked another opening feature that characterizes all other books in Mormon's abridgement—an initial notation before the main body of text that usually identifies the book's first record keeper and summarizes its content. For example, the Book of Alma opens with:

THE BOOK OF ALMA

THE SON OF ALMA

The account of Alma, who was the son of Alma, the first and chief judge over the people of Nephi, and also the high priest over the Church. An account of the reign of the judges, and the wars and contentions among the people. And also an account of a war between the Nephites and the Lamanites, according to the record of Alma, the first and chief judge.

The lack of any similar notation at the beginning of the Book of Mosiah again suggests that the earliest portion of the book was part of the lost manuscript.

Third, the book's present title—"The Book of Mosiah"—fails to match the pattern of how Mormon named the books in his abridgement, all of which bear the name of the *first* record keeper during the period covered by the book and *not* the name of the *main* record keeper during that period. The Book of Helaman, for example, is named after $Alma_2$'s grandson $Helaman_2$, who kept the record for the period covered by its first three chapters (Hel. 1–3), and not for $Helaman_2$'s son Nephi, who kept the record for the period covered by the remaining *thirteen* chapters (Hel. 4–16). Applying the title "The Book of Mosiah" to a book that began while Benjamin was the keeper of the records departs from Mormon's convention.[4] If the book's original title was lost and

---

4. It could be posited that the Book of Mosiah was named for $Mosiah_1$. This would resolve the anomaly of Oliver not naming the book after Benjamin—but only at the price of creating a still larger anomaly. As documented in Chapter 14, the importance of $Mosiah_1$ as a figure within Nephite history is enormous, and the volume of evidence for what was in his narrative in the lost manuscript is exceptionally high—by far the highest for any post-Nephi narrative in that manuscript. For the missing first two chapters of "The Book of $Mosiah_{[1]}$" to have contained the two narratives of conflict from Benjamin's reign related below *and* to have contained the *entire* narrative of $Mosiah_1$ would have required those chapters to have been anomalously large, rivaling in size the *books* within Mormon's abridgment.

forgotten along with the lost manuscript, then Oliver would have had to provide *some* title for the book as it went to press.[5] Selecting a name based on the identity of the primary ruler and chief record-keeper for the period covered by the book may have seemed a fitting choice to Oliver, but that was not the choice Mormon would have made, given the pattern of his other writings. Instead, the title that Mormon gave our Book of Mosiah was likely "The Book of Benjamin," named after that volume's initial record keeper.

Fourth, the Printer's Manuscript of the Book of Mosiah lacks a Chapter I and Chapter II. Instead, it oddly begins with "Chapter III." To adjust for this missing material Oliver crossed out part of the Roman numeral chapter number, changing "Chapter III" to "Chapter III," which then became in print "Chapter I."[6] Given that the Book of Mormon's original chaptering system (later revised in 1876) used chapters twice the length of present chapters, we can estimate that the present Book of Mormon is missing the equivalent of about four chapters of our present version from the early reign of king Benjamin.

---

5. When adding a name to this book on the Printer's Manuscript, Oliver likely did not get the name from Joseph Smith. The addition was made above the line and thus, as noted on the Joseph Smith Papers website, "possibly inserted after the time of the original inscription." Oliver would not have needed to add a title to this book until it was being prepared for typesetting around mid-October 1829, at which time Joseph was hundreds of miles away in Pennsylvania. The title's failure to align with Mormon's naming practices and the evidence about the size and significance of Mosiah₁'s narrative strongly suggest that Oliver selected a name for this book. For the chronology of the typesetting, see Royal Skousen, "Why Was One Sixth of the 1830 Book of Mormon Set from the Original Manuscript?" 93–103.

6. While acknowledging that there were missing chapters of our Book of Mosiah, Brant Gardner posits that Oliver Cowdery may have initially assigned this chapter the number III, continuing this numbering from the Book of Omni being labeled "Chapter I" and the Words of Mormon being labeled "Chapter 2.d." However, the crucial question here is the order in which these labels were assigned. The numbering of [Mosiah] "Chapter III" is logically prior to Oliver's confused numbering of the Words of Mormon as "Chapter 2.d," because, as Gardner notes, (1) "Chapter 2.d" was later added intrusively above the line, and (2) Oliver did not initially perceive the Words of Mormon as a distinct unit (either a book or a chapter) but merely part of the Book of Omni Chapter I. This means that Joseph Smith did not, per his usual practice, indicate a chapter break at this point in the translation. Oliver thus would not have had any reason to enumerate the Words of Mormon as a separate chapter until he encountered "Chapter III" at the end of the Words of Mormon. The Words of Mormon were thus assigned "Chapter 2.d" because the succeeding text had been designated "Chapter III" and not the other way around. See Brant A. Gardner, "When Hypotheses Collide: Responding to Lyon and Minson's 'When Pages Collide,'" 105–19.

Benjamin's Lost Narratives

Despite missing the original first two chapters of the Book of Mosiah (or Book of Benjamin), clues in the present first chapter point to what preceded it. For example, the published Book of Mosiah begins:

> And now there was *no more* contention in all the land of Zarahemla, among all the people who belonged to king Benjamin, so that king Benjamin had continual peace all the remainder of his days" (1:1)

Much can be teased out from this wording.

From this first verse of our Book of Mosiah 1 we can see that the prior material in the missing pages dealt with "contention" located "in . . . the land of Zarahemla, among . . . the people who belonged to king Benjamin." The word "contention" in Mormon's abridgement generally connotes a tense dispute rather than a military conflict (although the former often leads to the latter),[7] and the text here implies that the contention that occurred among Benjamin's people and in Zarahemla was an *internal* conflict between them.

In the small plates, Mormon opens his account of Benjamin's reign with just such a conflict: "And now, concerning this king Benjamin—he had somewhat of contentions among his *own* people" (W of M 1:12). Mormon further and separately notes that Benjamin dealt with an external military conflict between Benjamin's people and the Lamanites, but he distinguishes that martial conflict from the earlier, internal contention by introducing it (with "also") as an additional controversy:

> And it came to pass *also* that the armies of the Lamanites came down out of the land of Nephi, to battle against his people. But behold, king Benjamin gathered together his armies, and he did stand against them; and he did fight with the strength of his own arm, with the sword of Laban. And in the strength of the Lord they did contend against their enemies, until they had slain many thousands of the Lamanites. And it came to pass that they did contend against the Lamanites until they had *driven them out* of all the lands of their inheritance. (vv. 13–14)

In the Book of Omni, Amaleki gives a brief account of the same war:

> I have seen, in the days of king Benjamin, a serious war and much bloodshed between the Nephites and the Lamanites. But behold, the Nephites did obtain much advantage over them; yea, insomuch that king Benjamin did *drive them out* of the land of Zarahemla. (1:24)

---

7. For example, in Alma 19:28 "contention" is used to describe the dispute in the previous verses over whether Ammon was the "Great Spirit," was "sent by the Great Spirit," or was "a monster . . . sent by the Nephites" (vv. 25–27). Despite the severity of the contention, the narrative gives no indication of it turning violent.

In these accounts both Mormon and Amaleki describe the Nephites "driving out" the Lamanites from the Nephites' lands with their superior strength or advantage. However, Mormon also notes Benjamin's personal role in the combat and his wielding the sword of Laban in defense of his people, evoking the earlier imagery of Nephi's defensive conquest of the Nephite promised land (2 Ne. 5:14; see Chapter 10).

After describing Benjamin's military conflict with invading Lamanites, Mormon returns to the previously mentioned internal contention among the Nephites:

> And it came to pass that after there had been false Christs, and their mouths had been shut, and they punished according to their crimes; And after there had been false prophets, and false preachers and teachers *among the people*, and all these having been punished according to their crimes; and after there having been much contention and many dissensions away unto the Lamanites, behold, it came to pass that king Benjamin, with the assistance of the holy prophets who were among his people—For behold, king Benjamin was a holy man, and he did reign over his people in righteousness; and there were many holy men in the land, and they did speak the word of God with power and with authority; and they did use much sharpness because of the stiffneckedness of the people—Wherefore, with the help of these, king Benjamin, by laboring with all the might of his body and the faculty of his whole soul, and also the prophets, did once more establish peace in the land. (W of M 1:15–18)

This describes a spiritual conflict that in many ways paralleled the military conflict that preceded it. Benjamin throws himself forcefully into each conflict, "fight[ing] with the strength of his own arm" against the physical threat and "laboring with all the might of his body and the faculty of his whole soul" against the spiritual threat.

The resolution of the military conflict against an external adversary and of the spiritual conflict against an internal adversary share the exact same structure, and Benjamin triumphs in them by variations on the same two means. First, he wields an incisive weapon with his full personal strength—the *sword*—against the Lamanite invaders, and speaking with power and authority he wields another weapon—the *word*—against the false Christs, false prophets, and false preachers and teachers. Second, he joins with allies by gathering his armies against the military threat and working with true prophets against the spiritual threat. At the end of both conflicts, the victory is the same, with Benjamin restoring peace in the land.

These two parallel conflicts waged by Benjamin are the likely subjects of the missing first two chapters of the Book of Mosiah/Benjamin.[8] Chapters in

---

8. Jack Lyon and Kent Minson have asked how the conclusion of Benjamin's conflicts in the Words of Mormon is able to bring the narrative so precisely to where

the original Book of Mormon text were typically twice as long as chapters in the present Latter-day Saint editions and were divided along narrative units, with a single chapter generally providing a cohesive narrative. The two *narratives* of conflict from Benjamin's early reign would have thus nicely mapped onto the missing two *chapters* of Benjamin's book.

If these two narratives of conflict—one military, one spiritual—correspond to the two missing chapters, then the opening words of Chapter III (our Mosiah 1–2) pick up precisely where Chapter II left off. After Chapter II's conclusion with Benjamin's victory in the spiritual contention among his people in the land of Zarahemla, the opening verse of Chapter III would provide a perfect segue into the succeeding narrative: "And now *there was no more contention* in all the land of Zarahemla, among all the people who belonged to king Benjamin" (Mosiah 1:1). This suggests that the conflict concluded at the end of Chapter II was not the "serious war . . . between the Nephites and the Lamanites" but the spiritual "contention" that occurred among Benjamin's people.

---

our Book of Mosiah (1:1) picks up when Joseph resumes translating after the theft. Intriguingly, they argue that Joseph Smith "retained" a portion of the initial translation manuscript prior to Mosiah 1:1 and that Joseph added this translation remnant to the Words of Mormon as verses 12–18 to bridge a narrative gap between the small plates and where Mosiah 1:1 picked up. I critique the proposition of a "retained" portion as an anachronistic reading of D&C 10:41 in Chapter 5 note 10. I would add that it is uncharacteristic of Mormon to offer only a terse summary of these intensive conflicts. Such summary treatment better fits the context of the small plates, in which the verses actually appear and where they appear to belong. As Brant Gardner notes,

> Mormon's descriptions of events do not have this level of terseness until 4 Nephi. . . . These verses describe nothing short of the crucial events that led up to Benjamin's speech. They deal with an external war with the Lamanites, an internal civil war, and a religious crisis. Compare the treatment in this synopsis with similar topics in the book of Alma. These are things that Mormon cares about deeply.

Further clashing with Lyon and Minson's hypothesis, there is no evidence that Joseph Smith helped Oliver Cowdery understand and arrange this part of the manuscript, and Oliver's demonstrable confusion over it, noted by Lyon and Minson and described in note 5 above, suggests that Joseph did not. Oliver's confusion over "Chapter III" suddenly appearing in the manuscript is understandable when (1) we recognize that it would have been Martin Harris (per D&C 5:30), not Oliver, who was the scribe for that chapter, and (2) we understand Oliver to be arranging this material *without* Joseph's supervision. Yet, the question raised by Lyon and Minson is incisive. I will offer my own explanation of the Words of Mormon's summary of Benjamin's conflicts and its unexplained duplication of Omni 1:24 in future work. See Jack M. Lyon and Kent R. Minson, "When Pages Collide: Dissecting the Words of Mormon," 120–36; and Gardner "When Hypotheses Collide," 105–19.

The Expeditions to the Land of Nephi

Further clues to the contents of these lost chapters of this book appear at the end of the Book of Omni. Amaleki, last record keeper of Jacob's line, ends the Book of Omni as follows:

> And now I would speak somewhat concerning a certain number who went up into the wilderness to return to the land of Nephi; for there was a large number who were desirous to possess the land of their inheritance. Wherefore, they went up into the wilderness. And their leader being a strong and mighty man, and a stiffnecked man, wherefore he caused a contention among them; and they were all slain, save fifty, in the wilderness, and they returned again to the land of Zarahemla. And it came to pass that they also took others to a considerable number, and took their journey again into the wilderness. And I, Amaleki, had a brother, who also went with them; and I have not since known concerning them. And I am about to lie down in my grave; and these plates are full. And I make an end of my speaking. (Omni 1:27–30)

How do these expeditions relate to the war and spiritual contention among Benjamin's people, and where do they fall within the first two chapters of Benjamin's reign? The accounts in the Book of Omni and Words of Mormon provide clues.

First, in describing the war that likely comprised the first chapter, Mormon begins, "And it came to pass also that the armies of the Lamanites came down out of the land of Nephi" (W of M 1:13). The detail that the Lamanite armies came upon Zarahemla "out of the land of Nephi" is significant for relating this account to the expeditions mentioned by Amaleki. Describing the same expeditions, Zeniff later recounts that the second expedition was successful, resulting in the Lamanite king giving Zeniff's people the land of Nephi, which then they settled and successfully held against Lamanite attack (Mosiah 9–10). After this expedition, the land of Nephi was consistently held by *Nephite* settlers; thus, an attack involving Lamanites coming down from the land of Nephi would necessarily *precede* the Zeniff expedition.[9]

Second, the colonizing expeditions are connected to the war by a golden thread: the theme of "lands of inheritance." The war began with the Lamanites attacking "out of the land of Nephi" (W of M 1:13) and ended with the Lamanites being driven "out of the land of Zarahemla" (Omni 1:24). Mormon takes this further: the Nephites "did contend against the Lamanites until they had driven them out of *all the lands of their inheritance*" (W of M 1:14). This sequence implies probable causal relationships. The Lamanite attack from the Nephites' original, southern land of inheritance (Nephi) led to the Lamanites

---

9. Note Amaleki's presentation of the events in the same order: the war (Omni 1:24) and then the colonizing expeditions (1:27–29).

being driven out of the Nephites' present, northern lands of inheritance (Zarahemla, etc.) and back to the land of Nephi. With the Nephites having clear military superiority and the Lamanites having been weakened, some Nephites now wished to press their advantage. Countering the Lamanites' failed conquest of the Zarahemla and extermination of the Nephites, the first expedition attempted a conquest of the land of Nephi and extermination of the Lamanites (Mosiah 9:1). This comprised Chapter I of Benjamin's reign—a chapter focused entirely on struggles for lands of inheritance: narrating (1) the attempted Lamanite conquest, (2) the attempted Nephite counter-conquest, and (3) a second expedition to re-inherit the land of Nephi, this time non-violently.

Chapter II then narrated spiritual contentions in the land of Zarahemla. This narrative, like the narrative of war and expeditions comprising Chapter I, was complex and included multiple conflicts. The first was with a false Christ or Christs, ending with them having "their mouths . . . shut" and being "punished according to their crimes." Both these elements appear again in Alma's conflict with one person Mormon calls an "Anti-Christ" in his extant abridgment, Korihor (Alma 30:6, 9–12, 47–52), possibly suggesting a similar one-on-one conflict between Benjamin—who prefigures the true Christ— and a false Christ (W of M 1:15). This is followed by conflicts with "false prophets," in which a number of *true* "prophets" assist Benjamin (vv. 16–18). In the midst of all this are also "many dissensions away unto the Lamanites," indicating that internal cohesion within the Nephite community is restored in part by dissent being put down, but also in part by dissidents leaving (v. 16). The chapter then concluded with the restoration of peace, setting the stage for Mosiah 1:1, in which "there was *no more* contention."

Summaries of the Missing Chapters

The apparent structure for the missing first two chapters of Benjamin's reign in the book that may have borne his name is thus:

Chapter I: War and Expeditions for Lands of Inheritance
(A fuller version of the events in Omni 1:24 and Words of Mormon 1:13–14)

Chapter II: Contentions for Souls: Benjamin and the Prophets against the False Messiahs and False Prophets
(A fuller version of the events in Words of Mormon 1:12, 15–18)

As one Book of Mormon scholar has noted, "The Book of Mosiah is possibly the most carefully composed book in the Book of Mormon."[10] Thus, understanding its opening chapters may help us better understand that complexity and glean the book's overall message.

---

10. Gordon C. Thomasson, "Mosiah: The Complex Symbolism and Symbolic Complex of Kingship in the Book of Mormon," 21–38.

Benjamin and Messianic Expectations

It's important to note that Benjamin's settling of this contention that began with false Christs was the final narrative of the lost manuscript before it was stolen. The theme behind this conflict is thus one of messianic expectation. As discussed in Chapter 14, Benjamin's father, Mosiah$_1$, was a proto-messianic figure or precursor of the Messiah. As a prophet, priest, and king, a deliverer, lawgiver, and shepherd, Mosiah$_1$ pointed his people to the Messiah who was yet to come, thus stoking messianic hope and expectation. Given that their own king was a powerful prototype for the Messiah, it is possible that Mosiah$_1$'s people would have not only expected the Messiah but expected him *soon*.

This raises a question: Did some of this messianic expectation get centered on Mosiah$_1$'s own son in the missing narrative? Benjamin, like his father and as each ancient high priest, as Alma explained, served as a similitude of the Messiah, a finger pointing the people to him. But what if the people confused the pointing finger and that to which it pointed? This would account for why Benjamin would feel the need to quash any suspicions that he himself was the divine Messiah by opening his sermon to his people with the declaration, "I of myself am . . . a mortal man" and "am like as yourselves, subject to all manner of infirmities in body and mind" (Mosiah 2:10–11). The same fervent hope that the Messiah was at hand that led some to embrace false Christs could have led others among Benjamin's people to suspect that, as successor to Mosiah$_1$ who had pointed them to the Christ, Benjamin was that true Christ. The challenge confronting Benjamin, then, was to keep his people focused on active faith in the Christ-to-come without prematurely fixing that hope on a false messiah—to point them beyond the finger, the symbol, and to the substance to which it led.

In taking up the "sword of Laban" his father had delivered to him to defend his people, the young King Benjamin carried on a legacy that stretched back to Nephi, and before him to the patriarch Joseph, Benjamin's own forefather and the brother of his biblical namesake. In taking up the "the word of God with power and authority," young Benjamin taught his people God's word on the brass plates—again a legacy of Joseph, God's word on the golden plates—a legacy of Nephi, and God's word of continuing revelation through the Spirit and also through the interpreters—a legacy of his father. In all of this, Benjamin perpetuated and extended Mosiah$_1$'s reform and pointed the minds of the "people of Mosiah" forward to their Messiah (Mosiah 1:10).

INSIGHTS FROM WHAT WAS FOUND

When I first set out to learn what I could of the Book of Mormon's lost pages, I had no idea how deeply the complexity of the text would require me to keep going, or for how long—thus far for a decade and a half—and how completely that search would turn my life and my view of the world upside-down.

When I began this research on the lost pages I was losing my connection with the Restoration and was on my way out of the Church. Out of a desire for truth and a fascination with the subject, I continued my research while I was away from the Church, and what I found in that research led, ultimately, to a reappraisal of my direction. In conjunction with things I learned in studying Joseph Smith's First Vision, what I learned about the Book of Mormon by studying its lost pages opened the door to a new direction, another spiritual journey, one *back* to faith and to the Church. My research into the Book of Mormon's lost pages became the first step in my personal restoration *to* the Restoration.[1]

My research held many other surprises too. Some of them intertwined with my return to faith; all of them were transformative in how I have come to see the Restoration. Seven of these larger conclusions from my study of the lost pages merit fleshing out here.

1. A Jewish Book

One of the most striking and startling things about both the coming forth and the content of the Book of Mormon's lost text is how Hebraic, and even specifically Jewish, they were. In the buildup to the lost manuscript's translation, the watershed events in its coming forth were keyed to Jewish festival days (Chapters 1-3). The narrative history within the book itself appears to have begun with one of those feasts (Chapter 7). It also began at the opening of the great shaping condition of Jewish life across millennia: the Diaspora, the dispersion of Jews—whose very name means people of Judea—across a wider world. Although it appears to have largely escaped note, the

---

1. For readers who may be interested in brief glimpses of my personal journey and how it has intertwined with my scholarship, see Peggy Fletcher Stack, "The Rest Is History: How a Mormon Scholar Turned Doubter, then Believer"; Don Bradley, "Pillars of My Faith"; Don Bradley, "Joseph Smith's First Vision as Endowment and Epitome of the Gospel of Jesus Christ (or Why I Came Back to the Church."

Book of Mormon tells us that it began in the literal very first days of the Diaspora (Chapters 6-7). The lives of Lehi and Nephi were consequently devoted to solving, in part, the problem of Diaspora or Exile: if they could not remain perpetually in Judea could they create their own Judea and restore the wholeness of the original Jewish commonwealth that had existed there? The problem Lehi and Nephi sought to solve was thus a distinctively Jewish problem.

There is an academic idea that during the Book of Mormon's coming forth the Restoration was very Christian primitivist—focused selectively on the New Testament and restoring the primitive church like many movements around Joseph Smith at the time (such as the Stone-Campbell movement from which Sidney Rigdon emerged).[2] When we look at *the earliest part* of the Book of Mormon—the first half of Mormon's abridgment that was lost—we do indeed find a restorationist program being enacted by Lehi and Nephi; but rather than trying to build the New Testament church, they were trying to rebuild "Old Testament" Israel! The contents of the lost pages thus entirely buck scholarly expectation that the Book of Mormon will behave as a New Testament-focused, nineteenth-century Christian primitivist text.[3]

2. The Centrality of Temple Worship

Another of the more surprising things emerging from this research is how central *temple worship* was within the lost pages. As noted in Chapter 11, all the major early events of Lehi and Nephi's exodus culminate in *one* major event after Nephi's conquest: the re-establishment of the worship of Israel's God in the temple of Nephi. Lehi's prophesying, Nephi's conflict with Laban, Lehi's finding of the Liahona, the use of the Liahona during their wandering in the wilderness, Nephi taking David-like leadership of his older brothers— these all eventuate, as if by grand design, in Nephi being able to establish a temple like Solomon's that is led with royal priesthood authority and stocked with relics paralleling those of the Tabernacle and Jerusalem temple. In the lives of Lehi and Nephi, everything builds toward the temple.

Given that the Book of Mormon was so Judaic, it is not surprising that Jewish temple worship would be prominent in its pages. And that is indeed not the truly striking thing. What is striking is that through the lens of the lost pages we see that not only was temple worship characteristic of biblical

---

2. See discussion in Don Bradley, "American Proto-Zionism and the 'Book of Lehi': Recontextualizing the Rise of Mormonism."

3. For the Book of Mormon's lost text as a "Judaic primitivist" work, see Bradley, "American Proto-Zionism and the Book of Lehi."

Jews prominent in the Book of Mormon's lost pages, so was *temple worship as recognizable to Latter-day Saints.*

As we saw in the story of Aminadi (Chapter 13), temple worship among the Nephites was not only about sacrifice; it was also about the revelation of symbolic truths with lower and higher levels of meaning. As we saw in the story of Mosiah₁ (Chapter 14) and in the parallel account of the brother of Jared on Mount Shelem, temple worship in the Book of Mormon was about the testing of our faith and knowledge so we might be redeemed from the Fall and admitted into the presence of God. Then, as now, the temple was a place to seek God's presence and learn his truths.

3. The Mormon Book

An idea exists for many—an idea I once held—that the most distinctive doctrines of the Restoration are not in the Book of Mormon. This is sometimes expressed by critics of the Restoration in quips that "there is not much Mormonism in the Book of Mormon." Delving deeply into the Book of Mormon's clues about what was in its lost pages straightforwardly refutes this.

The Book of Mormon's lost text was the *earliest* contemporaneously recorded revelation of the Restoration. Before the Book of Abraham, before the Joseph Smith Translation, before the revelations of the Doctrine and Covenants, and before the Book of Mormon text we still have, the Book of Mormon's now-lost text was revealed to Joseph Smith. And when we look at this earliest recorded revelation of the Restoration, what do we find?

Already we find that the faith propounded there was not just a New Testament faith; it was a whole-Bible faith. Already we find that it was focused on the temple as not just as a place of sacrifice; it was a place to meet God, to encounter truths communicated in symbolic form, and to receive revelations of higher and higher levels of truth. Already we find that it was not just a sacred history of the past; it was about progressing to receive divine attributes like the wisdom embodied in the interpreters—an "all-seeing eye," the ability to see as God sees and thus to grow in the realization of our own divine potential.

The Restoration of the Gospel of Jesus Christ in its full bloom—what has been called "Nauvoo Mormonism"—is *original* and literal "Mormonism"; it is the very faith propounded by Mormon in his book, beginning in its lost pages with the first words of written revelation given to Joseph Smith. This is not only evident in what we can know of the lost text. Rather, in light of such findings about Mormon's *lost* abridgment, we can better understand what it is in Mormon's *available* abridgment—neither of which was meant to stand alone; each was part of a larger whole.

The Prophet Joseph Smith once said, "I have a key by which I understand the scripture—I enquire what was the question which drew out the answer."[4] Context provides vital information for understanding any passage of scripture, and, as with most books, the context of Mormon's abridgment was largely provided in the opening act that was lost. Glimpses into Mormon's lost abridgment may provide keys to unlocking some of the meanings Mormon intended to convey. The same is true of the book as a whole; understanding Mormon's abridgment—both the lost and published text—opens our understanding of the small plates and Moroni's writings. Thus, for example, grasping the temple context of the Nephite recovery of the interpreters opened my eyes to the temple context in the brother of Jared's recovery of the interpreters in Ether 3.

4. The Lost Pages and the Restoration.

While it may be surprising to us to learn that "Nauvoo" elements of the Restoration were already present in the Book of Mormon's lost pages, this would have been no surprise to Joseph Smith. With virtual certainty, we can see the seeds of later aspects of the Restoration arising in the lost pages and planted in Joseph. Thus, while the Book of Mormon's lost pages may be a mystery that we are just beginning to crack, for Joseph they were not a mystery but a *memory*. We know that until late into his relatively young life, Joseph recalled and reported to a number of Saints Ishmael's lineage from the tribe of Ephraim (Chapter 9). If the Prophet remembered this genealogical detail, he surely recalled larger and more consequential teachings and events of the lost manuscript.

As a book about restoration, the Book of Mormon facilitated the Prophet's work of Restoration. In its pages, particularly as it appeared in its now-lost manuscript, he would have found a template for restoration—specifically, the restoration of Israel. Here he would have first encountered in scripture the idea of a restoration of the temple. He would have learned just what worship in such a temple was to *look* like. He would have encountered the idea of actually *building* a New Jerusalem, as Nephi built his new Jerusalem.

The first half of Mormon's abridgment is an ever-present absence. In an important and powerful sense, the lost book of Mormon we are attempting to recover in these pages was never really gone. If you want to know what was in the lost pages, look at the Restoration effected by the Prophet Joseph Smith. He knew the Book of Mormon's lost contents and taught and enacted them in his continuing work of Restoration after translating the Book of Mormon.

---

4. Joseph Smith, sermon, January 29, 1843, reported by Willard Richards, in Andrew F. Ehat and Lyndon W. Cook, ed., *The Words of Joseph Smith: The Contemporary Accounts of the Nauvoo Discourses of the Prophet Joseph*, 161.

5. The Book of Mormon and the Bible.

Delving into the clues about what was in the Book of Mormon's lost pages brings into sharp relief the Book of Mormon's remarkable relationship with the Bible—how it begins in, extends, and integrates the Bible.

The Book of Mormon *begins* within the Bible—the larger narratives of Israel and the kingdom of Judah, and the specific narratives of Zedekiah and Jeremiah. This is made clear by attention to the lost pages' details about the post-Babylonian invasion, Passover setting of Lehi's vision, and its account of Zedekiah and his son Muloch.

The Book of Mormon then *extends* that story. If the Bible is the story of Israel, set in a small region of the Middle East, then by carrying Israel's story to the other side of the world, the Book of Mormon stretches the Bible and implicitly extends it to engulf the entire globe. It does this by not only carrying it geographically further but also by recapitulating all of the Bible's major events and re-building Israel on successively finer and finer levels. The events and figures of the Nephite world typologically mirror the events and figures of the biblical Israelite world. In demonstrating this more fully, the discernible contents of the lost pages make clearer a message that is intended to be revealed in the Book of Mormon: that just as there was and is a Judean Israel in the Old World, there was and is an American Israel in the New World, one with a similar pattern and purpose—and destiny.

In responding to its latter-day critics, the Book of Mormon itself implicitly notes how it extends the Bible (2 Ne. 29:3-14). In refuting as "fools" those who say, "A Bible! A Bible! We have got a Bible, and there cannot be any more Bible" (vv. 3) and "A Bible, we have got a Bible, and we need no more Bible" (vv. 6), the Book of Mormon embraces the idea that there is, in one sense, "more Bible" in its own pages.

The Book of Mormon also *integrates* the Bible with incredible depth. Only after closely studying the narratives of Nephi and Laban in the small plates account and in the clues left for us about the lost account, have I perceived much of the richness in the biblical narratives of David and Goliath and of David and Saul. Only after closely engaging the lost and extant narratives of the brass plates, the sword of Laban, and Nephi's conquest (Chapter 10) have I found myself understanding at any depth the biblical narrative of Joseph and his connection with the Exodus and Conquest. Close attention to the Book of Mormon narratives yields novel insight into the narratives of the Bible. The Book of Mormon's extensions of the biblical narratives make those narratives make more sense, both by *disclosing* depths of meaning that are already there and by *developing* those narratives further in recounting additional events along the trajectory on which the biblical account was going.

In its tendency to take biblical themes and extend them further, and to bring the Bible's narratives to more complete development and integration into one great divine whole, the Book of Mormon seems at times more biblical than the Bible itself, or rather, the Book of Mormon makes the Bible more biblical than it is by itself. In this way the Book of Mormon not only *reads* the Bible; it further *writes* the Bible, carrying its grand meta-narrative of Israel beyond the covers of the Old and New Testaments, across the hemispheres, and beyond the First Century, bringing the grand epic of Israel to us, and offering us a part in the great consummation of that narrative by its Author.

6. A Fractal Israel

Israel, as presented in the Book of Mormon, bears a pattern we can best describe using the mathematical and scientific concept of a fractal. A fractal is a pattern that repeats smaller and smaller copies of itself. At each successively smaller level, the structure remains the same. An example of a fractal structure in nature would be a tree. The pattern on which a tree trunk shoots forth boughs, which shoot forth branches, which shoot forth smaller branches, and so on, iterates over and over down to the finest level of the branching veins within each leaf.

The Book of Mormon nation of Israel, which fittingly describes itself as "a righteous branch unto the house of Israel" (2 Nephi 3:5), bears just such a structure. In the Book of Mormon, the process of apostasy and restoration by which a functionally independent Israelite nation is created is recursive and iterates over and over again. Thus, as seen in the Book of Mormon's published text, and even more crisply visible in what we can piece together of its lost text, under Lehi and Nephi's direction the Lehites recapitulated the larger history of Israel and thereby *re-created* Israel in miniature. They established a covenant, divided into tribes, made the exodus on which they gathered sacred relics for their temple, made a conquest of a new promised land, established a sacred dynasty, built a temple and a temple city—a new Jerusalem, and constructed a system of priesthood and temple worship remarkably parallel to that of First Temple Jerusalem. The Lehites, thus described, constitute a *part* of biblical Israel, yet *a part that contains all the features of and shares the structure of the whole.* The Lehites, while just a *part* of Israel, are functionally a *whole* Israel and thus a new Israel. They might thus best be described as a *sub*-Israel, and the Book of Mormon's own analogy to a branch, which shares the structure of its mother tree, seems particularly apropos.

This fractal-like repetition continues within the Book of Mormon as well. After those of this first Nephite nation fell into apostasy and broke their covenant, Mosiah₁ led them in the making of a new covenant, took them on a new exodus on which they found yet another relic for their temple, carried out a non-violent conquest and a new enumeration of tribes with the Mulochites (the seven Lehite tribes plus the Mulochites), established a new sacred dynasty, made the city of Zarahemla a *new* new Jerusalem, and established the worship of Israel's God at the temple of Mosiah, thereby re-capitulating again the founding events of Israel recorded in the Bible, and *re-creating Israel once more!*

Even the later colonizing expeditions to the land of Nephi attempted to iterate this process once more, carrying out an exodus and attempted conquest, establishing a new dynasty, rebuilding Nephi's sacred city and temple. However, this effort at recapitulation and re-creation was incomplete, and, thus perhaps not surprisingly, it failed.

At each successful new level, the process of recapitulating Israel's history leads to the creation of the previous Israel *in microcosm*, a smaller new Israel, or sub-Israel, an Israel within an Israel within an Israel. . . . Yet none of these sub-Israels can claim to *be* the true Israel over and against the rest of the house of Israel. Each is part of biblical Israel, established through God's covenants with Abraham, Isaac, and Jacob. To use an analogy from Joseph Smith, a branch cannot jump off from an apple tree and say, "I am the true tree."[5]

It is possible that this iterative process of the creation of new, finer branches of Israel is not only a duplicative process but a *progressive* process. Israel's Conquest was offensively violent. Nephi's conquest was defensively violent. Mosiah$_1$'s conquest was non-violent. Perhaps the same processes that create Israels or sub-Israels also tend to refine them.

7. A Messianic Manuscript

As we saw with the opening of the "Book of Benjamin," the lost manuscript ended on a note of Messianic expectation (Chapter 15). Hope for the coming Messiah ran so high that Nephites thought they saw him in false Christs and even in messianic forerunners like Benjamin himself.

The lost Book of Mormon manuscript thus ends where it began. Its narrative opened with Passover and the expectation of the Lamb of God—the Messiah and the redemption of the world (Chapter 7). Its narrative closes on the same note: messianic expectation, hope in Christ. This theme of hope in Israel's Messiah bookends the lost manuscript at each side. He was the lost manuscript's Alpha and Omega, its beginning and its end. The entire lost text of the Book of Mormon thus comprises an inclusio—a text that begins and ends on the same motif, a structure common to the Hebrew Bible and one that marks the text off as a discrete unit with a unified theme.

---

5. Joseph Smith, discourse, June 16, 1844, reported by Thomas Bullock, in Ehat and Cook, *Words of Joseph Smith*, 382.

The lost Book of Mormon manuscript was merely the part of Mormon's book that Joseph Smith happened to finish dictating before Martin Harris borrowed the incomplete manuscript. It was not intended either by Mormon or by Joseph Smith to comprise a complete literary unit, a work of scripture with a coherent and self-contained theological message. But a larger hand intervened. Despite its human author's failure to intend or plan as much, the lost manuscript *did* present a unified theological message, beginning and concluding on the same messianic note, a symmetry that gave it a kind of completeness and drove home its central message. If this wholeness cannot be attributed to the book's human author, who did not know where the lost manuscript would end, or even that there would be a manuscript loss, then the manuscript's elegant beginning and ending on the same note of messianic hope may be seen as a contribution to the work by the hoped-for one himself, an inclusio written by the finger of the one the Book of Mormon names "the author and the finisher of our faith" (Heb. 12:12).

BIBLIOGRAPHY

Abbreviation: *EMD* = Dan Vogel, *Early Mormon Documents.*

"$25 Reward." *Wayne Sentinel* (December 30, 1840): 4.

Adler, Herbert M. "The Jews in Southern Italy." *The Jewish Quarterly Review* 14, no. 1 (October 1901): 111–15.

Alvin Smith Gravestone. June 15, 1828, McKune Cemetery, Oakland, Susquehanna County, PA.

Anderson, Lavina Fielding, ed. *Lucy's Book: A Critical Edition of Lucy Mack Smith's Family Memoir.* Salt Lake City: Signature Books, 2001.

Anderson, Richard L. "The Mature Joseph Smith and Treasure Searching," *Brigham Young University Studies* 24, no. 4 (1984): 489–560.

Anthon, Charles. Charles Anthon to E. D. Howe, February 17, 1834. In E. D. Howe, *Mormonism Unvailed: or, A Faithful Account of That Singular Imposition and Delusion, from Its Rise to the Present Time,* 270–72. Painesville, Ohio: E. D. Howe, 1834.

———. Charles Anthon to Thomas Winthrop Coit, April 3, 1841. *Church Record* (April 17, 1841): 231–32. Reprinted in Vogel, *EMD,* 4:384.

———. Charles Anthon to William E. Vibbert, August, 12 1844. In "A Fact in the Mormon Imposture," *New York Observer* 23, no. 69 (May 3, 1845). Reprinted in Larry E. Morris, ed., *A Documentary History of the Book of Mormon,* 235. New York: Oxford University Press, 2019.

———. *A Classical Dictionary; Containing a Copious Account of all the Proper Names Mentioned in Ancient Authors.* New York: Harper and Brothers, 1842.

———. *A System of Ancient and Medieval Geography for the Use of Schools and Colleges.* New York: Harper and Brothers, 1850.

Armstrong, Karen. *The Great Transformation: The Beginning of our Religious Traditions.* New York: Knopf, 2006.

Attridge, Harold W., and Helmut Koester, eds. *Hebrews: A Commentary on the Epistle to the Hebrews.* Philadelphia: Fortress, 1989.

Austin, Emily M. *Mormonism; or, Life Among the Mormons.* Madison, WI: 1882.

Barrett, T. H. "On the Reconstruction of the Shenxian zhuan." *Bulletin of the School of Oriental and African Studies* 66, no. 2 (2003): 229–35.

Bennett, Richard E. "'Read This I Pray Thee': Martin Harris and the Three Wise Men of the East." *Journal of Mormon History* 36, no. 1 (Winter 2010): 178–216.

Bidamon, Emma Smith. Emma Smith Bidamon to Emma Pilgrim, March 27, 1870; reprinted in Vogel, *EMD,* 1:532.

Bishop, Francis Gladden. *An Address to the Sons and Daughters of Zion, Scattered Abroad, Through All the Earth.* Kirtland, OH: F. G. Bishop, 1851.

———. *A Proclamation from the Lord to His People, Scattered Throughout All the Earth.* Kirtland, OH: Np., 1851.

"Blessing from Joseph Smith Sr., 9 December 1834." The Joseph Smith Papers. Accessed November 8, 2019. https://www.josephsmithpapers.org/paper-summary/blessing-from-joseph-smith-sr-9-december-1834/2.

"Blessing from Oliver Cowdery, 22 September 1835." The Joseph Smith Papers. Accessed November 8, 2019. https://www.josephsmithpapers.org/paper-summary/blessing-from -oliver-cowdery-22-september-1835/1.

"Book of Commandments, 1833." The Joseph Smith Papers. Accessed November 7, 2019. https:// www.josephsmithpapers.org/paper-summary/book-of-commandments-1833.

The Book of Mormon: An Account Written by the Hand of Mormon, Upon Plates Taken from the Plates of Nephi. Palmyra, NY: E. B. Grandin, 1830.

The Book of Mormon: Another Testament of Jesus Christ. Salt Lake City: Church of Jesus Christ of Latter-day Saints, 1981.

Booth, Ezra. "Mormonism—No. III," *Ohio Star* (October 27, 1831).

Bradley, Don. "American Proto-Zionism and the 'Book of Lehi': Recontextualizing the Rise of Mormonism." MA thesis, Utah State University, 2018.

———. "Building the Temple of Nephi: Early Mormon Perceptions of Cumorah and the New Jerusalem." *Journal of Book of Mormon Studies* 27 (2018): 264–77.

———. "'The Grand Fundamental Principles of Mormonism,' Joseph Smith's Unfinished Reformation." *Sunstone*, April 2006, 32–41.

———. "Joseph Smith's First Vision as Endowment and Epitome of the Gospel of Jesus Christ (or Why I Came Back to the Church)." 2019 Fair Conference. Available online at https://www.fairmormon.org/blog/2019/09/09/fairmormon-conference-podcast- 40-don-bradley-joseph-smiths-first-vision-as-endowment-and-epitome-of-the-gospel- of-jesus-christ-or-why-i-came-back-to-the-church.

———. "Pillars of My Faith." Presentation, Sunstone Symposium, August 4, 2012, https:// www.sunstonemagazine.com/pillars-of-my-faith-2012/.

Bradley, Don, and Mark Ashurst-McGee. "Joseph Smith and the Kinderhook Plates." In *A Reason for Faith: Navigating LDS Doctrine and Church History*, edited by Laura Harris Hales, 93–115. Provo, UT: Religious Studies Center, 2016.

———. "'President Joseph Has Translated a Portion': Joseph Smith and the Mistranslation of the Kinderhook Plates." In *Producing Ancient Scripture: Joseph Smith's Translation Projects in the Development of Mormon Christianity*, edited by Michael Hubbard MacKay, Mark Ashurst-McGee, and Brian Hauglid, 452–523. Salt Lake City: University of Utah, 2019.

Briggs, Edmund C. "A Visit to Nauvoo in 1856." *Journal of History* 9 (January 1916): 454; reprinted in Vogel, *EMD*, 1:530–31.

Brown, S. Kent. "Lehi's Personal Record: Quest for a Missing Source." *BYU Studies* 24, no. 1 (1984): 19–42.

Brückle, Irene. "Historical Manufacture and Use of Blue Paper." *The Book and Paper Group Annual* 12 (Fall 1993). Available at https://cool.conservation-us.org/coolaic/sg/bpg/ annual/v12/bp12-02.html.

Bruno, Cheryl L. and Joe Steve Swick, III. *Method Infinite: Freemasonry and the Mormon Restoration*. Salt Lake City: Greg Kofford Books, forthcoming.

Bushman, Richard Lyman. *Joseph Smith: Rough Stone Rolling*. New York: Alfred A. Knopf, 2005.

Butterworth, C. E. "The Old Soldier's Testimony. Sermon preached by Bro. William B. Smith, in the Saints' Chapel, Detroit, Iowa, June 8th, 1884." *Saints' Herald* 31 (October 4, 1884): 643–44.

Campany, Robert F. *To Live as Long as Heaven and Earth: A Translation and Study of Ge Hong's Traditions of Divine Transcendents*. Berkeley: University of California Press, 2002.

Cannon, George Q. *The Life of Joseph Smith the Prophet*. Salt Lake City: Juvenile Instructor Office, 1888.

Caswall, Henry. *The City of the Mormons; or, Three Days at Nauvoo, in 1842*, 2nd ed. rev. and enl. London: J. G. F. & J. Rivington, 1843.

Cazier, Donald Arthur. "A Study of Nephite, Lamanite, and Jaredite Governmental Institutions and Policies as Portrayed in the Book of Mormon." MA thesis, Brigham Young University, 1972.

Chase, Willard. "Willard Chase Statement, Circa 11 December 1833." In E. D. Howe, *Mormonism Unvailed: or, A Faithful Account of That Singular Imposition and Delusion, from Its Rise to the Present Time*, 240–48. Painesville, Ohio: E. D. Howe, 1834.

Christensen, Kevin. "Paradigms Regained: A Survey of Margaret Barker's Scholarship and its Significance for Mormon Studies." *Occasional Papers* 2 (2001).

Clark, John A. *Gleanings by the Way*. Philadelphia: W. J. & J. K. Simon, 1842.

———. Letter to "Dear Brethren," August 24, 1840, *The Episcopal Recorder* 18 (September 5, 1840): 94; reprinted in Vogel, *EMD*, 2:264.

Coe, Truman. "Mormonism." *The Ohio Observer* (August 11, 1836): 1–2.

Cole, Abner. "Gold Bible, No. 6." *Palmyra Reflector* 2, no. 16 (March 19, 1831), 126–27.

Collingwood, Robin G. *The Idea of History*, rev. Oxford: Oxford University Press, 1946; 1993.

Conrad, Lawrence I. "Recovering Lost Texts: Some Methodological Issues." *Journal of the American Oriental Society* 113, no. 2 (Apr.–Jun. 1993): 258–63.

Cowdery, Oliver. "Left Kirtland on the 16th." *Latter Day Saints' Messenger and Advocate* 1 (October 1834): 3–6.

———. Letter to W. W. Phelps. *Latter Day Saints' Messenger and Advocate* 1, no. 5 (February 1835): 77–80.

Crapo, Richley. "Lehi, Joseph, and the Kingdom of Israel." *Interpreter: A Journal of Latter-day Saint Faith and Scholarship* 33 (2019): 289–304.

Dame, William H. Journal, typescript. Special Collections, Harold B. Lee Library, Brigham Young University, Provo, UT.

Damen, Mark L. "Reconstructing the Beginning of Menander's Adelphoi (B)." *Illinois Classical Studies* 12 (1987): 67–84

———. "Translating Scenes: Plautus' Adaptation of Menander's Dis Exapaton." *Phoenix* 46 (1992): 205–31;

Davidson, Karen Lynn, David J. Whittaker, Mark Ashurst-McGee, and Richard L. Jensen, eds. *Histories, Volume 1: Joseph Smith Histories, 1832–1844.* Vol. 1 of the Histories series of *The Joseph Smith Papers,* edited by Dean C. Jessee, Ronald K. Esplin, and Richard Lyman Bushman. Salt Lake City: Church Historian's Press, 2012.

Davis, Charles Thomas. *The Manufacture of Paper: Being a Description of the Various Processes for the Fabrication, Coloring, and Finishing of Every Kind of Paper*. Philadelphia: Henry Carey Baird, 1886.

Devine, Donn. "How Long Is a Generation?" *Ancestry Magazine*. Accessed March 18, 2019. http://www.ancestry.ca/learn/learningcenters/default.aspx?section=lib_generation,

Dille, David B. "Additional Testimony of Martin Harris (One of the Three Witnesses) to the Coming Forth of the Book of Mormon." *Millennial Star* 21, no, 34 (August 20, 1859): 545–46.

"Discourse, 1 May 1842, as Reported by Willard Richards." The Joseph Smith Papers. Accessed November 12, 2019. https://www.josephsmithpapers.org/paper-summary/discourse-1-may-1842-as-reported-by-willard-richards/1.

Dolansky, Shawna. "A Goddess in the Garden? The Fall of Eve." In *Milk and Honey: Essays on Ancient Israel and the Bible in Appreciation of the Judaic Studies Program at the University of California, San Diego*, edited by Sarah Malena and David Milano, 3–22. Winona Lake, IN: Eisenbrauns, 2007.

Donaldson, Lee L. "The Plates of Ether and the Covenant of the Book of Mormon." In *Fourth Nephi, From Zion to Destruction*, edited by Monte S. Nyman and Charles D. Tate Jr., 69–79. Provo, UT: Religious Studies Center, 1995.

Ehat, Andrew F., and Lyndon W. Cook, ed. *The Words of Joseph Smith: The Contemporary Accounts of the Nauvoo Discourses of the Prophet Joseph*. Provo, UT: Religious Studies Center, 1996.

Elliott, Mark C. *Emperor Qianlong: Son of Heaven, Man of the World*. New York: Longman, 2009.

Ferguson, P. Scott. "Mahonri's Model for Temple Worship: Rending the Veil of Unbelief." Perspective: Understand Great Teaching 8, no. 1 (Spring 2008):. 37–45.

Ford,Clyde. "The Origin of the Word of Wisdom." *Journal of Mormon History* 24 (Fall 1998): 129–54.

Friedman, Richard Elliot. *The Hidden Book in the Bible*. San Francisco: Harper, 1999.

———. *Who Wrote the Bible?*. San Francisco: Harper, 1997.

Gardner, Brant A. *The Gift and Power: Translating the Book of Mormon*. Salt Lake City: Greg Kofford Books, 2011.

———. *Second Witness: Analytical and Contextual Commentary on the Book of Mormon*, 6 vols. Salt Lake City: Greg Kofford Books, 2007.

———. "When Hypotheses Collide: Responding to Lyon and Minson's 'When Pages Collide.'" *Interpreter: A Journal of Latter-day Saint Faith and Scholarship* 5 (2013): 105–19.

"General Minutes, April 6, 1856, Provo Utah Central Stake." Provo Utah Stake General Minutes, 1849–1977. LR 9629 11, LDS Church History Library, Salt Lake City, UT.

Gervais, Timothy, and John L. Joyce. "'By Small Means': Rethinking the Liahona." *Interpreter* 30 (2018): 207–32.

Gilbert, John H. "Joe Smith. Something About the Early Life of the Mormon Prophet. Story of the Mormon Bible From the Man Who First Printed It. The Men Who Figured in Its Production and Publication," *Post and Tribune* (December 3, 1877): 3; reprinted in Vogel, *EMD*, 2:519.

———. John H. Gilbert to James T. Cobb, Feb 10, 1879. Theodore Schroeder Papers, Manuscript Division, NYPL; microfilm copy in LDS Church History Library.

Goff, Alan. "How Should We Then Read? Reading Mormon Scripture After the Fall." *FARMS Review* 21, no. 1 (2009): 137–78.

"Golden Bible." *Rochester Gem* 1 (September 5, 1829): 70–71.

Gutmann, Joseph. *The Jewish Sanctuary*. Leiden, Netherlands: E. J. Brill, 1983.

Hammer, Reuven. *Entering the High Holy Days: A Complete Guide to the History, Prayers, and Themes*. Philadelphia: Jewish Publication Society, 2005.

Hardy, Grant. *Understanding the Book of Mormon: A Reader's Guide*. New York: Oxford University Press, 2010.

Harris, Henry. "Statement." In Eber D. Howe, *Mormonism Unvailed: or, A Faithful Account of That Singular Imposition and Delusion, from Its Rise to the Present Time*, 251–52. Painesville, Ohio: E. D. Howe, 1834.

Harris, Lucy. "Statement." In Eber D. Howe, *Mormonism Unvailed: or, A Faithful Account of That Singular Imposition and Delusion, from Its Rise to the Present Time*, 254–57. Painesville, Ohio: E. D. Howe, 1834.

Harris, Martin. Interview in "A Witness to the Book of Mormon." *Iowa State Register* (August 28, 1870); reprinted in Vogel, EMD, 2:330.

———. Martin Harris to H. B. Emerson, November 23, 1870, *Saints' Herald* 22 (October 15, 1875): 630\.

Hart, James H. Letter to the Editor, March 18, 1884, *Bear Lake Democrat* (March 28, 1884); reprinted in Vogel, *EMD*, 5:108.

"History, 1838–1856, volume A-1 [23 December 1805–30 August 1834]." The Joseph Smith Papers. Accessed November 4, 2019. https://www.josephsmithpapers.org/paper-summary/history-1838-1856-volume-a-1-23-december-1805-30-august-1834.

History of Joseph Smith (Mulholland draft). MS 23153, LDS Church History Library, Salt Lake City, UT.

"History of the Church." *Times and Seasons* 3, no. 14 (May 16, 1842): 785.

Holbrook, Brett L. "The Sword of Laban as a Symbol of Divine Authority and Kingship." *Journal of Book of Mormon Studies* 2, no. 1 (1993): 39–72.

Howe, Eber D. *Mormonism Unvailed: or, A Faithful Account of That Singular Imposition and Delusion, from Its Rise to the Present Time.* Painesville, Ohio: E. D. Howe, 1834.

Humboldt, Alexander [von]. *Concerning the Institutions & Monuments of the Ancient Inhabitants of America, with Descriptions & Views of Some the Most Striking Scenes in the Cordilleras!,* trans. Helen Maria Williams. London: 1814.

Iser, Wolfgang. *The Act of Reading: A Theory of Aesthetic Response.* London: Routledge, 1978.

Jacob, Norton. Journal; reprinted Vogel, *EMD,* 1:225.

Jennings, Erin B. "Charles Anthon—The Man Behind the Letters." *John Whitmer Historical Association Journal* 32, no. 2 (Fall/Winter 2012): 171–72.

Jensen, Ole A. "Testimony of Martin Harris (One of the Witnesses of the Book of Mormon)," ca. 1918. MS 7814, LDS Church History Library, Salt Lake City, UT; reprinted in Vogel, EMD, 2:376.

"Joseph Smith, History, 1838–1856, Volume A-1 [23 December 1805–30 August 1834]." Joseph Smith Papers. Accessed October 27, 2019. https://www.josephsmithpapers.org/paper-summary/history-1838-1856-volume-a-1-23-december-1805-30-august-1834/40.

Journal of Discourses. 26 vols. London and Liverpool: LDS Booksellers Depot, 1854–86.

"Journal, December 1842–June 1844; Book 3, 15 July 1843–29 February 1844." The Joseph Smith Papers. Accessed November 15, 2019. https://www.josephsmithpapers.org/paper-summary/journal-december-1842-june-1844-book-3-15-july-1843-29-february-1844/17.

Kimball, Stanley. "The Anthon Transcript: People, Primary Sources, and Problems." *BYU Studies* 10, no. 3 (Spring 1970): 325–52.

Kitov, Eliyahu. *The Book of Our Heritage: The Jewish Year and its Days of Significance.* Jerusalem: Feldheim Publishers, 1978.

Knight, Joseph, Sr. "Manuscript of the History of Joseph Smith," c. 1835–1847; reprinted in Vogel, *EMD,* 4:14–18.

Landau-Tasseron, Ella "On the Reconstruction of Lost Sources." In *History and Historiography in Early Islamic Times: Studies and Perspectives,* edited by Lawrence I. Conrad. Princeton, NJ: Princeton University Press, 2003.

Lapham, Fayette. "Interview with the Father of Joseph Smith, the Mormon Prophet, Forty Years Ago. His Account of the Finding of the Sacred Plates." *Historical Magazine* [second series] 7 (May 1870): 305–9; reprinted in Vogel, *EMD,* 1:462.

Larsen, Val. "In His Footsteps: Ammon$_1$ and Ammon$_2$." *Interpreter: A Journal of Latter-day Saint Faith and Scholarship* 3 (2013): 85–113.

———. "Killing Laban: The Birth of Sovereignty in the Nephite Constitutional Order." *Journal of Book of Mormon Studies* 16, no 1 (2007): 26–41.

"The Last Witness Dead!" *Richmond Democrat* 16, no. 5 (January 26, 1888): 3.

Lemprière, J. *A Classical Dictionary; Containing a Copious Account of all the Proper Names Mentioned in Ancient Authors.* London: T. Cadell and W. Davies, 1820, 1822.

———. *A Classical Dictionary; Containing a Copious Account of all the Proper Names Mentioned in Ancient Authors,* corrected and improved by Charles Anthon. New York: E. Duyckinck, G. Long, 1825.

Levias, Caspar. "Number and Numerals." In *The Jewish Encyclopedia,* 12 vols., edited by Isidore Singer et al., 9:348–50. New York and London: Funk and Wagnalls, 1907.

Lewis, Joseph and Hiel Lewis, "Mormon History. A New Chapter, About to Be Published," *Amboy Journal* 24 (April 30, 1879): 1.

Lipton, Peter. *Inference to the Best Explanation,* 2d ed. London: Routledge, 2004.

"Look Out for a Swindler." *Wayne Sentinel* (August 20, 1830): 3.

Ludlow, Daniel H. *A Companion to Your Study of the Book of Mormon*. Salt Lake City: Deseret Book, 1981.

Lundquist, John M., and John W. Welch. "Kingship and Temple in 2 Nephi 5–10." In *Reexploring the Book of Mormon: A Decade of New Research*, edited by John W. Welch, 66–68. Provo, UT: FARMS, 1992.

Lyon, Jack M., and Kent R. Minson. "When Pages Collide: Dissecting the Words of Mormon," *BYU Studies* 51, no. 4 (2012): 120–36

MacKay, Michael Hubbard. "'Git Them Translated': Translating the Characters on the Gold Plates." In *Approaching Antiquity: Joseph Smith and the Ancient World*, edited by Lincoln H. Blumell, Matthew J. Grey, and Andrew H. Hedges, 83–116. Provo, UT: Religious Studies Center, 2015.

Magee, Frances. Oral History, interviewed by Mike George, n.d.;reprinted in Linda Sillitoe and Allen D. Roberts, *Salamander: The Story of the Mormon Forgery Murders*, 154. Salt Lake City: Signature Books, 1988.

"Manchester in the Early Days." *Shortsville Enterprise* (March 11–18, 1904); reprinted in Vogel, *EMD*, 3:229.

Marquardt, H. Michael. *The Joseph Smith Revelations: Text and Commentary*. Salt Lake City: Signature Books, 1999.

———. "Martin Harris: The Kirtland Years, 1831–1870." *Dialogue: A journal of Mormon Thought* 35, no. 3 (2002): 1–40.

Mather, Frederick G. "The Early Mormons. Joe Smith Operates at Susquehanna." *Binghamton Republican* (July 29, 1880); reprinted in Vogel, *EMD*, 4:355.

McGuire, Benjamin. "Benjamin or Mosiah? Resolving an Anomaly in Mosiah 21:28." Paper presented at the 2001 FAIR Conference. https://www.fairmormon.org/conference/august-2001/benjamin-or-mosiah-resolving-an-anomaly-in-mosiah-2128/.

———. "Nephi and Goliath: A Case Study of Literary Allusion in the Book of Mormon." *Journal of the Book of Mormon and Other Restoration Scripture* 18, no. 1 (2009): 16–31.

McKune, Hezekiah. "Statement, March 20, 1834." *Susquehanna Register and Northern Pennsylvanian* (May 1, 1834); reprinted in Vogel, *EMD*, 4:327.

Metcalf, Anthony. *Ten Years Before the Mast. Shipwrecks and Adventures at Sea! Religious Customs of the People of India and Burmah's Empire. How I Became a Mormon and Why I Became an Infidel!* [Malad City, Idaho]: n.p., [1888]; reprinted in Vogel, *EMD*, 2:348.

Metcalfe, Brent Lee. "The Priority of Mosiah." In *New Approaches to the Book of Mormon: Explorations in Critical Methodology*, edited by Brent Lee Metcalfe, 395–437. Salt Lake City, UT: Signature Books, 1993.

Miner, Alan C. "The Lord Redeems His Covenant Children: Alma 1 -- Alma 44." Step by Step Through the Book of Mormon. Accessed September 12, 2019. https://stepbystep.alancminer.com/alma_10.

———. "Out of Bondage through Covenants: Jarom -- Mosiah." Step by Step Through the Book of Mormon. Accessed September 12, 2019. https://stepbystep.alancminer.com/omni.

"Minutes, 25–26 October 1831." The Joseph Smith Papers. Accessed November 8, 2019. https://www.josephsmithpapers.org/paper-summary/minutes-25-26-october-1831/4

Mock, Cary J. et al. "The Winter of 1827–1828 over Eastern North America: A Season of Extraordinary Climatic Anomalies, Societal Impacts, and False Spring." *Climatic Change* 83 (2007): 87–115.

"The Mormon Creed." *Painesville Telegraph* 2, no. 44 (April 19, 1831). Reprinted in *Documentary History of the Book of Mormon*, compiled by Larry E. Morris, 37–40. New York: Oxford University Press, 2019.

"Mormonism. Authentic Account of the Origin of the Sect from One of the Patriarchs." *Kansas City Daily Journal* (June 5, 1881): 1.

"Mormonism in Its Infancy." *Newark Daily Advertiser* (ca. August 1856), in Charles Woodward, Scrapbook, 1:125. New York Public Library, NY; reprinted in Vogel, *EMD*, 3:61.

"Mormonism---No. II," *Tiffany's Monthly: Devoted to the Investigation of the Science of Mind, in the Physical, Intellectual, Moral and Religious Planes Thereof* 5 (August 1859): 163–70; reprinted in Vogel, *EMD*, 2:307.

Münnich, Maciej. "The Cult of Bronze Serpents in Ancient Canaan and Israel." In *Iggud: Selected Essays in Jewish Studies, Vol. I: The Bible and Its World, Rabbinic Literature and Jewish Law, and Jewish Law*, edited by B. J. Schwartz, A. Melamed, and A. Shemesh, 39–56. Jerusalem: World Union of Jewish Studies, 2008.

Nibley, Hugh W. *The Prophetic Book of Mormon*. Salt Lake City: Deseret Book, 1989.

———. *Since Cumorah*. Salt Lake City: Deseret Book, 1988.

———. *Temple and Cosmos*. Salt Lake City: Deseret Book, 2002.

"Old Newspapers--No. 24." *Palmyra Courier*, May 24, 1872; reprinted in Vogel, *EMD*, 2:342.

"Old Newspapers--No. 25." *Palmyra Courier*, May 31, 1872; reprinted in Vogel, *EMD*, 2:343.

Oppenheimer, Clive. "Climatic, Environmental and Human Consequences of the Largest Known Historic Eruption: Tambora Volcano (Indonesia) 1815," *Progress in Physical Geography* 27, no. 2 (2003): 230–59.

Oyer and Terminer Minutes, 1824–1845, 92. Wayne County Courthouse, Lyons, NY; reprinted in Vogel, *EMD*, 3:186.

Perkinson, Roy. "Summary of the History of Blue Paper," *The Book and Paper Group Annual* 16 (Fall 1997): https://cool.conservation-us.org/coolaic/sg/bpg/annual/v16/bp16-10.html.

Parry, Donald W. "Sinai as Sanctuary and Mountain of God." In *By Study and Also By Faith: Essays in Honor of Hugh Nibley on the Occasion of His Eightieth Birthday*, 2 vols., edited by John M Lundquist and Stephen David Ricks, 482–500. Provo, UT: FARMS. 1990.

Peterson, Daniel C. "Authority in the Book of Mosiah." *FARMS Review* 18, no. 1 (2006):149–85.

Peterson, J. W. "The Urim and Thummim." *The Rod of Iron* 1, no. 3 (February 1924):7

Phelps, W. W. "The Book of Ether." *The Evening and the Morning Star* 1, no. 3 (August 1832): 22.

Pilkington, William. Autobiography, 1934–1939. MS 1041, LDS Church History Library, Salt Lake City, UT.

———. "A Dying Testimony Given by Martin Harris." MS 8068, LDS Church History Library, Salt Lake City, UT.

Post, John D. *The Last Great Subsistence Crisis in the Western World*. Baltimore, MD: The Johns Hopkins University Press, 1977.

Poulson, P. Wilhelm. "Correspondence. Interview with David Whitmer." *Deseret Evening News* 11, no. 224 (August 16, 1878): 2.

Pratt, John P. "Book of Mormon Chronology." In *Encyclopedia of Mormonism*, 4 vols., edited by Daniel H. Ludlow, 169–71. New York: Macmillan, 1992.

———. "Lehi's 600-year Prophecy of the Birth of Christ," *Meridian Magazine*. March 31, 2000. http://johnpratt.com/items/docs/lds/meridian/2000/lehi6apr.html.

———. "The Nephite Calendar," *Meridian Magazine*. January 14, 2004. Available at https://www.johnpratt.com/items/docs/lds/meridian/2004/nephite.html.

———. "Passover: Was It Symbolic of His Coming?" *The Ensign*, January 1994, 38–45.

Pratt, Orson. *Divine Authenticity of the Book of Mormon*, 3 vols. Liverpool, England: Np., 1850–51.

"Printer's Manuscript of the Book of Mormon, circa August 1829–circa January 1830." The Joseph Smith Papers. Accessed November 8, 2019. https://www.josephsmithpapers.org/paper-summary/printers-manuscript-of-the-book-of-mormon-circa-august-1829-circa-january-1830/.

Proctor, Scot and Maurine Proctor. "Archaeological Dig: Was There a Holy Place of Worship at Nephi's Bountiful?" *Meridian Magazine*, February 29, 2016. https://latterdaysaint-mag.com/day-2-was-there-a-holy-place-of-worship-at-nephis-bountiful/.

"The Progress of Mormonism." *Philadelphia Album* 5, no. 22 (May 28, 1831): 173.

Purple, W. D. "Joseph Smith, the Originator of Mormonism. Historical Reminiscences of the Town of Afton," *Chenango Union* 30 (May 3, 1877): 3; reprinted in Vogel, *EMD*, 4:135.

Read, Lenet Hadley. "Joseph Smith's Receipt of the Plates and the Israelite Feast of Trumpets." *Journal of Book of Mormon Studies* 2, no.2 (Fall 1993): 110–20.

"Revelation, April 1829–B [D&C 8]." The Joseph Smith Papers. Accessed November 7, 2019. https://www.josephsmithpapers.org/paper-summary/revelation-april-1829-b-dc-8/1.

"Revelation, March 1829 [D&C 5]." The Joseph Smith Papers. Accessed November 15, 2019. https://www.josephsmithpapers.org/paper-summary/revelation-march-1829-dc-5/1

"Revelation, July 1828 [D&C 3]." The Joseph Smith Papers. Accessed November 8, 2019. https://www.josephsmithpapers.org/paper-summary/revelation-july-1828-dc-3/2

"Revelation Revisers." *St. Louis Republican* 77 (July 16, 1884): 7; reprinted in Vogel, *EMD* 5:129–30.

"Revelation, Spring 1829 [D&C 10]." The Joseph Smith Papers. Accessed November 8, 2019. https://www.josephsmithpapers.org/paper-summary/revelation-spring-1829-dc-10/6

Reynolds, George. *A Dictionary of the Book of Mormon, Comprising its Biographical, Geographical and other Proper Names.* Salt Lake City: Joseph Hyrum Parry, 1891.

———. "The Political Dimension in Nephi's Small Plates." *BYU Studies* 27, no. 4 (1987): 15–37.

Reynolds, Noel B. "Nephi's Political Testament." In *Rediscovering the Book of Mormon*, edited by John L. Sorenson and Melvin J. Thorne, 220–29. Provo: FARMS, 1991.

Richards, Franklin D. "Origin of American Aborigines." *The Contributor* 17, no. 7 (May 1896): 425–28.

Ricks Stephen D. "The Appearance of Elijah and Moses in the Kirtland Temple and the Jewish Passover." *BYU Studies* 23, no. 4 (1983): 1–4.

Roberts, B.H. *Defense of the Faith and the Saints*, 2 vols. Salt Lake City: Deseret News, 1907.

Robinson, James M. Paul Hoffmann, and John S. Kloppenborg, eds., *The Critical Edition of Q: Synopsis including the Gospels of Matthew and Luke, Mark and Thomas with English, German, and French Translations of Q and Thomas.* Minneapolis: Fortress Press, 2000.

Rolph, Daniel N. "Prophets, Kings, and Swords: The Sword of Laban and Its Possible Pre-Laban Origin." *Journal of Book of Mormon Studies* 2, no. 1 (1993): 73–79.

Rothbard, Murray N. *The Panic of 1819: Reactions and Policies.* New York: Columbia University Press, 1962.

Salisbury, Herbert S. "Things the Prophet's Sister Told Me," July 2, 1945; reprinted in Vogel, *EMD*, 1:524.

Salisbury, Katharine Smith. Letter to "Dear Sisters." *Saints' Herald* 33 (May 1, 1886): 260; reprinted in Vogel, *EMD*, 1:521–22.

Saunders, Lorenzo. Interviewed by E. L. Kelley, November, 12, 1884. E. L. Kelley Papers, "Miscellany." Community of Christ Library Archives, Independence, MO; reprinted in Vogel, *EMD*, 2:149.

Saunders, Richard L. "Francis Gladden Bishop and Gladdenism: A Study in the Culture of a Mormon Dissenter and his Movement." MA thesis, Utah State University, 1989.

Scholem, Gershom. *Kabbalah.* New York: Meridian, 1974.

Segal, Jerome M. *Joseph's Bones: Understanding the Struggle between God and Mankind in the Bible.* New York: Riverhead Books, 2007.

Shaughnessy, Edward L. *Rewriting Early Chinese Texts.* Albany: State University of New York Press, 2006.

Simmons, Verneil. *People, Places and Prophecies: A Study of the Book of Mormon*. Independence, MO: Zarahemla Research Foundation, 1981.

Skousen, Royal. *Analysis of Textual Variants of the Book of Mormon*, 6 vols. Provo, UT: Foundation for Ancient Research and Mormon Studies, 2006.

———, ed. *The Book of Mormon: The Earliest Text*. New Haven, CT: Yale, 2009.

———. "Critical Methodology and the Text of the Book of Mormon." *Review of Books on the Book of Mormon* 6, no. 1 (1994): 121–44.

———. "The Original Language of the Book of Mormon: Upstate New York Dialect, King James English, or Hebrew?" *Journal of Book of Mormon Studies* 3, no. 1 (1994): 28–38.

———. *The Original Manuscript of the Book of Mormon: Typographical Facsimile of the Extant Text*. Provo, UT: FARMS, 2001.

———. "The Original Text of the Book of Mormon and Its Publication by Yale University Press." *Interpreter: A Journal of Mormon Scripture* 7 (2003): 57–96.

———, ed. *The Printer's Manuscript of the Book of Mormon: Typographical Facsimile of the Entire Text in Two Parts*. Provo, UT: FARMS, 2001.

———. "Translating the Book of Mormon: Evidence from the Original Manuscript." In *Book of Mormon Authorship Revisited: The Evidence for Ancient Origins*, edited by Noel B. Reynolds, 61–93. Provo, Utah: FARMS, 1997.

———. "Why Was One Sixth of the 1830 Book of Mormon Set from the Original Manuscript?" *Interpreter: A Journal of Latter-day Saint Faith and Scholarship* 2 (2012): 93–103.

———. "Worthy of Another Look: John Gilbert's 1892 Account of the 1830 Printing of the Book of Mormon." *Journal of the Book of Mormon and Other Restoration Scripture* 21, no. 2 (2012): 58–72.

Sloan, David E. "The Book of Lehi and the Plates of Lehi." *Journal of Book of Mormon Studies* 6, no. 2 (1997): 269–72.

Smith, Ethan. *View of the Hebrews; or the Tribes of Israel in America*, 2d ed. Poultney, VT: Smith and Shute, 1825.

Smith, George Albert. "Sketch of the Autobiography of George Albert Smith." *Deseret News* (August 11, 1858): 101.

Smith, John. Journal, circa 1839. In Lucy Smith, *Biographical Sketches of Joseph Smith the Prophet and His Progenitors for Many Generations*. Liverpool: S. W. Richards, 1853, 154–7.

Smith, Joseph. "Church History." *Times and Seasons* 3 (1 March 1842): 706–10.

———. "Elder's Journal: Joseph Smith jr. Editor," *Elders' Journal* 1 no. 3 (July 1838), 42–44.

———. "History, circa Summer 1832." Joseph Smith Papers. Accessed September 4, 2019. https://www.josephsmithpapers.org/paper-summary/history-circa-summer-1832/.

———. History Draft, 1839; reprinted in Vogel, *EMD*, 1:54–144.

Smith, Joseph, et al. *History of the Church of Jesus Christ of Latter-day Saints*, edited by B. H. Roberts, 7 vols. Salt Lake City: Deseret News, 1904.

Smith, Joseph, III. "Last Testimony of Sister Emma." *Saints Herald* 26 (October 1, 1879): 289–90.

Smith, Lucy. *Biographical Sketches of Joseph Smith the Prophet, and His Progenitors for Many Generations*. Plano, Illinois: Reorganized Church of Jesus Christ of Latter Day Saints, 1880.

———. "Preliminary Manuscript." LDS Church History Library, Salt Lake City, UT; reprinted in *Lucy's Book: A Critical Edition of Lucy Mack Smith's Family Memoir*, edited by Lavina Fielding Anderson. Salt Lake City: Signature Books, 2001.

Smith, Simon. "Martin Harris' Testimony." *The Saints' Herald* 28, no. 3 (1 February 1881): 43.

Smith, William. Interview with J. W. Peterson and W. S. Pender, 1921. In *Opening the Heavens: Accounts of Divine Manifestations, 1820–1844*, edited by John W. Welch, PAGE #S. Provo, UT: BYU Press: 2005.

———. *William Smith on Mormonism*. Lamoni, IA: Herald Steam Book and Job Office, 1883.

Sorenson, John L. "The 'Brass Plates' and Biblical Scholarship." *Dialogue: A Journal of Mormon Thought* 10, no. 4 (1977): 31–39.

Spackman, Randall P. "The Jewish/Nephite Lunar Calendar." *Journal of Book of Mormon Studies* 7, no. 1, (1998): 48–59.

Spencer, Joseph M. *For Zion: A Mormon Theology of Hope.* Salt Lake City: Greg Kofford Books, 2014.

Sperry, Sidney B. *Book of Mormon Compendium.* Salt Lake City: Bookcraft, 1970.

Stack, Peggy Fletcher. "The Rest Is History: How a Mormon Scholar Turned Doubter, then Believer." *Salt Lake Tribune*, September 4, 2012, https://archive.sltrib.com/article. php?id=54790798&itype=cmsid.

Staker, Mark Lyman, and Robin Scott Jensen. "David Hale's Store Ledger: New Details about Joseph and Emma Smith, the Hale Family, and the Book of Mormon." *BYU Studies Quarterly* 53, no. 3 (2014): 77–112.

"Statement of J. W. Peterson Concerning William Smith," May 1, 1921. Miscellaneous Letters and Papers, Community of Christ Library-Archives, Independence, MO; reprinted in Vogel, *EMD*, 1:508–9.

Stevenson, Edward. "One of the Three Witnesses." *Deseret Evening News* 15, no. 20 (December 13, 1881): 4.

Stout, Meg. "The Beaver Skin Hat: How Joseph Interpreted the Plates." Millennial Star (blog). January 22, 2015. https://www.millennialstar.org/the-beaver-skin-hat-how -joseph-interpreted-the-plates/

Tate, George S. "The Typology of the Exodus Pattern in the Book of Mormon." In *Literature of Belief: Sacred Scripture and Religious Experiences*, edited by Neal E. Lambert, 245–62. Provo: BYU Religious Studies Center, 1981.

"Testimony of Martin Harris, 1870." Dictated to Edward Stevenson, September 4, 1870. MS 4806, Edward Stevenson Collection, 1849–1922, LDS Church History Library, Salt Lake City, UT.

Thomas, John Christopher *A Pentecostal Reads The Book of Mormon: A Literary and Theological Introduction.* Cleveland, TN: CPT Press, 2016.

Thomas, M. Catherine. "The Brother of Jared at the Veil." In *Temples of the Ancient World: Ritual and Symbolism*, edited by Donald W. Parry, 388–98. Salt Lake City: Deseret Book, 1994).

Thomasson, Gordon C. "Mosiah: The Complex Symbolism and Symbolic Complex of Kingship in the Book of Mormon." *Journal of Book of Mormon Stories* 2, no. 1 (1993): 21–38

Thompson, Charles B. "A Correspondent Writes." *Zion's Harbinger and Baneemy's Organ* 2, no. 3 (March 1852): 22.

———. *Evidence in Proof of the Book of Mormon Being a Divinely Inspired Record, Written by the Forefathers of the Natives whom We Call Indians (Who are a Remnant of the Tribe of Joseph).* Batavia, NY: C. B. Thompson, 1841.

Townsend, Colby. "Rewriting Eden with the Book of Mormon: Joseph Smith and the Reception of Genesis 1–6 in Early America." MA thesis, Utah State University, 2019.

Townsend, Jesse. Letter to Phineas Stiles, December 24, 1833, in Pomeroy Tucker, *Origin, Rise, and Progress of Mormonism*, 288–91. New York: D. Appleton and Co., 1867.

Traughber, J. L., Jr. "Testimony of David Whitmer." *Saints' Herald* 26, no. 22 (November 15, 1879): 341.

Troll, Rich. "Samuel Tyler Lawrence: A Significant Figure in Joseph Smith's Palmyra Past." *Journal of Mormon History* 32, no. 2 (Summer 2006): 38–86.

Tucker, Pomeroy *Origin, Rise, and Progress of Mormonism.* New York: D. Appleton and Co., 1867.

Tvedtnes, John A. *The Most Correct Book: Insights from a Book of Mormon Scholar.* Salt Lake City: Cornerstone Publishing, 1999.

Turner, Orsamus. *History of the Pioneer Settlement of Phelps and Gorham's Purchase.* Rochester, NY: William Alling, 1851; reprinted in Vogel, *EMD*, 3:52.

Van Dam, Cornelis. *The Urim and Thummim: A Means of Revelation in Ancient Israel.* Winona Lake, Indiana, Eisenbrauns, 1997.

Van Wagoner, Richard S., and Steven C. Walker. "Joseph Smith: 'The Gift of Seeing.'" *Dialogue: A Journal of Mormon Thought* 15, no. 2 (Summer 1982): 49–68.

Vogel, Dan, ed. *Early Mormon Documents.* 5 vols. Salt Lake City: Signature Books, 1998–2003.

———. *Joseph Smith: The Making of a Prophet.* Salt Lake City: Signature Books, 2004.

Wadsworth, Nathaniel Hinckley. "Copyright Laws and the 1830 Book of Mormon." *BYU Studies* 45, no. 3 (2006): 77–96.

Walker, Kyle R. "Katharine Smith Salisbury's Recollections of Joseph's Meetings with Moroni." *BYU Studies* 41, no. 3 (2002): 5–17.

Walker, Ronald W. "Joseph Smith: The Palmyra Seer." *BYU Studies* 24, no. 4 (Fall 1984): 461–72.

———. "The Persisting Idea of American Treasure Hunting." *BYU Studies* 24, no. 4 (Fall 1984): 427–59.

Washburn, Jesse Nile. *The Contents, Structure and Authorship of the Book of Mormon.* Salt Lake City: Bookcraft, 1954.

Watson, Elden. "Approximate Book of Mormon Translation Timeline." Elden Watson's Home Page. April 1995. http://eldenwatson.net/BoM.htm, accessed October 29, 2019.

Wayne County. Indenture, Martin Harris and Lucy Harris to Flanders Dyke, June 30, 1828. Wayne County, New York. New York Land Records, Wayne County, Deeds 1827–1828, Vol. 7:26–27.

Webster, Noah. *An American Dictionary of the English Language,* 2 vols. New Haven, CT: 1828.

Welch, John W. "Benjamin's Covenant as a Precursor of the Sacrament Prayers." In *King Benjamin's Speech: "That Ye May Learn Wisdom,"* edited by John W. Welch and Stephen D. Ricks, 295–314. Provo, UT: FARMS, 1998.

———. "Doubled, Sealed, Witnessed Documents: From the Ancient World to the Book of Mormon." In *Mormons, Scripture, and the Ancient World,* edited by Davis Bitton, 391–444. Provo, UT: FARMS, 1998.

———. "Lehi's Last Will and Testament: A Legal Approach." In *The Book of Mormon: Second Nephi, the Doctrinal Structure,* edited by M. Nyman and C. Tate, 61–82. Provo, UT: Religious Studies Center, 1989.

———. "The Miraculous Timing of the Translation of the Book of Mormon." In *Opening the Heavens: Accounts of Divine Manifestations, 1820–1844,* 2nd ed., edited by John W. Welch, 79–125. Salt Lake City: Deseret Book, 2017.

———, ed. *Opening the Heavens: Accounts of Divine Manifestations, 1820–1844,* 2nd ed. Provo, UT: BYU Studies, 2017.

———. "Our Nephite Sacrament Prayers." In *Reexploring the Book of Mormon: A Decade of New Research,* edited by John W. Welch, 286–89. Provo, UT: FARMS, 1992.

Wells, Anita Cramer. "Lost—But Not Forgotten—116 Pages: What the Book of Mormon Might Have Included." Unpublished manuscript in possession of author.

White, William Wallace. Journal. Photographs in possession of author. Original in private possession.

Whitelam, Keith W. "Israelite Kingship: The Royal Ideology and Its Opponents." In *The World of Ancient Israel: Sociological, Anthropological And Political Perspectives,* edited by R. E. Clements, 119–40. Cambridge: Cambridge University Press, 1989.

Whitmer, David. *An Address to All Believers in Christ.* Richmond, MO: David Whitmer, 1887.

———. "Revelation Revisers." *St. Louis Republican* 77 (July 16, 1884): 7; reprinted in Vogel, *EMD,* 5:129–30.

SCRIPTURE INDEX

SUBJECT INDEX

A

Aaron's rod, 150–51
Abinadi, 227–28
All Saints Day, 19
Alma$_1$
    founds church, 206
    performs first baptisms, 206
Alma$_2$
    appoints chief judge, 202
    authority derived from king, 196
    gives the Liahona to Helaman, 148, 150
    high priest, 202
    on Liahona, 150, 152, 155–56
    priesthood of, 199–200
Amaleki
    describes Benjamin, 279
    describes Mulochites, 258
    gives plates to Benjamin, 199
    on Mosiah$_1$, 243
Amaron, 221–22
Aminadi
    ancestor of Amulek, 223
    differs from other wisdom figures, 229
    interprets writing, 229–31
    in lost manuscript, 233
    and Nephite temple, 234–40
    time of, 224–25
    as wisdom figure, 225–26, 229
    and year 320, 232
Ammon$_1$
    discovers people of Zeniff, 250
    tells Limhi about interpreters, 197, 244
    reverses Mosiah$_1$, 251
Ammon$_2$
    inversion of Mosiah$_1$, 245, 266
    shepherd, 245
Amulek, 223
Anthon transcript, 20–24
    not Caractors document, 21
    stolen by Lucy Harris, 64–65
Anthon, Charles
    and biblical scholarship, 31–32

condemned, 33
describes transcript, 5, 21–22
devout Christian, 33
learned, 32
tears certificate, 28
on transcript, 26–35
ark, 3–4
    containing Joseph of Egypt's remains, 179
    Nephite, 200, 204–5
    of Joseph, 205–6
Ark of the Covenant, 179, 195, 201–2, 236
    taken, 147
Armstrong, Karen, 135
Austin, Emily Colburn, 30
Aztec calendar, 22

B

Babylonian invasion, 116, 128, 147, 260
Benjamin
    defeats false Christs, 280
    defeats Lamanites, 279
    ends contention, 279
    people take on name of Christ, 264
    length of reign, 95
    lost narratives, 279–83
    meaning of name, 275
    and Messianic expectation, 284
    name changed to Mosiah, 197
    possessed interpreters, 197–98
    renews Mosiah$_1$'s covenant, 269–70
    shares Mosiah$_1$'s teachings., 248
Bible, 289–90
Bishop, Francis Gladden
    claims angel took manuscript, 70
    describes manuscript, 83–84
    describes plates, 5n5, 23
    on Liahona, 149
    on sword of Laban, 141, 177
    supported by Martin Harris, 141–42
Book of Benjamin, 278
Book of Mormon
    hybrid text, 85

Also available from
GREG KOFFORD BOOKS

Authoring the Old Testament: Genesis–Deuteronomy

David Bokovoy

Paperback, ISBN: 978-1-58958-588-1
Hardcover, ISBN: 978-1-58958-675-8

For the last two centuries, biblical scholars have made discoveries and insights about the Old Testament that have greatly changed the way in which the authorship of these ancient scriptures has been understood. In the first of three volumes spanning the entire Hebrew Bible, David Bokovoy dives into the Pentateuch, showing how and why textual criticism has led biblical scholars today to understand the first five books of the Bible as an amalgamation of multiple texts into a single, though often complicated narrative; and he discusses what implications those have for Latter-day Saint understandings of the Bible and modern scripture.

Praise for *Authoring the Old Testament*:

"*Authoring the Old Testament* is a welcome introduction, from a faithful Latter-day Saint perspective, to the academic world of Higher Criticism of the Hebrew Bible. . . . [R]eaders will be positively served and firmly impressed by the many strengths of this book, coupled with Bokovoy's genuine dedication to learning by study and also by faith." — John W. Welch, editor, *BYU Studies Quarterly*

"Bokovoy provides a lucid, insightful lens through which disciple-students can study intelligently LDS scripture. This is first rate scholarship made accessible to a broad audience—nourishing to the heart and mind alike." — Fiona Givens, co-author, *The God Who Weeps: How Mormonism Makes Sense of Life*

"I repeat: this is one of the most important books on Mormon scripture to be published recently. . . . [*Authoring the Old Testament*] has the potential to radically expand understanding and appreciation for not only the Old Testament, but scripture in general. It's really that good. Read it. Share it with your friends. Discuss it." — David Tayman, The Improvement Era: A Mormon Blog

Second Witness: Analytical and Contextual Commentary on the Book of Mormon

Brant A. Gardner

Second Witness, a new six-volume series from Greg Kofford Books, takes a detailed, verse-by-verse look at the Book of Mormon. It marshals the best of modern scholarship and new insights into a consistent picture of the Book of Mormon as a historical document. Taking a faithful but scholarly approach to the text and reading it through the insights of linguistics, anthropology, and ethnohistory, the commentary approaches the text from a variety of perspectives: how it was created, how it relates to history and culture, and what religious insights it provides.

The commentary accepts the best modern scholarship, which focuses on a particular region of Mesoamerica as the most plausible location for the Book of Mormon's setting. For the first time, that location—its peoples, cultures, and historical trends—are used as the backdrop for reading the text. The historical background is not presented as proof, but rather as an explanatory context.

The commentary does not forget Mormon's purpose in writing. It discusses the doctrinal and theological aspects of the text and highlights the way in which Mormon created it to meet his goal of "convincing . . . the Jew and Gentile that Jesus is the Christ, the Eternal God."

Praise for the *Second Witness* series:

"Gardner not only provides a unique tool for understanding the Book of Mormon as an ancient document written by real, living prophets, but he sets a standard for Latter-day Saint thinking and writing about scripture, providing a model for all who follow. . . . No other reference source will prove as thorough and valuable for serious readers of the Book of Mormon."

-Neal A. Maxwell Institute, Brigham Young University

1. 1st Nephi: 978-1-58958-041-1
2. 2nd Nephi–Jacob: 978-1-58958-042-8
3. Enos–Mosiah: 978-1-58958-043-5

4. Alma: 978-1-58958-044-2
5. Helaman–3rd Nephi: 978-1-58958-045-9
6. 4th Nephi–Moroni: 978-1-58958-046-6

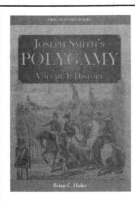

Joseph Smith's Polygamy, 3 Vols.

Brian Hales

Hardcover
Volume 1: History 978-1-58958-189-0
Volume 2: History 978-1-58958-548-5
Volume 3: Theology 978-1-58958-190-6

Perhaps the least understood part of Joseph Smith's life and teachings is his introduction of polygamy to the Saints in Nauvoo. Because of the persecution he knew it would bring, Joseph said little about it publicly and only taught it to his closest and most trusted friends and associates before his martyrdom.

In this three-volume work, Brian C. Hales provides the most comprehensive faithful examination of this much misunderstood period in LDS Church history. Drawing for the first time on every known account, Hales helps us understand the history and teachings surrounding this secretive practice and also addresses and corrects many of the numerous allegations and misrepresentations concerning it. Hales further discusses how polygamy was practiced during this time and why so many of the early Saints were willing to participate in it.

Joseph Smith's Polygamy is an essential resource in understanding this challenging and misunderstood practice of early Mormonism.

Praise for *Joseph Smith's Polygamy*:

"Brian Hales wants to face up to every question, every problem, every fear about plural marriage. His answers may not satisfy everyone, but he gives readers the relevant sources where answers, if they exist, are to be found. There has never been a more thorough examination of the polygamy idea." —Richard L. Bushman, author of *Joseph Smith: Rough Stone Rolling*

"Hales's massive and well documented three volume examination of the history and theology of Mormon plural marriage, as introduced and practiced during the life of Joseph Smith, will now be the standard against which all other treatments of this important subject will be measured." —Danel W. Bachman, author of "A Study of the Mormon Practice of Plural Marriage before the Death of Joseph Smith"

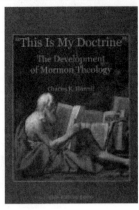

"This is My Doctrine": The Development of Mormon Theology

Charles R. Harrell

Hardcover, ISBN: 978-1-58958-103-6

The principal doctrines defining Mormonism today often bear little resemblance to those it started out with in the early 1830s. This book shows that these doctrines did not originate in a vacuum but were rather prompted and informed by the religious culture from which Mormonism arose. Early Mormons, like their early Christian and even earlier Israelite predecessors, brought with them their own varied culturally conditioned theological presuppositions (a process of convergence) and only later acquired a more distinctive theological outlook (a process of differentiation).

In this first-of-its-kind comprehensive treatment of the development of Mormon theology, Charles Harrell traces the history of Latter-day Saint doctrines from the times of the Old Testament to the present. He describes how Mormonism has carried on the tradition of the biblical authors, early Christians, and later Protestants in reinterpreting scripture to accommodate new theological ideas while attempting to uphold the integrity and authority of the scriptures. In the process, he probes three questions: How did Mormon doctrines develop? What are the scriptural underpinnings of these doctrines? And what do critical scholars make of these same scriptures? In this enlightening study, Harrell systematically peels back the doctrinal accretions of time to provide a fresh new look at Mormon theology.

"This Is My Doctrine" will provide those already versed in Mormonism's theological tradition with a new and richer perspective of Mormon theology. Those unacquainted with Mormonism will gain an appreciation for how Mormon theology fits into the larger Jewish and Christian theological traditions.

Beholding the Tree of Life:
A Rabbinic Approach to
the Book of Mormon

Bradley J. Kramer

Paperback, ISBN: 978-1-58958-701-4
Hardcover, ISBN: 978-1-58958-702-1

Too often readers approach the Book of Mormon simply as a collection of quotations, an inspired anthology to be scanned quickly and routinely recited. In Beholding the Tree of Life Bradley J. Kramer encourages his readers to slow down, to step back, and to contemplate the literary qualities of the Book of Mormon using interpretive techniques developed by Talmudic and post-Talmudic rabbis. Specifically, Kramer shows how to read the Book of Mormon closely, in levels, paying attention to the details of its expression as well as to its overall connection to the Hebrew Scriptures—all in order to better appreciate the beauty of the Book of Mormon and its limitless capacity to convey divine meaning.

Praise for *Authoring the Old Testament*:

"Latter-day Saints have claimed the Book of Mormon as the keystone of their religion, but it presents itself first and foremost as a Jewish narrative. *Beholding the Tree of Life* is the first book I have seen that attempts to situate the Book of Mormon by paying serious attention to its Jewish literary precedents and ways of reading scripture. It breaks fresh ground in numerous ways that enrich an LDS understanding of the scriptures and that builds bridges to a potential Jewish readership." — Terryl L. Givens, author of *By the Hand of Mormon: The American Scripture that Launched a New World Religion*

"Bradley Kramer has done what someone ought to have done long ago, used the methods of Jewish scripture interpretation to look closely at the Book of Mormon. Kramer has taken the time and put in the effort required to learn those methods from Jewish teachers. He explains what he has learned clearly and carefully. And then he shows us the fruit of that learning by applying it to the Book of Mormon. The results are not only interesting, they are inspiring. This is one of those books that, on reading it, I thought 'I wish I'd written that!'" — James E. Faulconer, author of *The Book of Mormon Made Harder* and *Faith, Philosophy, Scripture*

Whom Say Ye That I Am?
Lessons from
the Jesus of Nazareth

James W. McConkie
and Judith E. McConkie

Paperback, ISBN: 978-1-58958-707-6

"This book is the most important Jesus study to date written by believing Mormons for an LDS audience. It opens the door for Mormons to come to know a Jesus most readers will know little about—the Jesus of history." — David Bokovoy, author of *Authoring the Old Testament: Genesis–Deuteronomy*

"Meticulously documented and researched, the authors have crafted an insightful and enlightening book that allows Jesus to speak by providing both wisdom and council. The McConkies masterfully weave in sources from the Gospels, ancient and modern scholars, along with Christian and non-Christian religious leaders." — *Deseret News*

The story of Jesus is frequently limited to the telling of the babe of Bethlehem who would die on the cross and three days later triumphantly exit his tomb in resurrected glory. Frequently skimmed over or left aside is the story of the Jesus of Nazareth who confronted systemic injustice, angered those in power, risked his life for the oppressed and suffering, and worked to preach and establish the Kingdom of God—all of which would lead to his execution on Calvary.

In this insightful and moving volume, authors James and Judith McConkie turn to the latest scholarship on the historical and cultural background of Jesus to discover lessons on what we can learn from his exemplary life. Whether it be his intimate interactions with the sick, the poor, women, and the outcast, or his public confrontations with oppressive religious, political, and economic institutions, Jesus of Nazareth—the son of a carpenter, Messiah, and Son of God—exemplified the way, the truth, and the life that we must follow to bring about the Kingdom of Heaven.

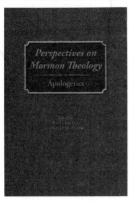

Perspectives on Mormon Theology: Apologetics

Edited by Blair G. Van Dyke and Loyd Isao Ericson

Paperback, ISBN: 978-1-58958-580-5
Hardcover, ISBN: 978-1-58958-581-2

This volume in the PERSPECTIVES ON MORMON THEOLOGY series is an exploration of Mormon apologetics—or the defense of faith. Since its very beginning, various Latter-day Saints have sought to utilize evidence and reason to actively promote or defend beliefs and claims within the Mormon tradition. Mormon apologetics reached new levels of sophistication as believers trained in fields such as Near-Eastern languages and culture, history, and philosophy began to utilize their knowledge and skills to defend their beliefs.

The contributors to this volume seek to explore the textures and contours of apologetics from multiple perspectives, revealing deep theological and ideological fissures within the Mormon scholarly community concerning apologetics. However, in spite of deep-seated differences, what each author has in common is a passion for Mormonism and how it is presented and defended. This volume captures that reality and allows readers to encounter the terrain of Mormon apologetics at close range.

Hugh Nibley:
A Consecrated Life

Boyd Jay Petersen

Hardcover, ISBN: 978-1-58958-019-0

Winner of the Mormon History Association's Best Biography Award

As one of the LDS Church's most widely recognized scholars, Hugh Nibley is both an icon and an enigma. Through complete access to Nibley's correspondence, journals, notes, and papers, Petersen has painted a portrait that reveals the man behind the legend.

Starting with a foreword written by Zina Nibley Petersen and finishing with appendices that include some of the best of Nibley's personal correspondence, the biography reveals aspects of the tapestry of the life of one who has truly consecrated his life to the service of the Lord.

Praise for *A Consecrated Life*:

"Hugh Nibley is generally touted as one of Mormonism's greatest minds and perhaps its most prolific scholarly apologist. Just as hefty as some of Nibley's largest tomes, this authorized biography is delightfully accessible and full of the scholar's delicious wordplay and wit, not to mention some astonishing war stories and insights into Nibley's phenomenal acquisition of languages. Introduced by a personable foreword from the author's wife (who is Nibley's daughter), the book is written with enthusiasm, respect and insight. . . . On the whole, Petersen is a careful scholar who provides helpful historical context. . . . This project is far from hagiography. It fills an important gap in LDS history and will appeal to a wide Mormon audience."
    —Publishers Weekly

"Well written and thoroughly researched, Petersen's biography is a must-have for anyone struggling to reconcile faith and reason."
    —Greg Taggart, Association for Mormon Letters

Textual Studies of the
Doctrine and Covenants

The Plural Marriage Revelation

William Victor Smith

Textual Studies of
the Doctrine and Covenants:
The Plural Marriage Revelation

William Victor Smith

Paperback, ISBN: 978-1-58958-690-1
Hardcover, ISBN: 978-1-58958-691-8

Joseph Smith's July 12, 1843, revelation on plural marriage was the last of his formal written revelations and a transformational moment in Mormonism. While acting today as the basis for the doctrine of eternal nuclear families, the revelation came forth during a period of theological expansion as Smith was in the midst of introducing new temple rituals, radical doctrines on God and humanity, a restructured priesthood and ecclesiastical hierarchy, and, of course, the practice of plural marriage.

In this volume, author William V. Smith examines the text of this complicated and rough revelation to explore the motivation for its existence, how it reflects this dynamic theology of the Nauvoo period, and how the revelation was utilized and reinterpreted as Mormonism fully embraced and later abandoned polygamy.

Praise for *Textual Studies*:

"No Mormon text is as ritually important and as fundamentally mysterious as Doctrine and Covenants 132. William V. Smith's work is a fine example of what a serious-minded and meticulous blend of source and redaction critical methods can tell us about the revelations produced by Joseph Smith. This is a model of what the future of Mormon scriptural studies should be."
— Stephen C. Taysom, author of *Shakers, Mormons, and Religious Worlds: Conflicting Visions, Contested Boundaries*

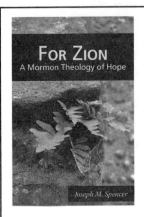

For Zion:
A Mormon Theology of Hope

Joseph M. Spencer

Paperback, ISBN: 978-1-58958-568-3

What is hope? What is Zion? And what does it mean to hope for Zion? In this insightful book, Joseph Spencer explores these questions through the scriptures of two continents separated by nearly two millennia. In the first half, Spencer engages in a rich study of Paul's letter to the Roman to better understand how the apostle understood hope and what it means to have it. In the second half of the book, Spencer jumps to the early years of the Restoration and the various revelations on consecration to understand how Latter-day Saints are expected to strive for Zion. Between these halves is an interlude examining the hoped-for Zion that both thrived in the Book of Mormon and was hoped to be established again.

Praise for *For Zion*:

"Joseph Spencer is one of the most astute readers of sacred texts working in Mormon Studies. Blending theological savvy, historical grounding, and sensitive readings of scripture, he has produced an original and compelling case for consecration and the life of discipleship." — Terryl Givens, author, *Wrestling the Angel: The Foundations of Mormon Thought*

"*For Zion: A Mormon Theology of Hope* is more than a theological reflection. It also consists of able textual exegesis, historical contextualization, and philosophic exploration. Spencer's careful readings of Paul's focus on hope in Romans and on Joseph Smith's development of consecration in his early revelations, linking them as he does with the Book of Mormon, have provided an intriguing, intertextual avenue for understanding what true stewardship should be for us—now and in the future. As such he has set a new benchmark for solid, innovative Latter-day Saint scholarship that is at once provocative and challenging." — Eric D. Huntsman, author, *The Miracles of Jesus*